MICROSOFT® OFFICE POWERPOINT® 2003 QuickSteps

CAROLE [illegible]

McGraw-Hill/Osborne

New York Chicago San Francisco
Lisbon London Madrid Mexico City
Milan New Delhi San Juan
Seoul Singapore Sydney Toronto

McGraw-Hill/Osborne
2100 Powell Street, 10th Floor
Emeryville, California 94608
U.S.A.

To arrange bulk purchase discounts for sales promotions, premiums, or fund-raisers, please contact **McGraw-Hill**/Osborne at the above address. For information on translations or book distributors outside the U.S.A., please see the International Contact Information page immediately following the index of this book.

This book was composed with Adobe® InDesign®

MICROSOFT® OFFICE POWERPOINT® 2003 QUICKSTEPS

7890 QPD QPD 01987

ISBN 0-07-223230-7

PUBLISHER / Brandon A. Nordin

VICE PRESIDENT AND ASSOCIATE PUBLISHER / Scott Rogers

ACQUISITIONS EDITOR / Roger Stewart

ACQUISITIONS COORDINATOR / Jessica Wilson

TECHNICAL EDITOR / John Cronan

COPY EDITORS / Harriet O'Neal, Chara Curtis

PROOFREADERS / Chara Curtis, Kellen Diamanti, Harriet O'Neal

INDEXER / Kellen Diamanti

LAYOUT ARTISTS / Laura Canby, Bailey Cunningham

ILLUSTRATORS / Kathleen Edwards, Pattie Lee

SERIES DESIGN / Bailey Cunningham

COVER DESIGN / Pattie Lee

To Marty and Michael

How grateful I am that we share this journey together.

To Marty: for immeasurable patience and love, and always being there for me.

To Michael: for your wonderful, bright self, and the joy you bring to my life.

About the Author

Carole Boggs Matthews has been involved with computers for over 35 years. During that time she has been a programmer, systems analyst, technical consultant, and founder, co-owner, and Vice-President of a software company. She is familiar with all aspects of computer software products, having been a designer and builder, and now, in her business, an accomplished user of software. Together with Marty Matthews, her husband, she has authored or co-authored over 40 books, including *Microsoft Office FrontPage 2003, The Complete Reference; Office 2000 Answers;* and *The Official Guide to CorelDraw 6*.

Carole lives on an island with her husband, Marty; son, Michael; cats, Domino and Tortoise; and dog, Tank.

Contents at a Glance

Contents

1

2

5

6

Acknowledgments

We had an awesome team putting this book together. Although at times it seemed like a cast of thousands, it was only a few, very talented and professional team-workers that turned this daunting task into a done deal. And with good humor and patience to boot! Many, many thanks.

John Cronan, technical editor extraordinaire (plus an excellent writer), was exceedingly reliable, accurate, and very astute in his pursuit of the truth! My thanks also to Faye, who must have felt like a single person during the long hours that John gave to both technical editing and writing of some of the books in the QuickSteps series.

Harriet O'Neal and **Chara Curtis,** copy editors/proofreaders, shared the task of attending to the details of my imperfectly written words, always on the alert for those awkward or unintelligible phrases, and then transforming them. Harriet, your knowledge and experience is very reassuring. Chara, your contributions and sense of humor were a delight during those long hours. The books are so much better because of both of you.

Laura Canby and **Bailey Cunningham**, layout artists, have talents I truly admire. Laura, you laid out my manuscript with great skill and had incredible patience for my endless changes. Your vision and artistic flair added so much to the book. Bailey, your design skills and excellent help during a tight schedule was so appreciated.

Kellen Diamanti, indexer/proofreader, in addition to proofreading some chapters, did the indexing for all the books in the series. How did you do it, Kellen? I so admire your abilities to pay attention to detail, knowing that in the details lies the excellence of the book. And you did it with such grace.

Marty Matthews, author, partner in writing and in life, and originator of the QuckSteps idea. How you kept us all organized is beyond me. We are a demanding group, and "crisis" is our middle name! Yet you kept us sane and together. Just as you do for me "in real life!"

Roger Stewart and **Scott Rogers**, and all the others at Osborne who gave us the opportunity to produce this series of books.

Introduction

QuickSteps books are recipe books for computer users. They answer the question "how do I..." by providing quick sets of steps to accomplish the most common tasks with a particular program. The sets of steps are the central focus of the book. QuickSteps sidebars show you how to quickly do many small functions or tasks that support the primary functions. Notes, Tips, and Cautions augment the steps, yet they are presented in such as manner as to not interrupt the flow of the steps. The brief introductions are minimal rather than narrative, and numerous illustrations and figures, many with callouts, support the steps.

QuickSteps books are organized by function and the tasks needed to perform that function. Each function is a chapter. Each task, or "How To," contains the steps needed for its accomplishment along with the relevant Notes, Tips, Cautions, and screenshots. Tasks will be easy to find through:

- The Table of Contents, which lists the functional areas (chapters) and tasks in the order they are presented
- A How To list of tasks on the opening page of each chapter
- The index with its alphabetical list of terms used in describing the functions and tasks
- Color-coded tabs for each chapter or functional area with an index to the tabs just before the Table of Contents

Conventions Used in this Book

Microsoft Office PowerPoint QuickSteps uses several conventions designed to make the book easier for you to follow. Among these are:

- A in the Table of Contents or the How To list in each chapter references a QuickSteps sidebar in a chapter.
- **Bold type** is used for words on the screen that you are to do something with, such as click **Save as** or open **File**.
- *Italic type* is used for a word or phrase that is being defined or otherwise deserves special emphasis.
- Underlined type is used for text that you are to type from the keyboard
- SMALL CAPITAL LETTERS are used for keys on the keyboard such as **ENTER** and **SHIFT**.
- When you are expected to enter a command, you are told to press the key(s). If you are to enter text or numbers, you are told to type them.
- When you are to open a menu, such as the Start menu or the File menu, you are told to "open **Start**" or "open **File**."

How to...

- *Use the Start Menu to Load PowerPoint*
- *Starting PowerPoint*
- *Open a Presentation*
- *Open Slide Sorter View*
- *Using the Slide Sorter Toolbar*
- *Change Opening Default View*
- *Displaying Views*
- *Remove the Startup Task Pane*
- *Display a Toolbar*
- *Start a Slide Show*
- *Using Task Panes*
- *Select Another Task Pane*
- *Show Toolbars on Two Rows*
- *Customize a Toolbar*
- *Using Toolbars*
- *Open Help Three Ways*
- *Access Offline Help*
- *Using Help*
- *Do Research*
- *Save a Presentation Automatically*
- *Saving a Presentation*
- *Close a Presentation Session*

Chapter 1 Stepping into PowerPoint

Chapter 1, Stepping Into PowerPoint, explains how to open PowerPoint, understand its screens and toolbars, and set them up according to your personal needs. You will learn how to get help from Microsoft's Office Online Help, from Offline Help, and by using Internet research to search for help in subjects of your choice. You will learn how to manage your task panes and toolbars, even how to customize your own toolbar. You will be able to display or hide the Office Assistant. This chapter will also tell you how to close your presentation and then end a PowerPoint session.

Start PowerPoint

I assume that you already know how to turn on the computer and load Windows, and that PowerPoint has been installed on your computer. Once PowerPoint is installed, you may start it as you would any other program. There are several ways to do this. For example, the quickest way may be to simply double-click on the PowerPoint icon on your desktop. However, the most common way is to use the Start menu.

1 2 3 4 5 6 7 8 9 10

Use the Start Menu to Load PowerPoint

To load PowerPoint using the Start menu on the Windows task pane:

1. Start your computer and log on to Windows, if necessary.
2. Click **Start.** The Start menu opens.
3. Select **All Programs**, choose **Microsoft Office**, and click **Microsoft Office PowerPoint 2003**. The PowerPoint window will open, as shown in Figure 1-1.

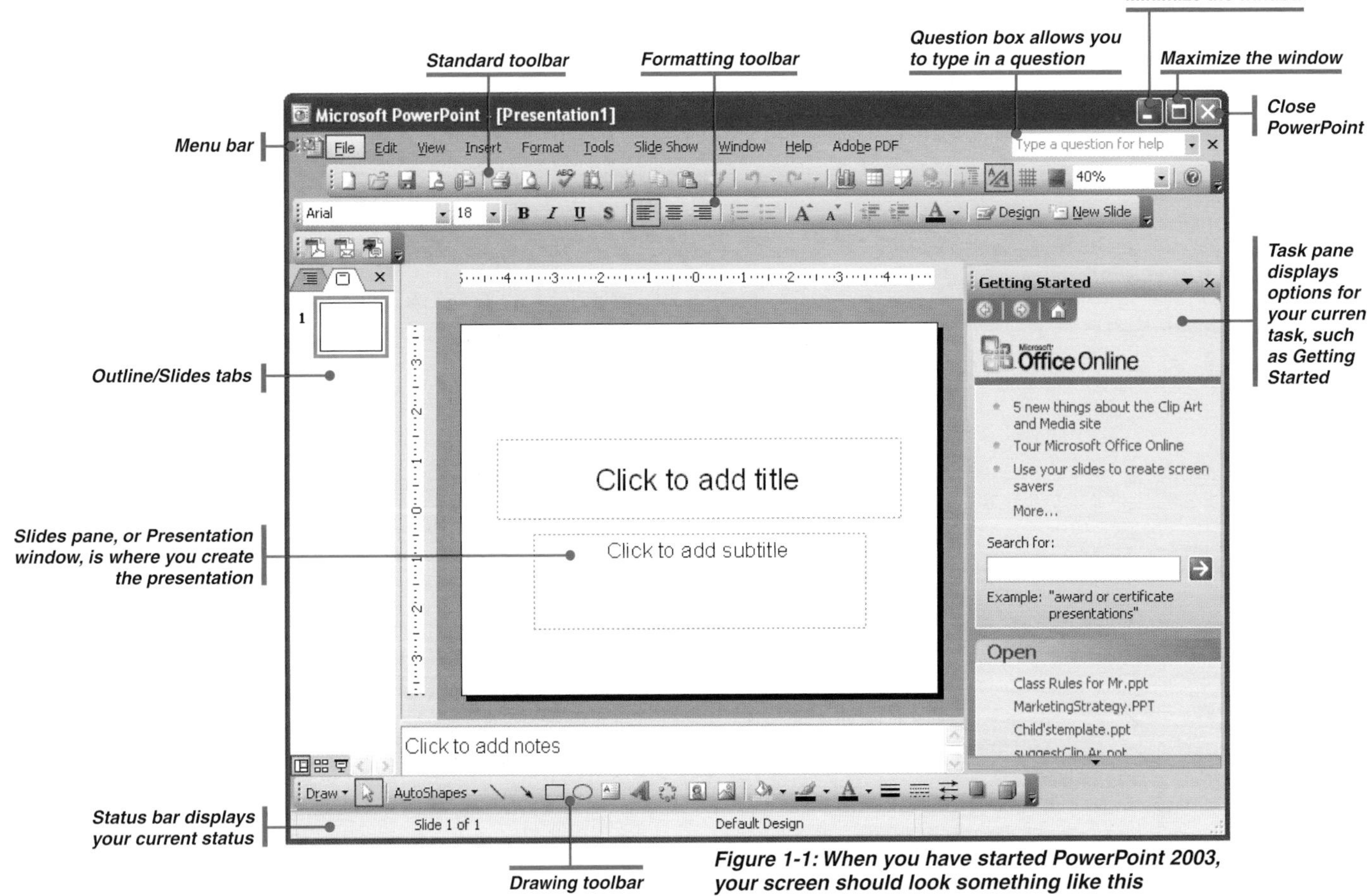

Figure 1-1: When you have started PowerPoint 2003, your screen should look something like this

QUICKSTEPS

STARTING POWERPOINT

START POWERPOINT FROM THE KEYBOARD

1. Press **CTRL+ESC**, or press the Windows flag key on your keyboard to open the Start menu.
2. Press **P** to select the All Programs menu, and press **RIGHT ARROW** to open it.
3. Press **DOWN ARROW** until Microsoft Office is selected. Then press **RIGHT ARROW** to open it.
4. Press **DOWN ARROW** until Microsoft Office PowerPoint is selected. Then press **ENTER** to start it.

CREATE A SHORTCUT TO START POWERPOINT

Another way to start PowerPoint is first to create a shortcut icon on your desktop.

1. Open **START** and select **All Programs**.
2. Choose **Microsoft Office**, and right-click **Microsoft Office PowerPoint 2003**.
3. Select **Send To** and click **Desktop** (create shortcut).

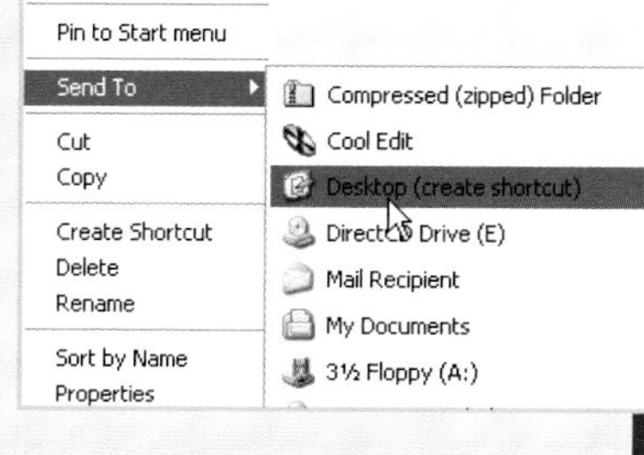

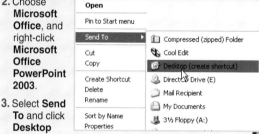

START POWERPOINT FROM THE SHORTCUT

Double-click the shortcut icon on your desktop.

Open a Presentation

The initial PowerPoint window, shown in Figure 1-1, gives you the Getting Started task pane. It introduces you to PowerPoint, but it does not present you with the alternatives available for creating presentations. Presentations are begun in several ways: you can create a new one from scratch, use a template that defines a design for a slide, use a wizard to create a complete model presentation, or open an existing presentation and modify it.

CREATE A NEW PRESENTATION

Although you can create a new presentation by just typing in the Title and Subtitle boxes of the blank slide, shown in Figure 1-1, you have more options available to you in the New Presentation task pane.

1. Open **File** and select **New**. The New Presentation task pane is displayed, as shown in Figure 1-2.
2. Under **New**, select the type of presentation you want.
   - **Blank Presentation** allows you to create a slide show from scratch. The Slide Layout task pane provides many layout designs from which to choose, allowing you to create your own slide layout structure and look.
   - **From Design Template** presents a blank slide and the Slide Design task pane, which displays a variety of design templates to choose from.
   - **From AutoContent Wizard** offers a choice of predefined presentations, which after minimal input from you, automatically creates a complete presentation to use as a starting point.
   - **From Existing Presentation** brings up a New From Existing Presentation dialog box that allows you to find an existing presentation. Once you have selected and opened the presentation, you can modify it to suit your purposes.

Figure 1-2: The New Presentations task pane allows you to choose the way to create a new presentation

See Chapter 2 to continue with the creation of a presentation.

TIP

To show the full menus instead of the shortened menus (prioritized by how often you use the commands), Open **Tools,** select **Customize,** and click the **Options** tab. Click **Always Show Full Menus** to place a check mark next to it.

OPEN AN EXISTING PRESENTATION

Once you have created a presentation, you will have to find it and reopen it to make changes, to print or display it. To open an existing presentation:

1. Open **File** and click **Open**.
2. In the Open dialog box, find the location of the PowerPoint presentation. You can open the Look In drop-down list or click My Recent Documents, Desktop, My Documents, My Computer, or My Network Places.
3. When you have located the folder containing the presentation, double-click the presentation to open it. You should see the presentation appear, as shown in Figure 1-3.

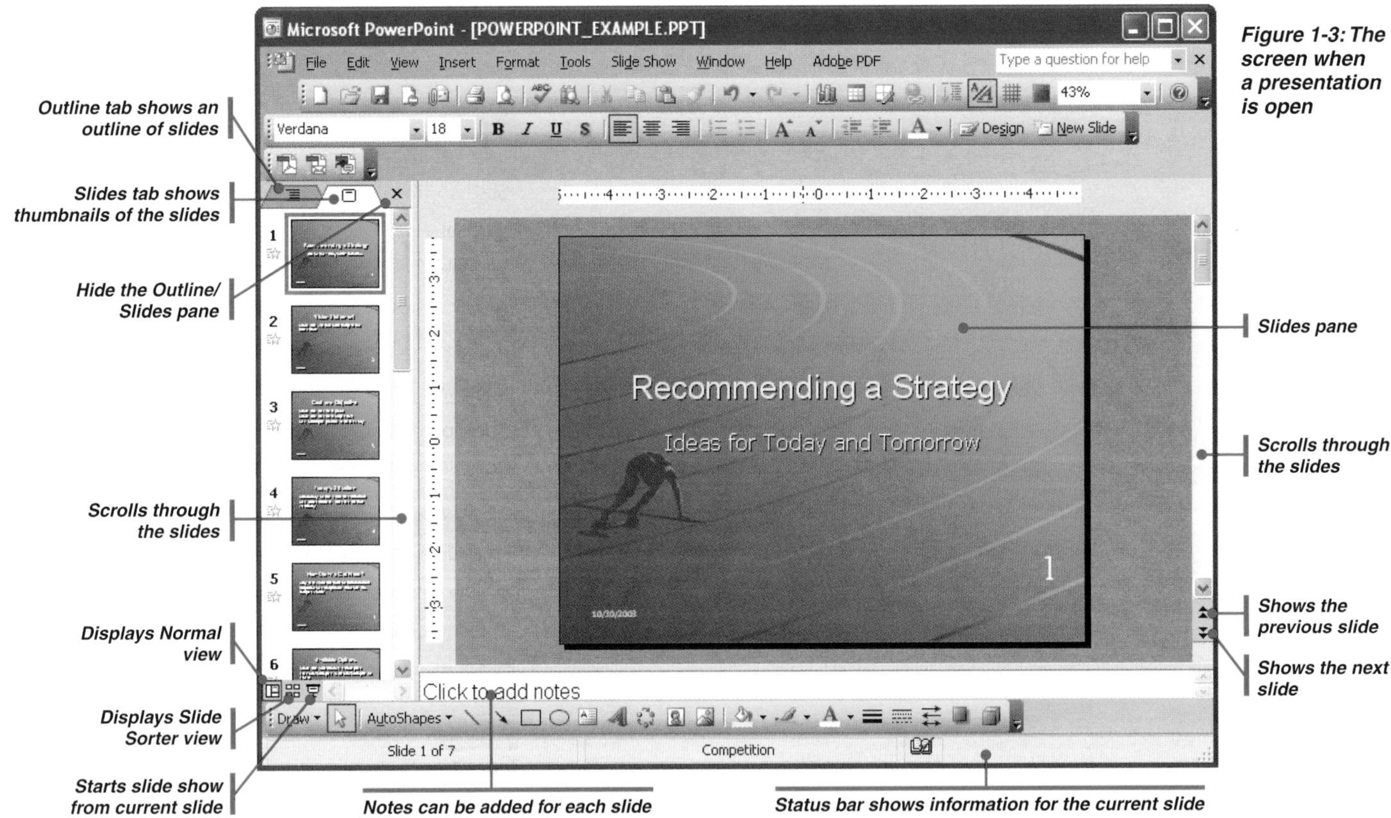

Figure 1-3: The screen when a presentation is open

NOTE

To get back to the Normal view from another view, you can either click the **Normal View** button or select **Normal** from the View menu.

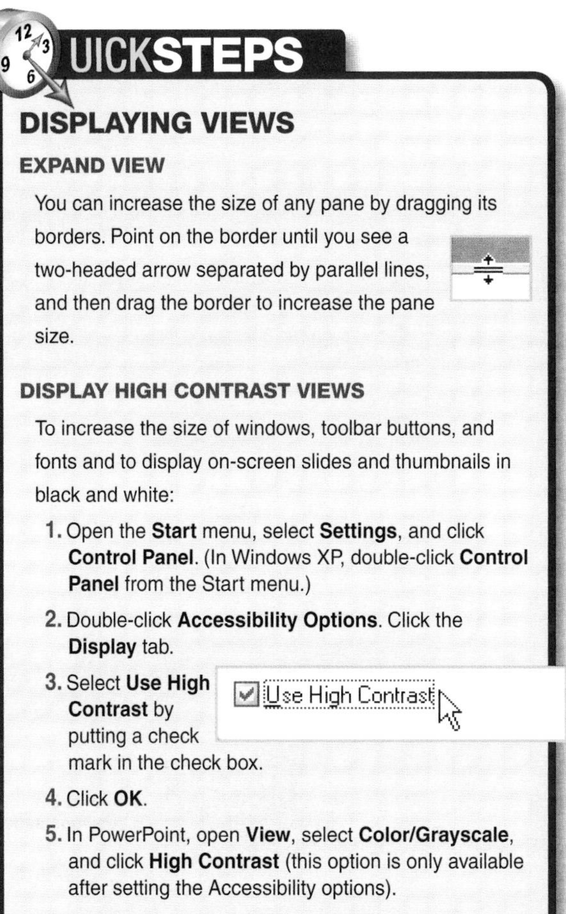

QUICKSTEPS

DISPLAYING VIEWS

EXPAND VIEW

You can increase the size of any pane by dragging its borders. Point on the border until you see a two-headed arrow separated by parallel lines, and then drag the border to increase the pane size.

DISPLAY HIGH CONTRAST VIEWS

To increase the size of windows, toolbar buttons, and fonts and to display on-screen slides and thumbnails in black and white:

1. Open the **Start** menu, select **Settings**, and click **Control Panel**. (In Windows XP, double-click **Control Panel** from the Start menu.)
2. Double-click **Accessibility Options**. Click the **Display** tab.
3. Select **Use High Contrast** by putting a check mark in the check box.

4. Click **OK**.
5. In PowerPoint, open **View**, select **Color/Grayscale**, and click **High Contrast** (this option is only available after setting the Accessibility options).

Change Opening Default View

You can change the default view of a document when it is first displayed.

1. Open **Tools** and click **Options**. The Options dialog box will open.
2. Select the **View** tab, as shown in Figure 1-4.
3. Under **Default View**, open the list box, and click the view you want to see when you open all presentations.

Figure 1-4: The Options dialog box presents several alternatives to PowerPoint's default opening view

USING THE SLIDE SORTER TOOLBAR

HIDE A SLIDE

Click **Hide Slide**. You will still see the slide, but its slide number will be crossed out, and it will not be displayed in the slide show.

RUN A TIMING REHEARSAL

Click **Rehearse Timings** to run and time a slide show.

CREATE A SUMMARY SLIDE

To create a summary slide, click **Summary Slide**.

OPEN NOTES PAGE

To open the Notes page, click **Notes**.

DISPLAY THE SLIDE TRANSITION TASK PANE

To work with transitions between slides, display the Slide Transition task pane by clicking **Transition**.

DISPLAY THE DESIGN TASK PANE

To display the Slide Design task pane, click **Design**.

INSERT A NEW SLIDE

To insert a new slide, select the slide preceding the one to be inserted, and click **New Slide**.

New Slide

Open Slide Sorter View

The Slide Sorter view displays the slides in thumbnail view, as shown in Figure 1-5, and allows you to rearrange them. Either:

- Click the **Slide Sorter view** icon at the bottom of the screen.

–Or–

- Open **Views** and click **Slide Sorter**.

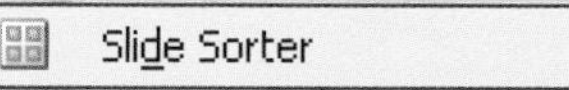

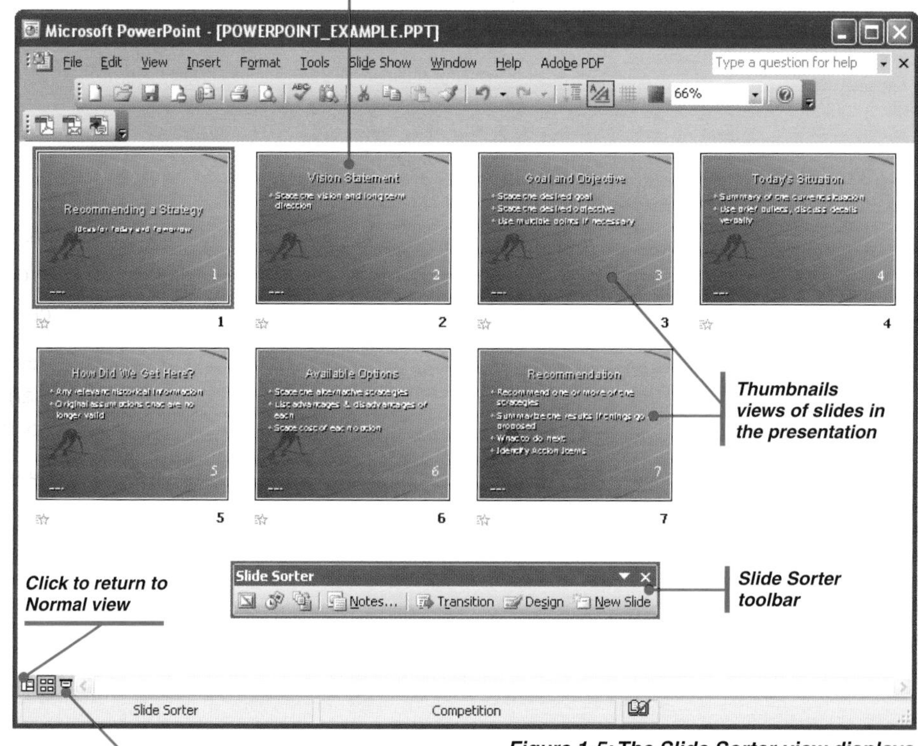

Figure 1-5: The Slide Sorter view displays thumbnails of the slides in a presentation

TIP

Click the slide screen to advance the presentation from one slide to another. To close the slide show and return to the previous view, press **ESC** on your keyboard.

QUICKSTEPS

USING TASK PANES

OPEN/CLOSE THE TASK PANE

To toggle between displaying the task pane and not, press **CTRL+F1**, or open **View** and click **Task Pane.**

CLOSE THE TASK PANE

To close the task pane, click **Close** on the task pane title bar, or press **CTRL+F1.**

SCROLL THROUGH TASK PANES BEING USED

To move back and forth through task panes you're working with, click the **Back** and **Forward** arrows on the task pane toolbar. The rightmost icon displays the Home task pane, which, by default, is the Getting Started task pane.

DISPLAY THE GETTING STARTED TASK PANE

To display the Getting Started task pane, click **Home** on the task pane toolbar.

NOTE

You can start a slide show using My Computer or Windows Explorer without bringing up PowerPoint. Right-click the presentation file name, and click **Show** from the context menu.

Start a Slide Show

Start a slide show in one of three ways:

- Click **Slide Show From Current Slide**.

  –Or–

- Open **View** and click **Slide Show**.

  –Or–

- Press **F5**.

Personalize PowerPoint

You can personalize PowerPoint by changing the display of task panes, toolbars, and menus.

Select Another Task Pane

To select a different task pane (if your task pane is not open, you can open it by opening **View** and clicking **Task Pane**):

1. Open **Other Task Panes** (the down arrow on the task pane title bar). The menu of task panes will open, as shown in Figure 1-6:
2. Click the task pane you want.

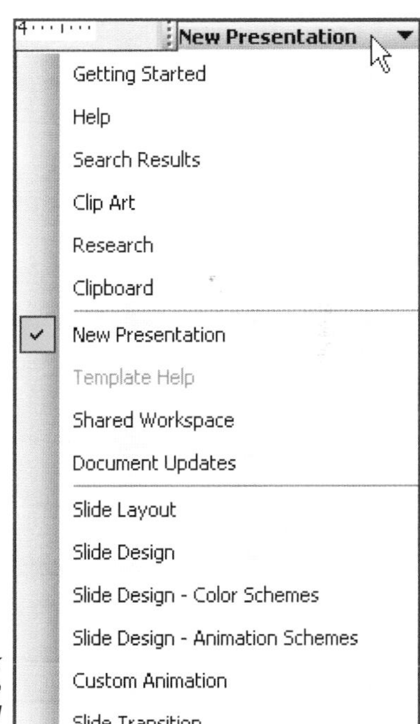

Figure 1-6: Click the Other Task Panes button to see alternative task panes you can use to build a presentation

NOTE

Task panes present options for doing whatever task is at hand. Here are some of your task pane options:

- **Getting Started** suggests beginning tasks to do when you first load PowerPoint.
- **Help** displays ways you can search for help online or offline.
- **Search Results** allows you to search for Microsoft Office Help, training, and templates.
- **Clip Art** allows you to search for clip art by subject name, location, and file types.
- **Research** searches your computer or Microsoft online references for typed text.
- **Clipboard** displays the contents of the Clipboard, which you can then paste or clear.
- **New Presentation** displays ways to get started when creating a new presentation.
- **Template Help** allows you to search for useful templates.
- **Shared Workspace** displays information relevant to sharing workspace with others, such as document Status, Members, Tasks, Documents, Links, and Document Information. You can create the workspace here as well.
- **Document Updates** is displayed when a document is shared in a Document Workspace and has been updated.

Continued...

TIP

Another way to display a toolbar is to open **Tools,** select **Customize,** and choose the **Toolbar** tab. Then click the toolbar name to place a check mark next to it, and click **Close**.

Remove Startup Task Pane

When you start PowerPoint, the Getting Started task pane automatically appears. To suppress showing the task pane upon startup:

1. Open **Tools** and select **Options**.
2. Open the **View** tab.
3. Remove the check mark next to **Startup Task Pane**, as shown here:

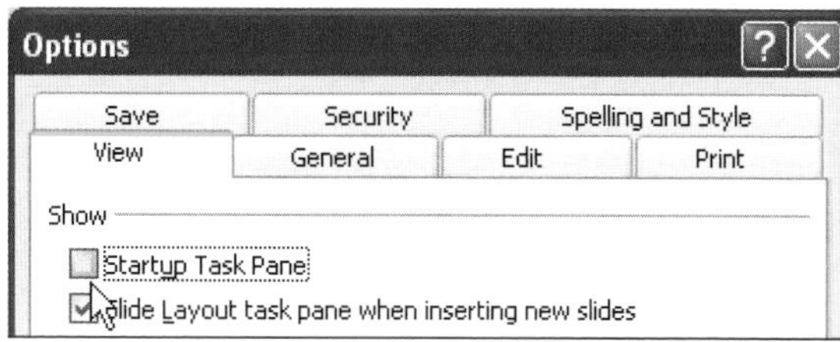

Display a Toolbar

To display a toolbar:

1. Open **View** and select **Toolbars**. The Toolbars menu will be displayed, as shown in Figure 1-7.
2. Click the toolbar you want to display to place a check mark there.

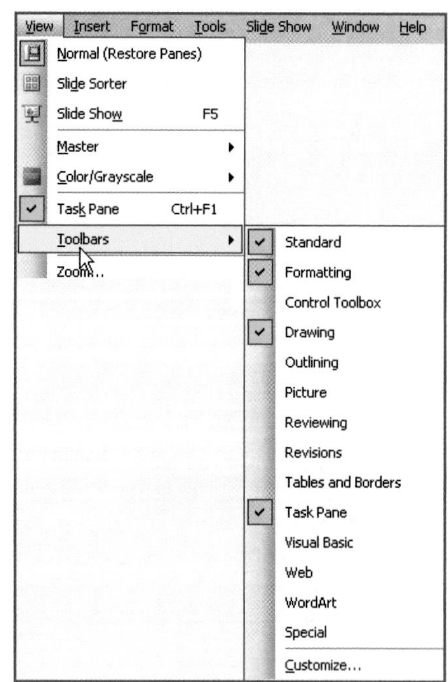

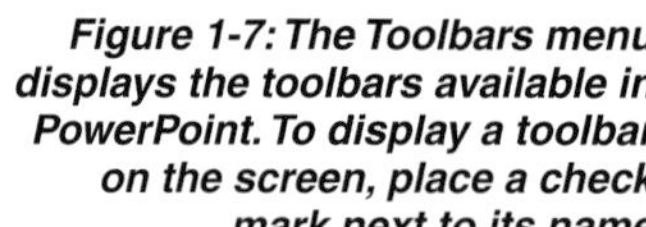

Figure 1-7: The Toolbars menu displays the toolbars available in PowerPoint. To display a toolbar on the screen, place a check mark next to its name

NOTE

(CONTINUED)

- **Slide Layout** displays a menu of layout options for creating a new slide or modifying an existing one.
- **Slide Design,** displays a menu of slide design options, including layout, color, and design element.
- **Slide Design – Color Schemes** displays various colors that can be used to change the color scheme for a specific slide design.
- **Slide Design – Animation Schemes** displays a menu of animations, which may be added to an element of a slide.
- **Custom Animation** is used to create a custom animation on an element of a slide.
- **Slide Transition** displays a menu of visually interesting transitions that can be used to vary how one slide gives way to the next.

NOTE

The Standard and Formatting toolbars are initially shown on one row, which limits the number of commands that can be displayed. Click **Toolbar Options** (the downward pointing arrow on the right of the toolbar) to see additional commands.

Show Toolbars on Two Rows

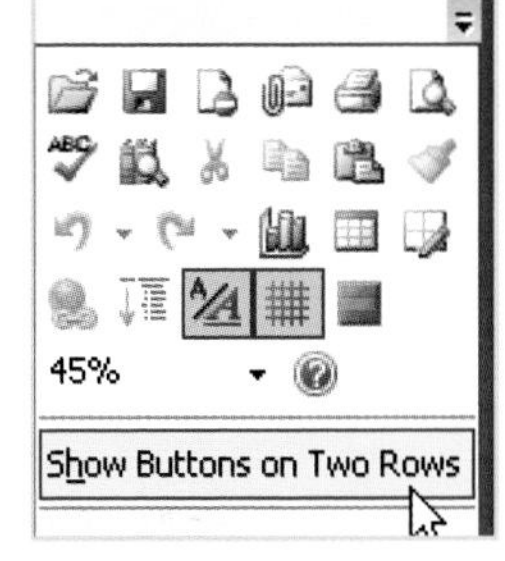

1. Click **Other Options** (the arrow at the right end of the toolbar).
2. Select **Show Buttons On Two Rows**.

–Or–

1. Open **Tools** and select **Customize.**
2. On the **Options** tab, click **Show Standard And Formatting Toolbars On Two Rows**.

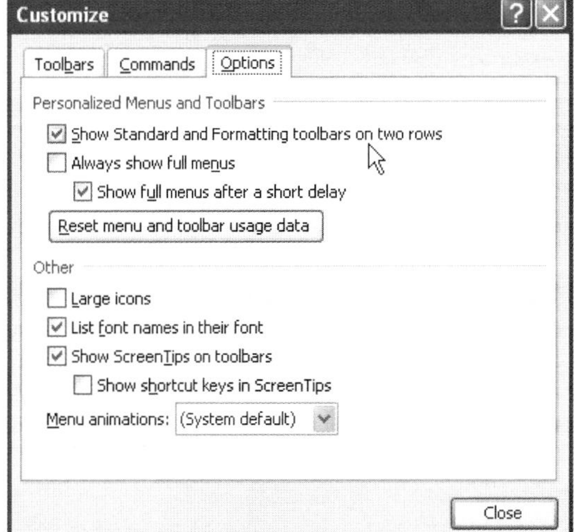

Customize a Toolbar

You can customize a toolbar or menu either by adding commands or menus to it, or by creating a new custom toolbar and adding commands to that.

ADD COMMANDS TO THE TOOLBAR

If you find the toolbar buttons are not as convenient as you would like, or if you frequently use a feature that is not on one of the toolbars, you can rearrange the buttons or add commands to a toolbar.

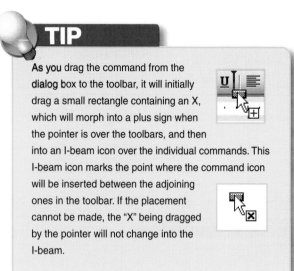

TIP

As you drag the command from the dialog box to the toolbar, it will initially drag a small rectangle containing an X, which will morph into a plus sign when the pointer is over the toolbars, and then into an I-beam icon over the individual commands. This I-beam icon marks the point where the command icon will be inserted between the adjoining ones in the toolbar. If the placement cannot be made, the "X" being dragged by the pointer will not change into the I-beam.

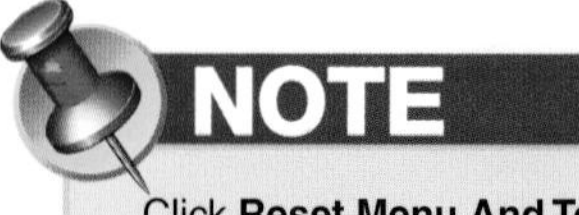

NOTE

Click **Reset Menu And Toolbar Usage Data** on the **Options** tab to restore the menus and toolbars to default settings.

TIP

To drag a menu command to a toolbar, open **Tools** and select **Customize**. Open the **Commands** tab and select **Built-in Menus** from the Categories list. Drag the commands you want to the toolbar.

1. Open **Tools,** select **Customize,** and click the **Commands** tab.
2. Under **Categories**, select the category where the command will be found.

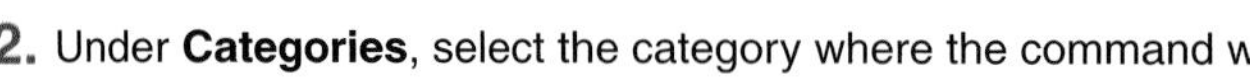

3. Under **Commands**, find the command, and drag it from the dialog box to the toolbar.

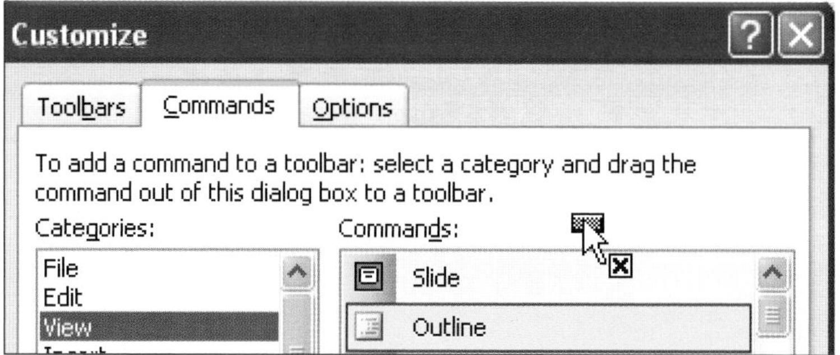

4. Click **Close** when you are finished.

CREATE A CUSTOM TOOLBAR

You can create a custom toolbar of your most frequently used commands and avoid displaying several toolbars. Omitting some of the toolbars creates more open space for the presentation. Here's how:

1. Open **Tools,** select **Customize,** and click the **Toolbars** tab.
2. Click **New** to open the New Toolbar dialog box.

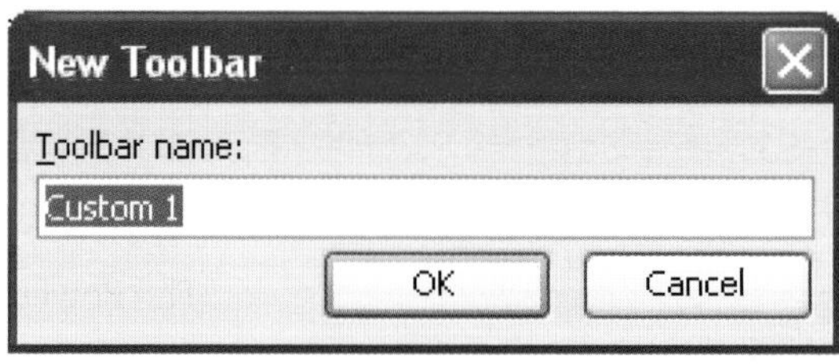

3. Enter the name of the new toolbar, and click **OK**. A small toolbar will appear on the screen.
4. Open the **Commands** tab. In the **Categories** list, select the toolbar containing a command you want to copy to the new toolbar.

QUICKSTEPS

USING TOOLBARS

DISPLAY A TOOLBAR

Right-click a toolbar or menu bar, and click the toolbar you want to be displayed.

MOVE A TOOLBAR

- When the toolbar is *docked* (attached to the edge of the screen), place your pointer on the handle at the left of the toolbar, and drag it to the new location.
- When the toolbar is *floating* (not attached to the edge, but somewhere on your screen), place your pointer on the title bar of the toolbar, and drag it to the new location.

HIDE A TOOLBAR

1. Right-click the toolbar.
2. Click the toolbar name to clear the check mark.

DELETE A TOOLBAR

Only custom toolbars that you create can be deleted.

1. Open **Tools** and select **Customize.** Choose the **Toolbars** tab.
2. Click the custom toolbar to be deleted.
3. Click **Delete**. You will be asked if you really want to delete the toolbar.
4. Click **OK** and click **Close.**

TIP

When you drag a toolbar next to the edge of the window, it will automatically attach itself to the window and become docked.

5. From the **Commands** list, drag the command to the new toolbar.
6. Click **Close** when you are finished.

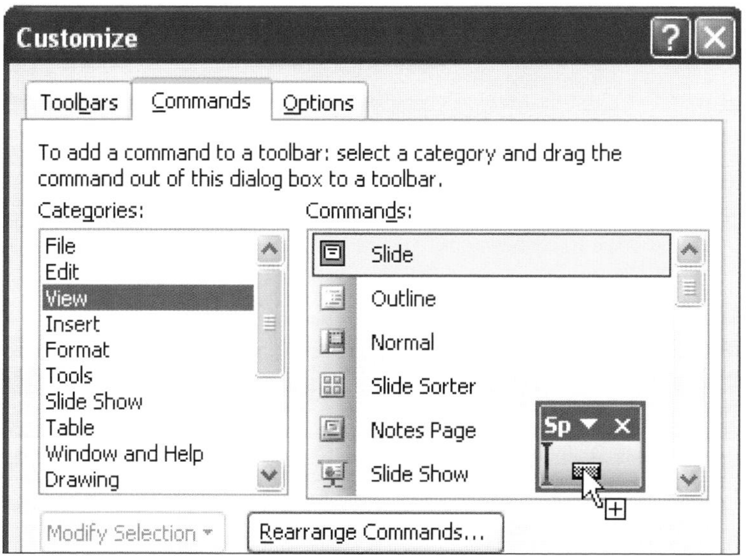

Get Help

Help can be accessed both online from Microsoft servers and offline on your own computer. A different kind of help which provides the Thesaurus and Research features is also available.

Open Help Three Ways

The PowerPoint Help system is maintained online at Microsoft. It is easily accessed using one of three techniques. The first two display the PowerPoint Help task pane. Here you can Search for specific information or click on one of the task pane's options, as seen in Figure 1-8. The third technique allows you to type a question, which will display a list of possible answers:

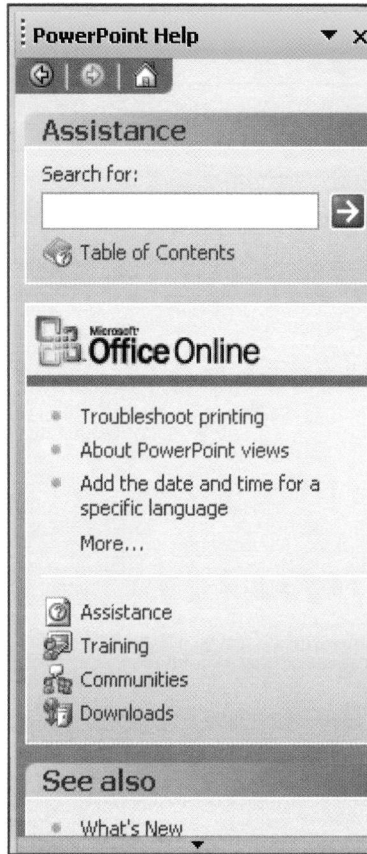

Figure 1-8: The PowerPoint Help task pane offers quick access to help from Microsoft's Online Help System

- Open **Help** and select **Microsoft Office PowerPoint Help**.

–Or–

- Click the **Microsoft Office PowerPoint Help** icon on the Standard toolbar

–Or–

- Type your question in the **Type A Question For Help** text box.

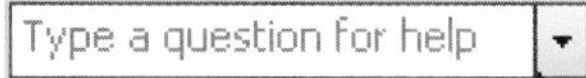

Access Offline Help

Microsoft by default searches the Microsoft's Online Help System first. You can change the default so that offline Help is primary.

1. Click **Help** and select **Microsoft Office PowerPoint Help**.
2. On the PowerPoint Help task pane, click **Also See** at the bottom of the pane.
3. Select **Online Content Settings**. The Service Options dialog box will open, as shown in Figure 1-9.
   - To search offline first, click **Search Online Content When Connected** to remove the check mark.
   - To disable Online Help, click **Show Content and Links From Microsoft Office Online** to remove the check mark. This will force Office application to always access Offline Help.

NOTE

When you reset the Help defaults in the Service Options dialog box, it will apply to all Office products. Any Office applications open, including PowerPoint, will not be affected until they are closed and opened again.

USING HELP

PRINT A HELP TOPIC

Click the **Print** icon in the Help dialog box. 

HIDE THE TYPE A QUESTION FOR HELP BOX

To suppress the display of the Type A Question For Help box:

1. Open **Tools** and select **Customize**. The Customize dialog box will open.
2. With the dialog box open, right-click the **Type A Question For Help** box on the menu bar.
3. Click the **Show Ask a Question Box** text to deselect it.
4. Click **Close** in the dialog box. When the dialog box is closed, the text box will be removed from the menu bar.

HIDE/SHOW THE OFFICE ASSISTANT

Open the **Help** menu, select **Hide The Office Assistant** or **Show The Office Assistant** depending on whether you want to hide or show it.

When you suppress the display of the Office Assistant or the Type a Question For Help box, you are not deleting it. You are just hiding it.

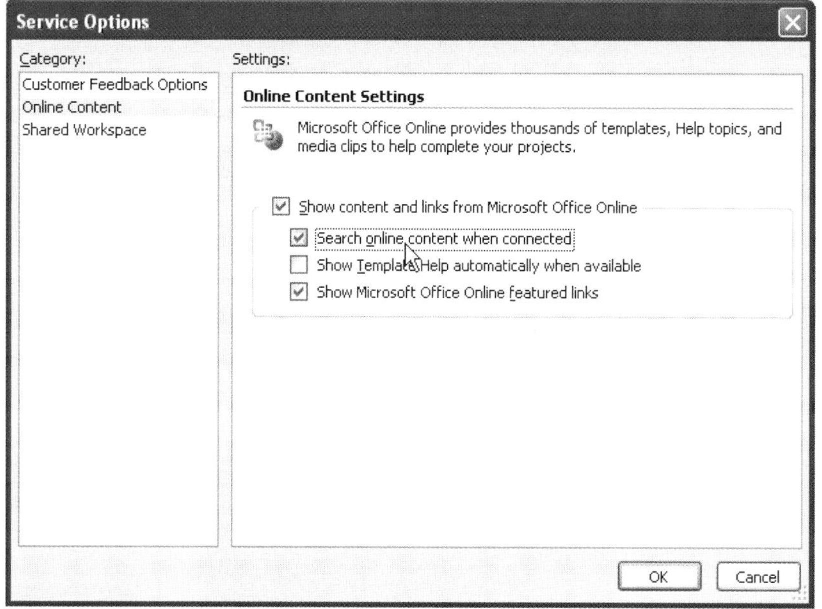

Figure 1-9: The default set in the Service Options dialog box establishes the online help as the first resource available to you

Do Research

You can do research on the Internet using PowerPoint's Research command. This displays a Research task pane that allows you to enter your search criteria and specify references to search.

1. Open **Tools** and select **Research.**
2. Enter your search criteria in the **Search For** text box.
3. Beneath the text box, a reference source is selected. To change the reference source, open the list box, and click a reference to be searched, as shown here:

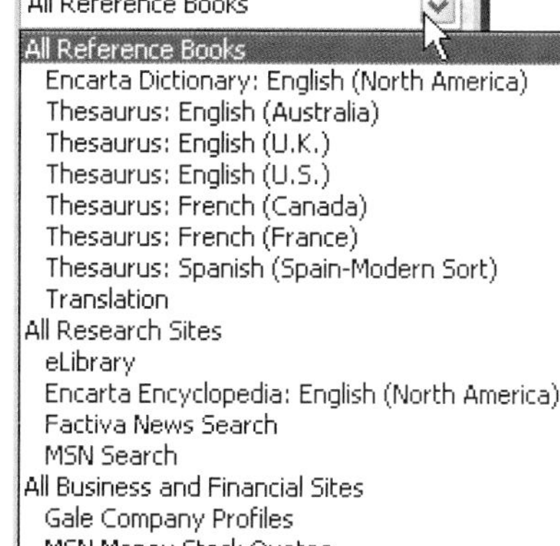

NOTE

When you are working offline, only the reference tools provided with PowerPoint, such as the Thesaurus and bilingual language references, are available.

TIP

Click to remove the check mark next to **Save AutoRecover Info Every** if you want to stop automatically saving your presentations.

NOTE

When you first open PowerPoint, the save interval is set to a default of 10 minutes. You also use these steps to change the default save interval to another time interval.

TIP

If this is your first time saving the file, the Save As dialog box will open. Enter the name of your presentation and the Save In *path*, or location where you would like to store the file.

End Your PowerPoint Presentation

When you have finished your presentation, you need to save it and close PowerPoint. One way to make this more efficient is to have PowerPoint save it automatically while you work.

Save a Presentation Automatically

It is important to periodically save a presentation as you work. Having PowerPoint save it automatically will reduce the chance of losing data in case of a power failure or other interruption. Follow these steps to save your files automatically.

1. Open **Tools** and select **Options**.
2. Choose the **Save** tab.
3. Click **Save AutoRecover Info Every** to place a check mark next to it.
4. In the Minutes box, enter a time for how often PowerPoint is to save your presentation.
5. Click **OK** to close the dialog box.

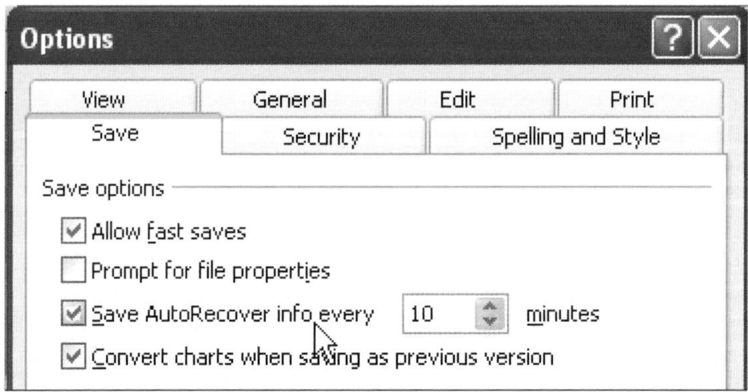

QUICKSTEPS

SAVING A PRESENTATION

SAVE A PRESENTATION

To save a file:

- Open **File** and click **Save**.

  –Or–

- Click the **Save** toolbar button.

  –Or–

- Press **CTRL+S**.

SAVE A COPY OF YOUR PRESENTATION

When you save a presentation under a different name, you create a copy of it. Both the original presentation and the newly named one will remain. To create a copy with a new name:

1. Open **File** and choose **Save As**.
2. In the Save As dialog box, as shown in Figure 1-10, enter the **File Name.** Then open the **Save In** list box, and find the path to the folder you want.
3. Click **Save.**

SAVE A PRESENTATION AS A TEMPLATE

To save a newly created presentation as a template from which to create new presentations:

1. Open **File** and select **Save As**.
2. Enter a **File Name** for your template.
3. In the **Save As Type** box, select **Design Template**.
4. Click **Save**.

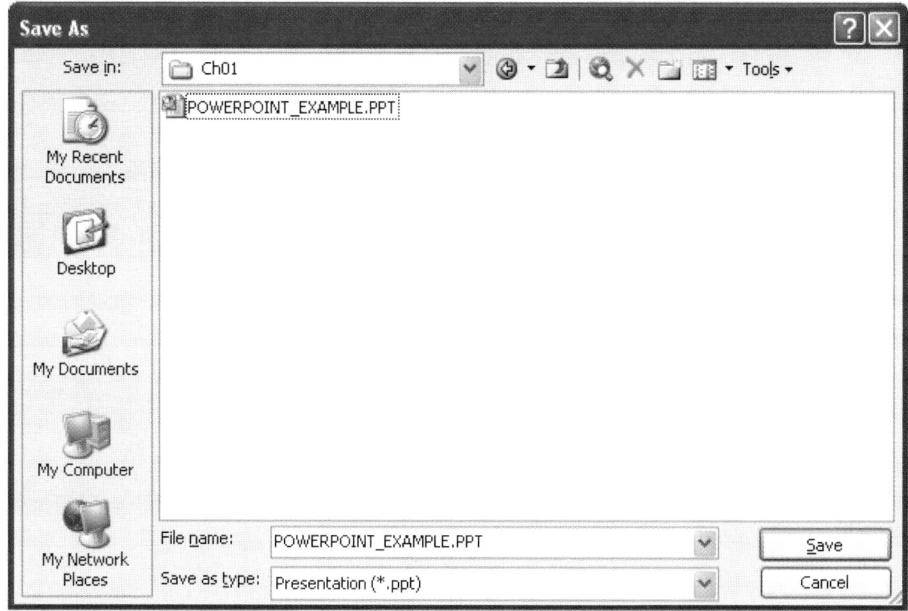

Figure 1-10: The Save As command is a way to make a copy of your presentation so that you can modify it to meet new requirements without changing the original

Close a Presentation Session

When you have completed your work for the day, or you want to use another application, you must "officially" close your presentation and then close PowerPoint.

Closing a presentation removes the presentation from the PowerPoint window, and closing PowerPoint stops the program from using your computer's memory. If the presentation has been saved, nothing will be lost. However, if you have not saved your work, you could lose all the work you have produced since the last time you saved your presentation. (See Saving A Presentation.)

1

2

3

4

5

6

7

8

9

10

CLOSE THE PRESENTATION

After you have saved all changes to your presentation, you can close your presentation and then exit PowerPoint. To do this:

- Open **File,** choose **Close,** and click **Yes** to save the presentation.

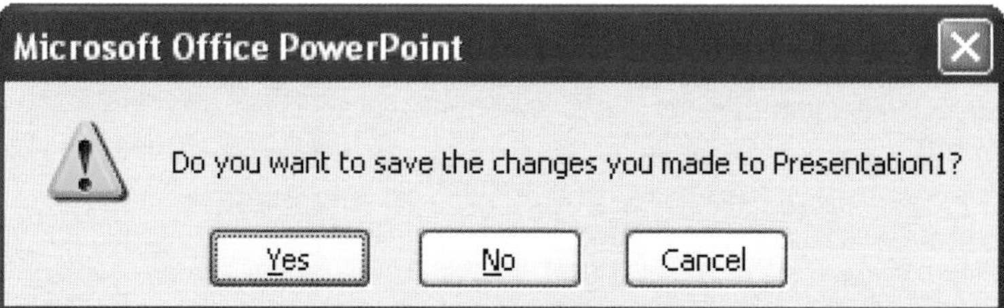

–Or–

- Click **Close**. 

CLOSE POWERPOINT

- To close PowerPoint, open **File** and select **Exit.**

–Or–

- Click **Close**. 

How to...

- *Create a PowerPoint Folder*
- *Change the Default Save Folder*
- *Create a Presentation Using AutoContent Wizard*
- *Add a Template to the Wizard*
- *Create a Presentation Using a Design Template*
- *Working with Templates*
- *Create a Template*
- *Create a Presentation from Another Presentation*
- *Choosing Layout and Design Elements*
- *Create a Presentation from Scratch*
- *Adding Content to a Slide*
- *Create an Outline*
- *Indenting with the Keyboard*
- *Insert an Outline from Other Sources*
- *Using the Outlining Toolbar*
- *Preview the Outline*
- *Print the Outline*
- *Insert a Hyperlink in the Outline*
- *Dealing With Permissions*
- *Send the Outline to Microsoft Word*

Chapter 2
Creating the Presentation

Chapter 2 describes how to prepare for your presentation by setting up a folder for it and deciding what layout and Design template you will use. You will learn to create a presentation in four ways: using the AutoContent Wizard to build a complete presentation which you then can modify; using a Design Template that predefines a color scheme, fonts, layout, and some design elements; using another presentation which closely matches what you want to do; and creating your presentation from scratch. Finally, you will see how to organize and manage your slides by creating and working with a presentation outline.

Prepare to Create a Presentation

Before you build a presentation, you can ease the creation process by creating a folder to store your presentation in and determining some basic design qualities for your presentation.

Create a PowerPoint Folder

You prepare a folder to store your presentation so that you won't have to search for the presentation when you need it. If you don't have a special need that requires storing your presentations in a unique location (for example, if you have a project or task folder where you want the presentation to be stored), you may want to create a folder within My Documents, where you can also direct PowerPoint to save your presentations by default. Create a PowerPoint folder by using Windows Explorer.

1. Open **Start** and select **All Programs**.
2. Choose **Accessories** from the menu, and then click **Windows Explorer**. The Windows Explorer window will open. Next you'll add a folder to your hard disk.
3. Find and click the name of the drive where you want the folder to be created. It will probably be the C:\ drive.
4. If necessary, click the name of the folder within which the presentation folder will be placed.
5. Open **File** and select **New**, and then click **Folder**.
6. In the text box, replace the words "New Folder" with the name you want for your presentation folder. Then press **ENTER**.

TIP

If you are unsure what the disks are on your computer, click **My Computer** in the Folders pane on the left of the Explorer window to display the drives on your machine as shown here.

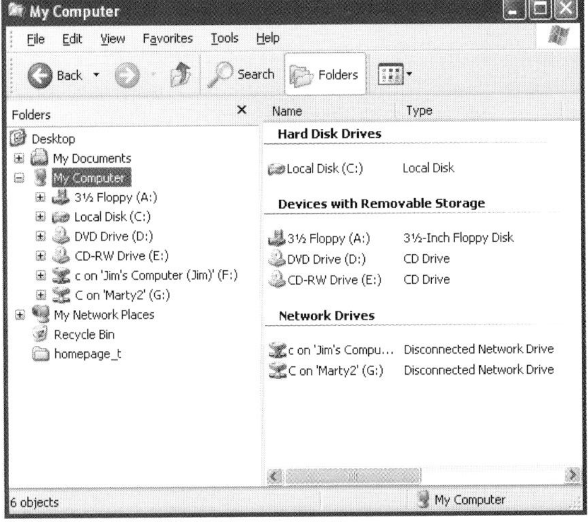

Change the Default Save Folder

To store all your PowerPoint presentation files in one place, direct PowerPoint to save your files in a default folder. Follow these steps:

1. Assuming PowerPoint is started, open **Tools** and select **Options**.
2. In the Options dialog box, click the **Save** tab.
3. Under **Default File Location,** shown in Figure 2-1, enter the path to the folder you want to be the default storage place.

TIP

You can set the time interval that a file Save will automatically take place. Open **File**, select **Options,** and then click the **Save** tab. In the **Save AutoRecover Info Every __ Minutes**, enter the number of minutes that you want the automatic save to occur.

CAUTION

Do not rely on AutoRecovery to back up your files. This is something *you* need to do on a regular basis to keep from losing data. For example, if your computer fails and you have to reboot, AutoRecovery will attempt to save the document you're working in and recover as much of it as it can, but—I can sadly tell you—that it seldom saves everything you've done. And if you elect to not save the recovered file, you will lose everything you've entered since you last saved your data. Saving your data rules!

NOTE

To speed your file saves, specify that only the changes will be saved when you click Save. To do this, open **Tools** and select **Options**. Click the **Save** tab. Select the **Allow Fast Saves** check box, as seen in Figure 2-1. Then, when you are through for the day, you can clear the check mark. Saving with this option unselected will save the whole presentation.

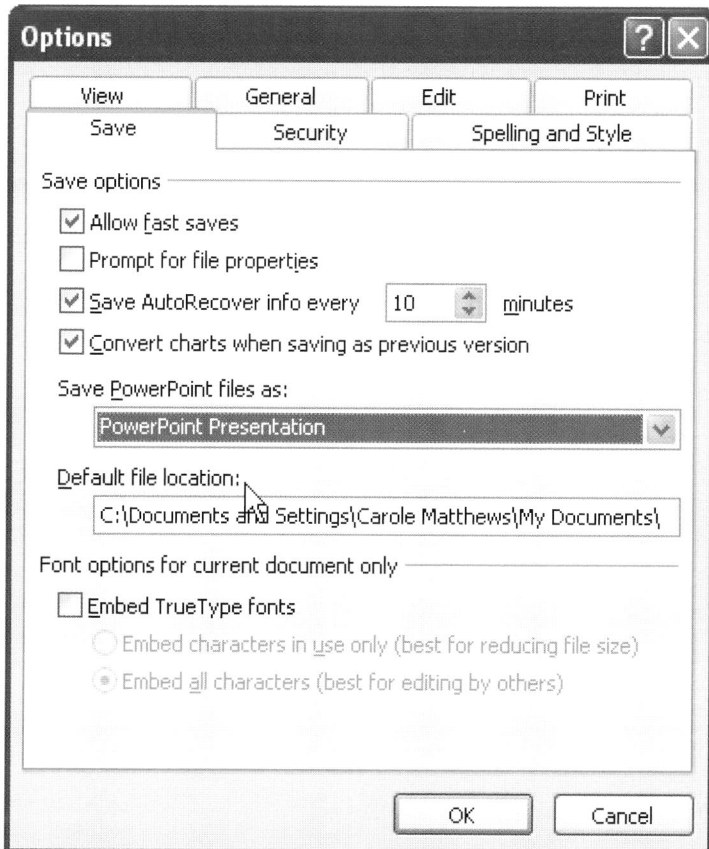

***Figure 2-1:** You can set up one location to be the default Save location for all your PowerPoint presentations*

Create a Presentation

There are four ways to begin creating your presentation: using the AutoContent wizard to build a complete presentation which you then can modify, using a template that defines the design and layout of a slide, using another existing presentation and then modifying it, and starting from scratch.

Create a Presentation Using AutoContent Wizard

The AutoContent Wizard creates a complete presentation, including text, and requires only minimal input from you. You select the presentation type from a menu of options, establish the output mode for the presentation (such as a web presentation, on-screen presentation, black and white overheads, color overheads, or 35 mm slides), give it a title and select some options (such as a footer), and choose whether you want to display the date last modified and slide number.

Figure 2-2: The AutoContent Wizard guides you through creating a predefined presentation that can be modified to suit your needs. Here you select the type of presentation you want to build

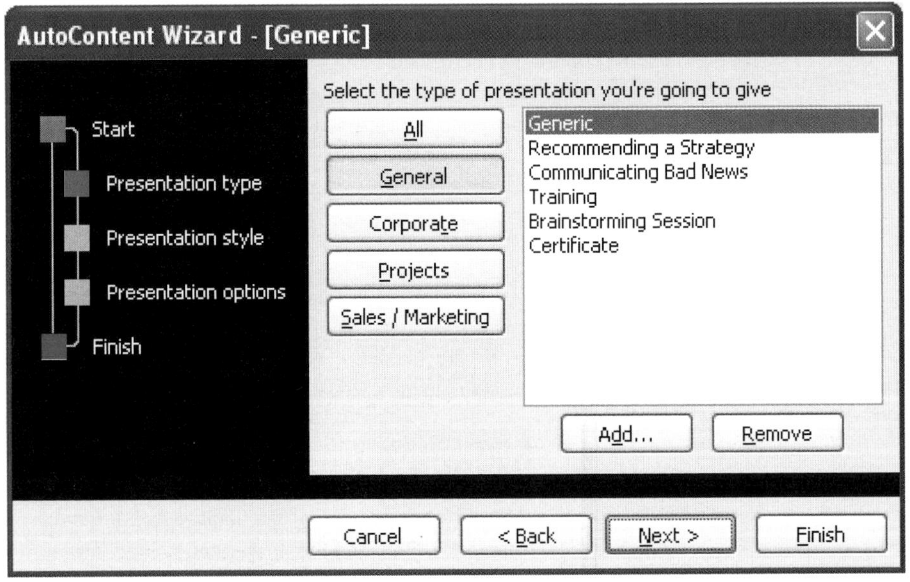

1. Select **File** and click **New** to bring up the New Presentation tasks pane.
2. Click **From AutoContent Wizard** in the New Presentation tasks pane. The AutoContent Wizard dialog box will be displayed and will lead you through a series of dialog boxes that define your complete presentation.
3. Click **Next** to begin the wizard's process. You are asked to select the type of presentation you're going to give, as seen in Figure 2-2. To see the choices available to you, click the type of presentation:
   - **All**, to see all the presentations available
   - **General**, shown in Figure 2-2, for broad, general topics
   - **Corporate**, for business, financial, and employee presentations
   - **Projects**, for project management and report presentations
   - **Sales/Marketing**, for sales and marketing types of presentations
4. Select a type and click **Next**.
5. You will be asked what type of output you will use. Select an option and click **Next**.

NOTE

When you select the type of presentation you're going to give, you may get a message from Microsoft PowerPoint that the template is not installed. Click **Yes** to install it. PowerPoint will find the template and install it for you. You may need your installation CD to install the template.

6. Type the Presentation Title and whether to include a Footer, Date Last Updated, and Slide Number. If you choose to include a footer, you must type the Footer text. When you're finished, click **Next**.
7. Click **Finish** to view the completed presentation.
8. To modify the presentation, type your own words over those suggested by PowerPoint; add graphics, charts, or other visual effects; add or delete slides; and add other changes as required. (Chapters 4 through 9 contain detailed information on how to do some of these tasks.)

Add a Template to the Wizard

To add a template to those that the AutoContent Wizard will create:

1. Open **File** and click **New** for the New Presentation tasks pane.
2. Click **From AutoContent Wizard** to start the wizard.
3. Click **Next**. Select the Type of Presentation You're Going To Give that the new template will be assigned to.
4. Click **Add**.
5. Find and select the template, as shown in Figure 2-3, and click **OK**.
6. To end the session, click **Cancel** to end the Auto-Content Wizard. To create a presentation from the new template, continue to number 7.
7. Select your template from the Type of Presentation You're Going to Give and click **Next.**
8. The Wizard process will continue with your new template. Continue to supply needed input as described under Create a Presentation Using Auto-Content Wizard.

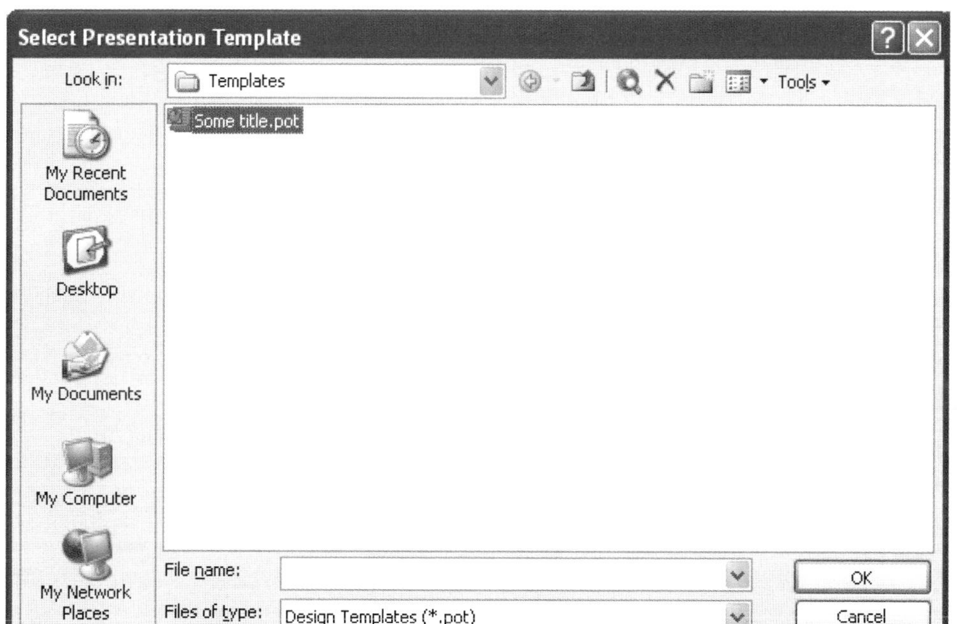

Figure 2-3: You can add your own template to the presentation choices offered by the wizard

NOTE

The Design button on the Formatting toolbar above the tasks pane will immediately open the Slide Design tasks pane.

TIP

By default, the design template will apply to all slides of a presentation unless you specify otherwise. See "Working With Templates" to see how to apply the design to selected slides.

TIP

To enlarge the thumbnail preview and more clearly see the detail, point to a thumbnail and click the down arrow that appears on the right side of it. Then select **Show Large Previews** from the context menu.

CAUTION

If you "click" the thumbnail rather than "point to" it, the design will be applied to the current slide.

Create a Presentation Using a Design Template

A *design template* is a predefined slide with fonts, color scheme, layout design, and art elements that you can copy to give your new presentation a unified design. The design template can be one that PowerPoint offers or a slide that you design and save as a template. Follow these steps:

1. If needed, open **File** and click **New** to display the New Presentation tasks pane.
2. On the tasks pane, click **From Design Template**.
3. In the Slide Design tasks pane, shown in Figure 2-4, click the design thumbnail preview you want to see.
4. Repeat the steps below to create your presentation, slide by slide.
   - Fill in the text for your presentation either on the slide or in the Outline tab. (See "Create an Outline" in this chapter on using the outline approach.)
   - To vary the layout for a slide, select **Format** and click **Slide Layout**. Click the layout you want for the slide you're working on.
   - Click **New Slide** to insert another blank slide. New Slide
   - Add clip art, graphics, and other content.
5. After you have finished, save your presentation. Select **File** and click **Save As**. Enter a name for your presentation and click **Save**. The presentation will be saved in the PowerPoint default folder.

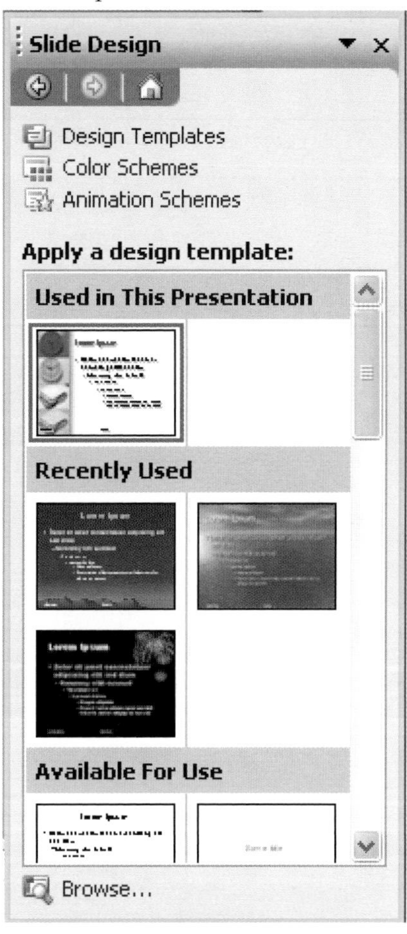

Figure 2-4: The Slide Design tasks pane offers a selection of templates that you can copy onto your slides to give them a unified and professional look

QUICKSTEPS

WORKING WITH TEMPLATES

FIND OTHER MICROSOFT TEMPLATES

1. Scroll to the last thumbnail of the Slide Design tasks pane and click **Design Templates on Microsoft Office Online**.

Design Templates on Microsoft Office Online

2. Click the link to the template you want. Follow the download instructions to install the template. The new template will appear on a blank slide in PowerPoint.

APPLY A TEMPLATE TO ALL SLIDES IN A PRESENTATION

Use the context menu for the template thumbnail to select the option to apply the template to all slides.

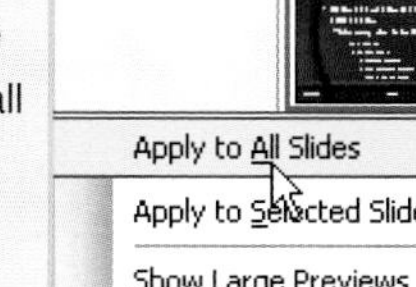

1. Right-click the template thumbnail.
2. Click **Apply To All Slides**.

APPLY A TEMPLATE TO SELECTED SLIDES

1. To select the slides to which the template will be applied, either:
   - Press CTRL and click the thumbnail in the Slides tab.

   -Or-

   - Press CTRL and click slides in the Slide Sorter view.
2. Right-click the template, or point to the template and click the down arrow on the right side of the template thumbnail in the tasks pane.
3. Click **Apply To Selected Slides**.

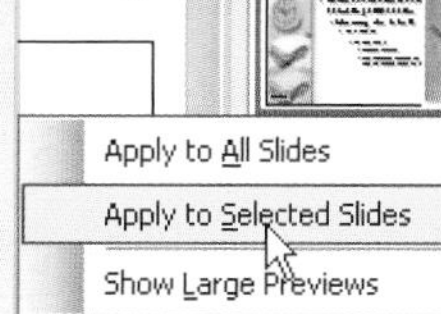

SET A DEFAULT TEMPLATE TO APPLY A TEMPLATE TO ALL FUTURE PRESENTATIONS:

1. Under Available For Use in the Slide Design tasks pane, right-click the thumbnail you want.
2. Select **Use For All New Presentations**.

Create a Template

After you have designed a slide with your desired color scheme, layout, and fonts, you can save it as a template to use in formatting and adding color and design elements to new presentations. Here's how:

1. Create a slide or presentation using one of the techniques in this chapter.
2. When you are satisfied with the results, select **File** and click **Save As**.
3. In the **File Name** box, type a name for the new template.
4. In the **Save As Type** drop-down list box, click **Design Template**.

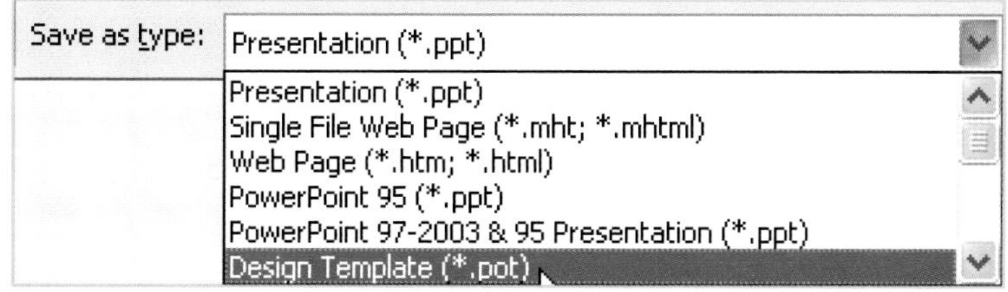

5. Click **Save**.

The template will be saved in the default template folder where PowerPoint design templates are stored and will appear in the Design Template tasks pane.

Create a Presentation from Another Presentation

To copy a presentation, rename it, and then modify it according to your needs:

1. Select **File** and click **New**.
2. On the New Presentation tasks pane, click **From Existing Presentation**.
3. Select the name of the presentation or template you want to use and click **Create New**, as displayed in Figure 2-5.

UICKSTEPS

CHOOSING LAYOUT AND DESIGN ELEMENTS

CHOOSE A SLIDE LAYOUT

Before you start designing and creating your presentation, you will want to familiarize yourself with the slide layouts that come with PowerPoint. Click the tasks pane title bar and select **Slide Layout**. Scroll through the layout options. (If the tasks pane is not showing, select **View** and click **Tasks Pane**.)

CHOOSE A DESIGN TEMPLATE

The Design template contains predefined color schemes, fonts, slide layouts, and other design elements. Click the **tasks pane title bar** and select **Slide Design**. Scroll through the options. To see them more clearly, right-click a thumbnail and choose **Show Large Previews**.

TIP

PowerPoint uses Title and Slide Masters to establish a common look throughout the presentation. Use the Title Master and Slide Master to format those aspects that you want to be present throughout the presentation—such as logo placement, title and footer placement, fonts, and so on. (See Chapter 3.)

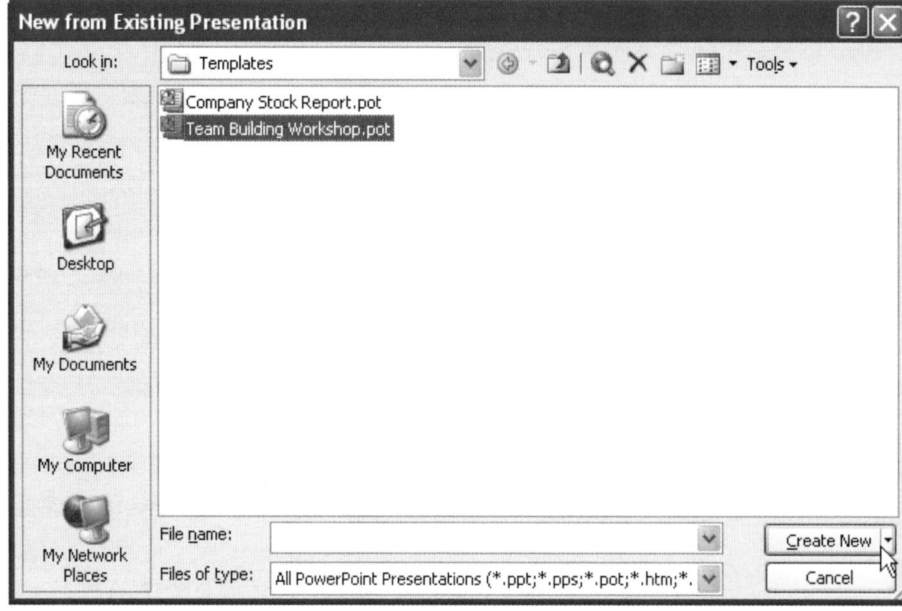

Figure 2-5: In this dialog box, you find the presentation and create a new copy of it

4. Modify the presentation by highlighting text and replacing it with your own; deleting unnecessary slides; inserting new slides; inserting your own graphics, charts, and art; and rearranging the slides according to your needs.
5. Select **File** and click **Save As**. Enter a name for the presentation and click **Save.**

Create a Presentation from Scratch

When you create a presentation from scratch, you'll begin with blank slides and add layouts, color schemes, fonts, graphics and charts, other design elements, and text.

1. Select **File** and click **New**. The New Presentations tasks pane will be displayed.
2. Click **Blank Presentation** from the tasks pane. A blank title page slide will be displayed.
3. Click and type over **Click To Add Title** to enter the title of your presentation. If you want to add a subtitle, click and type over **Click To Add Subtitle**.

QUICKSTEPS

ADDING CONTENT TO A SLIDE

The following elements are available to help you design the look of your slides.

DEFINE FONTS

To assign fonts to text, highlight the text by dragging the pointer over it. Then select **Format** and click **Font**. Select the Font, Font Style, Font Size, and click **OK**. (See Chapter 4 for additional information on fonts.) Font, Font Style, and Font Size are also available on the Formatting toolbar.

SELECT A LAYOUT

Click the tasks pane title bar and click **Slide Layout**. Click the layout thumbnail you want. To apply the layout to more than one slide, right-click the thumbnail and click **Apply To Selected Slides** or **Use For All New Presentations**.

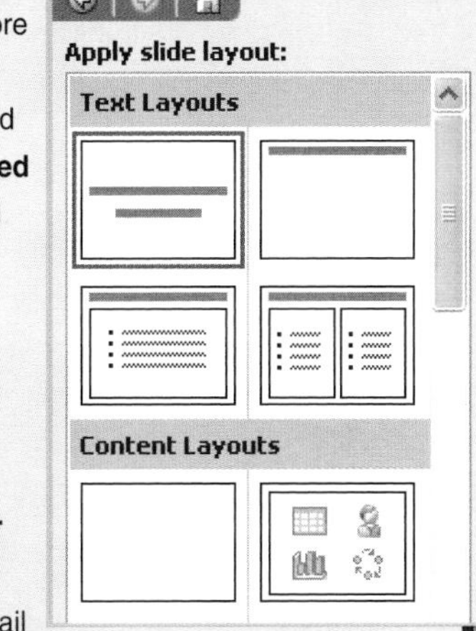

ADD COLOR SCHEMES

Click the tasks pane title bar and click **Slide Design – Color Schemes**. Click the color scheme thumbnail you want. To apply the color scheme to more than one slide, right-click the thumbnail and click the appropriate option on the context menu. (See Chapter 3 for more information.)

Continued...

4. When you are satisfied with the slide, click **New Slide**, normally above the tasks pane, to insert another blank slide.
5. Add text and other content to your slides.
6. Repeat steps 4 through 5 for as many slides as you have in your presentation.
7. Save the presentation. Select **File** and click **Save As**. Enter a name and click **Save**.

Outline a Presentation

Since PowerPoint is more easily managed when you have an outline of what your main points will be, I recommend that you create an outline before you start building your presentation. The outline should contain:

- Main points you want to make which will become the titles of the slides
- Subsidiary points that support the main points and will become the bulleted content of each slide

Your main and subsidiary points are essential to the presentation. Although not essential at this point, certain secondary considerations are beneficial in flushing out your main points and the "feel" of your presentation, and the more you think these through initially, the more smoothly your presentation will flow.

- What graphics will you want to use on each slide? Do you have charts or graphs that tell the story? Are there photos that will take up part of the slide? Will you have a logo or other mandated identification on the chart?
- What color schemes might you want to use? Are there company colors that you want to use or colors you want to stay away from? While this seems like a later step, one of the first jobs you will do is select a design template for your slides where color schemes are provided. If you don't have a clue to begin with, don't worry. Color and layouts are easy to implement and to change. The points you want to make are most important.

Create an Outline

The outline is created, modified, and viewed using the Outline tab, shown in Figure 2-6. An outline is created in three ways: from scratch, using the AutoContent Wizard, or inserting text from other sources.

ADDING CONTENT TO A SLIDE

(Continued)

SELECT AN ANIMATION SCHEME

To display animated text on your slide, click the tasks pane title bar and click **Slide Design - Animation Schemes**. Find the animation scheme you want and click it. (See Chapter 8 for more information.)

INSERT ART AND GRAPHICS

Open **Insert** and click the name of the art or graphic object you want to insert. Drag the object where you want it and resize it as needed.

-Or-

Create and insert your own drawing. (See Chapter 8 for additional information.)

INSERT A TABLE

Insert a table to present more organized data. You can insert a table by creating one from scratch, or you can import one from Excel. (See Chapter 5 for more information.)

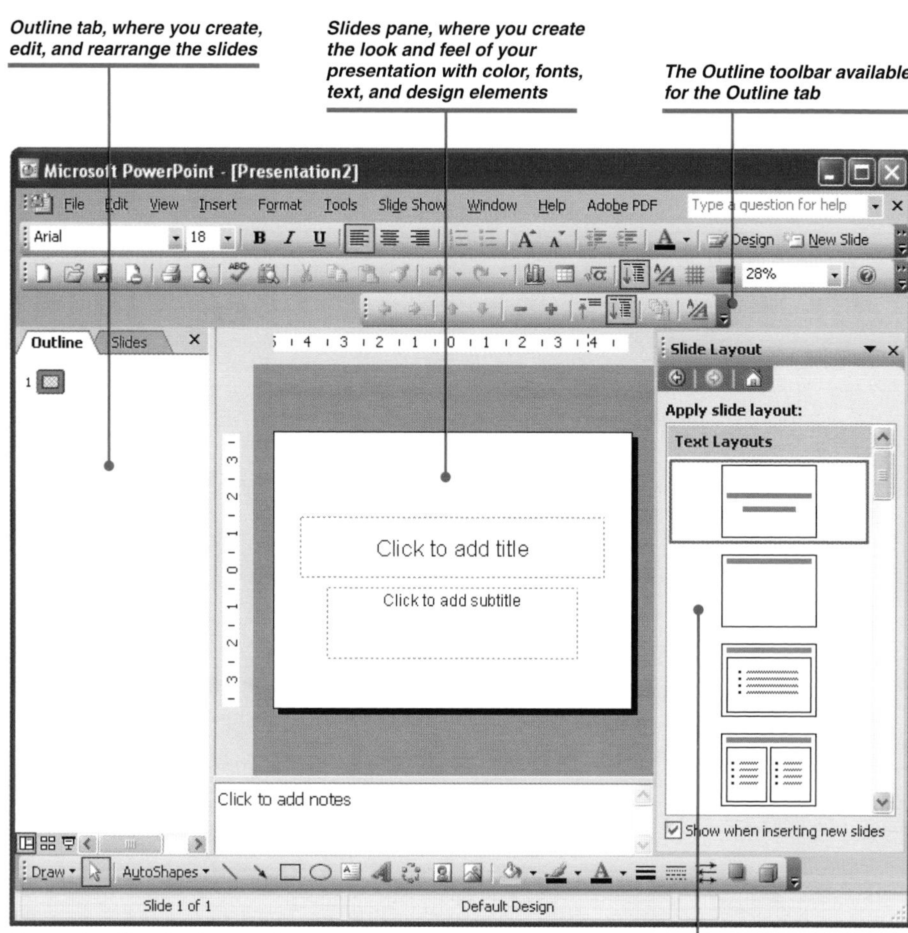

Figure 2-6: The Outline tab is where you can work with your slides to organize, create, and modify your presentation

TIP

If you don't see your Outline tab, open **View** and click **Normal** (Restore Panes).

NOTE

Instead of using the Promote and Demote buttons, you can also press **ENTER** to create a a new bulleted line. When you press **TAB**, the bulleted line will be indented. If you press **SHIFT+TAB**, the indent will be removed. Pressing **CTRL+ENTER** will create a new slide.

TIP

For more typing room in the Outline tab, expand the tab by dragging its inside edge into the Slides pane.

CREATE AN OUTLINE FROM SCRATCH

To create a fresh outline, type your text into the Outline tab.

1. To open a blank presentation, open **File** and click **New**.
2. Display the Outlining toolbar by opening **View**, selecting **Toolbars**, and clicking **Outlining**.
3. Click **Blank Presentation** from the New Presentations tasks pane.
4. Click the **Outline** tab.
5. Click to the right of the Outline slide icon to place the insertion point.
6. Type the title of your presentation. Press **ENTER** to insert a new slide.
7. Type your first topic or main point. Press **ENTER** when you are done. Click **Demote** on the Outlining toolbar to enter sub-points into the presentation.
8. Click **Promote** on the Outlining toolbar to move to the next slide.
9. Continue typing and pressing **ENTER, Promote,** and **Demote** to move the text into headings and bulleted points until the presentation is outlined.

CREATE AN OUTLINE WITH AUTOCONTENT

To start with an outline that is similar to what you need, use an AutoContent presentation, which you can then modify.

1. Create a presentation using AutoContent (see "Create a Presentation Using AutoContent Wizard" earlier in this chapter). Follow the instructions to find and create a presentation that is closest to that which you are trying to build. The presentation and its outline will be displayed. (See sample shown in Figure 2-7.)

1 2 3 4 5 6 7 8 9 10

QUICKSTEPS

INDENTING WITH THE KEYBOARD

INCREASE INDENTS

Press **TAB.**

–Or–

Press **ALT+SHIFT+RIGHT ARROW.**

DECREASE INDENTS

Press **SHIFT+TAB.**

–Or–

Press **ALT+SHIFT+LEFT ARROW.**

MOVE UP A LEVEL

Press **ALT+SHIFT+UP ARROW.**

MOVE DOWN A LEVEL

Press **ALT+SHIFT+DOWN ARROW.**

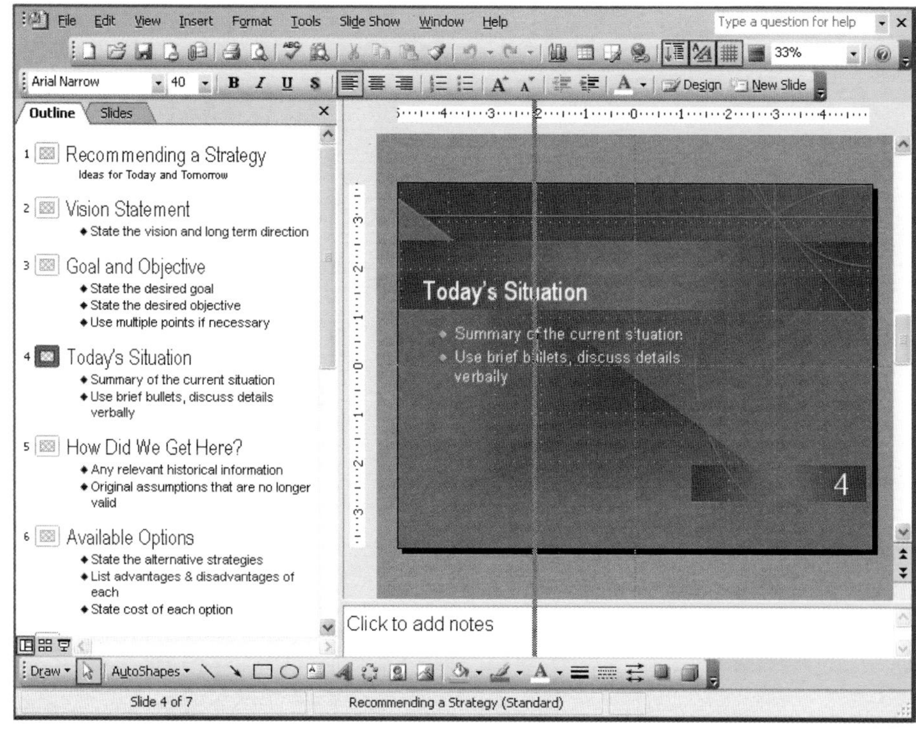

Figure 2-7: When you create a presentation using an AutoContent presentation, an outline is already available which can be easily modified to suit your needs

2. Expand the Outline tab by dragging the edge into the Slides pane, as shown in Figure 2-7.
3. Highlight the text to be replaced and type your own text. As you type, your new text will appear on the slide. You can skip back and forth between the slide and the outline as you make your changes.

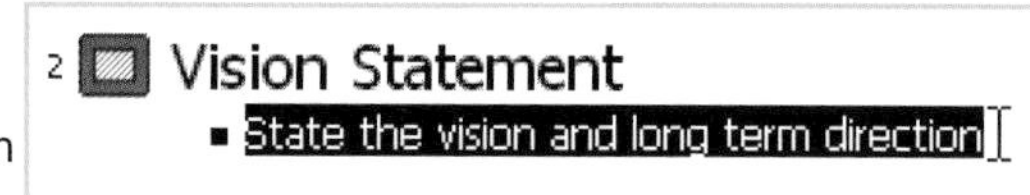

4. To delete slides that are not needed, right-click the slide icon in the Outline tab and click **Delete Slide.**
5. To insert a new slide, click the slide icon preceding where you want the new one inserted, and click **New Slide** on the Formatting toolbar.

New Slide

6. To save your presentation, select **File** and click **Save As**. Give the presentation a new name and click **Save**.

TIP

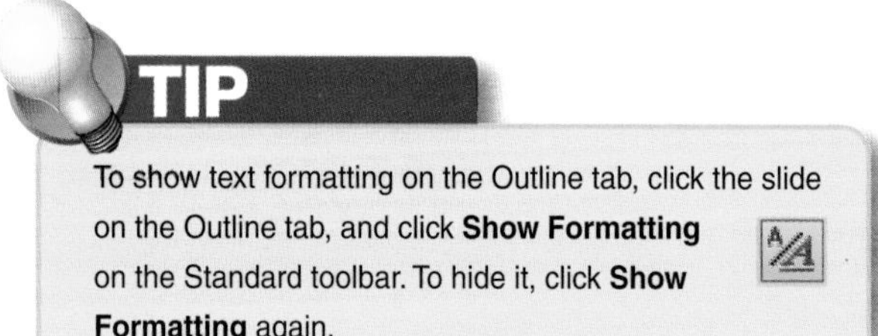

To show text formatting on the Outline tab, click the slide on the Outline tab, and click **Show Formatting** on the Standard toolbar. To hide it, click **Show Formatting** again.

CAUTION

PowerPoint looks to the formatting of outlines in the source document, such as a Word .doc file, to establish its slide content. The outline must be formatted as headings. Up to 5 levels of headings are recognized by PowerPoint. If you use normal text, it may not be recognized by PowerPoint.

Insert an Outline From Other Sources

You can create slides from an outline you have previously created in another document. Depending on the format of the text, the formatting retained and used by PowerPoint will differ.

- A **Microsoft Word (.doc) or Rich Text Format (.rtf)** outline will use paragraph breaks to mark the start of a new slide. Each paragraph will become a slide title. However, if the document is formatted with headings, Heading 1 will become the title of the slide, Heading 2 will be the second level, Heading 3 the third level, and so on. (See Figure 2-8.)

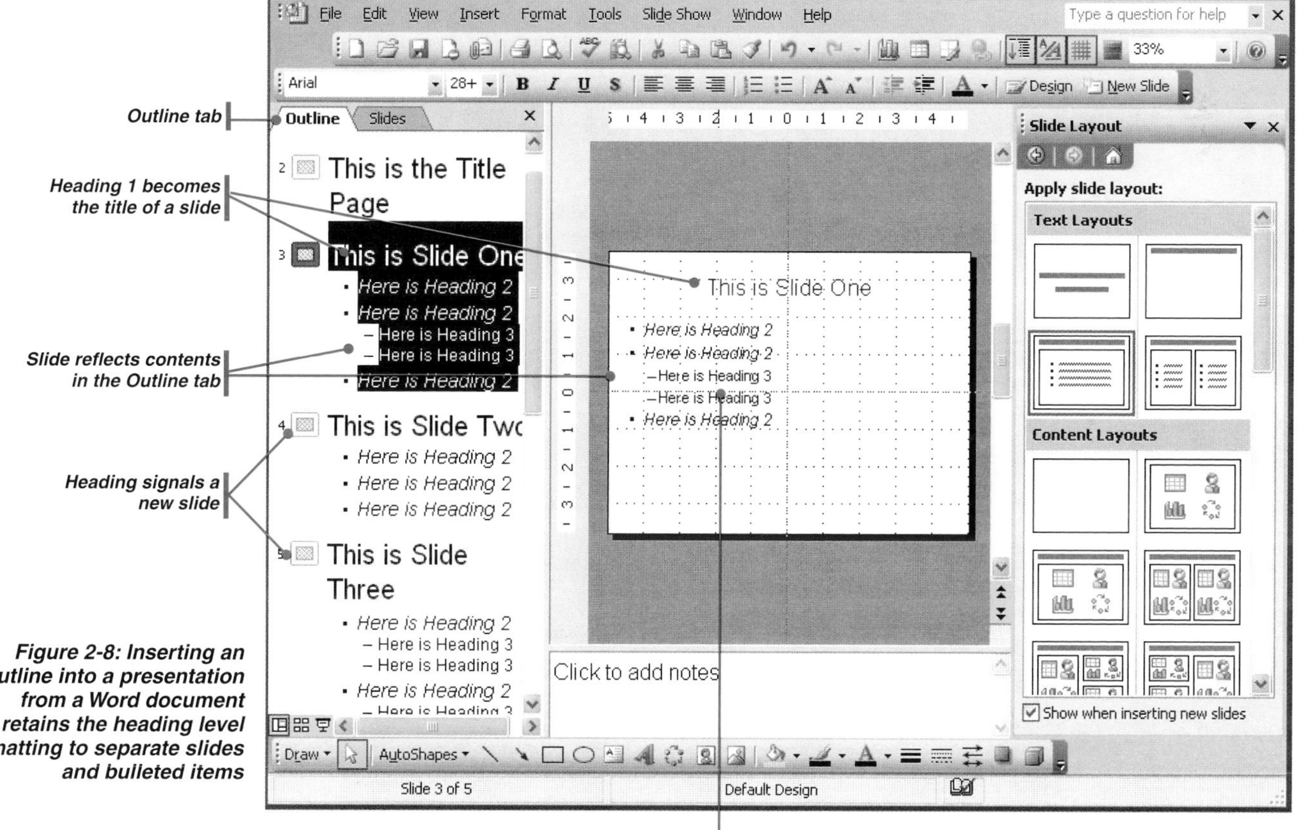

Figure 2-8: Inserting an outline into a presentation from a Word document retains the heading level formatting to separate slides and bulleted items

QUICKSTEPS

USING THE OUTLINING TOOLBAR

DISPLAY THE OUTLINING TOOLBAR

Although some of the Outlining toolbar buttons are available on the Standard and Formatting toolbars, you can display all the buttons in one convenient toolbar: Select **View**, choose **Toolbars**, and click **Outlining**.

PROMOTE OR DEMOTE OUTLINE TEXT

- Click **Promote** to move the selected text in a slide up one level.
- Click **Demote** to move the selected text in a slide down one level.

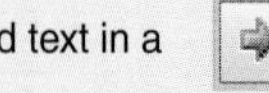

MOVE UP OR MOVE DOWN OUTLINE TEXT

- Click **Move Up** to move the selected text of a slide up one line or item.
- Click **Move Down** to move the selected text of a slide down one line or item.

COLLAPSE OR EXPAND A SLIDE

- Click **Collapse** to hide the detail beneath the title of a selected slide.
- Click **Expand** to show the detail beneath a title of a selected slide.

–Or–

- On the outline itself, right-click a slide and click either **Collapse** or **Expand.**

COLLAPSE ALL OR EXPAND ALL

- Click **Collapse All** to hide all the detail lines in the outline.
- Click **Expand All** to show all the detail lines in the outline.

Continued...

- An **HTML** outline will retain its formatting; however, the text will appear in a text box on the slide and can only be edited in the Slides pane, not in the Outline tab. In addition, you must create a separate HTML file for each slide. (To see the HTML file in the Insert Outline dialog box, you may have to select .htm as the Files of Type.)
- A **Plain Text** (.txt) outline will adopt the styles of the current presentation. PowerPoint will use paragraph separations to start a new slide.

To insert an outline from another source:

1. Select **Insert** and click **Slides From Outline**.
2. In the Insert Outline dialog box, find the location and name of the outline to be used, select it, and click **Insert**.

Preview the Outline

To preview an outline and then print it:

1. Click Expand All on the Outlining toolbar to expand the entire outline so that all detail is showing.
2. Select **File** and click **Print Preview**.
3. Open the **Print What** drop-down list box, and click **Outline View**.
4. Click **Print**.
5. Click **OK** in the Print dialog box.

Print the Outline

To print the outline without previewing it:

1. Open **File** and click **Print**.
2. In the Print dialog box, open the **Print What** drop-down list box. Click **Outline View**.
3. Click **OK** to print.

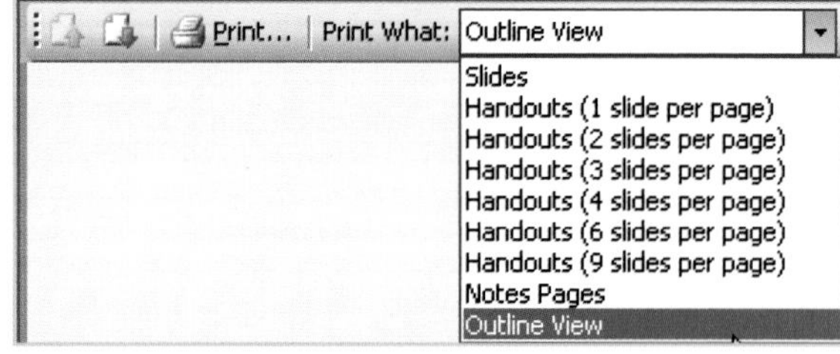

USING THE OUTLINING TOOLBAR

(Continued)

CREATE A SUMMARY SLIDE

To create a separate slide that displays the titles of selected slides, click the slides you want to include and then click **Summary Slide**. Note that all selected slides must be contiguous in the Outline tab. To create a summary slide of non-contiguous slides, use the Slide Sorter view.

SHOW FORMATTING

Click **Show Formatting** to toggle between showing and not showing the formatting in the outline text.

TIP

If you find that you cannot get a pointer or gray box that signals your ability to drag-and-drop text, the option may be turned off. Open **Tools**, select **Options** and click the **Edit** tab. Place a check mark in the **Drag-And-Drop Text Editing** check box. Then click **OK**. Now when you select the text and point to it with your pointer, a gray box should appear, indicating that you can drag the text.

Insert a Hyperlink in the Outline

To insert a hyperlink in the outline:

1. In your outline, highlight the text that you want to contain the hyperlink.
2. Right-click your highlighted text and click **Hyperlink**.
3. In the Insert Hyperlink dialog box, find the destination for the link. If it is within the outline itself, click **Place In The Document** and click the slide, as seen in Figure 2-9.
4. Click **OK**.

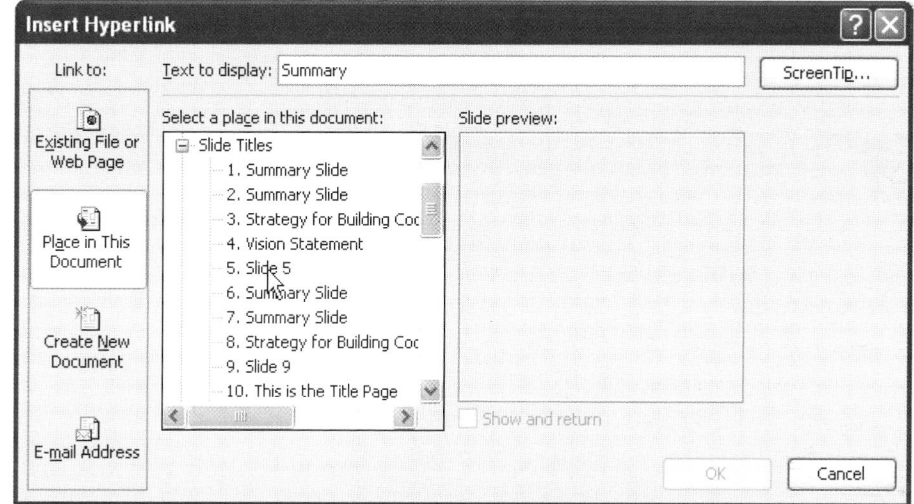

Figure 2-9: Hyperlinks can provide a means to "jump" from one part of an outline to another

QUICKSTEPS

DEALING WITH PERMISSIONS

Permission to view a presentation can be restricted by the author only. Also, only the author can remove restrictions for viewing a presentation. Even viewing the permissions is restricted to the author or persons they specify. Note that the Rights Management (RM) must be installed in order for this to be available to you, and you must download an RM account certificate. To install it and download the certificate, you must have a Microsoft Passport and be the system administrator.

VIEW PERMISSIONS FOR A PRESENTATION

To see the permissions for a presentation:

- Right-click the task pane title bar, and click **Shared Workspace**.
- From the Shared Workspace task pane, click the **Status** tab.

RESTRICT PERMISSION TO VIEW A PRESENTATION

- From the File menu, select **Permission** and click **Do Not Distribute**.
- In the Permission dialog box, place a check mark next to **Restrict Permission To This Presentation**.
- In the Read and Change boxes, supply the names or e-mail addresses of persons with permission to view the presentation.

REMOVE PERMISSION RESTRICTIONS

- From the File menu, select **Permission**.
- Click **Unrestricted Access**.

Send the Outline to Microsoft Word

To send the outline to Microsoft Word for additional editing or formatting:

1. Select **File**, choose **Send To**, and click **Microsoft Office Word**.

2. In the Send To Microsoft Office Word dialog box, click **Outline Only**.
3. Click **OK**.

Microsoft Word will open and the outline will be displayed.

How to...

- *Navigate from Slide to Slide*
- *Navigating with the Keyboard*
- *Insert a Slide*
- *Moving or Copying Slides*
- *Display Two or More Presentations at Once*
- *Using a Keyboard with Slides*
- *Duplicate a Slide*
- *Copy a Design Using Browse*
- *Create a Color Scheme*
- *Use a Slide Layout*
- *Copy Color with Format Painter*
- *Using Headers and Footers on Slides*
- *Work with Hyperlinks*
- *Create a Note*
- *Using Headers and Footers on Notes and Handouts*
- *Print Notes and Handouts*
- *Preview Speaker Notes*
- *Manage Slide and Title Masters*
- *Working With Slides Masters*
- *Work with the Notes Master*
- *Change the Handout Master*

Chapter 3
Working with Slides, Notes, and Masters

In this chapter you will find how to work with presentations at the slide level. In addition to navigating through the slides in various views of PowerPoint, you will learn to insert, delete, rearrange, and copy slides, as well as to work with permissions, hyperlinks, and colors. This chapter also covers using Notes for preparing speaker and handout notes. It addresses using Slide and Title Masters to make overall changes to your presentation.

Work with Slides

Working with slides enables you to find your way around PowerPoint and to manipulate the slides, both individually and globally. This section addresses how to insert and delete slides, display slides in a variety of ways, move and duplicate slides, work with the color or color schemes of a presentation, and how to work with hyperlinks.

QUICKSTEPS

NAVIGATING WITH THE KEYBOARD

MOVE FROM PANE TO PANE

To move from the Slides pane to the Task pane, to the Notes pane, to the Slides tab, in that order, press **F6**; press **SHIFT + F6** to move in the reverse order.

MOVE TO THE NEXT AND PREVIOUS SLIDE

You have two ways on the keyboard to move to the next or previous slide on the Slides pane and the Slides tab:

- To move to the previous slide, press **PAGE UP** or press the **UP ARROW**.
- To move to the next slide, press **PAGE DOWN** or press the **DOWN ARROW**.

MOVE TO FIRST AND LAST SLIDE

Press **CTRL+HOME** to move to the first slide.

Press **CTRL+END** to move to the last slide.

MOVE TO NEXT PLACEHOLDER (DOTTED BOX)

Press **CTRL+ENTER**.

OPEN AND CLOSE THE TASK PANE

Press **CTRL+F1**.

START AND END SLIDE SHOWS

- To start a slide show on the current slide, press **SHIFT+F5**.
- To start a slide show beginning with the first slide, press **F5**.
- To close the slide show and return to Normal view, press **ESC**.
- To switch between the slide show and the Normal view (or vice versa), press **ALT+TAB**.

Navigate from Slide to Slide

To move between the slides, you can use the Slides pane, the Outline tab, or the Slides tab to select and move to the slide you want.

- On the Slides tab, click the thumbnail of the slide you want.
- On the Outline tab, click the icon of the slide you want.
- On the Slides pane or either tab, click the vertical scroll bar to move to the next or previous slide.
- On the Slide Sorter view, click the vertical scroll bar to move to the next screen of thumbnails. Click the scroll bar to move more slowly. Click the up or down arrows on the scroll bar to move row by row. Click on each slide to select it.
- On the Slides pane or either tab, drag the scroll bar to move to the slide indicated by the label.

Insert a Slide

You can insert a new blank slide from several places in PowerPoint. The most common ways are:

- On the Formatting toolbar, click **New Slide**.
- In the Slide Layout task pane, right-click a layout and click Insert New Slide.
- In the Outline tab, when entering bulleted text, press **CTRL+ENTER**.
- In the Slides tab, right-click the slide before the one you want to insert, and click **New Slide** or press **ENTER**.
- In the Slide Sorter view, right-click the slide preceding the new one, and click **New Slide** or press **CTRL+M**.

INSERT A SLIDE FROM ANOTHER FILE

To insert a slide duplicated from another presentation, you must find and open the file that contains the slide, then select the slide or slides that you want to copy into your current presentation.

1. Click the slide in the Slides tab positioned immediately before the one to be inserted.
2. Select **Insert** and click **Slides From Files**. The Slide Finder dialog box will be displayed.
3. Click **Browse** to find the file. When found, select the file and click **Open**. The Slide Finder dialog box, illustrated in Figure 3-1, will be displayed.

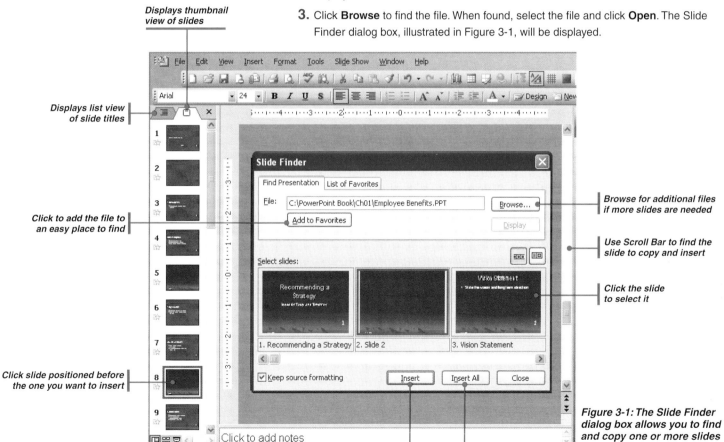

Displays thumbnail view of slides

Displays list view of slide titles

Click to add the file to an easy place to find

Click slide positioned before the one you want to insert

Browse for additional files if more slides are needed

Use Scroll Bar to find the slide to copy and insert

Click the slide to select it

Click to insert one slide or all the slides of the presentation

Figure 3-1: The Slide Finder dialog box allows you to find and copy one or more slides from another presentation into your current one

1

2

3

4

5

6

7

8

9

10

TIP

Before closing the dialog box, you can work back and forth between the Slides tab and the Slide Finder dialog box to select a positioning slide from the Slides tab and then find the next slide to be inserted in the Slide Finder dialog box. If you want to copy slides from additional presentations, you can Browse for other files and insert slides from them without closing the dialog box.

NOTE

To insert a complete presentation, follow steps 1 through 4 in "Insert a Slide from Another File." After you have found the presentation, click **Insert All** in the Slide Finder dialog box. The complete presentation will be inserted into the destination presentation immediately following the selected slide.

TIP

To delete a slide from the Slide Sorter view, the Outline tab, or the Slides tab: click the thumbnail slide to select it, and press **DELETE**. You can also right-click the thumbnail slide, and click **Delete Slide**. Or lastly, select a slide, select **Edit,** and click **Delete Slide**.

4. To retain the formatting from the source presentation, click **Keep Source Formatting**. If you do not select this, the formatting of the destination presentation (the one you are currently working in) will be used.
5. To view the slides in order to select them, you can click an icon to see two views, as shown here: to see the slides only, click the leftmost icon. To see the titles and a preview of the slide, click the rightmost icon.

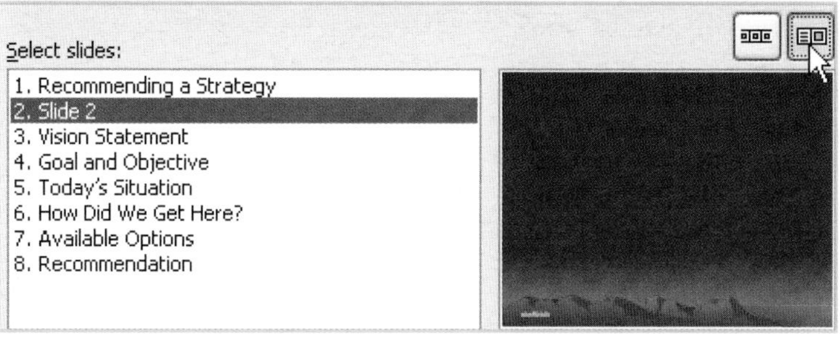

6. To copy selected slides, click the slides you want to insert into your current presentation, and then click **Insert**. In the list view, either press **CTRL** while clicking non-contiguous slides to add them, or press **SHIFT** while clicking contiguous slides to add them.
7. To copy all the slides, click **Insert All**.
8. When you have inserted all the slides you want, click **Close**.

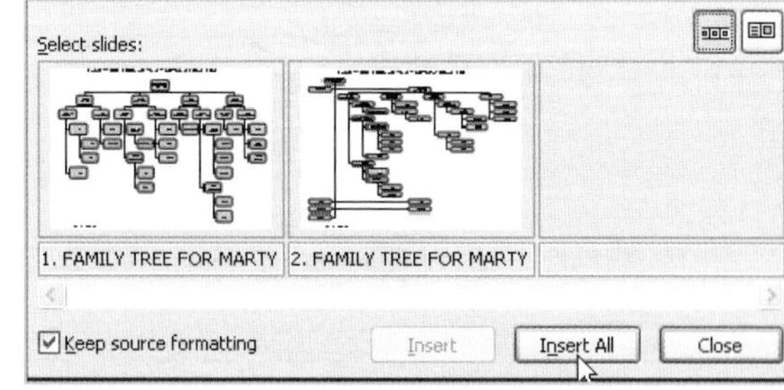

QUICKSTEPS

MOVING OR COPYING SLIDES

You can move or copy your slides most easily from the Outline tab, the Slides tab, or the Slides Sorter View.

- To copy a slide on the Outline tab, right-click the slide to be copied, and click **Copy** on the context menu. Right-click the slide preceding where you want the new slide to go, and click **Paste** on the context menu.
- To move a slide on the Outline tab, click the slide icon to be moved, and drag it to the new location. You can select and drag multiple slides at the same time if they are contiguous. To select more than one slide at a time, press **SHIFT**, and then click the first and last slide icon. Drag the slides while pressing **SHIFT**.
- To copy a slide on the Slides tab or the Slide Sorter view, right-click the slide to be copied, and click **Copy** on the context menu. Right-click the slide preceding where you want the new slide to go, and click **Paste** on the context menu.
- On the Slides tab or Slides Sorter view, click one or more thumbnail slides to be moved, and drag them to a new location. (To select more than one non-contiguous slide at a time, press **CTRL** when you click the slide thumbnails. If you are selecting contiguous slides to be moved, press **SHIFT**, and click the first and last slide.) Drag while pressing **CTRL** or **SHIFT**. The insertion point line will show you where the slide will be inserted.

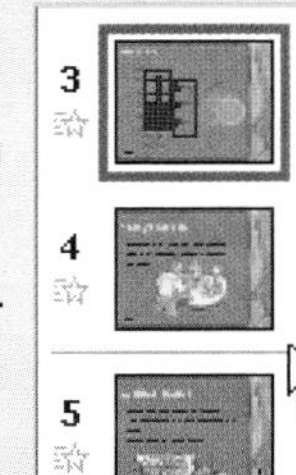

NOTE

To copy rather than move on the thumbnail slides, you can also right-click the selected slides and drag to the new location. Then click **Copy** on the context menu that will appear.

Display Two or More Presentations at Once

Opening and displaying two or more presentations opens many possibilities for dragging one slide from one presentation to another, copying color or formatting from one slide or presentation to another, and for comparing the presentations or slides side by side.

1. Open the presentations. Open **File**, click **Open,** and complete the sequence of locating and opening the presentations. (See Chapter 1 for how to open a presentation.)
2. To arrange the display of the windows:
   - Open **Window,** and click **Arrange All** to display each presentation window side by side, as seen in Figure 3-2.

   –Or–

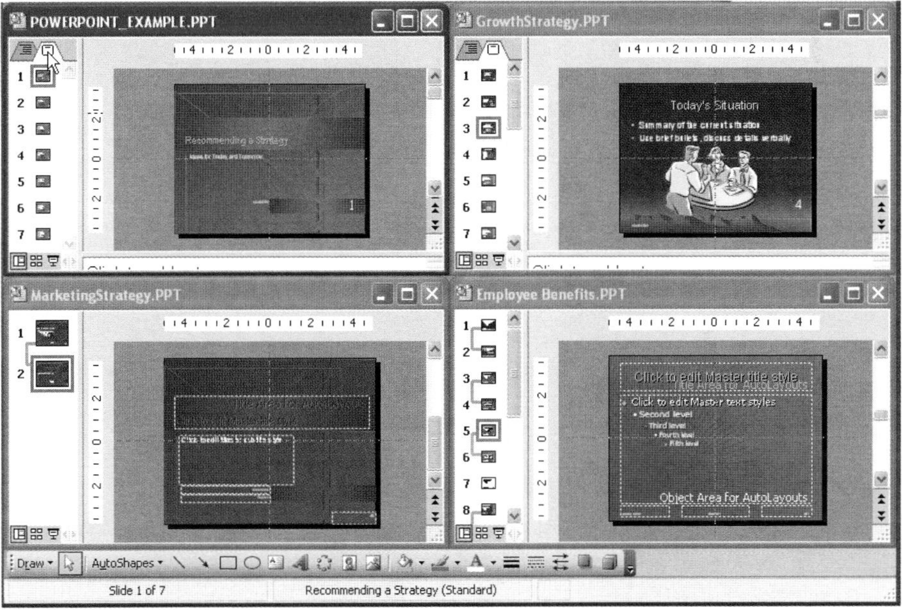

Figure 3-2: You can see each window separately by using the Arrange All command

USING A KEYBOARD WITH SLIDES

INSERT A NEW SLIDE

Press **CTRL+N**.

REMOVE A SLIDE

Press **DELETE** or press **CTRL+X**.

COPY A SLIDE

1. Click a thumbnail to select it, and press **CTRL+C**.
2. Click where you want the copied slide inserted, and press **CTRL+V**.

COPY THE CONTENTS OF A SLIDE

1. Click a thumbnail to select it, select the text to be copied, and press **CTRL+C**.
2. Move the insertion point to where you want the items copied, and press **CTRL+V**.

Where you place the insertion point will determine where the new slide will be positioned. It's possible to insert a slide into the middle of another one, splitting its contents unintentionally. Make certain you place the insertion point precisely where you want the new slide to go.

4 Revenue for Last Year
5 Available Options
State the alternative strategies
State cost of each option

- Open **Window**, and click **Cascade** to see the windows cascading, as seen in Figure 3-3.

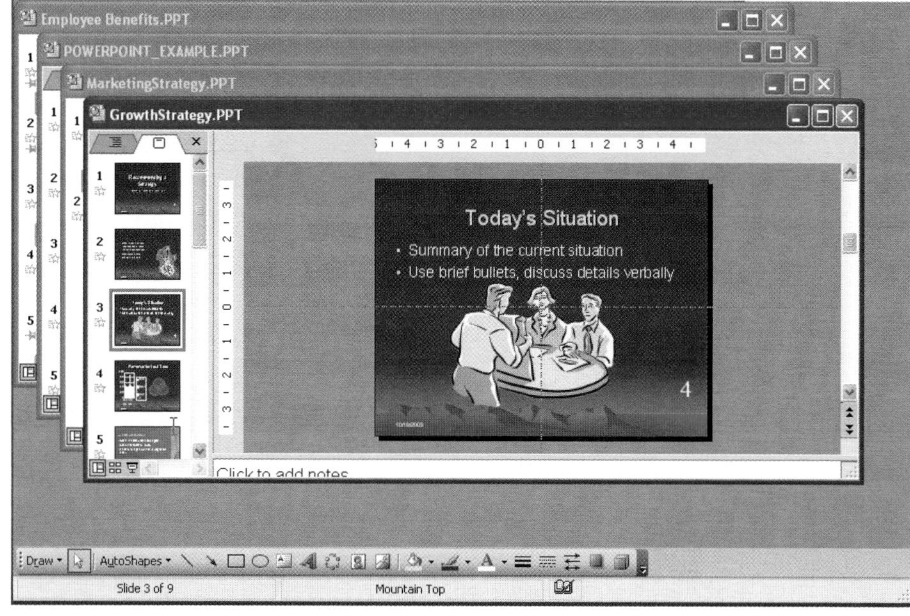

Figure 3-3: Using the Cascade command, you can arrange the presentations in a cascading sequence

3. Click each window, and place it in the view you want by opening **View** and clicking the view you want.

Duplicate a Slide

To copy or duplicate a slide:

1. In the Slide Sorter view, the Outline tab, or the Slides tab, select the slide you want to copy. To copy multiple slides in the thumbnail views or the Outline tab, press **CTRL** while you click the slides to select them. For contiguous slides, you can press **SHIFT** and click the first and last slide in the range. In Normal view, the active slide is the one that is selected.
2. Open **Insert** and click **Duplicate Slide**.

Copy a Design Using Browse

To copy just the design (and not the content) of a presentation, use the Browse feature of the task pane.

1. Open in Normal View the presentation to which you will apply the design of another presentation.
2. To open the Task pane (if it is not already opened), click the task pane title bar, and then click **Slide Design**.
3. In the Slides tab, select the slides to which the design will be applied in one of these ways:
   - Select one slide if the design is to apply to all slides having the same design as the selected slide.
   - Select all the slides to which the design is to apply.
4. Click **Browse** on the bottom of the task pane. The Apply Design Template dialog box will be displayed.

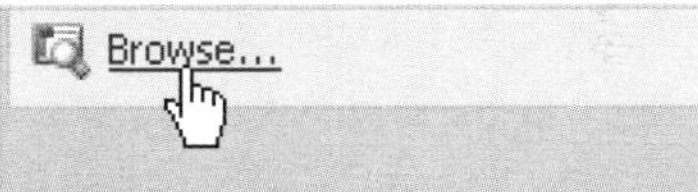

5. Select the file containing the design you want, and click **Apply**.

NOTE

If you have more than one design template applied to a presentation, the first one will be copied, and if you haven't opened the presentation recently, you will be asked if you want the remaining templates to be made available.

Create a Color Scheme

You can change the color scheme of a single slide or the whole presentation by working with the Design Templates task pane.

1. Click the task pane title bar, and click **Slide Design – Color Schemes**.
2. Click **Edit Color Schemes**. The Edit Color Scheme dialog box will open. Click the **Custom** tab (shown in Figure 3-4). It will contain a thumbnail preview of the current slide and a list of colors used for design elements on that slide.
3. To alter one of the scheme colors, click the element in the Scheme Colors list, and click **Change Color**. The Background Color dialog box will appear, as shown in Figure 3-5a.
4. Click one of the color units, as shown in Figure 3-5a, and you will see the comparison between the current color and the new color on the lower right side. You can play with the colors, clicking color units until you find the right one.

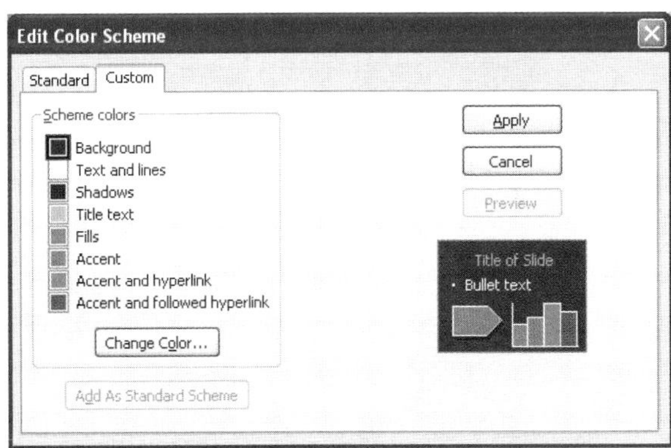

Figure 3-4: The Edit Color Scheme dialog box allows you to change the colors of slide design elements

1 2 3 4 5 6 7 8 9 10

Figure 3-5a: With Background Color you can change colors very precisely by clicking the color unit you want

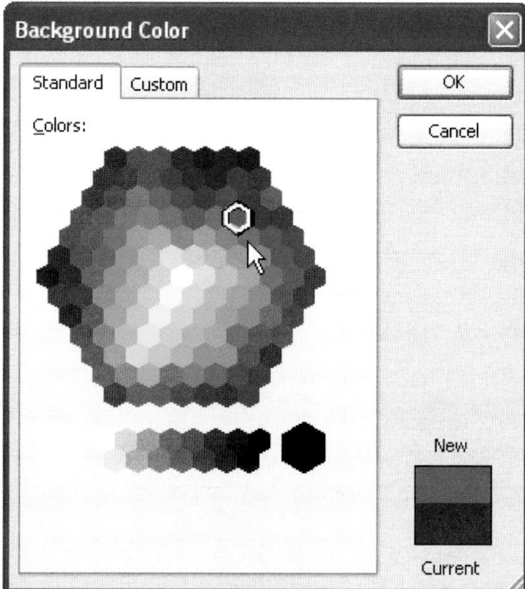

NOTE

Color is handled in several places in PowerPoint. For instance, you can get Fill Color from the Drawing toolbar; from the Edit Color Schemes link on the Slide Design – Color Schemes task pane; choosing Background on the Format menu; opening Format, choosing Font, and clicking Color; from the Font Color button on the Formatting toolbar; opening Format, choosing Placeholder, and clicking Color; and more. They all have a common Colors dialog box that is displayed by clicking **More Colors**. Figure 3-5a shows the Standard tab for the Colors dialog box used for Background Color. Figure 3-5b shows the Custom tab. The Colors dialog box works similarly for all the color commands.

5. When you are finished, click **OK**. The Edit Color Scheme dialog box will be redisplayed.
6. Click **Apply** to change the color in the presentation.

USE CUSTOM COLORS

You can create your own color mix for slides and objects. Here is how you work with custom colors.

1. Select the slides to be colored, whether all of them or a selected few.
2. Click the task pane and click **Slide Design – Color Schemes**. The task pane will appear. (If the task pane is not showing, open **View** and click **Task Pane**.)
3. Click **Edit Color Schemes**. The Edit Color Scheme dialog box will open. Click the **Custom** tab (shown earlier in Figure 3-4).
4. Click the element to be changed. You can change the Background, Text And Lines, Shadows, Title Text, Fills, Accent, Accent And Hyperlink, or Accent And Followed Hyperlink.
5. Click **Change Color**. Click the **Custom** tab. You will see the dialog box that is displayed in Figure 3-5b.
6. Click somewhere on the color rainbow to get the approximate color. Then drag the slider to get precisely the color you want. You will see it displayed in the New preview pane.

   –Or–

   Click the **Red**, **Green**, or **Blue** up arrow or down arrow to get the precise color mix you want. Displayed is RGB (Red, Green, Blue color standard) color, but you can

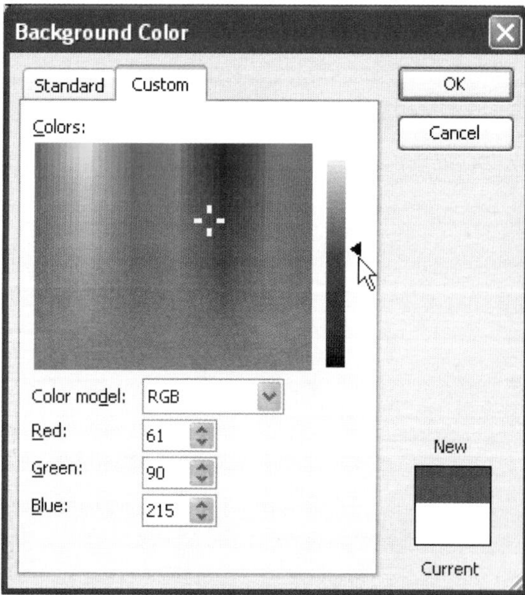

Figure 3-5b: You can create your color from the Custom tab by dragging the slider

also select other color types, such as HSL (Hue, Saturation, and Luminosity color standard).

7. When you are finished, click **OK** to close the Background Color dialog box. Click **Apply** to close the Edit Color Schemes dialog box.

TIP

To add the color scheme to those available in the Slide Design – Color Scheme task pane, click **Add As Standard Scheme**. This will make it available as a standard choice on the task pane.

CHANGE PRESENTATION COLOR

If you want to change the color scheme for a presentation to one of the standards already established and available in the task pane, follow these steps:

1. Open the Slide Design task pane by clicking the task pane title bar and clicking **Slide Design – Color Schemes**.
2. Click **Edit Color Schemes** at the bottom of the task pane. The Edit Color Scheme dialog box will open.
3. Click the **Standard** tab, shown in Figure 3-6.
4. Click one of the standard color schemes, and click **Apply**. All slides in the presentation will be changed.

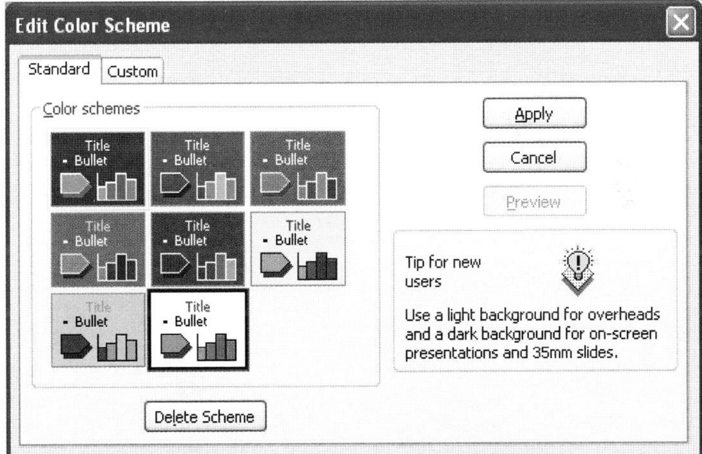

Figure 3-6: The Standard tab of the Edit Color Scheme dialog box allows you to choose another standard color combination for your presentation

CHANGE BACKGROUND COLOR

You can change the slide background on one or all slides in a presentation.

1. Open **Format** and click **Background**. The Background dialog box will appear.

2. Click the Color drop-down box to see the colors that can be chosen.

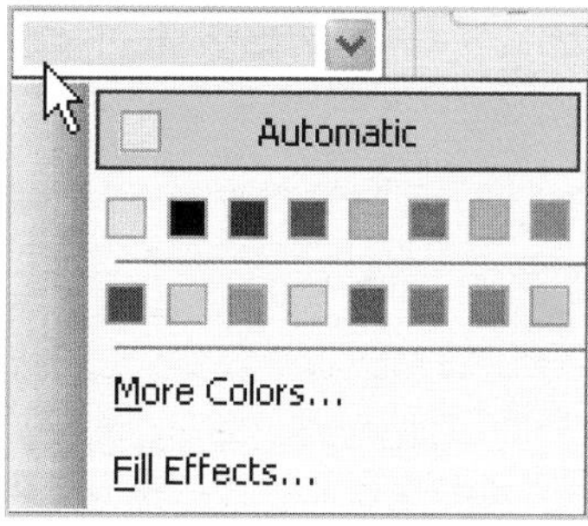

3. Click a color to see it in the thumbnail display. To see the slide in the background displayed, click **Preview**. You can drag the dialog box to one side to see the current slide in the new background color.
4. When you have chosen a color, click **Apply To All** to change the background color for all slides. Click **Apply** to change only the current slide.

TIP

To see a full range of colors, click **More Colors** from the color drop-down box. The Colors dialog box will be displayed. Click the **Custom** tab, and then click the rainbow of colors to get in the range of colors you want. Then slide the arrow to the right of the colors up or down to get the precise color. When you are finished, click **OK**.

NOTE

See Chapter 8, "Special Effects and Drawing in PowerPoint," for information on how to create gradient backgrounds, insert patterns or textures, or insert a picture into the background using Fill Effects.

TIP

If the new slide is part of a presentation, it may have some elements of the design assigned to it. In that case, you may not get the Slide Layout task pane. If you want to change the layout from what it is, click the **task pane title bar** and click **Slide Layout** to display it.

Use a Slide Layout

When you open a new blank slide, you will see the Slide Layout task pane. From this, you can choose the layout you want for your slide. For example, you may want bulleted text, graphics, a chart, pictures, or tables.

1. Click **New Slide** to get a new slide.
2. The Slide Layout task pane will be displayed.
3. Find the layout you want for the slide, and click it.
4. You will see one or more placeholder boxes containing an icon describing the content you want in the placeholder. Options are tables, graphs, clip art, pictures, diagram or organizational chart, and media clip, as seen in Figure 3-7.

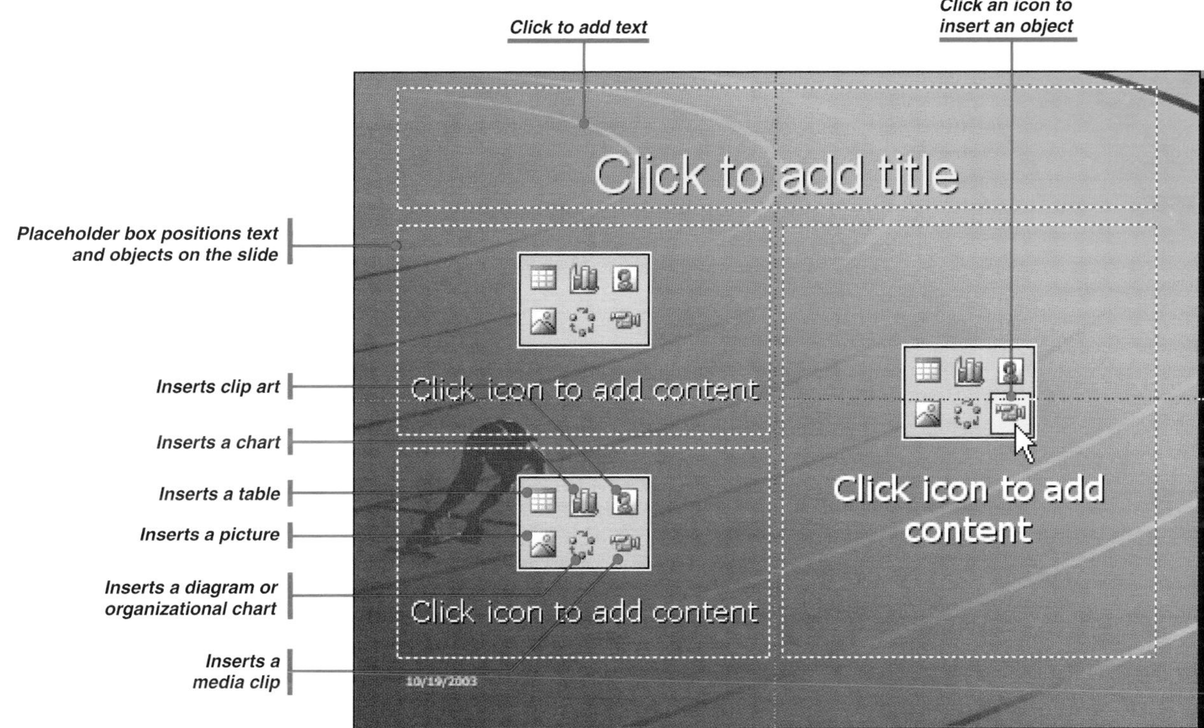

Figure 3-7: The Slide Layout placeholder boxes and icons make it easy to add content to your slides

1
2
3
4
5
6
7
8
9
10

TIP

To turn on or off the Automatic Layout option that automatically places an inserted object, Open **Tools** and click **AutoCorrect Options**. Click the **AutoFormat As You Type** tab. Click **Apply As You Work** option for Automatic Layout For Inserted Objects. If the check box contains a check mark, the option is activated.

NOTE

To copy colors in one presentation to all the slides in another, open both presentations in Master Slide view (click a presentation window, open **View**, choose **Master,** and then click **Master Slide**). Then select the Slide Master of the source presentation by clicking it, click **Format Painter**, and click (select) the destination Slide Master. Do the same with the Title Master. Check that the colors have been copied appropriately in Normal View. See "Manage Slide and Title Masters," later in this chapter, for additional information.

5. Click the placeholder text box to add text.
6. Click the icon to add content. A dialog box will be displayed for you to find the object you want and open it. Chapters 4 through 9 cover details on adding specific kinds of content.
   - Right-click the object to find options for working with the object.
   - Delete an object and replace it with another if you want.
   - Right-click the slide to redisplay a task pane, edit contents, add content, or look something up.
   - Drag an object to a new location.

Copy Color with Format Painter

The Format Painter can be used to copy colors from one slide to another as well as from one presentation to another.

COPY COLORS BETWEEN SLIDES

To copy colors between slides, you select the first slide (or source slide), select the Format Painter, and then select the second (destination) slide.

1. Display the slides in Slides tab or Slide Sorter view.
2. Find and click the source slide containing the color to be copied.
3. Click **Format Painter** once to copy the source format to one slide. If you want to use the source slide to reformat several other slides, double-click **Format Painter** to turn it on until you click it again to turn it off.
4. Find the destination slide and click it to receive the new color.
5. If you are copying the source color to multiple slides, continue to find the destination slides and click them.
6. When you are finished, click **Format Painter** to turn it off.

COPY COLORS BETWEEN PRESENTATIONS

To copy colors from one presentation to another, you must first display both presentations in the Slides pane.

QUICKSTEPS

USING HEADERS AND FOOTERS ON SLIDES

DISPLAY HEADER AND FOOTER DIALOG BOX

To work with any aspect of headers and footers, you need to display the Headers and Footers dialog box (shown in Figure 3-7b). To display this dialog box, follow these three steps; then do the fourth one to complete the selection.

1. Select the slide or slides that need headers or footers.
2. Open **View** and click **Header And Footer**.
3. Click the **Slide** tab for headers and footers for slides. (See "Using Headers and Footers on Notes and Handouts" in this chapter.)
4. When you have finished making your selections, click **Apply** to apply the choices to selected slides only, or click **Apply To All** for all slides.

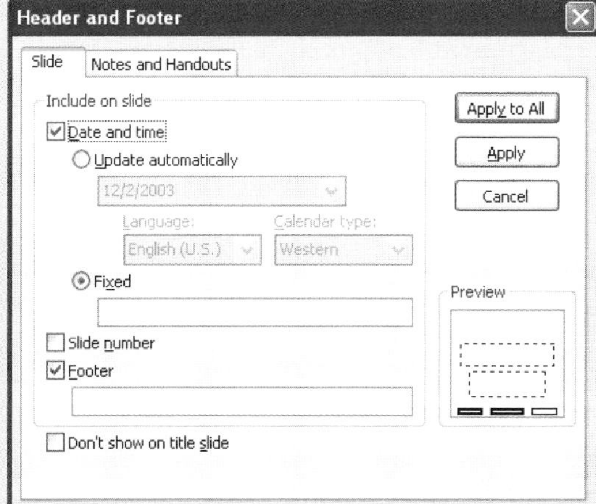

Figure 3-7b: The Header and Footer dialog box is used to set up your header and footer information for slides

Continued...

1. In the Slides pane, open **File** and click **Open**. Choose the source presentation to be opened. Then repeat for the destination presentation. Continue for as many presentations as you need to have open.
2. Open **Window** and click **Arrange All**. The Slides pane will be divided into two windows, as shown in Figure 3-8.

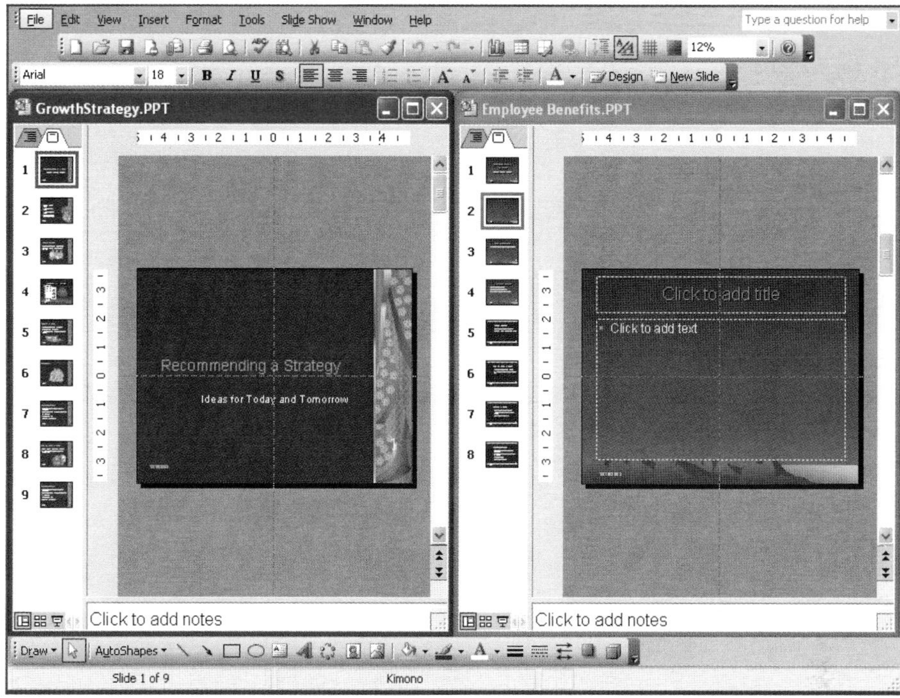

Figure 3-8: The first step in using the Format Painter to copy color is to arrange your presentations in the Slides pane

3. To copy the color of one slide to one or more slides in the destination presentation, open **View**, and click **Normal** in both presentations to make sure you can see the slides.
4. Click the slide containing the color you want to copy.
5. Click **Format Painter**. Click it once to use for one application of color. Double-click it to turn it on for multiple uses. 
6. Click the destination slide or slides you want to copy the color to.

1
2
3
4
5
6
7
8
9
10

> **USING HEADERS AND FOOTERS ON SLIDES** *(Continued)*
>
> **DISPLAY TIME OR DATE**
>
> You must first display the Headers and Footers dialog box, as described above:
>
> - To apply a time or date that reflects the actual time, select **Update Automatically** by placing a check mark in the check box. From the drop-down list box, click the date only, time only, or time and date format you prefer.
>
>
>
> - To apply a fixed time or date, or other text, select **Fixed**. In the Fixed text box, type the text that will always appear in the footer.
>
>
>
> *Continued...*

> **TIP**
>
> To remove both the object or text and the hyperlink, select the text or object, and press **DELETE**.

Work with Hyperlinks

Inserting hyperlinks in a presentation allows you to link to other presentations or to another slide within the current presentation.

INSERT A HYPERLINK

To insert a hyperlink for text or an object:

1. Highlight the text or select the object that will contain the hyperlink
2. Open **Insert** and click **Hyperlink**. The Insert Hyperlink dialog box will be displayed.
3. Find the hyperlink destination.
   - Click **Existing File Or Web Page** to view other presentations.
   - Click **Place In This Document** to see a slide in the current presentation
4. Click **OK** to insert the Hyperlink.

REMOVE A HYPERLINK

To remove a hyperlink from text or an object:

1. Right-click the text or object containing the hyperlink.
2. Select **Remove Hyperlink** from the context menu.

CHANGE A HYPERLINK COLOR

To change the color of hyperlinks:

1. Open **Format** and click **Slide Design**.
2. Click **Color Schemes** and then, at the bottom of the task pane, click **Edit Color Schemes**. Click the **Custom** tab.
3. Under Scheme Colors, click **Accent and Hyperlink** or **Accent and Followed Hyperlink**.

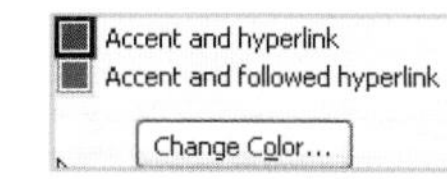

4. Click **Change Color**, and modify the color in one of two ways:
   - Click **Standard** tab. Click the color unit you want. Click **OK**.
   - Click the **Custom** tab. Click the color rainbow, and then drag the lever to the precise color you want. Click **OK**.
5. Click **Apply**.

USING HEADERS AND FOOTERS ON SLIDES *(Continued)*

ENTER A FOOTER

After displaying the Headers and Footers dialog box:

1. Select Footer by placing a check mark in the check box.

☑ Footer

2. In the Footer text box, type the text for the footer.

DO NOT SHOW HEADERS AND FOOTERS ON TITLE PAGE

Once you have displayed the Headers and Footers dialog box; place a check mark in the **Don't Show On Title Slide** check box.

☑ Don't show on title slide

REMOVE HEADERS OR FOOTERS

Once you have displayed the Headers and Footers dialog box:

1. Clear the check boxes for Date And Time, Slide Number, and Footer.
2. To remove the header and footer for selected slides, click **Apply**.

   –Or–

3. To remove the header and footer for all slides, click **Apply To All**.

TIP

If you use more of the Notes pane than is available, PowerPoint will reduce the font size and line spacing so the text will fit.

Work with Notes

Notes are used to create speaker notes that aid a speaker during a presentation and to create handouts given to the audience so that it can follow the presentation easily. The notes do not appear on the slides during a Slide Show presentation; they are only visible for the presenter's benefit.

Create a Note

To create speaker notes which can also be used as handouts, you can either use the Notes pane in Normal View (as shown in Figure 3-9) or the Notes Page (shown in Figure 3-10). In both views you are able to see a thumbnail of the slide with your notes about that slide. Each slide has its own note page. You can

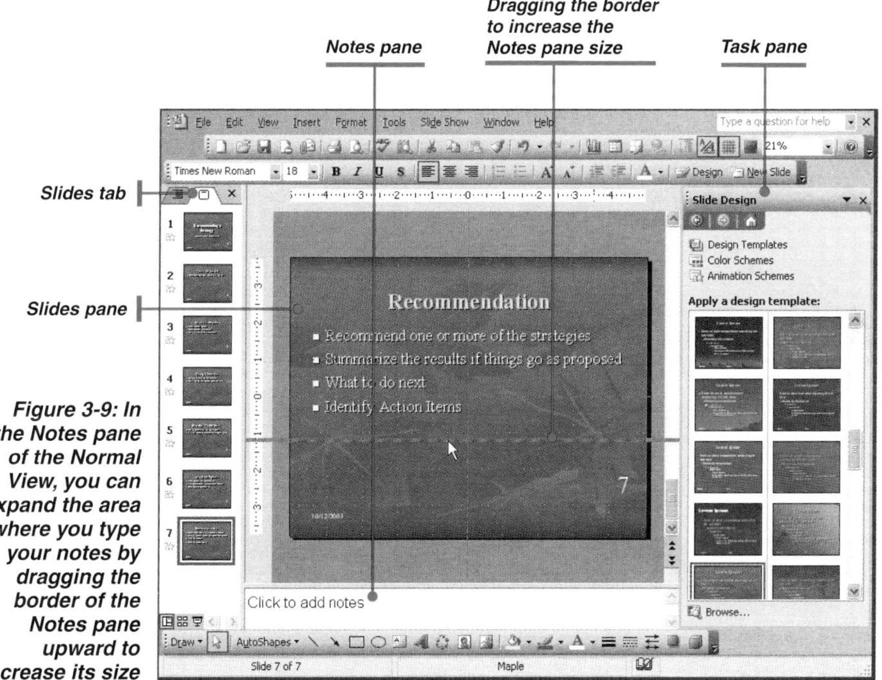

Figure 3-9: In the Notes pane of the Normal View, you can expand the area where you type your notes by dragging the border of the Notes pane upward to increase its size

1 2 3 4 5 6 7 8 9 10

TIP

To show the text formatting in the Notes Pane, click **Show Formatting**. This only works in the Normal View.

TIP

You can add an object, such as a picture, graph, chart, or organizational chart to the notes. Click in the Notes Page where the object is to be inserted. Open **Insert**, and click the object to be inserted from the menu. Drag the object to where you want it on the page.

TIP

To create a note in the Notes pane, open **Normal** view and click in the **Click To Add Notes**. Then type your notes.

TIP

To change the background of one or all notes, open **View**, and click **Notes Page**. Open **Format**, click **Notes Background,** and select your options. (See Chapter 8.)

Notes Background...

also add charts, graphs, or pictures to the notes. To add or change attributes or text to all notes in a presentation, make changes to the Note Master.

CREATE A NOTE IN THE NOTES PAGE

1. To open the Notes Page, open **View** and click **Notes Page**. The Notes Page opens, as shown in Figure 3-10.

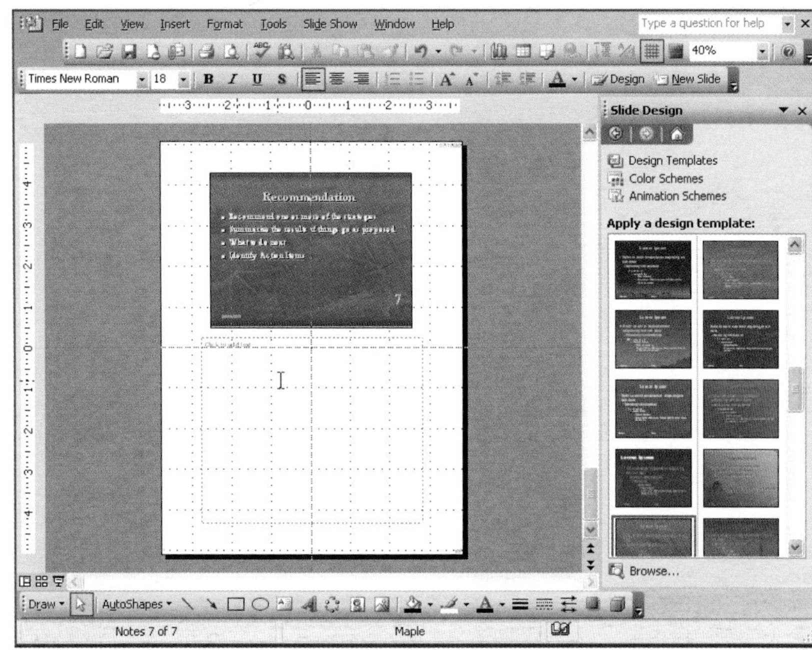

Figure 3-10: The Notes Page displays what the printout will look like before entering your notes and allows you to zoom the image to have more editing space

2. To increase the size of the notes area, open **View** and click **Zoom**.
3. Click the zoom magnification you want, and click **OK**.
4. To move to another slide, drag the scroll bar on the Notes Page.

TIP

You can send the speaker notes or handout notes to Microsoft Word where you can work with them more easily. Select **File**, select **Send To,** and click **Microsoft Office Word**. In the Send To Microsoft Office Word dialog box, select the layout you want, and click **OK**.

TIP

To Zoom in on an area of a slide, first select the area on the Outline tab, the Slides tab, or the Slides pane. Click the **Zoom** down arrow on the Standard toolbox, and select the magnification you need. (If you click the Zoom box rather than the arrow, you select the current magnification and can type in a new one.) If you want to see the whole slide on the screen, click **Fit**.

100%

Preview Speaker Notes

To preview and then print your notes:

1. Click **Print Preview**.
2. From the Print What drop-down list box, click **Notes Pages** (shown in Figure 3-11).

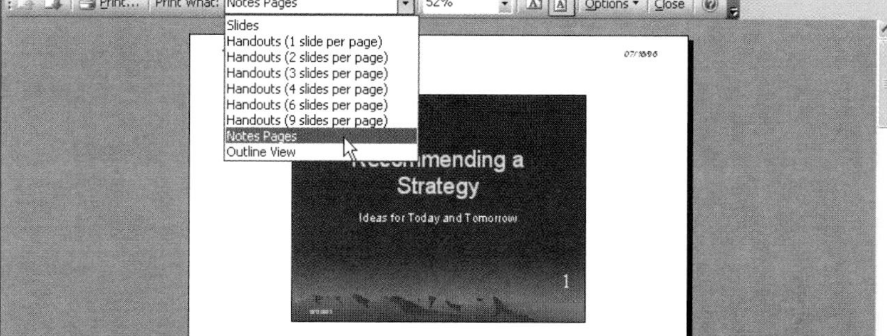

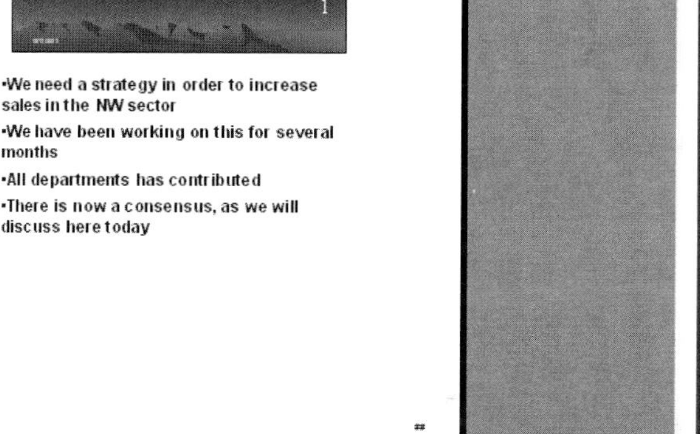

Figure 3-11: The Print Preview Notes Pages displays speaker notes with the accompanying slide and allows you to print from this view

3. Click **Print** for the Print dialog box. Enter the slide numbers for specific slide ranges, and enter the number of copies.
4. Click **OK** to print.

QUICKSTEPS

USING HEADERS AND FOOTERS ON NOTES AND HANDOUTS

To put headers and footers on Notes and Handouts:

1. Open **View** and click **Header And Footer**.
2. Click the **Notes And Handouts** tab.
3. Choose the items you want by placing a check mark next to them.
   - For a date/time entry, click **Date And Time**, and choose between **Update Automatically**, for a time/date that updates according to the current date, and **Fixed**, for a time/date or other text that remain the same.
   - Click **Header**, and enter the header text for notes and handouts.
   - Click **Footer**, and enter footer text.
   - Click **Page Number** to place a page number on the note or handout page.
4. Click **Apply To All**.

Print Notes and Handouts

Speaker Notes and Handouts are printed in a similar way.

PRINT SPEAKER NOTES

To print your notes:

1. Open **File** and click **Print**. The Print dialog box will be displayed. (See Figure 3-12.)
2. From the **Print What** drop-down list box, click **Notes Pages**.
3. Click **Preview** to see the Notes Page. Click **Print** to return to the Print dialog box.
4. To print specific slides, click **Slides** and enter the slide range numbers. For multiple copies, enter the number you wish to print under **Number Of Copies**.
5. Click **OK** to print.

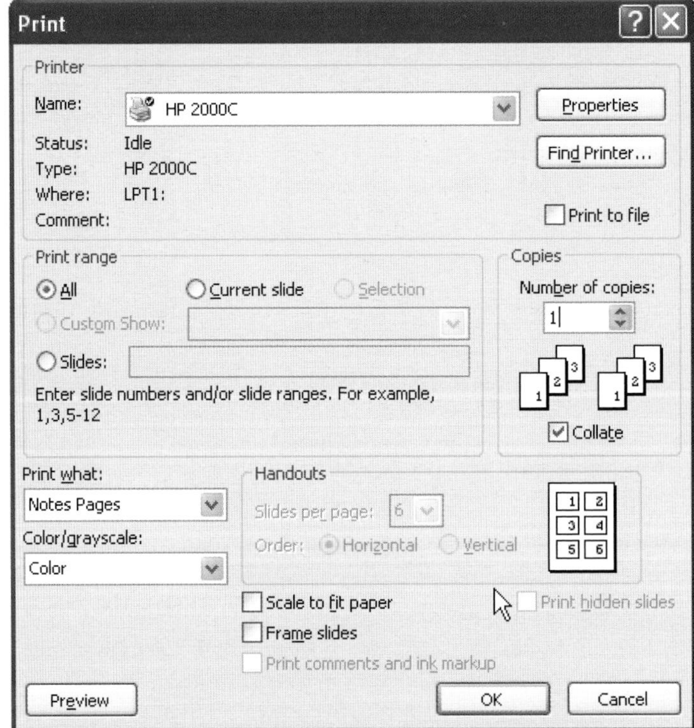

Figure 3-12: The Print dialog box allows you to select specific slides and speaker notes to print and to preview before printing

TIP

To number slides beginning with a number other than one, open **File** and click **Page Setup**. Click the **Number Slides From** up and down arrows to set the beginning number.

Number slides from: 1

NOTE

To avoid numbering the title slide and to begin numbering the following slide with number 1, set 0 (zero) to be your beginning page number in the Page Setup, Number Slides From box. Then open **View**, select **Header And Footer**, and click the **Slide** tab. Place a check mark in the **Don't Show On Title Slide**. Click **Apply To All**.

PRINT HANDOUTS

A printed handout contains a number of thumbnail slides; an example can be seen in Figure 3-13.

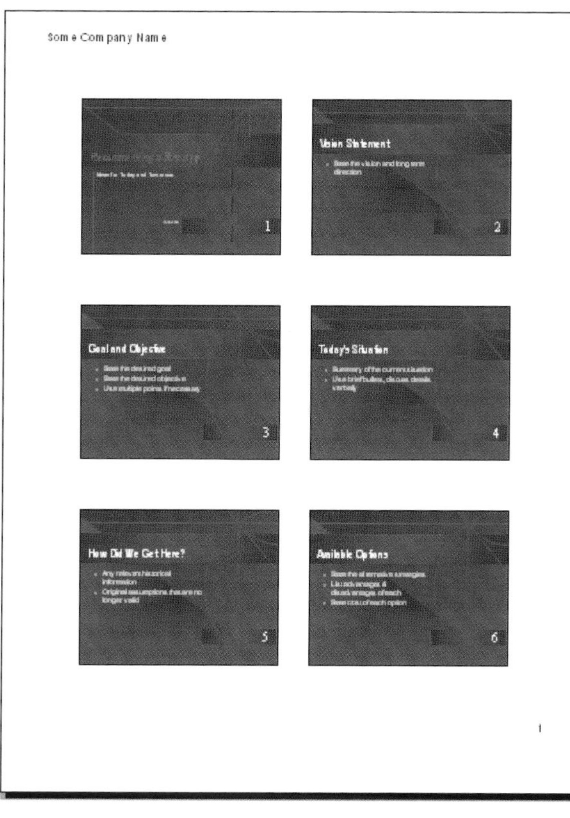

Figure 3-13: A preview of the printed handouts contains miniatures of slides and allows you to select the number of slides displayed on a page

1. Open **File** and click **Print**. The Print dialog box will be displayed.
2. To print only some of the slides, click **Slides** and enter the slide numbers or ranges.
3. Click **Handouts** in the **Print What** drop-down list box.
4. Type the **Slides Per Page** if the number is incorrect.
5. Make other adjustments as needed. Click **Preview** to see what the printout will look like, and then click **Print** to return to the Print dialog box.
6. Click **OK** to print.

1 2 3 4 5 6 7 8 9 10

Work with Slide and Title, Note and Handout Masters

Working with masters gives you an opportunity to change a presentation globally. PowerPoint gives you four types of masters to work with: slide and title masters control the slides and title slide of a presentation, the note master controls the global aspects of notes, and the handout master controls the handouts. You do not have to have masters for title and regular slides, but if design templates are used, your presentation will automatically be assigned one or more. Note and Handout Masters are created if you want to use global attributes for them.

Manage Slide and Title Masters

A presentation has a Slide Master and, sometimes, a Title Master that contains formatting and other design elements that apply to all slides in a presentation. The Slide Master applies formatting and elements to all slides, except that the title slide may have its own Title Master for unique positioning of page components, formatting, headings, and design elements. The Slide and Title Masters may get their specific formatting from a design template that you used, and you can change the masters without changing the original template. This is one way you can customize your presentation even after using a suggested template to get you going.

TIP

To remove the borders that are automatically placed around the thumbnail slides, click **Frame Slides** in the Print dialog box, and remove the check mark.

TIP

To hide a slide, first display the slides in Normal view. On the Slides tab, select the slide to be hidden. Right-click the thumbnail, and click **Hide Slide**. A faint rectangle will appear to the left of the hidden slide in the Slide tab. The rectangle contains a slash across it and the number of the slide. Although it is still in your presentation, the slide will not appear in the slide show. To show the hidden slide again, just right-click the slide, and click **Hide Slide** to turn the hide feature off.

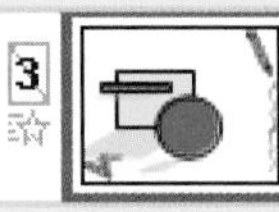

1
2
3
4
5
6
7
8
9
10

EDIT A SLIDE MASTER

Editing a Slide Master changes all the slides to which it applies.

1. Open **View**, choose **Master**, and click **Slide Master**. The Slide Master will be displayed. See Figure 3-14.

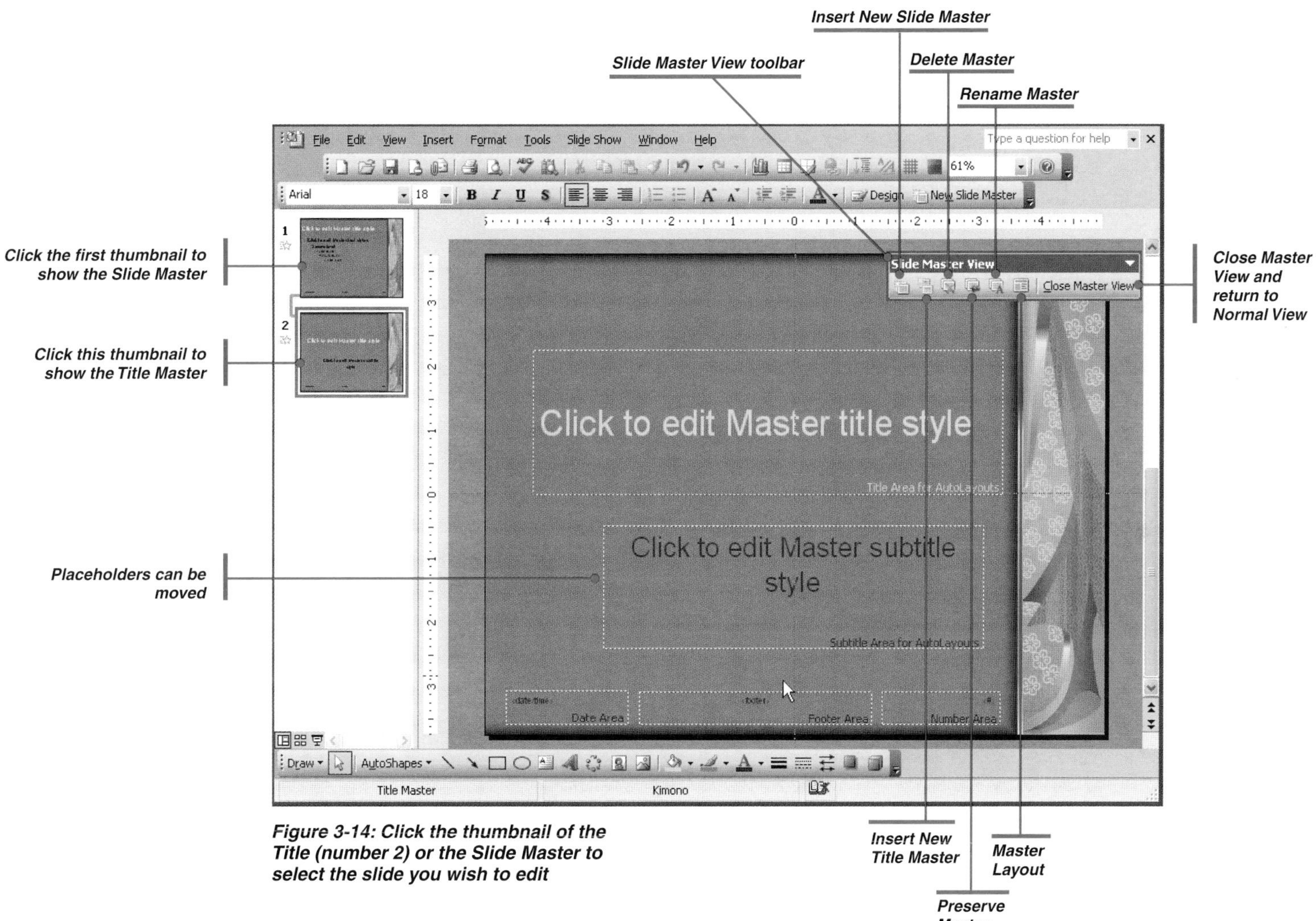

Figure 3-14: Click the thumbnail of the Title (number 2) or the Slide Master to select the slide you wish to edit

TIP

If you apply a design template to a presentation, Slide and Title Masters will be automatically created.

QUICKSTEPS

WORKING WITH SLIDES MASTERS

DUPLICATE A SLIDE MASTER

To duplicate a Slide Master:

1. Open **View** and choose **Master**. Click **Slide Master**.
2. Select the Slide Master to duplicate by clicking the thumbnail in the left pane. If you select one of a Title and Slide Master pair, both will be selected.
3. Open **Insert** and click **Duplicate Slide Master**. The new master (or masters) will appear in the thumbnail pane.

INSERT A TITLE MASTER

To make the format of your title page different from the rest of your slides, create a Title Master to contain its unique formatting or design elements.

1. Open **View**, choose **Master**, and click **Slide Master**.
2. From the Slide Master View toolbar, click **Insert New Title Master**.

PROTECT A MASTER

To protect a Slide and Title Master from being changed or deleted, use the Preserve Master button.

1. Select the Slide Master to be protected.
2. Click **Preserve Master** on the Slide Master View toolbar to protect both the Slide and Title Master. You will see gray thumbtacks or pushpins beside the master and title thumbnail slides.

2. Add text, format text, add graphics or background color, add headers or footers, or other elements of the Slide Master just as you would a normal slide. Here are some of the editing and formatting changes you can make:

- To change the font size, click a master thumbnail to specify the slides to be changed, click a text placeholder to select it (you may have to click directly on the placeholder text to select it, such as on <date/ time> in the Date Area placeholder), click the Font Size down arrow, and type in or select the size you want from the drop-down list.
- To insert a different bullet shape, click the line of text containing the bullet to be changed. Open **Format** and click **Bullets And Numbering**. In the dialog box, change the Size, Color, or shape of the bullet. To insert a picture that serves as a bullet, click **Picture**, and click the bullet picture you want. Then click **OK**. To insert a symbol, click **Customize**, and then choose the font and symbol you want. Click **OK**.
- To change the font style, click the placeholder text and open **Format**. Choose **Font**, and select the style changes you want. You can also click **Bold**, **Italic**, or **Underline** or select a font style from the font drop-down list on the Formatting toolbar.

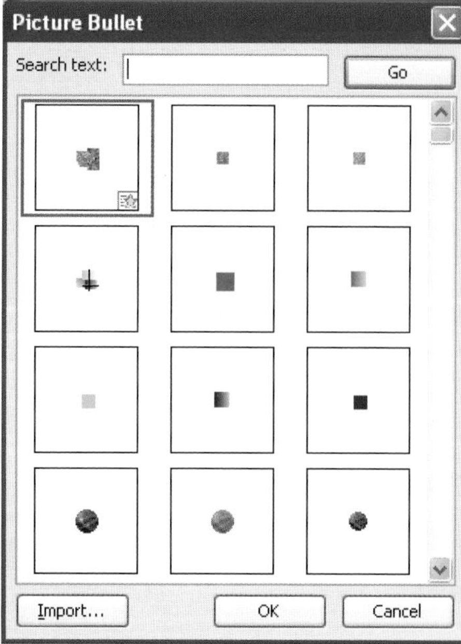

NOTE

When a design template is used to create more than one section in order to create multiple "looks" for the presentation, a Title and Slide Master will be automatically created for it. You can then modify the masters as needed to create a unique look.

TIP

To prevent multiple masters from being used in a presentation, you can disable the ability to do it. Open **Tools**, choose **Options**, and click the **Edit** tab. Under Disable New Features, deselect **Multiple Masters**.

Disable new features

- [ ] New animation effects
- [x] Multiple masters
- [ ] Password protection

NOTE

Your Title Master will contain the formatting from the Slide Master by default. However, if you change the formatting on the Title Master, it will be preserved.

CREATE MULTIPLE SLIDE AND TITLE MASTERS

Multiple Slide and Title Masters (illustrated in Figure 3-15, which shows three sets of Title and Slide Masters) can be used in one presentation to create different looks in layout or formatting for sections of the presentation.

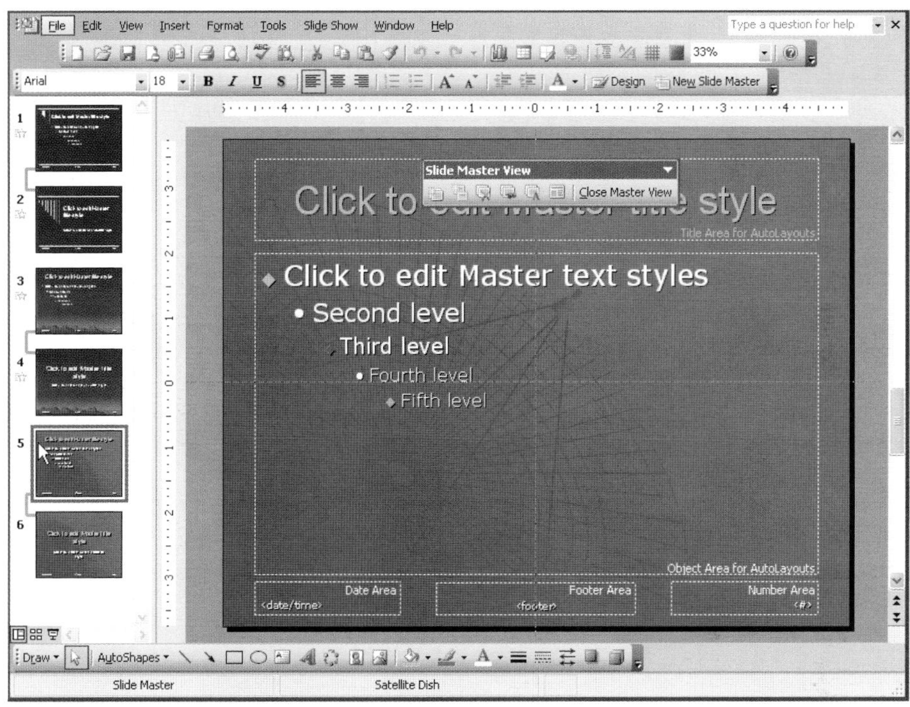

Figure 3-15: You can have multiple sets of Title and Slide Masters in one presentation

To create additional new Slide Masters:

1. Open **View**, choose **Master**, and click **Slide Master**.
2. If the Slide Master View toolbar is not showing, click the **Slides pane** to display it.
3. Click **Insert New Slide Master**.
4. If you need a Title Master, click **Insert New Title Master**.
5. Make any changes or incorporate different design templates to the new master pair as needed.

Figure 3-16: The Notes Master is used to globally change such note features as headers, footers, note text formatting, and placement of note elements

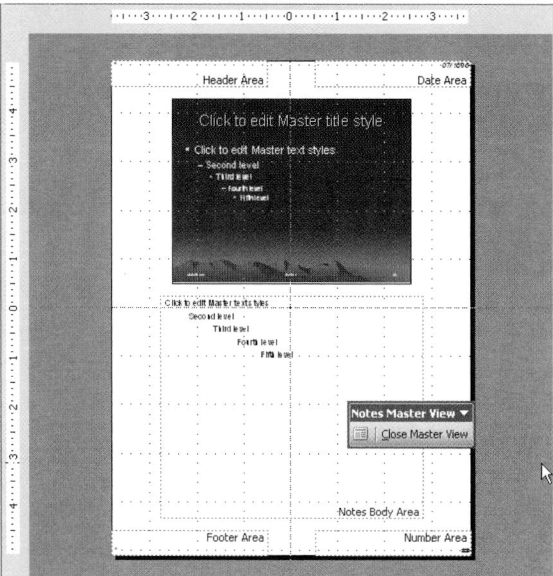

Work with the Notes Master

For each presentation, there will be a Notes Master that records the positioning of page components, formatting, headings, and text design elements within the notes. To create global modifications that appear on all notes in a presentation, you can change the Notes Master.

MODIFY THE NOTES MASTER

To change the placement of text on the slide, format text, add bullets, change indents, or add text:

1. Open **View** and select **Master**. Click **Notes Master**. The Notes Master will be displayed, as shown in Figure 3-16.
2. To adjust the Zoom, open **View** and click **Zoom**. Choose the magnification and click **OK**.
3. You may change the master as follows:
   - Change the formatting of the text elements, such as font size or style, or add bullets or indents.
   - Move the position of the slide or note text placeholder (dotted box).

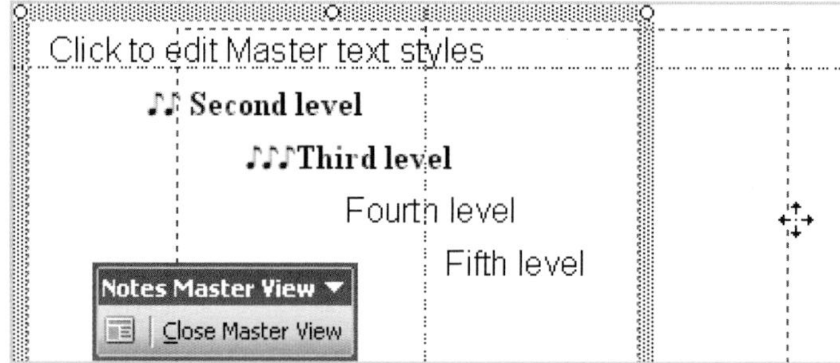

   - Change the size of the slide or note text placeholder.
   - Add text that will appear on all notes, such as page number, date, or title.
4. Click **Close** on the Notes Master View toolbar to close the Notes Master.

TIP

The Title Master and Slide Master are protected as pairs. Selecting either one for protection will automatically select the other for protection as well. Note: To remove the protection, click **Preserve Master** on the Slide Master View toolbar.

NOTE

You can also open **Format** and click **Notes Master Layout**.

ADD LAYOUT TO THE NOTES MASTER

If you want to add elements to the layout of the Notes Master or restore elements that have been removed, use the Notes Master Layout dialog box. It lists those items missing in your Notes Master. When you add an element to the Notes Master, it will appear on all note pages.

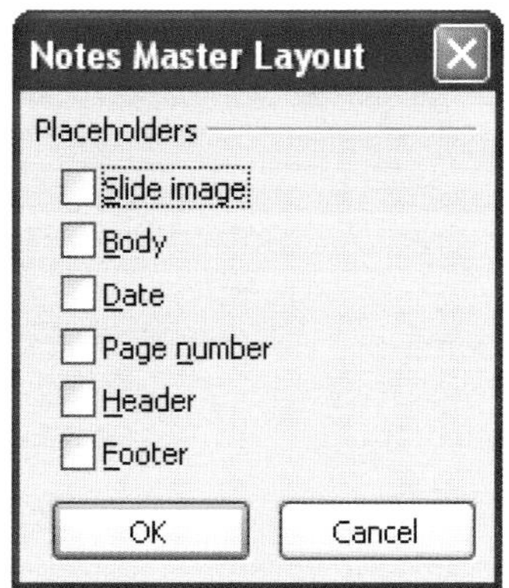

1. To display the Notes Master, open **View** and select **Master**, and click **Notes Master**.
2. From the Notes Master View toolbar, click **Notes Master Layout**.
3. Click the placeholders you want on the Notes Master, and click **OK**.

Change the Handout Master

Handouts display thumbnails of the slides on a printed page. You can have one to nine slides per page. To prepare your handouts for printing, use the Handout Master.

1. Open **View**, choose **Master**, and click **Handout Master**. The Handout Master will be displayed, as shown in Figure 3-17.
2. On the Handout Master View toolbar, click the number of slides to be displayed in the handout: one, two, three, four, six, or nine.
3. Make changes to the Handout Master as needed. For example, you might add titles for each slide, add graphics for the background, add a border around the slides, or make other changes. See Chapters 4 through 8 to learn how to make these changes.
4. To close the Handout Master, click **Close Master View** on the toolbar.

1 2 3 4 5 6 7 8 9 10

TIP

When you first open a Notes Master Layout, the options may be grayed out, signifying that they are unavailable. That is because the Placeholder is already available on the Note Master layout.

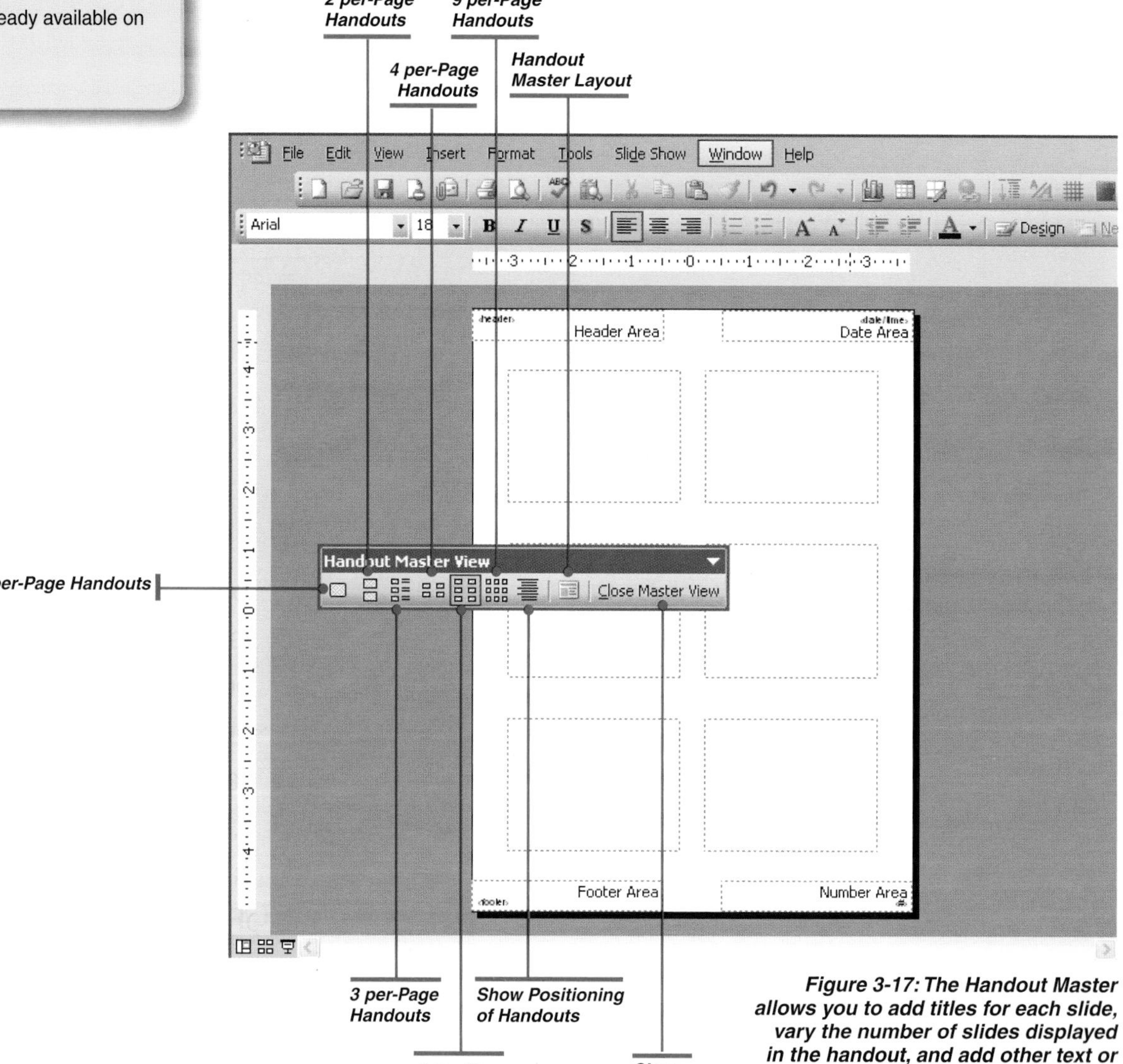

Figure 3-17: The Handout Master allows you to add titles for each slide, vary the number of slides displayed in the handout, and add other text or objects as needed on slides

How to...

- *Select a Layout*
- *Use Text Placeholders*
- *Setting Margins, Word Wrap, Anchor Points, and Rotating Text*
- *Set and Change Tab Setting*
- *Change Line and Paragraph Spacing*
- *Using Lists*
- *Editing Slide Text*
- *Change Capitalization*
- *Use the Font Dialog Box*
- *Change Fonts, Font Size, Color, Style, and Effects*
- *Moving or Copying Text*
- *Align Text*
- *Use AutoFit*
- *Copy Formatting with Format Painter*
- *Using the Office Clipboard*
- *Use AutoCorrect*
- *Use Spell Check*

Chapter 4 Modifying Slide Text

This chapter discusses the specifics of how to work with slide text. This includes selecting a layout, using text box placeholders to contain text, and setting defaults for text boxes—such as margins, word wrap, and anchor points. Positioning plain, bulleted, and numbered text is addressed as well as setting tabs, controlling line and paragraph spacing, and using lists. Modifying text would not be complete without discussions on editing, moving, copying, and deleting text. Working with capitalization and all aspects of working with fonts are discussed. The Office Clipboard is covered, as is spell checking with standard and foreign languages. Special features, like AutoFit and AutoCorrect, are also addressed.

Select a Layout

To create the "look" of your presentation, you will want to insert text, columns, graphics, charts, logos, and other pictures in a consistent way. This is referred to as the *layout* of a presentation. One of the ways you modify text is by positioning it on the slide. You use layouts for this purpose. Chapters 1 and 2 discussed layouts in more detail.

TIP

The layout will be applied to the current slide. If you have not created a new slide, the layout will be applied to whichever slide is selected.

Select a Layout

When you create a new blank slide, you must choose whether to use an existing layout that Microsoft provides, or to create your own layout. Here is how you use what is available.

1. Open **File**, and click **New**.
2. On the New Presentation task pane, click **Blank Presentation**. You will see a slide with a basic layout assigned to it. The Layout task pane will open, as shown in Figure 4-1.

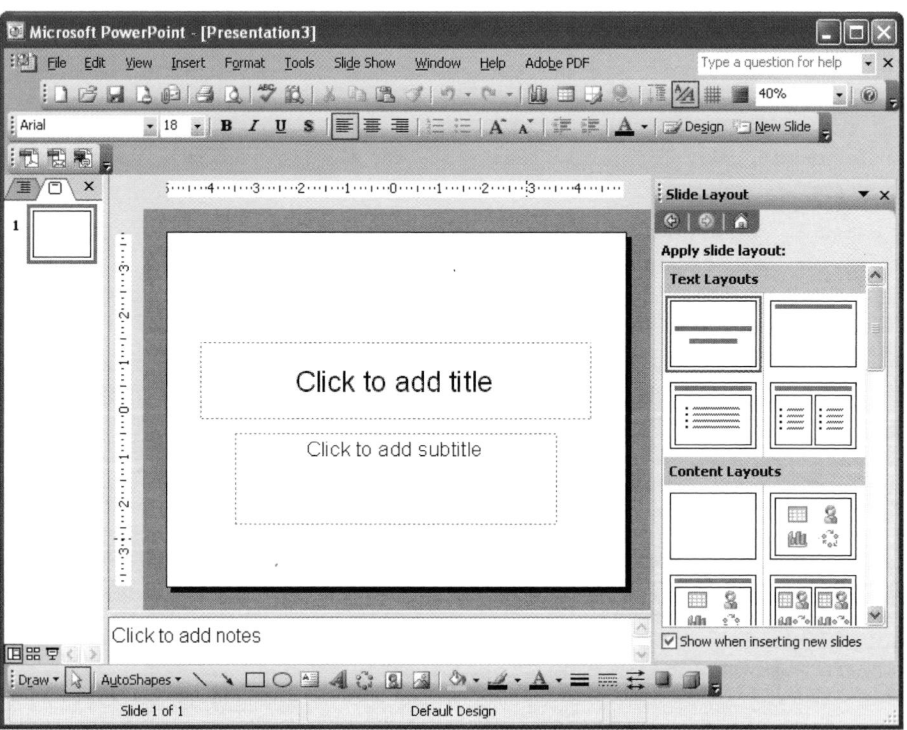

Figure 4-1: The Slide Layout task pane offers a variety of possibilities for placing text boxes

NOTE

If you use the AutoContent wizard, you will get an entire presentation that contains a consistent look, based on a combined design and layout, as described in Chapters 1 and 2. If you create a presentation or slide and apply a design template to it, you will get defined layout, design, color, and graphics for the slides selected. The layout templates are used for positioning title, text, and content.

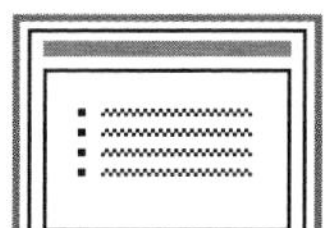

Title and Text *in one bulleted column*

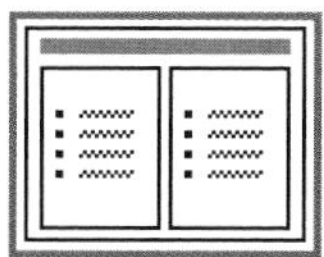

Title and 2-column *bulleted text*

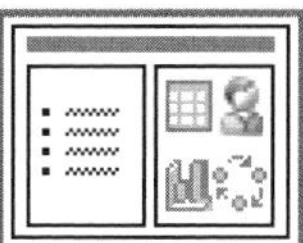

Title, Text, and Content, *where the text and content placeholders are beneath the title in two columns*

Title, Text, and 2 Content *placeholders, where the text placeholder is in one column beside two placeholders for content beneath the title box*

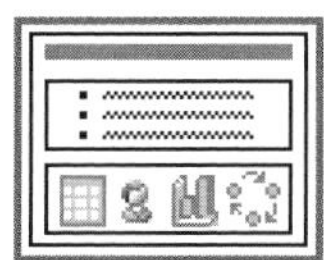

Title and Text over Content, *where the text is in a horizontal box over the content and beneath the title placeholder*

TIP

PowerPoint refers to text boxes that have been created by a template as AutoShapes. AutoShapes are created shapes that can be manipulated and include many shapes besides text boxes.

3. Click the scroll bar on the Slide Layout task pane to find the layout you want. Look for the placement of text, titles, and content. Examples of text placeholders are illustrated at the left.
4. Click the layout you want.
5. Click the title or text placeholders to begin entering text. See "Use Text Placeholders." (See Chapters 5 through 8 to get more information on working with the content placeholders).

Use Text Placeholders

PowerPoint uses *text placeholders* to contain text. Text placeholders are text boxes that contain text and other objects. Text boxes can be moved or rotated. You can create a new one or use an existing one from a template.

INSERT NEW TEXT BOX

Even when you use a predefined layout that Microsoft provides, you will find times when you want to insert a new text box. Here's how:

1. Display the slide within which you will place the text box.
2. Open **Insert** and click **Text Box**. The pointer at first will turn into a line pointer.

3. Place the pointer about where you want to locate the text box, and drag it into a text-box shape. As you drag, the pointer will morph into a crosshair shape. Don't worry about where the box is located, as later you can drag it into a precise location. When you release the pointer, the slant-line border and insertion point within the text box tell you that you can begin to type text.
4. Type the text you want.
5. When you are finished, click outside the text box to confirm the typing.

NOTE

The border of a placeholder tells what can be done with it. If the border contains slanted lines, the text area is selected, and you can enter or edit text. If the border is dotted, the placeholder itself is selected and can be moved or manipulated.

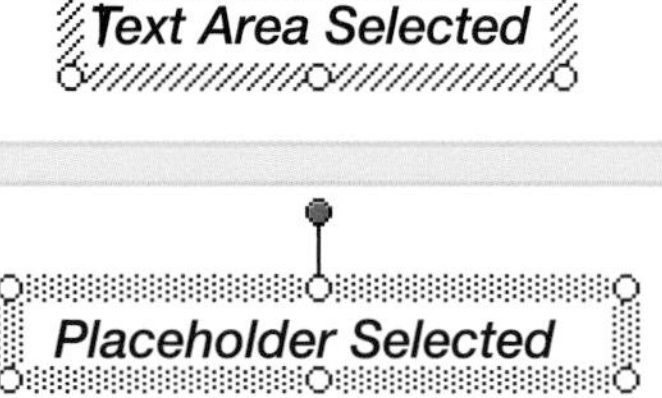

TIP

As you type and the text reaches the edges of the text box, it will expand vertically so that the text fits. You can then drag the handles to the shape you want. Drag left or right to change the width of the text box. Drag up or down to change the height of the text box

ENTER TEXT INTO A TEXT BOX

To enter text into a text box, simply click inside the text box; the border of the text box now appears as slanted lines. An insertion point also appears, indicating that you can now type text.

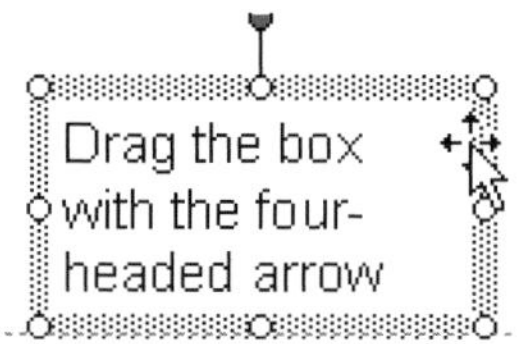

MOVE A TEXT BOX

To move a text box, you drag the border of the placeholder.

1. Click the text within a text box to display the outline of the text box.
2. Click the border of the text box. The border will become dotted. The pointer will be a four-headed arrow.
3. Place the pointer on the border between the handles, and drag it where you want.

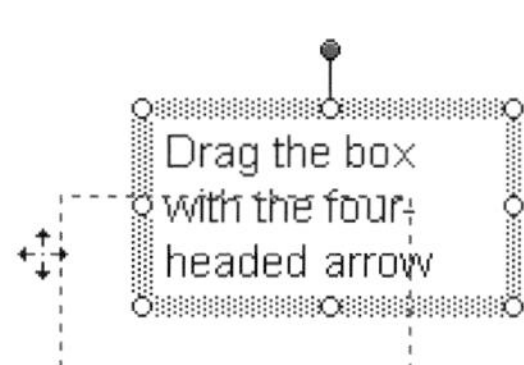

RESIZE A PLACEHOLDER

To resize a placeholder, you drag the sizing handles of the text box.

1. Click the text to display the text box border. Click the border of the placeholder. The border will become dotted. The pointer will be a four-headed arrow.
2. Place the pointer on the border over the handles so that the pointer becomes a two-headed arrow.
3. Drag the sizing handle in the direction you want the text box expanded or reduced in size. As you drag, the pointer will morph into a crosshair.

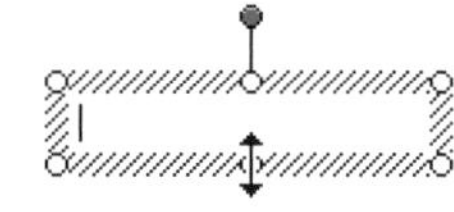

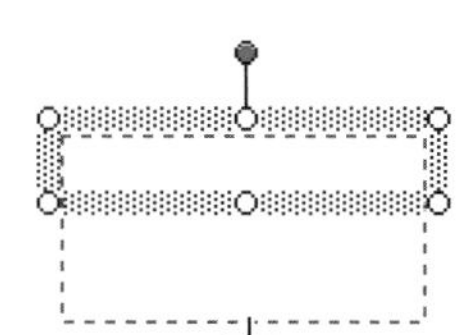

DELETE A TEXT BOX

To delete a text box:

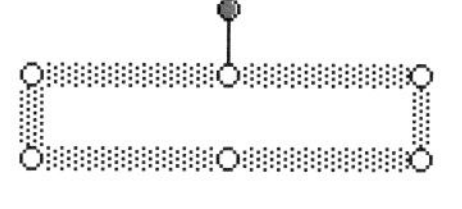

1. Click the text within the text box to display the border. Click the border of the text box to select it (the border will be dotted).
2. Press **DELETE**. If there is text in the text box, you may see "Click To Add Text." Press **DELETE** again.

COPY A TEXT BOX

To copy a text box with its contents and drag it to another part of the slide:

1. Click the text within the text box.
2. Place the pointer on the border of the text box where it becomes a four-headed arrow (not over the handles).
3. Drag the text box while pressing **CTRL**. The pointer will have a "+" when it can be copied.

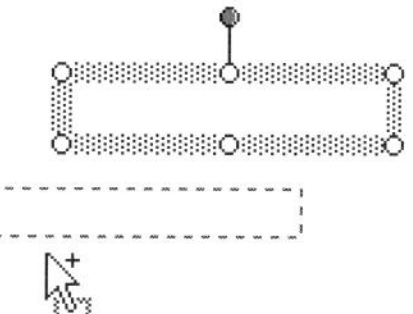

TIP

To rotate a text box or AutoShape that doesn't have a rotate handle, open **Draw**, select **Rotate** or **Flip**, and click **Free Rotate**. Rotating handles will appear on the text box. Place the pointer over the handles, and drag the text box to rotate it.

ROTATE A TEXT BOX

When you first insert a text box (or click on it to select it), a rotate handle allows you to rotate the box in a circle.

1. Place the pointer over the rotate handle.
2. Drag it in the direction it is to be rotated.
3. Place the pointer on the selection handles to drag the text box where you want it to appear on the slide.
4. Click outside the text box to confirm the rotation.

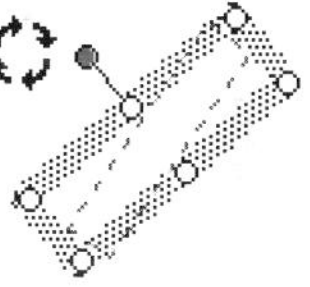

NOTE

If the text box has been inserted on the slide by a template, and you double click the text, the name of the dialog box will be Format AutoShapes.

TIP

If none of the colors is exactly right, click **More Colors**, and click the **Standard** tab. Click a color unit to select it. In the preview box you can see the New color compared to the Current color. Click **OK** twice to see the color change in the text box.

POSITION A TEXT BOX

To set the position of a text box precisely on a slide, follow these steps:

1. Double-click the text box border to get the Format Text Box dialog box. (AutoShape text boxes will show a Format AutoShape dialog box.)
2. Click the **Position** tab.

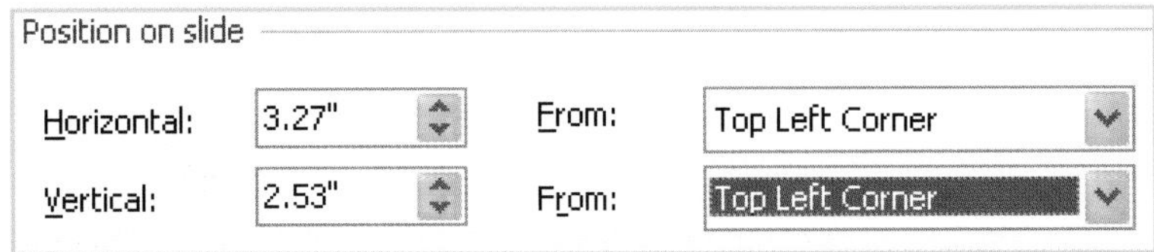

3. Set the Position On Slide settings for **Horizontal** and **Vertical** in inches.
4. In the **From** drop-down list boxes, choose between **Top Left Corner** and **Center**.
5. Click **OK**.

CHANGE THE FILL COLOR IN A TEXT BOX

To change the background color of a text box, you use the Format Text Box dialog box.

1. Click the text box to be changed.
2. To open the Format Text Box dialog box, double-click the border of the text box (the four-headed arrow must be showing). The dialog box will open.
3. Click the **Colors And Lines** tab, as shown in Figure 4-2.
4. Click the **Color** drop-down box to select a color. Click the color and click **OK**.

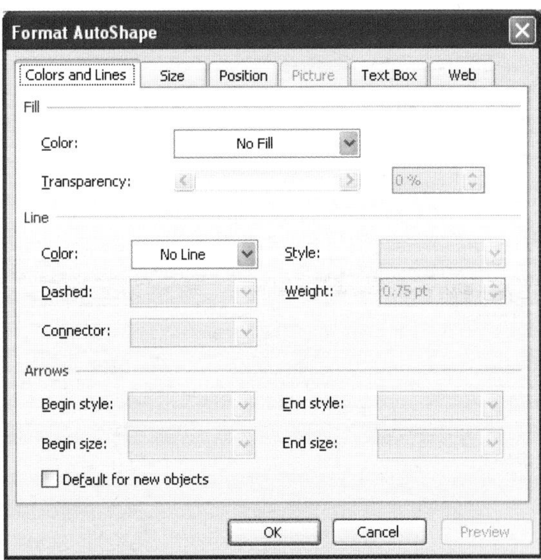

Figure 4-2: The Format Text Box (or Format AutoShapes) dialog box is where you can fill the text box with color or place a border around it

QUICKSTEPS

SETTING MARGINS, WORD WRAP, ANCHOR POINTS, AND ROTATING TEXT

All of these QuickSteps make use of the Format Text Box dialog box. To display it, double-click the border of a text box. When it opens, click the **Text Box** tab.

SET MARGINS IN A TEXT BOX

To change the margins in a text box, change the Internal Margin setting for **Left**, **Right**, **Top**, and **Bottom**

DISABLE WORD WRAP FOR TEXT

To disable (or enable) the word wrap feature for text in a text box, click **Word Wrap Text in AutoShape**. A check mark in the check box indicates that Word Wrap is turned on.

Word wrap text in AutoShape

ANCHOR TEXT IN A TEXT BOX

To anchor the text within a text box, select the position where the text will start, open the **Text Anchor Point** drop-down box, and click the position to which you want the text anchored.

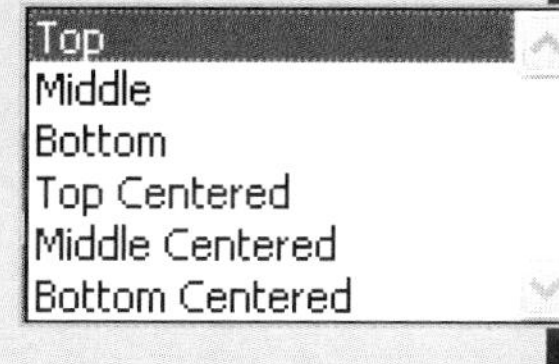

ROTATE TEXT WITHIN A TEXT BOX

To rotate text sideways (or 90 degrees) within a text box, click **Rotate Text Within AutoShape By 90°**.

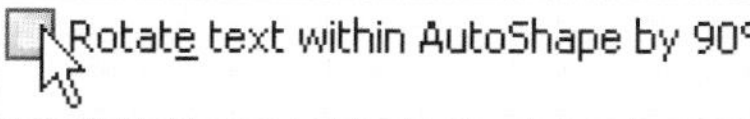

Set and Change Tab Settings

- To display the ruler if it isn't showing, open **View** and click **Ruler**. To see the tab markers on the ruler, you must click some text.
- To change a default tab setting, drag the small gray marker to the position you want. All other tabs on the line will realign to preserve the new positioning.
- To set a custom tab, click the tab at the left of the ruler until you see the type of tab you want:

  left,

  right,

  center, or

  decimal.

  Then click the ruler at the position you want the tab inserted.

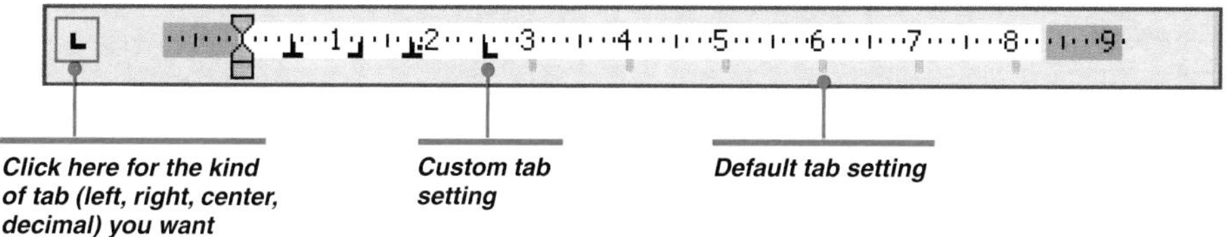

Click here for the kind of tab (left, right, center, decimal) you want

Custom tab setting

Default tab setting

- To remove a tab, simply drag it off the ruler.

Change Line and Paragraph Spacing

You can choose line spacing and determine the spacing before and after paragraphs. The line-spacing changes can be made in the text box, on a slide, or in the Outline tab. If you want to change the spacing for the presentation, not just the selected text, use the Slide Master. (See Chapter 3 for how to work with masters.)

1. Select the text for which you want to change the line spacing.

TIP

When you adjust the line spacing, the AutoFit feature, which is on by default, may cause the text to be resized to fit within the text box.

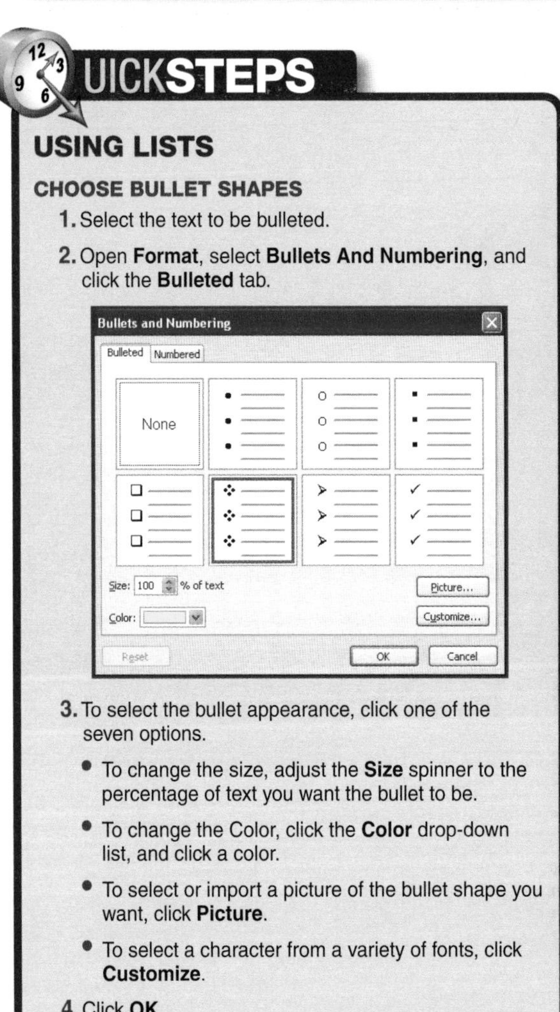

QUICKSTEPS

USING LISTS

CHOOSE BULLET SHAPES

1. Select the text to be bulleted.
2. Open **Format**, select **Bullets And Numbering**, and click the **Bulleted** tab.

3. To select the bullet appearance, click one of the seven options.
   - To change the size, adjust the **Size** spinner to the percentage of text you want the bullet to be.
   - To change the Color, click the **Color** drop-down list, and click a color.
   - To select or import a picture of the bullet shape you want, click **Picture**.
   - To select a character from a variety of fonts, click **Customize**.
4. Click **OK**.

Continued...

2. Open **Format** and click **Line Spacing**. The Line Spacing dialog box will open.

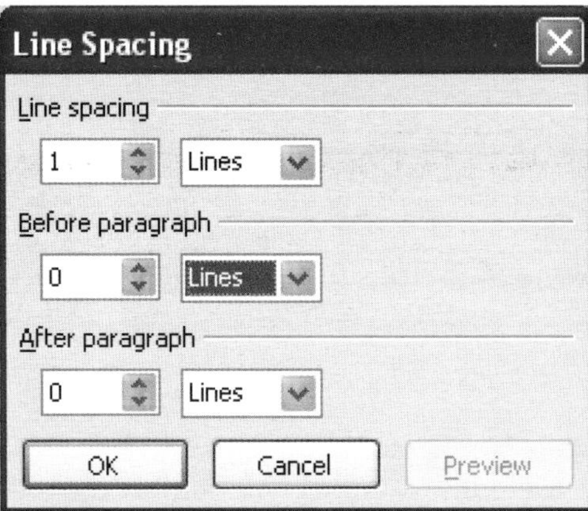

3. Choose one or more of the following:
   - To vary Line Spacing, click the **Down Arrow**, and choose between **Lines** and **Points** (one inch = 72 points). Use the scroll arrows to change the number to what you want.
   - To set the spacing Before Paragraph, click the **Down Arrow**, and choose between **Lines** and **Points**. Use the scroll arrows to set the number that will be used to space before a paragraph.
   - To set the spacing After Paragraph, click the **Down Arrow**, and choose between **Lines** and **Points**. Use the scroll arrows to set the number that will be used to space after a paragraph.
4. Click **Preview** to see if the setting is what you want.
5. Click **OK** to confirm the settings.

USING LISTS *(Continued)*

CHANGE NUMBERING STYLES

1. Select the text to be numbered.
2. Open **Format**, select **Bullets And Numbering**, and click the **Numbered** tab.
3. To select the numbering style, click one of the seven options.
   - To change the size, adjust the **Size** spinner to the percentage of text's size you want the numbering to be.
   - To change the color, click the **Color** drop-down list, and click a color.
   - To set a beginning number or letter, change **Start At**.
4. Click **OK**.

ALIGN LISTS

To change the alignment between the bullets and the text, you use the ruler at the top of the Slides pane, as shown in Figure 4-3.

1. To display the ruler, open **View** and click **Ruler**.
2. Click within the placeholder containing the list to be realigned.
   - Drag the first line indent to move the bullet or number.
   - Drag the left indent to move the text.
   - Drag the square beneath the left indent to move text and bullets or numbers together.

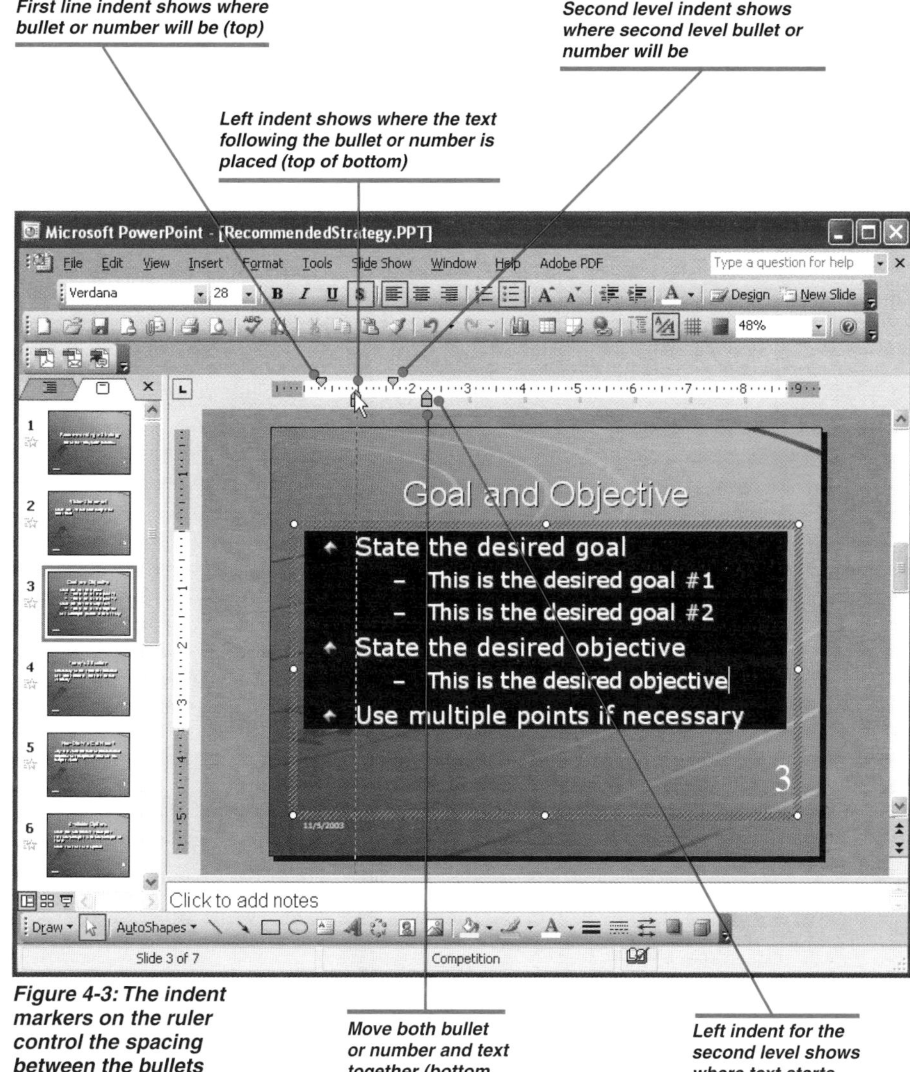

First line indent shows where bullet or number will be (top)
Second level indent shows where second level bullet or number will be
Left indent shows where the text following the bullet or number is placed (top of bottom)
Microsoft PowerPoint - [RecommendedStrategy.PPT]
Goal and Objective
State the desired goal
This is the desired goal #1
This is the desired goal #2
State the desired objective
This is the desired objective
Use multiple points if necessary
Click to add notes
Slide 3 of 7
Competition
Move both bullet or number and text together (bottom of bottom)
Left indent for the second level shows where text starts

Figure 4-3: The indent markers on the ruler control the spacing between the bullets and the text; there are separate indent markers for each level of bullets

EDITING SLIDE TEXT

Working with text in PowerPoint is similar to working with text in Microsoft Word. Here are some familiar ways to move the pointer, and to select, delete, and insert text.

MOVE THE POINTER WITHIN YOUR TEXT

- For the beginning of the line, press **HOME**.
- For the end of a line, press **END**.
- To skip to the next word, press **CTRL+RIGHT ARROW**.
- To skip to the previous word, press **CTRL+LEFT ARROW**.

SELECT TEXT

- To select all text contained within a text box, press **CTRL+A**.
- To select a word, double-click the word.

You can select text in a couple ways. You can double-click a word, or click three times for text in a paragraph. Or you can drag the pointer across text, highlighting it.

- To select a paragraph, click within the paragraph three times.
- To select all text to the end of the line, press **SHIFT+END**.
- To select all text to the beginning of the line, press **SHIFT+HOME**.
- To select multiple lines, press **SHIFT+UP ARROW** or **DOWN ARROW**.
- To select one character at a time, press **SHIFT+LEFT ARROW** or **RIGHT ARROW**.

Continued...

Change Capitalization

To set your capitalization standard, or to correct text typed in the wrong case:

1. Select the text you want to change the case on.
2. Open **Format** and choose **Change Case**. The Change Case dialog box will open.

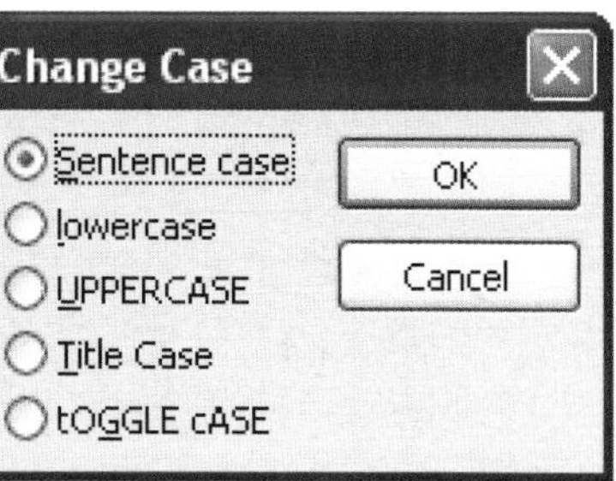

3. Select one of the following options:
   - **Sentence case**, to capitalize the first word in a sentence
   - **lowercase**, to make all text lowercase
   - **UPPERCASE**, to make all text uppercase
   - **Title Case** to capitalize all words except short articles, prepositions, and conjunctions, such as *in*, *and*, *of*, *the*, *to*, *at*, or *on*
   - **tOGGLE cASE** to switch upper- and lowercase letters, for instance, when you have accidentally typed text in the wrong case
4. When you have selected an option, click **OK**.

Use the Font Dialog Box

To change multiple font and character attributes at once, or to set the standard for a slide, it is easier to use the Font dialog box than individual buttons:

1. Open **Format** and click **Font**. The Font dialog box will open, as shown in Figure 4-4.
2. Choose the options you want and click **OK**.

EDITING SLIDE TEXT *(Continued)*

- To select other text as needed, drag the pointer across the text, highlighting it.

You can select text in a couple ways. You can double-click a word, or click three times for text in a paragraph. Or you can drag the pointer across text, highlighting it.

DELETE TEXT

- To delete the character to the right, press **DELETE**.
- To delete the character to the left, press **BACKSPACE**.
- To delete other text as needed, drag the pointer across the text, highlighting it, and press **DELETE**.

INSERT TEXT

To insert one or more characters within a text box, click within the text box, place the pointer where you want to type, then type.

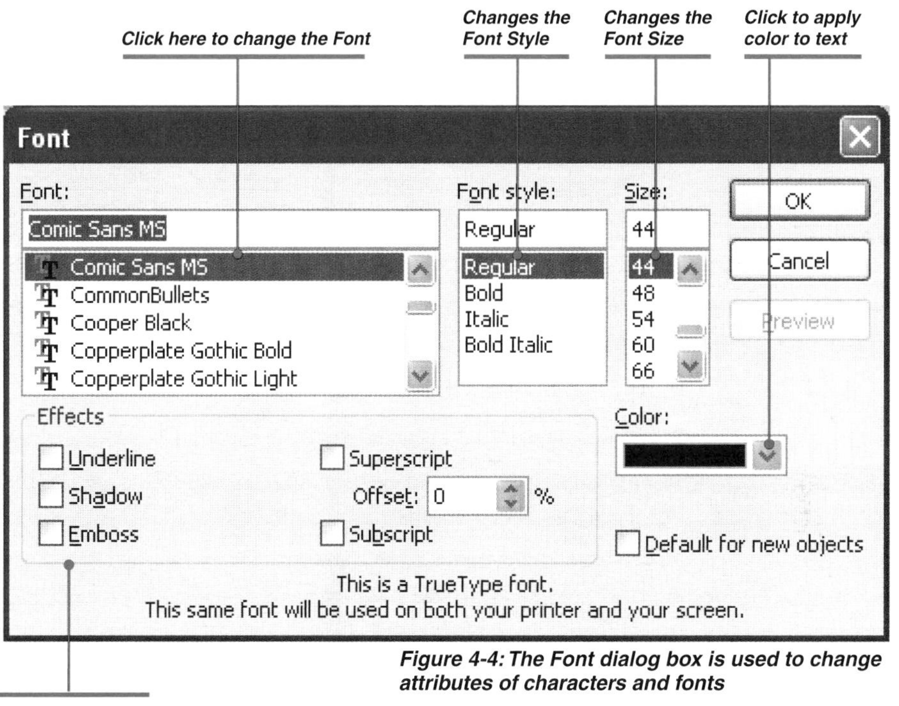

Figure 4-4: The Font dialog box is used to change attributes of characters and fonts

Change Fonts, Font Size, Color, Style, and Effects

You change the various font attributes either individually with the Formatting toolbar buttons or with the Font dialog box. Here's how to use the buttons:

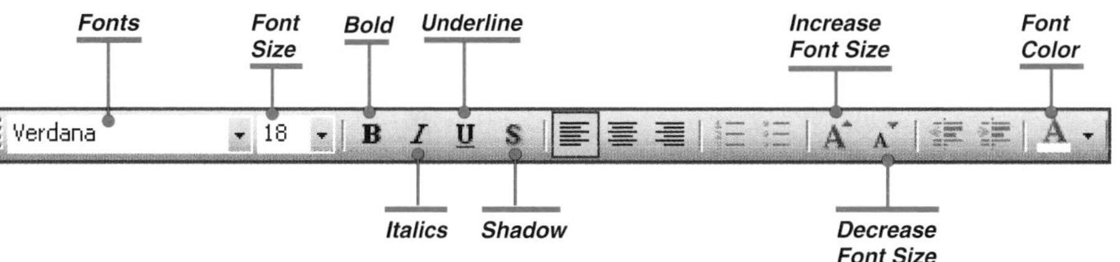

MOVING OR COPYING TEXT

There are at least four ways you can move text. You can use the Cut and Paste technique, the Edit menu, right-click from a context menu, or use the drag-and-drop technique. Here's how:

CUT AND PASTE TEXT WITH THE KEYBOARD

1. Select the text to be moved, and press **CTRL+X** to cut the text.
2. Click the pointer to place the insertion point, and press **CTRL+V** to paste the text in the new location.

CUT AND PASTE WITH THE EDIT MENU

1. Select the text to be moved.
2. Open **Edit** and click **Cut**.
3. Click the pointer to place the insertion point, and press **CTRL+V** to paste the text in the new location.
4. Open **Edit** and click **Paste**.

CUT AND PASTE WITH A CONTEXT MENU

1. Select the text to be moved or copied.
2. Right-click the selected text, and click **Cut**.
3. Click the pointer to place the insertion point, and press **CTRL+V** to paste the text in the new location; or right-click the new location, and click **Paste**.

Continued...

NOTE

All the Cut and Paste techniques can also be used to copy information. Just select **Copy** instead of Cut from the context or Edit menus, or press **CTRL+C**.

1. Select the text to be reformatted.
2. Click the button for the style effect you want:
   - To change the font, open the **Font** drop-down list, and click the font you want.

   - To change font size, open the **Font Size** drop-down list, and click the size you want.

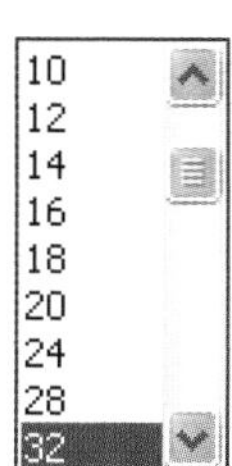

   - To change the font color, open the **Font Color** button, and click the color you want. From then on, to apply the same color to selected text, you can just click the button without opening it.
   - Click the appropriate style button. Click it both to apply the style and to remove it: **Bold** *Italics*
   - To underline or remove underlining from selected text, click the **Underline** button.

NOTE

To *justify* a paragraph is to space it so that both the left and right edges are evenly aligned.

MOVING OR COPYING TEXT *(Continued)*

USE DRAG AND DROP

To use the drag-and-drop technique to move text within the same text box, to other text boxes, or to other slides (when moving to other slides, you can only use the Outline tab):

1. Select the text to be moved.
2. Using the pointer, drag the text to the new location. An insertion point shows you where the text is about to be moved.

Drag and drop allows you to select text and then drag it to a new location within the same text. Here is text to move to another spot.

3. Release the pointer when the insertion point is in the correct location.

TIP

When text in a paragraph is first resized with AutoFit, the AutoFit button appears to its left. Click the **AutoFit** button, and click **Stop Fitting Text To This Placeholder**. Temporarily, AutoFit will be turned off for the selected placeholder during the current PowerPoint session. It does not reset the AutoFit settings in the AutoCorrect dialog box.

Align Text

You align text by centering, left-justifying, right-justifying, or justifying it. All four options are available from the Alignment option on the Format menu. Three are available on the Formatting toolbar.

1. Select the text to be aligned.
2. Choose one of these options:
   - To center, click **Center** on the Formatting toolbar; or open **Format**, choose **Alignment**, and click **Center**.
   - To left-align, click the **Align Left** button on the Formatting Toolbar; or open **Format**, choose **Alignment**, and click **Align Left**.
   - To right-align, click the Align Right button; or open Format, choose Alignment, and click **Align Right**.
   - To justify, open **Format**, select **Alignment**, and click **Justify**.

Use AutoFit

AutoFit is used to make text fit within a text box or AutoShape. It often resizes text to make it fit. You can turn it on or off:

1. Open **Tools**, and click **AutoCorrect Options**. The AutoCorrect dialog box will open.
2. Click the **AutoFormat As You Type** tab.
3. Under Apply As You Type, click **AutoFit Body Text To Placeholder**. If the check mark is in the check box, AutoFit is turned on.

1
2
3
4
5
6
7
8
9
10

If you want to copy more than one text selection, double-click the **Format Painter** to turn it on. You can copy multiple text selections, one after the other. To turn it off, click **Format Painter** again.

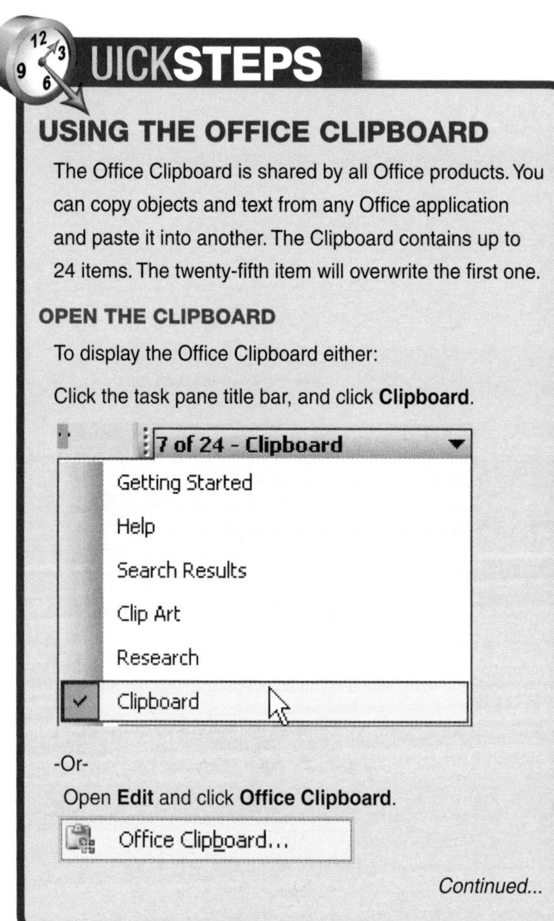

USING THE OFFICE CLIPBOARD

The Office Clipboard is shared by all Office products. You can copy objects and text from any Office application and paste it into another. The Clipboard contains up to 24 items. The twenty-fifth item will overwrite the first one.

OPEN THE CLIPBOARD

To display the Office Clipboard either:

Click the task pane title bar, and click **Clipboard**.

-Or-

Open **Edit** and click **Office Clipboard**.

Continued...

Copy Formatting with Format Painter

To copy all formatting attributes from one placeholder to another, you use Format Painter. With it you can copy fonts, font size and style, line and paragraph spacing, color, alignment, bullet selection, and character effects.

1. Select the text containing the formatting attributes to be copied.
2. Click **Format Painter**. 
3. Find the destination text to contain the copied attributes, and drag the paintbrush pointer over the text to be changed.

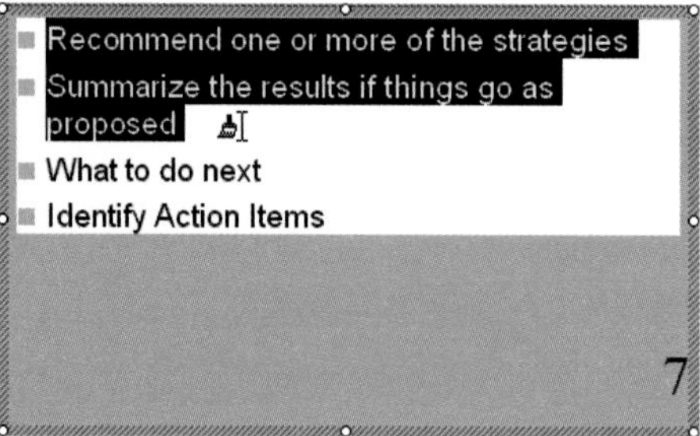

Use AutoCorrect

AutoCorrect is a feature that helps you type information correctly. For example, it corrects simple typing errors and makes certain assumptions about what you want to type. You can turn it off or change its rules.

TURN AUTOCORRECT OPTIONS ON OR OFF

The AutoCorrect feature assumes that you will want certain corrections always to be made while you type. Among these corrections are: change two initial capital letters to the first one only, capitalize the first letter of each sentence, capitalize the first letter of table cells and names of days, correct accidental use of the CAPS LOCK key, and replace misspelled words with the results it assumes you want. (See "Change AutoCorrect Spelling Corrections" to retain the correction of misspelled words but to change the correction made.) To turn off the automatic spelling corrections that PowerPoint makes, follow these steps:

USING THE OFFICE CLIPBOARD

(Continued)

ADD TO CLIPBOARD

When you Cut or Copy text, it is automatically added to the Office Clipboard

1. Select the text to be copied or cut.
2. Press **CTRL+X** to cut or **CTRL+C** to copy.

COPY CLIPBOARD TO PLACEHOLDER

To paste one item:

1. Click to place the insertion point in the text box or placeholder where you want the item on the Office Clipboard inserted.
2. Click the item on the Clipboard to be inserted.

–Or–

1. With the Clipboard item selected but no insertion point placed, right-click where you want the item.
2. Select **Paste** from the context menu.

To paste all items:

1. Click to place the insertion point in the text box or placeholder where you want the items on the Office Clipboard inserted.
2. Click **Paste All** on the Clipboard.

DELETE ITEMS ON THE CLIPBOARD

- To delete all items, click **Clear All** on the Clipboard task pane.
- To delete a single item, click the arrow next to the item, and click **Delete**.

Continued...

1. Open **Tools** and click **AutoCorrect Options**.
2. Click the **AutoCorrect** tab, as shown in Figure 4-5.

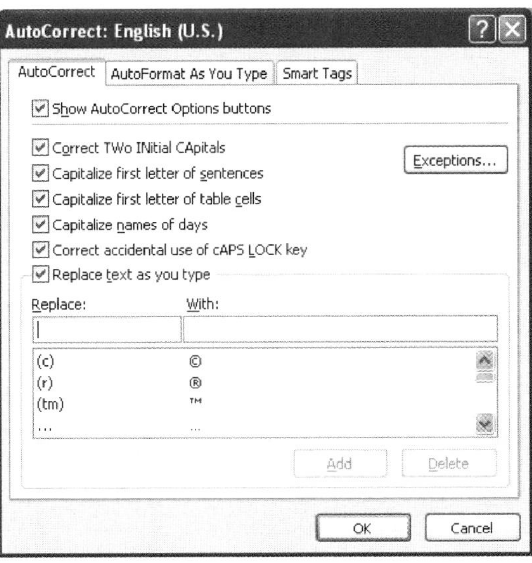

Figure 4-5: The AutoCorrect dialog box defines the automatic corrections that occur while you are typing. You can turn them off or on or change the spelling substitutions.

3. Find the option you want to turn off or on, and click the check box. If a check mark is in the box, the option is enabled. If it is not, the option is turned off.

CHANGE AUTOCORRECT SPELLING CORRECTIONS

You can add a new spelling correction, replace a current spelling correction with a new one, or replace the result that is now used. When you first open the dialog box, both the Replace and With boxes are blank (unless you have some text selected, then it's in the With box). In this case, you simply add what you want. To replace an entry, you first delete an entry—one that is not a mistake you typically make—and then you replace it with a typing error you commonly do make. To replace a current spelling result, you type over the current result with the correction you want. Make these changes like this:

Open **Tools**, select **AutoCorrect Options**, and click the **AutoCorrect** tab.

- To add a new entry when both the Replace and With boxes are blank, fill in the **Replace** and **With** boxes, and click **Add**.

1 2 3 4 5 6 7 8 9 10

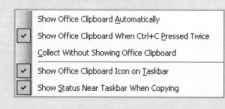

NOTE

The Exception button is used to provide exceptions to the capitalization rules. Clicking the button provides an opportunity to add to a list of either initially capitalized exceptions or exceptions about when to capitalize a word, such as after an abbreviation.

USING THE OFFICE CLIPBOARD

(Continued)

SET CLIPBOARD OPTIONS

1. Open **Edit**, and select **Office Clipboard**. The Office Clipboard will open.
2. Click **Options** on the Clipboard task pane.
3. Click an option to select or deselect it:
   - **Show Office Clipboard Automatically** always shows the Office Clipboard when copying.
   - **Show Office Clipboard When CTRL+C Pressed Twice** shows the Office Clipboard when you press CTRL+C twice to make two copies (in other words, two items on the clipboard will cause the Clipboard to be displayed).
   - **Collect Without Showing Office Clipboard** copies items to the Clipboard without displaying it.
   - **Show Office Clipboard Icon On Taskbar** displays the icon when the Clipboard is being used.
   - **Show Status Near Taskbar When Copying** displays a message about the items being added to the Clipboard as copies are made.

Show Office Clipboard Automatically
Show Office Clipboard When Ctrl+C Pressed Twice
Collect Without Showing Office Clipboard
Show Office Clipboard Icon on Taskbar
Show Status Near Taskbar When Copying

- To replace an entry in the Replace and With boxes, double-click the text in each box, and replace it with your new entry. Click **Add**. The "old" text will be not be deleted; it is still in the list. You must use the **DELETE** button to actually get rid of an entry in the list.
- To replace only one of the two related entries in either the Replace or With box, click the spelling entry to be changed.
- To replace an entry in the Replace box, first delete the current one by clicking **DELETE**, and then type the new spelling option. Click **Add**.

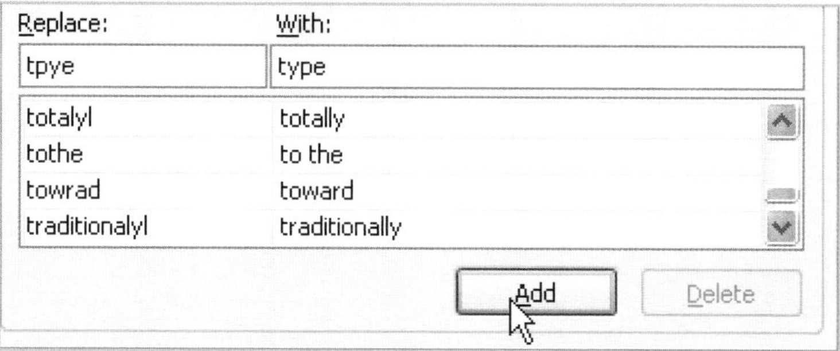

- To replace an entry in the With box with another word, type the new entry over the text currently there. Click **Replace**. Click **Yes** to redefine the entry.

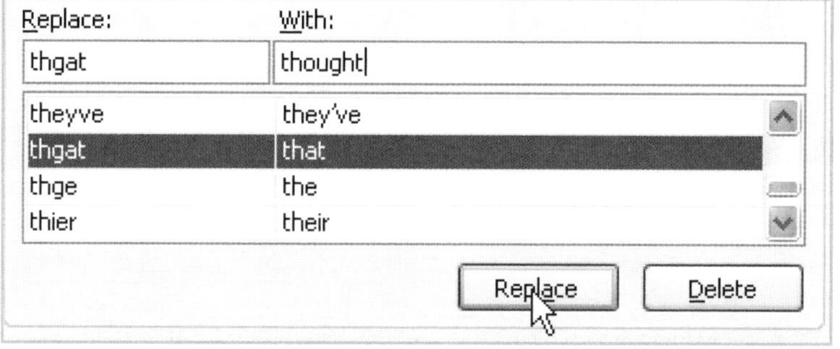

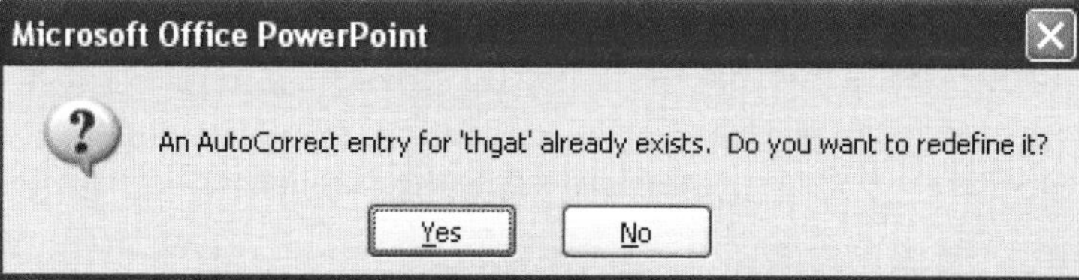

TIP

To quickly use spelling checker, right-click the misspelled word. A context menu will display several options for correct spellings. Click the correct word if it is on the list. You can also choose **Ignore All Instances** of the misspelling or **Add To Dictionary**. The Look Up feature searches the Internet or selected reference books to find matches. Finally, you can bring up the Spelling dialog box.

Use Spell Check

One form of the spelling checker automatically flags words that it cannot find in the dictionary as potential misspellings. It identifies the words with a red underline. However, even when the automatic function is turned off, you can still use the spelling checker by manually opening it.

SPELL CHECK A PRESENTATION

The spelling checker goes through all text in all placeholders on a slide looking for words that are not in the spelling dictionary. When it finds one, it displays the Spelling dialog box, seen in Figure 4-6. Here is how it works.

1. To bring up spelling checker, open **Tools** and click **Spelling**. The Spelling dialog box will be displayed when it finds a word that is not in the dictionary.
2. Choose any of these options to use the spelling checker:
   - If the word is incorrect, check **Suggestions** to see if the correct word is listed. If it is, select it and click **Change**. Click **Change All** to change all occurrences of that same word.
   - If the identified word is correct but not in the dictionary, either you can add the word to a custom dictionary by clicking **Add Words To CUSTOM.DIC**, or you can skip the word by clicking **Ignore** or **Ignore All** (to skip all occurrences of the same word).
   - To continue searching for words without taking any action, click **Resume**.
   - Click **AutoCorrect** to add the word to the AutoCorrect list of automatic spelling changes that will be made as you type. Immediately the word will be placed in the AutoCorrect list.
   - Click **Suggest** to get additional alternative suggestions.
3. Click **Close** to end the search for spelling errors. When spelling checker has finished, a message will be displayed. Click **OK** to confirm that it is finished.

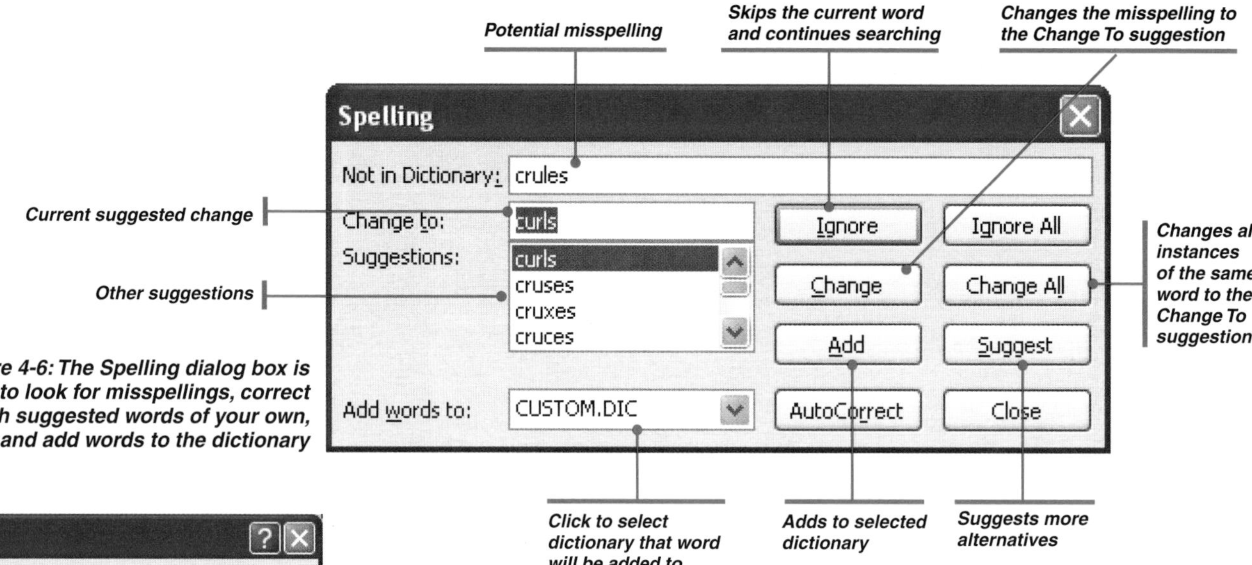

Figure 4-6: The Spelling dialog box is used to look for misspellings, correct them with suggested words of your own, and add words to the dictionary

Figure 4-7: The Spelling And Style tab offers several options for fine-tuning the spelling checker

SET SPELLING DEFAULTS

Set these options that determine how the spelling checker works.

1. Open **Tools** and click **Options**, and click the **Spelling And Style** tab. The Options dialog box opens, shown in Figure 4-7.
3. Select or deselect these options:
   - **Check Spelling As You Type** determines whether the spelling checker will automatically check spelling in a presentation. If this is deselected, you can still spell check your text, but it will not be done automatically.
   - **Hide All Spelling Errors** will display the red line beneath the misspelled words.
   - **Always Suggest Corrections** will display alternative suggestions.
   - **Ignore Words in UPPERCASE** determines whether uppercase words will be checked for spelling.
   - **Ignore Words With Numbers** determines whether words containing numbers will be checked for spelling.
4. Click **OK** to accept any changes.

How to...

- *Inserting a Table from Scratch*
- *Insert a Table*
- *Aligning Text*
- *Enter Text*
- *Format Text*
- *Rotating Text in Cells*
- *Delete a Table*
- *Use the Tables and Borders Toolbar*
- *Selecting Table Components*
- *Insert Columns and Rows*
- *Change Size of Columns and Rows*
- *Deleting Columns and Rows*
- *Work with Borders*
- *Merging or Splitting Cells*
- *Shade Cells, Columns, Rows, or a Table*
- *Use Special Effects in the Table Background*
- *Use a Picture in Your Table*
- *Enter Formulas*

Chapter 5

Creating Tables in Slides

This chapter will address how to create tables in slides. This includes how to insert tables into slides, enter text into tables, select text, and adjust columns and rows, or add or delete more columns and rows. It addresses how to format and align text held within tables, how to add borders, and how to work with cells, including how to shade, merge/split them, or rotate text within the cells. You will learn to enter formulas.

Create Tables

Creating tables is easily handled in PowerPoint. You give the Insert Table command, specify the number of rows and columns you want, and then fill in the data. That's just about all there is to it. Of course, thinking about what data will be included is a decision that PowerPoint can't do much to help with. But once you have answered those basic questions, PowerPoint offers a wide variety of choices about how to present that data clearly and professionally.

QUICKSTEPS

INSERTING A TABLE FROM SCRATCH

To insert a basic table onto a slide:

1. Click **New Slide** to insert a new slide into the presentation. The Slide Layout task pane will be displayed.
2. If need be, clear any default layout elements from the slide by clicking the Blank or the Title Only thumbnail.
3. Open **Insert** and click **Table**. The Insert Table dialog box is displayed.
4. Fill in the number of columns and rows, and click **OK**.

TIP

An alternate way to get an Insert Table dialog box is to click the Insert Table button on the Standard Toolbar.

Insert a Table

There are four ways to create a table on a slide. You can insert one from the Layout templates, directly insert a table from scratch, draw a table, or insert one from Microsoft Word.

INSERT A TABLE FROM A LAYOUT

The most common way to create a table is to use one from the various templates that Microsoft provides:

1. To create a new slide, open **File**, and click **New**. The New Presentation task pane will be displayed, along with a basically formatted slide.
2. Click **Blank Presentation** to display the Slide Layout task pane.
3. In the task pane, find a layout thumbnail that contains a table in the format you want. Your choices are:

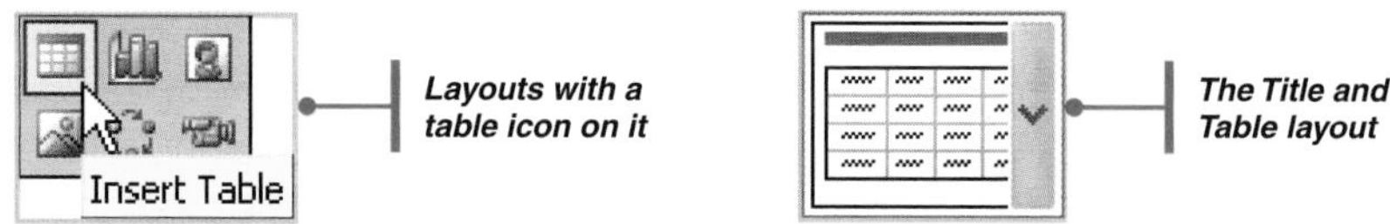

4. Click the thumbnail to apply it to the current slide.
5. Double-click the thumbnail on the slide. An Insert Table dialog box will be displayed. It asks for the number of columns and rows in the table.

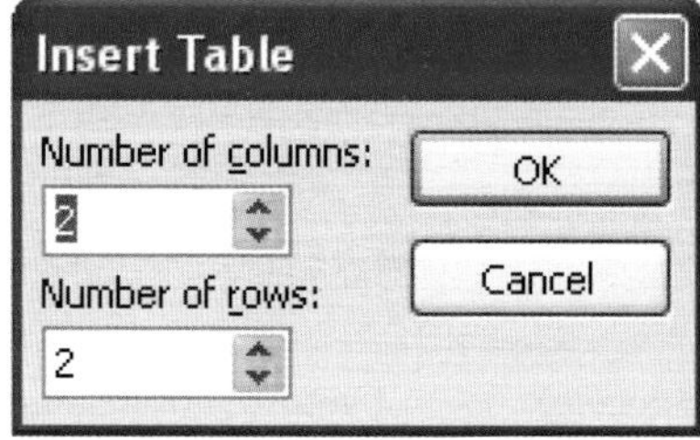

6. Enter the number of columns and rows, and click **OK**. The table will be inserted onto your slide, as shown in Figure 5-1.

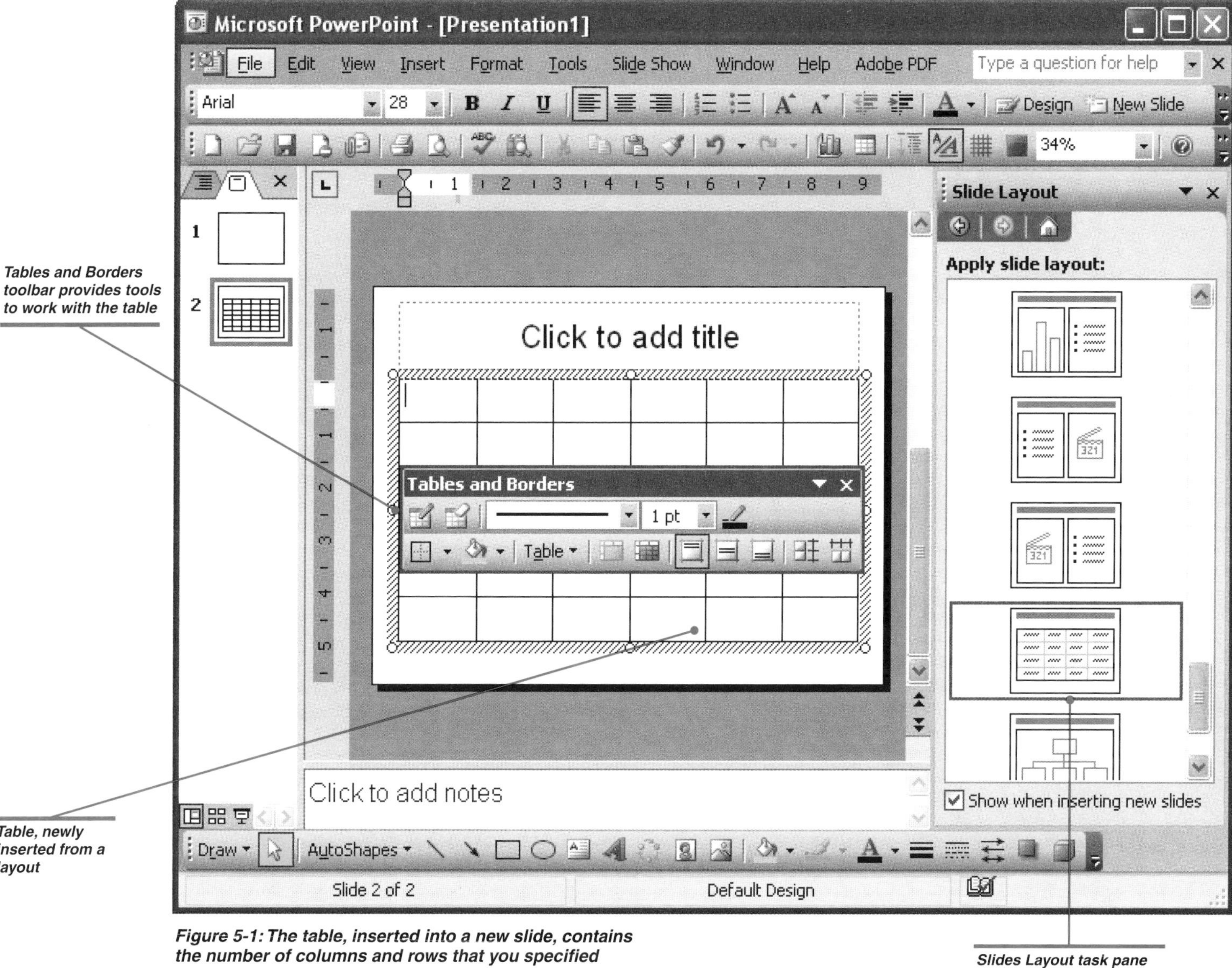

Figure 5-1: The table, inserted into a new slide, contains the number of columns and rows that you specified

1 2 3 4 5 6 7 8 9 10

Figure 5-2: The Grid and Guides dialog box allows you to insert a grid and guides on the slide to help in drawing a table

DRAW A TABLE

To draw a table, you must first display the Tables And Borders toolbar. You then draw the boundaries and interior design of the table:

1. If you need a clear slide, click **New Slide**, and click **Blank** or **Title Only** on the Slide Layout task pane, or choose a suitable layout for your table.
2. To display the toolbar, click **Tables And Borders** on the Standard toolbar. (See the section entitled "Use the Tables and Borders Toolbar," later in this chapter.)

3. To display a grid on the slide, open **View** and click G**rid and Guides**. (Or just click Show/Hide Grid on the Standard toolbar.) The Grid and Guides dialog box will be displayed, as shown in Figure 5-2.

4. Fill in the spacing, and place a check mark in the **Display Grid On Screen** check box. (See "Display Grid and Guides" in Chapter 6.) Click **OK**.
5. Click **Draw Table** on the Tables And Borders toolbar. The pointer will change into a pencil shape.

6. Drag the outline of the table in this way:
   - Drag the pointer diagonally across the slide to define the outside border of the table. When you release the pointer, a selected placeholder box will be in place.
   - Begin to draw the table you want. Draw vertical and horizontal lines. When you start a line, it will be extended in the direction you want until it reaches a border.

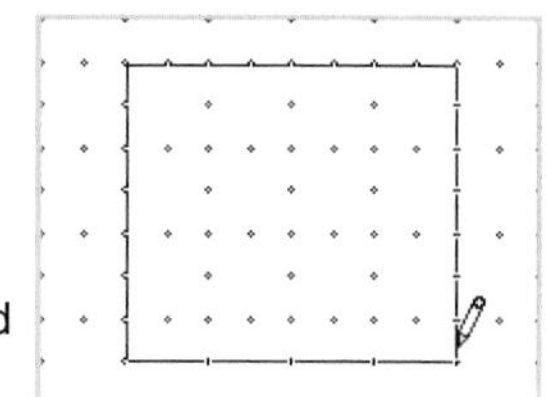

   - To turn off Draw Table, click **Draw Table** again. To turn off the grid, click **Show/Hide Grid**.
   - To insert color into the columns and rows you have drawn, highlight the cells to be colored, and click **Fill Color**. Click the color you want.

Figure 5-3 shows an example of a table drawn in PowerPoint.

TIP

To erase a line, click the **Eraser**, and then click the line to be removed.

NOTE

Tables are made up of columns and rows. The intersection between a row and a column is called a cell. You enter data into individual cells.

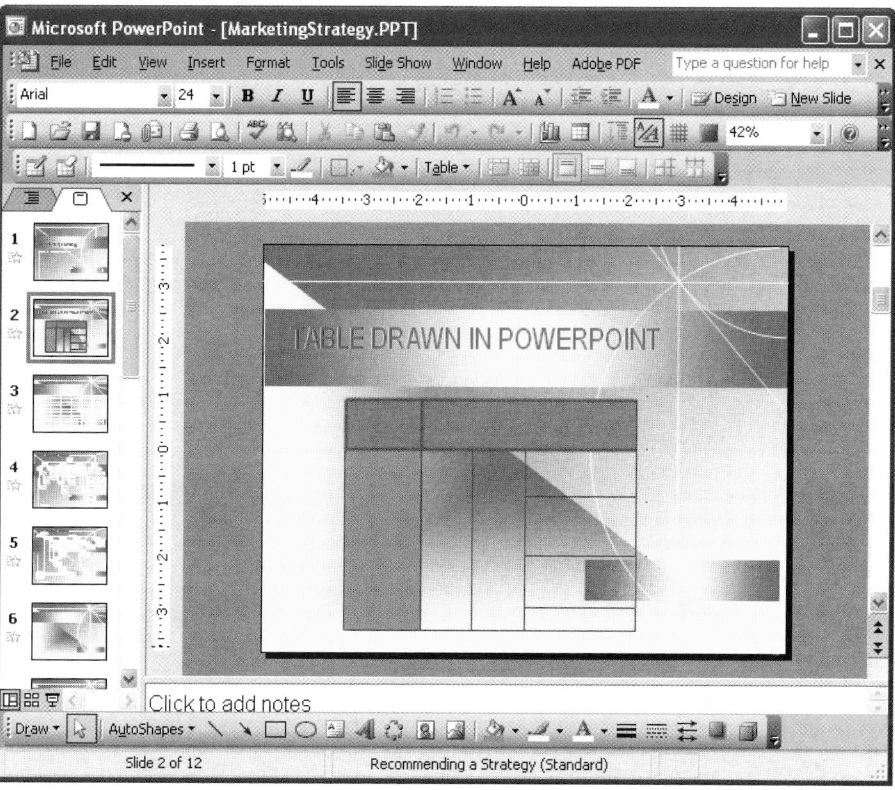

Figure 5-3: A table drawn in PowerPoint can have irregular column and row sizes and be placed in creative ways

While you are working in Word, you can use the AutoFormat feature to create special table looks. Open **Table** and click **Table AutoFormat**. Then scroll the styles, and select a table style to try. You will see the selected style previewed below in the Preview pane. Click **Apply** to apply the one you want to your table.

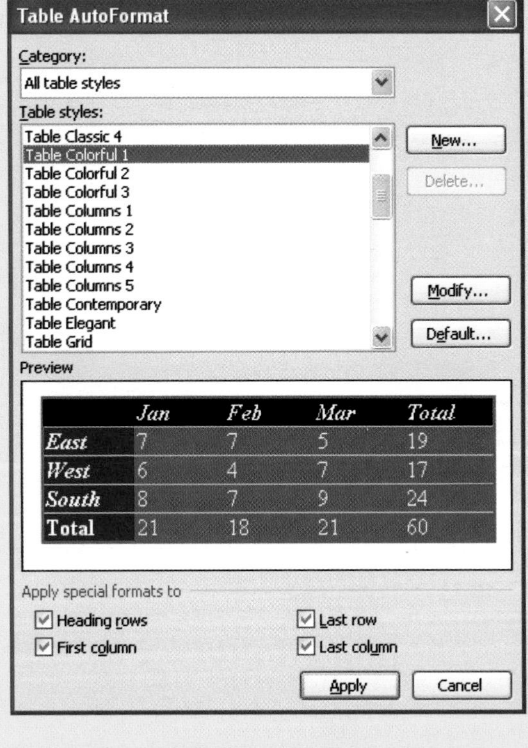

CREATE A TABLE FROM WORD IN POWERPOINT

You can bring up Microsoft Word and create a table while you are working on a presentation in PowerPoint. Here's how:

1. In PowerPoint, create a slide that is to contain your Word table. Click **New Slide**, and click the **Title Only**, **Blank**, or a layout you want from the Slide Layout task pane. The slide may contain color or other design elements based on your presentation.
2. Open **Insert** and choose **Object**. From the list, click **Microsoft Word Document**. Microsoft Word will open a window, as shown in Figure 5-4. The Word menus are available to you.
3. Open **Table** on the Tables and Borders toolbar, choose **Insert**, and click **Table**. The Insert Table dialog box will open.
4. Fill in the number of columns and rows, and click **OK**.
5. Type data into your table, and format it the way you want (see the Note).
6. When you are done and your table is ready, click outside the Word window. The Word window will close, and the table will remain on your PowerPoint slide.

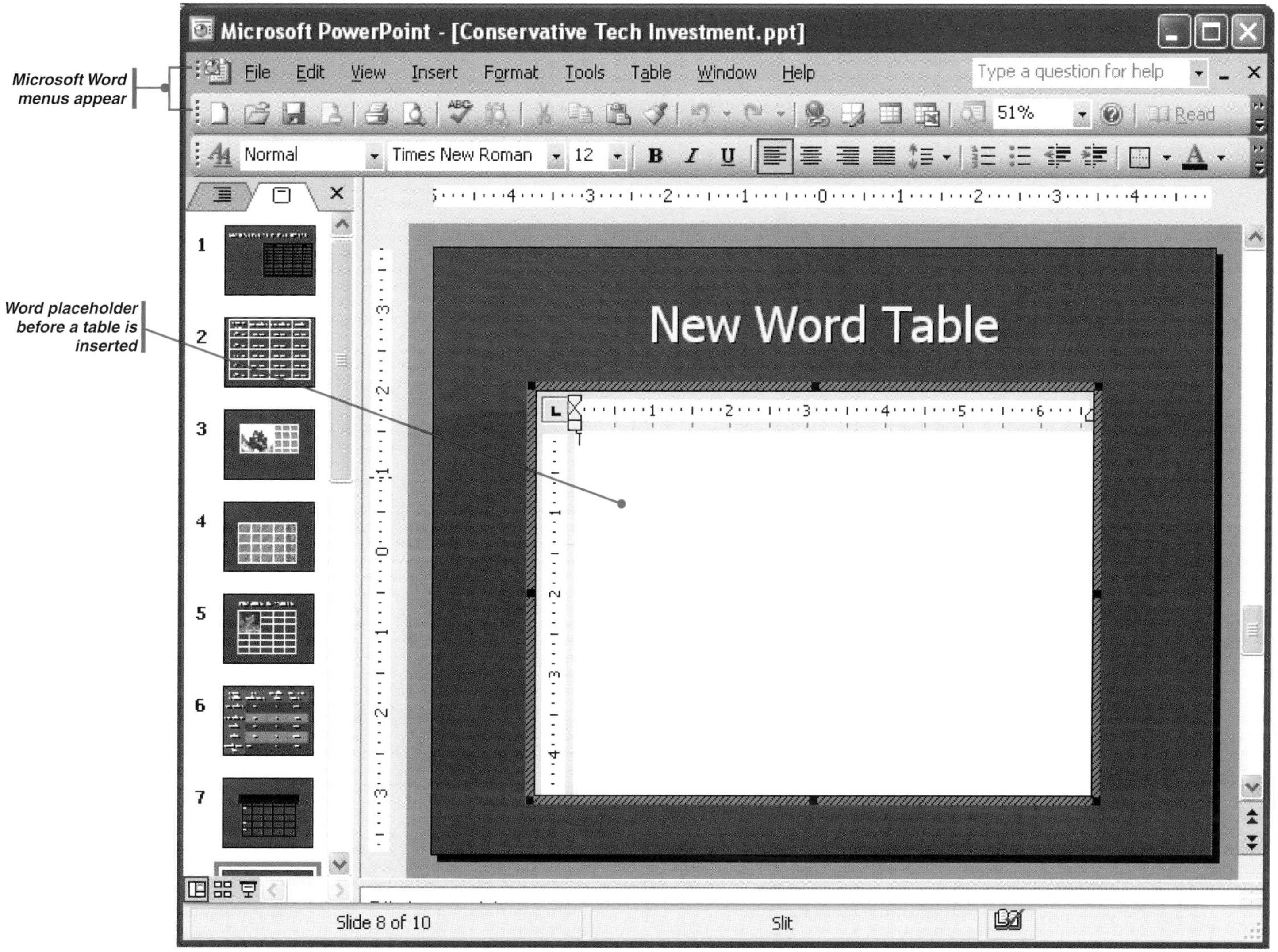

Microsoft Word menus appear

Word placeholder before a table is inserted

Figure 5-4: Microsoft Word opens a window within PowerPoint and is ready for you to create a table with Word menus

1 2 3 4 5 6 7 8 9 10

TIP

Double-click the Word table, and Word will open so you can edit the table in a Word window.

You may notice that text from a table is not showing on your Outline tab. Only text in text boxes shows up on the Outline tab. Text from tables, placeholders, and AutoShape objects do not show up on the Outline tab.

INSERT A TABLE FROM MICROSOFT WORD

You can insert a table created with Microsoft Word by inserting it as an object.

1. In Microsoft Word, use the Table menu commands to create a table the way you want it. Save the file.
2. In PowerPoint, open **Insert** and click **Object**. The Insert Object dialog box will be displayed.

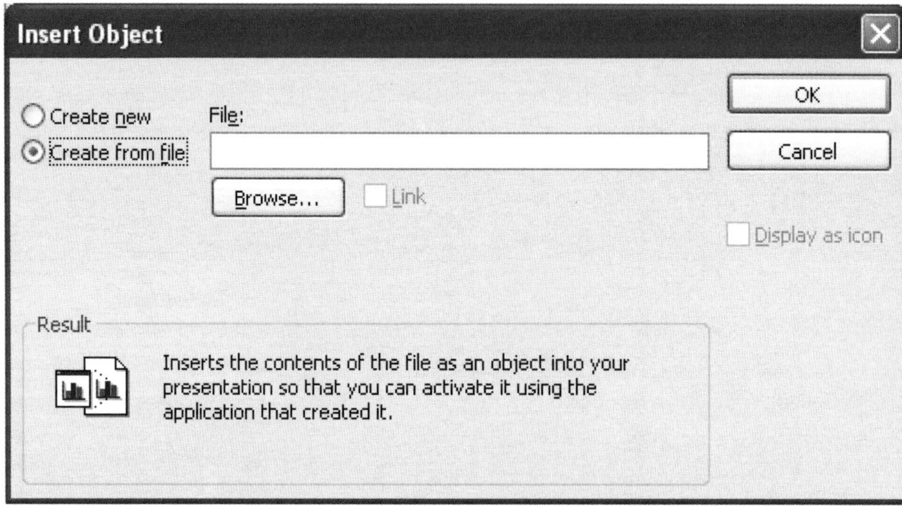

3. Click **Create From File**, and click **Browse** to find the Microsoft Word file containing the table. Select the file, and click **OK** twice to close the Browse and the Insert Object dialog boxes. The table will be inserted into the PowerPoint slide.
4. Use the sizing handles to drag the borders of the table to the size you want. Figure 5-5 shows an example.

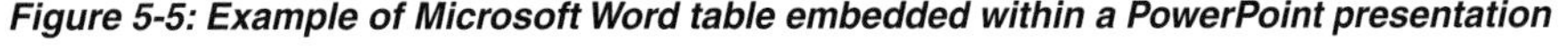

Figure 5-5: Example of Microsoft Word table embedded within a PowerPoint presentation

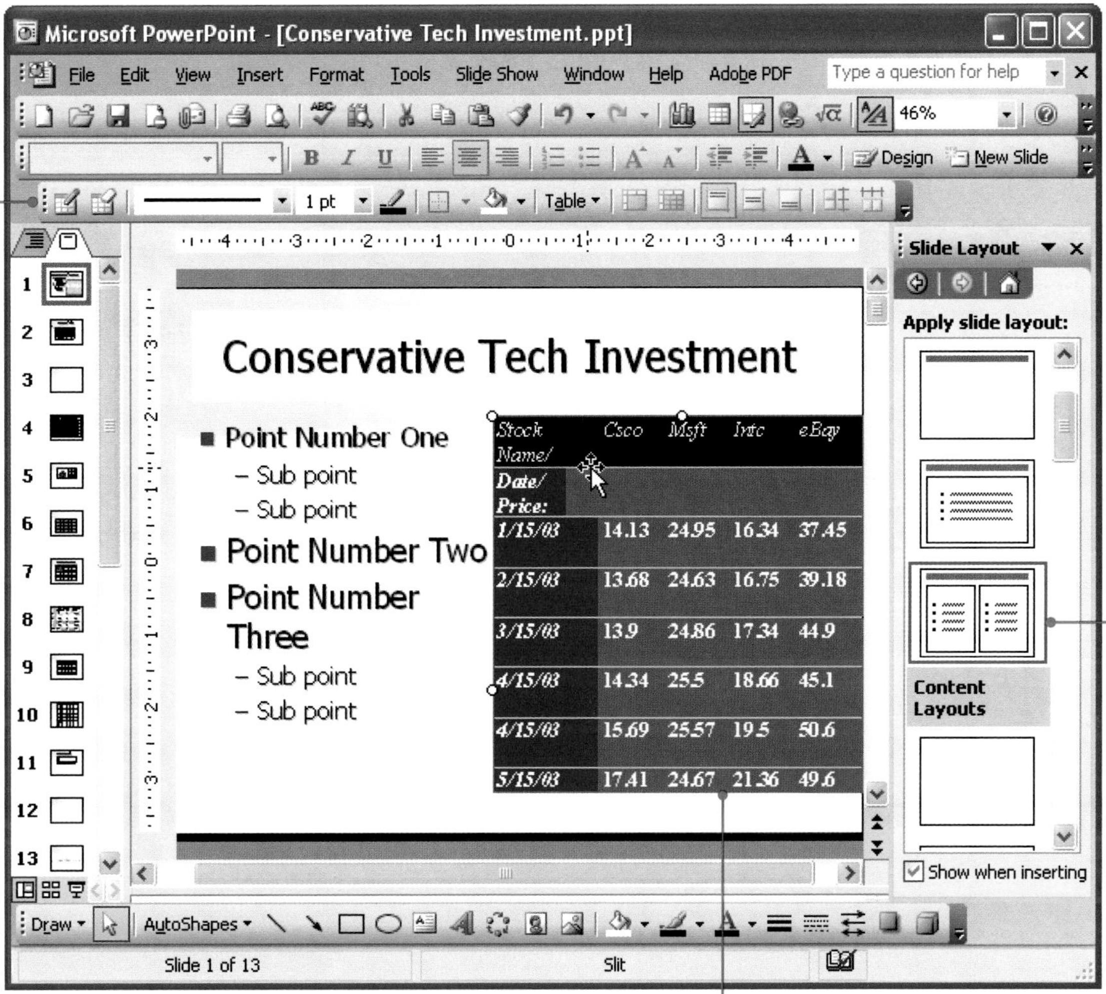

Table and Border toolbar

Layout used for slide

Microsoft Word table inserted into PowerPoint

QUICKSTEPS

ALIGNING TEXT

Text is aligned in the upper-left corner of a cell by default, as shown in Figure 5-6. You can align text vertically and horizontally within a cell:

ALIGN TEXT HORIZONTALLY

First, select the text by dragging over it or double-clicking it. The tools for horizontally aligning text can be found in the Standard toolbar.

Align Left Align Right

Center

- Click Center to center align text.

Marketing	Operations	Admin

- Click Align Left to left align text.

Marketing	Operations	Admin

- Click Align Right to right align text.

Marketing	Operations	Admin

Continued...

TIP

To insert a **TAB** in a table cell, press **CTRL+TAB**.

Enter Text

To enter text into a table cell, you have several navigational tips to keep in mind:

- To add data to a table, click a cell and type. If you type to the end of the cell, your text will wrap to the next line, making the cell taller.
- Press **TAB** to move the pointer to the next cell on the right in the same row.
- When you are at the last cell in a row, **TAB** will move the pointer to the first cell of the next row. If you are in the last cell in a table, **TAB** will insert a new row and place the pointer in the first cell of that row.
- Press **DOWN ARROW** or **UP ARROW** to move the pointer up or down one row in the same column.
- Press **ENTER** to insert another line within a cell—that is, to make the cell taller by one line.

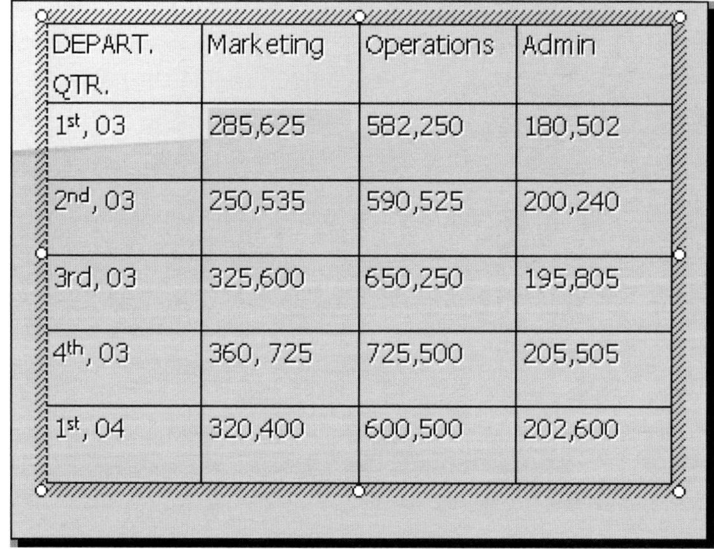

DEPART. QTR.	Marketing	Operations	Admin
1st, 03	285,625	582,250	180,502
2nd, 03	250,535	590,525	200,240
3rd, 03	325,600	650,250	195,805
4th, 03	360, 725	725,500	205,505
1st, 04	320,400	600,500	202,600

***Figure 5-6:** Text is initially aligned in the upper-left of a cell, but you can adjust it both horizontally and vertically within a cell*

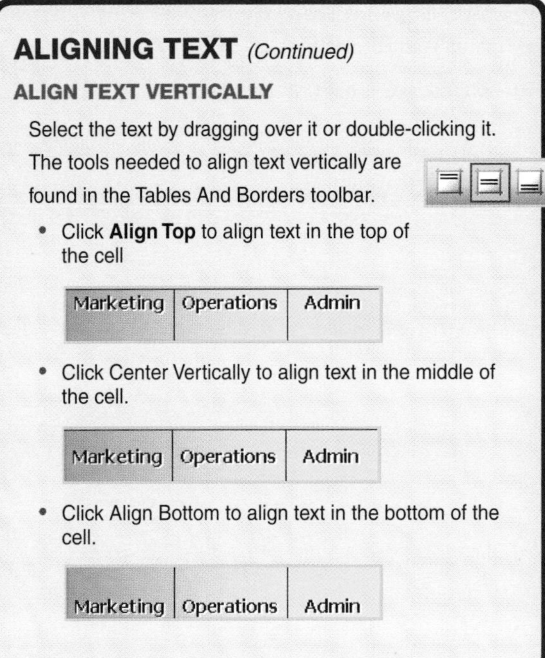

ALIGNING TEXT *(Continued)*

ALIGN TEXT VERTICALLY

Select the text by dragging over it or double-clicking it. The tools needed to align text vertically are found in the Tables And Borders toolbar.

- Click **Align Top** to align text in the top of the cell

- Click Center Vertically to align text in the middle of the cell.

- Click Align Bottom to align text in the bottom of the cell.

NOTE

To change the margins for the cells, select the cells to be changed, open **Format**, and select **Table**. In the Format Table dialog box, click the **Text Box** tab. Under Internal Margin, change the measurements as needed.

Internal margin			
Left:	0.1"	Top:	0.05"
Right:	0.1"	Bottom:	0.05"

Format Text

To format text, that is, to change fonts and font style, font size, font color, and character effects (such as **Bold**, Underline, and *Italics*), you can either use the Font dialog box, shown in Figure 5-7, or the Formatting toolbar, shown in Figure 5-8.

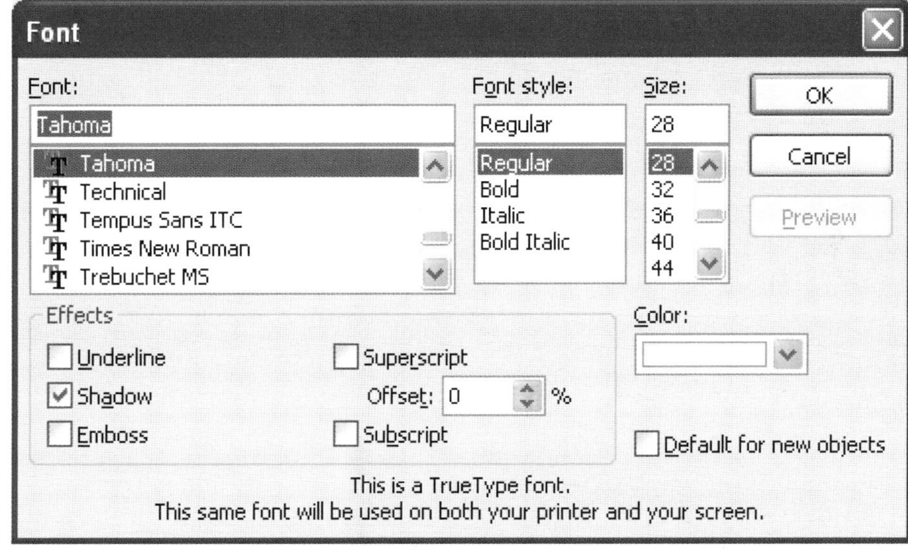

Figure 5-7: The Font dialog box allows you to select attributes for text

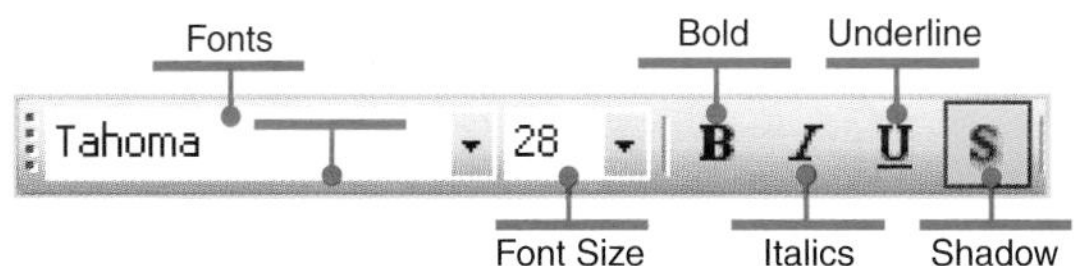

Figure 5-8: The Formatting toolbar places formatting commands a click away

QUICKSTEPS

ROTATING TEXT IN CELLS

You can rotate text 90 degrees clockwise within the cells of a table. This can help you in displaying information in a more efficient manner. Here's how:

1. Select the text which is to be rotated, such as you have here:

North	2002	2003	2004	2005
South				
West				
East				
HQRS				

2. Open **Format**, select **Table**, and click **Text Box**.
3. Place a check mark in the **Rotate Text Within Cell By 90 Degrees** check box, and click **OK**.
4. The text will be rotated, as shown here:

North	2002	2003	2004	2005
South				
West				
East				
HQRS				

TO USE THE FONT DIALOG BOX:

1. Select the text you want to format by highlighting it.
2. Open **Format** and click **Font**. The Font dialog box, shown in Figure 5-7, will open.
3. Click the format options you need.
4. Click **OK**.

TO USE THE FORMATTING TOOLBAR:

1. Select the text by highlighting it.
2. Click the button you want on the Formatting toolbar.

Delete a Table

To delete a table and its contents:

1. Select the table placeholder so that the border is a dotted line.
2. Click **DELETE**.

Use the Tables And Borders Toolbar

The Tables And Borders toolbar is an important tool in working with tables. It provides tools to manipulate the table and to format it. Table 5-1 shows the functions of the toolbar.

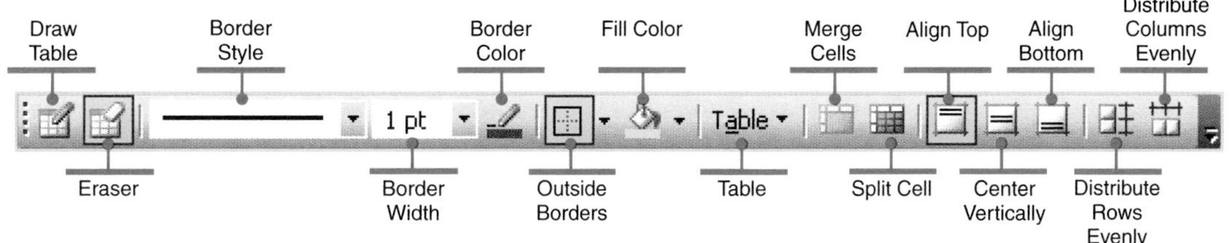

A floating Tables and Borders toolbar can be dragged on the screen for access where you need it

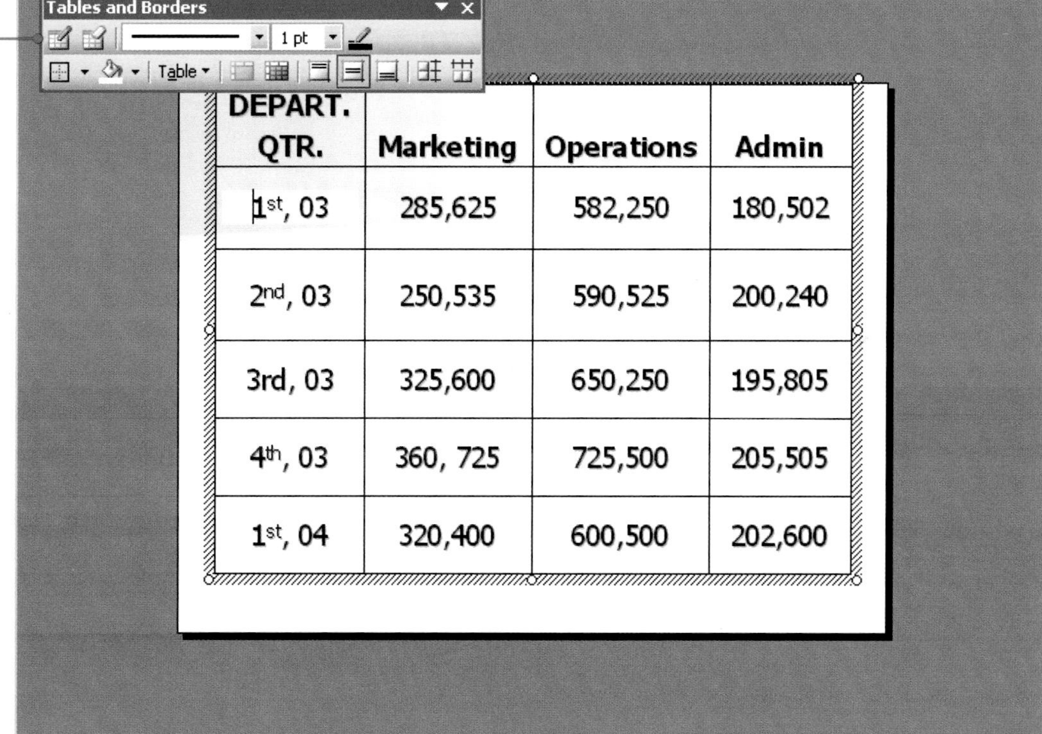

DEPART. QTR.	Marketing	Operations	Admin
1st, 03	285,625	582,250	180,502
2nd, 03	250,535	590,525	200,240
3rd, 03	325,600	650,250	195,805
4th, 03	360, 725	725,500	205,505
1st, 04	320,400	600,500	202,600

1

2

3

4

5

6

7

8

9

10

TABLE 5-1: TOOLS ON THE TABLES AND BORDERS TOOLBAR

TOOL NAME	DESCRIPTION	LOOK HERE FOR MORE INFORMATION
Draw Table	Use to draw a table with irregular columns and row sizes.	Insert a Table
Eraser	Erases lines as you click them	
Border Style	Displays a menu of border styles	Work with Borders
Border Width	Displays a menu of border sizes in points	Work with Borders
Border Color	Converts lines to a selected color when you click them	Work with Borders
Outside Borders	Use to choose which lines in the table will be displayed.	Work with Borders
Fill Color	Displays a menu of fill colors. You can fill a table or selected cells with a selected color. Through options, you can also fill with gradient colors, patterns, textures, or a picture.	Use Special Effects in the Table Background
Table	Displays a menu of options for inserting, deleting, or selecting columns or rows, plus other options.	Insert Columns and Rows, Delete Columns and Rows
Merge Cells	Merges two or more selected cells into one.	Merge or Split Cells
Split Cells	Splits a selected cell into two cells. The contents will be in one cell.	Merge or Split Cells
Align Top	Aligns the contents of selected cells on the top of the cells.	Aligning Text
Center Vertically	Aligns the contents of selected cells in the middle of the cells.	Aligning Text
Align Bottom	Aligns the contents of selected cells at the bottom of the cells.	Aligning Text
Distribute Rows Evenly	Makes rows the same height, and adjusts the contents accordingly	Change the Size of Columns and Rows
Distribute Columns Evenly	Makes columns the same width; adjusts the contents accordingly	Change the Size of Columns and Rows

SELECTING TABLE COMPONENTS

SELECT ONE OR MORE CELLS

- Click in a cell.
- Press **TAB** to select the next cell; press **SHIFT+TAB** for the previous cell.
- Drag the pointer across the cells you want to select.

DEPART. QTR.	Marketing	Operations	Admin
1st, 03	285,625	582,250	180,502
2nd, 03	250,535	590,525	200,240
3rd, 03	325,600	650,250	195,805
4th, 03	360, 725	725,500	205,505
1st, 04	320,400	600,500	202,600

SELECT THE TABLE

- Open **Edit** and click **Select All**.
- Right-click the table, and click Select **Table**.
- Click the **Table** button on the Tables And Borders toolbar. From the menu, click **Select Table**.

Table ▾

Select Table
Select Column
Select Row

SELECT A ROW

- Click a cell in the row you want to select. Click the Table button on the Tables And Borders toolbar. From the menu, click Select Row.
- Drag the pointer across the row. To select more than one row, drag the pointer up or down as well as across.

Continued...

Insert Columns and Rows

You may find that you need to add rows or columns to your table.

To insert a row:

- Click in the row above or below where the new row is to be inserted. On the Tables And Borders toolbar, click **Table**, and click **Insert Rows Above** or **Insert Rows Below**, as shown in Figure 5-9.

  –Or–

- Click in the row below where the new row is to be inserted. Right-click the table, and click Insert Rows. The row will be inserted above the selected one.

To insert a column:

- Click in a column next to where you want the new column. On the Tables And Borders toolbar, click **Table**, and click **Insert Columns To The Left** or **Insert Columns To The Right**, shown in Figure 5-9.

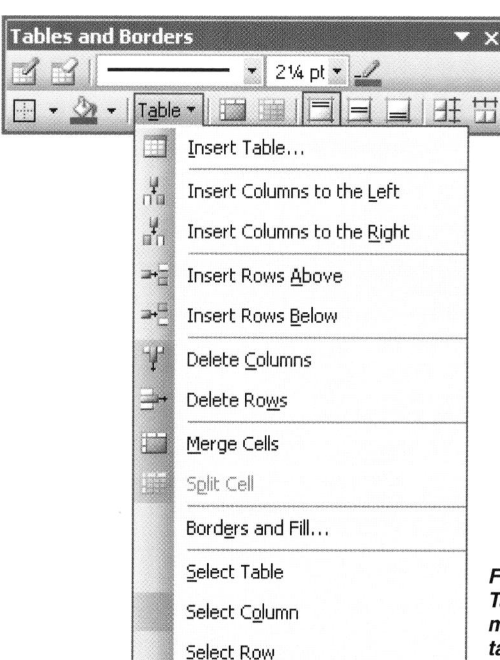

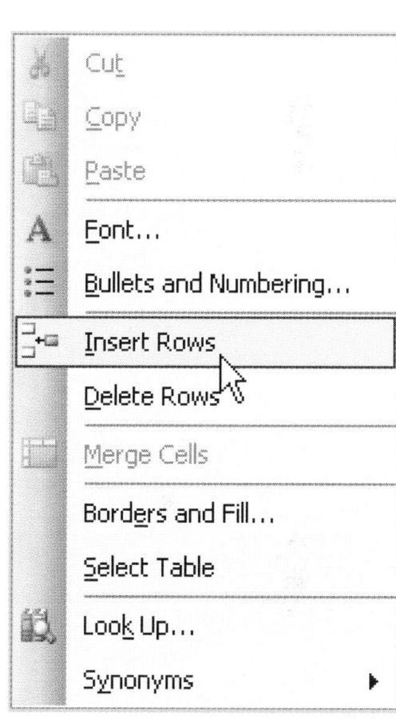

Figure 5-9: The Table button on the Tables And Borders toolbar offers many commands for working with tables

SELECTING TABLE COMPONENTS

(Continued)

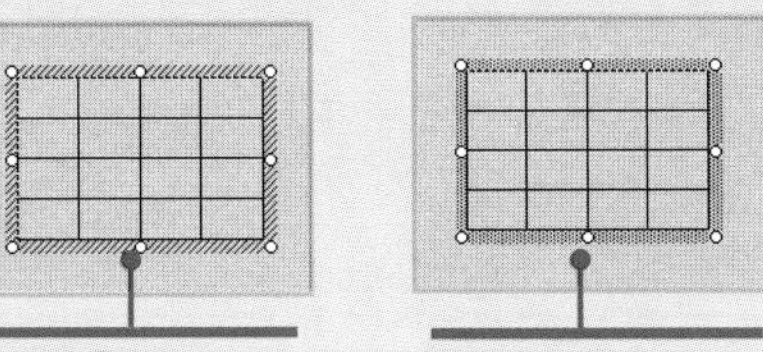

Dotted lines on placeholder tell you that the table itself is selected

Slanted lines on placeholder tell you that the contents are selected

SELECT A COLUMN

- Click a cell in the row you want to select. Click the **Table** button on the Tables And Borders toolbar. From the menu, click **Select Column**.
- Click the table to select it, and place the pointer above the column but outside the placeholder, as shown in Figure 5-10. When the pointer morphs into an arrow, click it. The column will be highlighted. To select multiple columns, drag the pointer across the top of the columns.

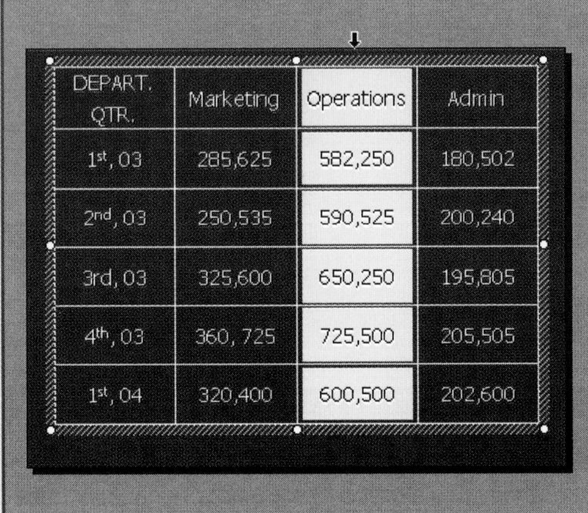

DEPART. QTR.	Marketing	Operations	Admin
1st, 03	285,625	582,250	180,502
2nd, 03	250,535	590,525	200,240
3rd, 03	325,600	650,250	195,805
4th, 03	360, 725	725,500	205,505
1st, 04	320,400	600,500	202,600

Figure 5-10: To select an entire column, click the pointer (when it becomes an arrow) above the column

–Or–

- Highlight the column to the right of where you want the new column inserted. Right-click the table, and click **Insert Columns**. The column will be inserted to the left of the selected one.

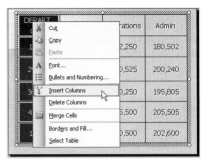

Change Size of Columns and Rows

You can change the width of columns and the height of rows using manual techniques of dragging the border of the column or row, or you can let PowerPoint do it automatically.

CHANGE COLUMN WIDTH

To adjust the size of the column, first click outside the table to deselect any cells:

- Place your pointer on the right border of a column so that it morphs into a two-headed arrow. Drag the border right or left to increase or decrease the size.

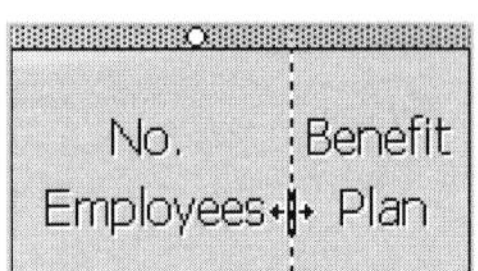

–Or–

- Click the table. Click **Distribute Columns Evenly** on the Tables and Borders toolbar. This makes the columns the same width and adjusts the content to fit.

–Or–

- Place your pointer on the right border of a column so that it morphs into a two-headed arrow. Double-click the column border for PowerPoint to adjust it.

TIP

You can open **Edit** and click **Undo** (or you can press **CTRL-Z**) to reverse the previous action. You can undo up to 20 previous actions in this way.

QUICKSTEPS

DELETING COLUMNS AND ROWS

You can easily delete rows or columns on your table.

DELETE A ROW:

- Click in the row or highlight multiple rows to be deleted by dragging over them. On the Tables And Borders toolbar, click **Table**, and click **Delete Rows**.

  –Or–

- Click the row to be deleted (or highlight multiple rows). Right-click the table, and click Delete Rows. The row (or rows) will be deleted.

DELETE A COLUMN:

- Click in the column (or highlight multiple columns) to be deleted. On the Tables And Borders toolbar, click **Table**, and click **Delete Columns**.

  –Or–

- Highlight the column (or columns) to be deleted. Right-click the table, and click **Delete Columns**. The selected column (or columns) will be deleted.

CHANGE ROW HEIGHT

To adjust the size of rows, first click outside the table to deselect any cells:

- Place your pointer on the lower border of a row so that it morphs into a two-headed arrow. Drag the border up or down to increase or decrease the size.

  –Or–

- Click the table. Click **Distribute Rows Evenly** on the Tables And Borders toolbar. This makes the rows the same height and adjusts the content to fit.

  –Or–

- Place your pointer on the lower border of a row so that it morphs into a two-headed arrow. Double-click the row border for PowerPoint to adjust it.

Work with Borders

You can vary the style, size, and color of table borders. You can also define which outside borders appear on the screen. Here's how:

CHANGE BORDER STYLE

To change the style or appearance of a border:

1. Display the Tables And Borders toolbar by clicking **Tables And Borders** on the Standard toolbar.

2. Open the **Border Style** drop-down box, and click the border you want. The pointer will morph into a pencil.
3. With the pencil icon, click the borders you want to have the new style.

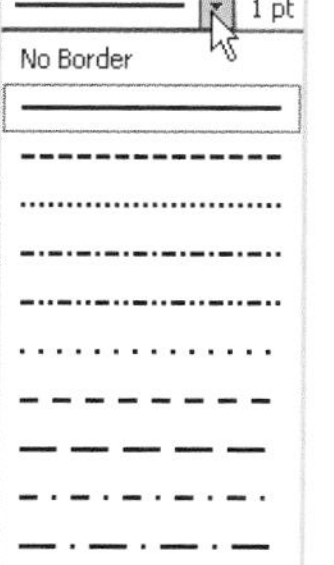

NOTE

You can also use the **Borders And Fill** option on the Table menu. Select the **Fill** tab, and select the fill color you want.

TIP

To change the fill color back to its default color, click **Automatic** on the Fill Color menu. To remove all fill colors, click **No Fill**.

CHANGE BORDER SIZE

To change the size of a border:

1. Display the Tables And Borders toolbar by clicking **Tables And Borders** on the Standard toolbar.

2. Open the **Border Width** drop-down box and click the point size you want. The pointer will morph into a pencil.
3. With the pencil, click the borders you want to have the new size.

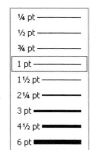

CHANGE BORDER COLOR

To change the color of a border:

1. Display the Tables And Borders toolbar by clicking **Tables And Borders** on the Standard toolbar.
2. Open the **Border Color** drop-down box, and click the border you want. The pointer will morph into a pencil.

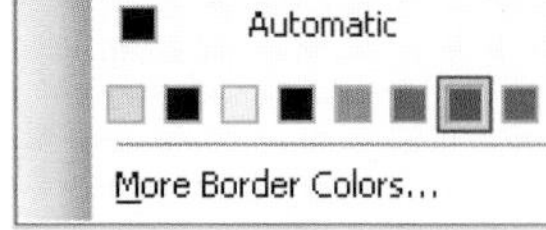

3. With the pencil pointer, click the borders that you want to have the new color.

DISPLAY OR NOT, INSIDE AND OUTSIDE BORDER LINES

To change the appearance of the borders (or cells) by controlling which inside or outside border lines appear:

1. Display the Tables And Borders toolbar by clicking **Tables And Borders** on the Standard toolbar.
2. Click the table border to select it (or select a cell to change its borders).

3. Click **Outside Borders** on the toolbar. (The button name changes to reflect the current chosen border style. It might not be Outside Borders. It might be All Borders.)
4. Click the border configuration you want. If you selected the table, the whole table will conform to the new border selection. If you selected one or more cells, only the cell's outline will change.

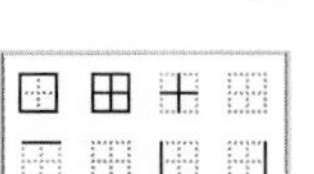

TIP

If you want to remove border lines selectively, open **Border Style** on the Tables And Borders toolbar, and click **No Borders**. With the pencil icon, click the cell borders that you want to remove.

TIP

You can also click the **Eraser** and erase the line between the cells.

CHANGE BORDERS ALL IN ONE

To change the style, size, color, and border lines with one dialog box, use the Format Table dialog box

1. Display the Tables And Borders toolbar by clicking **Tables And Borders** on the Standard toolbar.
2. Click **Table** on the toolbar, and click **Borders And Fill**. The Format Table dialog box will be displayed, as shown in Figure 5-11.
3. Click **Borders** where you will see choices to set border Style, Width (size), Color, or to determine which lines in the table to display.
4. Click the **Fill** tab, and open **Fill Color**. Click the color you want to use as a fill for the cell, cells, or the whole table, depending on what is selected.

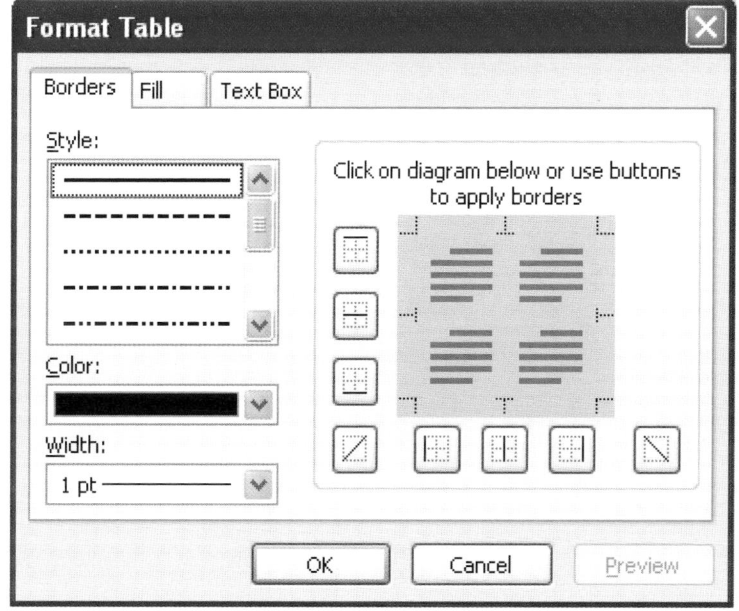

Figure 5-11: The Format Table dialog box can be used to change style, size, color, and borders, as well as to insert color fill into cells or the table as a whole

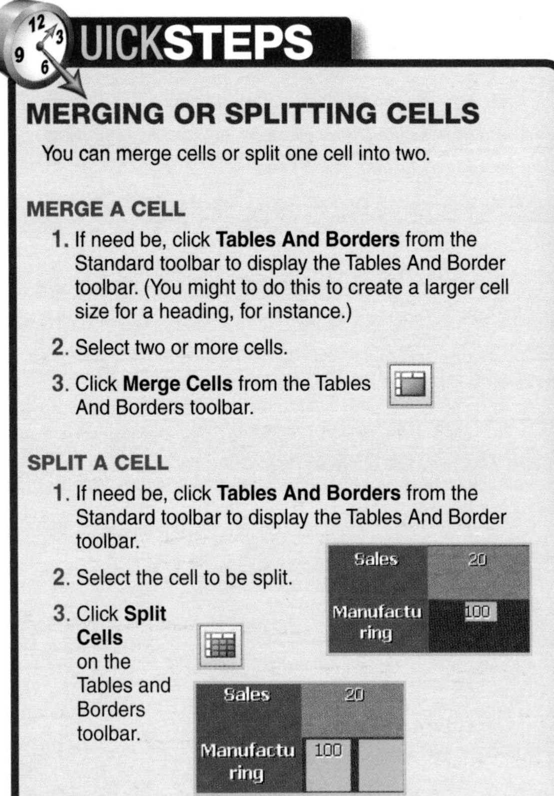

QUICKSTEPS

MERGING OR SPLITTING CELLS

You can merge cells or split one cell into two.

MERGE A CELL

1. If need be, click **Tables And Borders** from the Standard toolbar to display the Tables And Border toolbar. (You might to do this to create a larger cell size for a heading, for instance.)
2. Select two or more cells.
3. Click **Merge Cells** from the Tables And Borders toolbar.

SPLIT A CELL

1. If need be, click **Tables And Borders** from the Standard toolbar to display the Tables And Border toolbar.
2. Select the cell to be split.
3. Click **Split Cells** on the Tables and Borders toolbar.

Shade Cells, Columns, Rows, or a Table

Figure 5-12 shows an example of a table with shaded columns and rows to make it more readable. Here is how to add shading:

1. Select the row, column, or cell to be shaded. To select the whole table, click the border so that the table is contained in a dotted border.
2. On the Tables And Borders toolbar, open **Fill Color**, and click the color you want. The selected area will be filled with the color.

Dept/ Profile	No. Employees	Benefit Plan	Incr. Over Last Yr.
Marketing	10	A	15%
Operations	55	B	5%
Admin	25	A	15%
Sales	20	C	25%
Manufacturing	100	B	6%

Figure 5-12: Shaded row and columns help make a table more readable

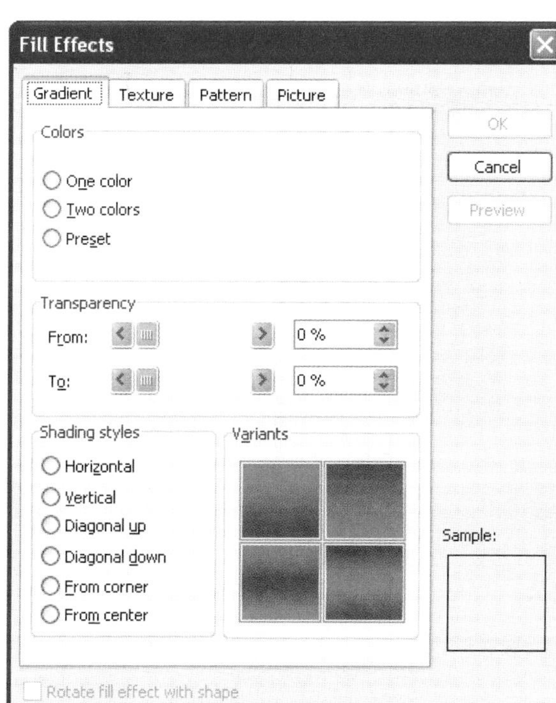

Figure 5-13: You can use the Fill Effects dialog box to fill your cells or background with gradient colors, textures, patterns, or one or more pictures

Use Special Effects in the Table Background

You can use some special effects, such as gradient colors, texture, and patterns, in the table background. (See Chapter 8 for additional information.) Here is how:

1. Select the cells you want to have the special effect, or select the whole table.
2. Bring up the Fill Effects dialog box either by clicking the **Fill Colors** button on the Tables And Borders toolbar, or by opening **Table** on the toolbar and selecting **Borders And Fill** and clicking the **Fill** tab.
3. Click **Fill Effects**. The Fill Effects dialog box, shown in Figure 5-13, will be displayed.
4. Click on the tab you want: Gradient, Texture, or Pattern:
5. When you are done, click **OK**.

Use a Picture in Your Table

You can add pictures to your table. The picture will be entered into a cell. You enlarge the picture by merging cells.

1. Select the cells to contain the picture.
2. Open the **Fill Colors** menu on the Tables And Borders toolbar. (If it is not showing, click **Tables And Borders** on the Standard toolbar.)

3. Select **Fill Effects**, and click the **Picture** tab.
4. Click **Select Picture**. The Select Picture dialog box will open.
5. Search for the picture you want. Select it, choose **Insert**, and then click **OK**. The picture will be inserted into the cells of your tables, as shown here:

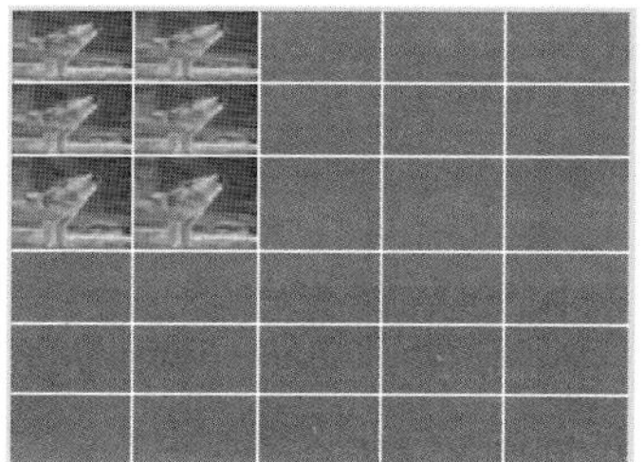

1 2 3 4 5 6 7 8 9 10

6. To combine the pictures into one larger one, select the cells containing the picture.
7. Click **Merge Cells** on the Tables And Borders toolbar. Figure 5-14 shows the effect of merging the pictures in cells. 

TIP

To add a picture to your slide without making it part of the Table, open **Insert** and click **Picture**. Complete the instructions to bring a picture onto your slide.

Figure 5-14: The pictures can be combined into a larger one by merging the cells containing the picture

Enter Formulas

To create formulas to display on slides and in tables, you use the Equation Editor. This is a separate application that interfaces closely with PowerPoint. The formulas are only for display. They do not calculate anything.

1. Open Insert and select Object.
2. In the Insert Object dialog box, click Microsoft Equation 3.0 and click OK. The Equation Editor will open, as shown in Figure 5-15.

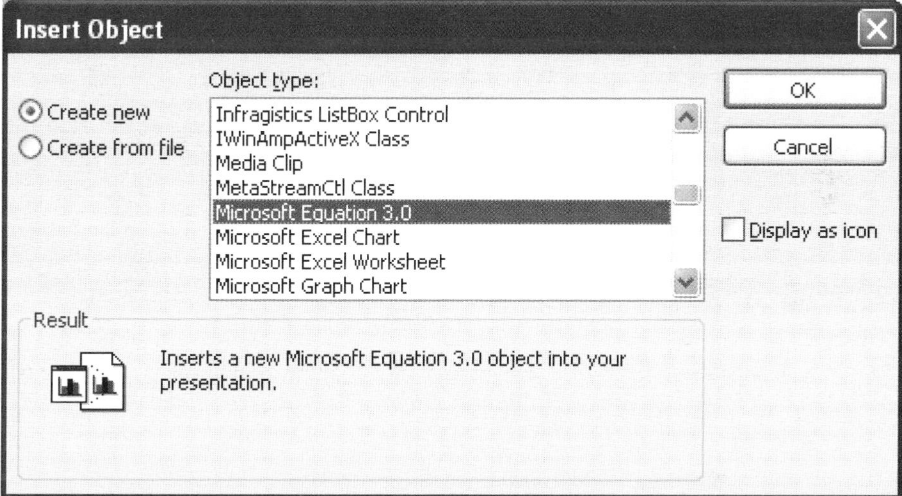

3. From the bottom row of the toolbars, click a template. From the top toolbar, click the symbols you need, and type the text you need to complete the equation or formula.
4. When you are finished with the equation, double-click outside the equation. You will be returned to PowerPoint, and the equation will be inserted on your slide. You can also return by opening **File** and clicking **Exit And Return To *file name*** where ***file name*** is the name of your presentation.

NOTE

If you do not have Equation Editor 3.0 on your toolbar, you can install it by opening **View** and choosing **Toolbars**. Select **Customize** to open the Customize dialog box. Click the **Commands** tab, and select **Insert** in Categories. Then select **Equation Editor** in Commands. Drag the editor to a toolbar, and click to install.

TIP

You can nest templates by clicking a template, and then clicking another template within the first.

TIP

To edit the equation once it is in PowerPoint, just double-click it, and the Equation Editor will open.

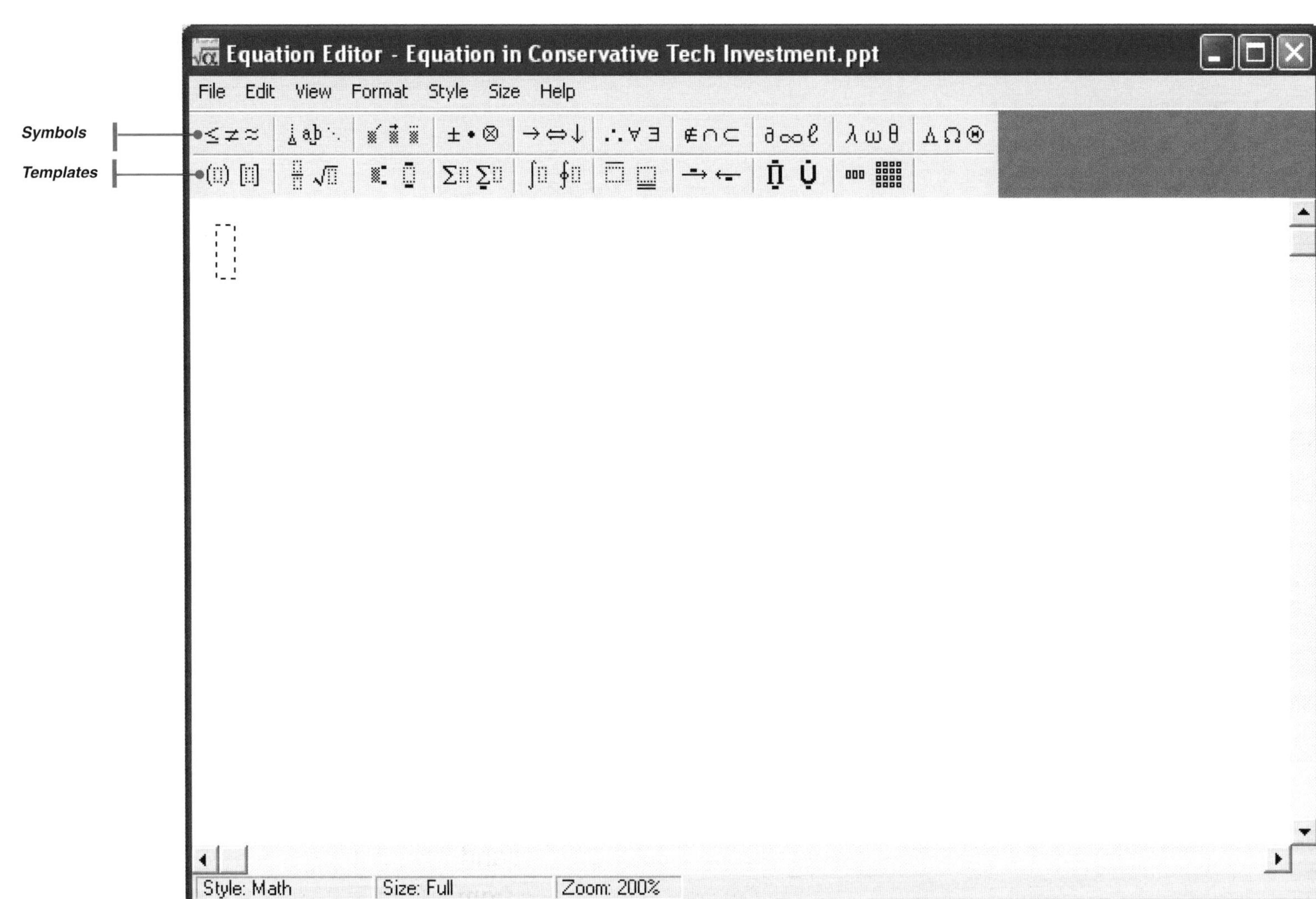

Figure 5-15: The Equation Editor is used to display equations and formulas in PowerPoint

How to...

- *Find and Insert Clip Art*
- *Change the Color of Clip Art*
- *Crop a Picture*
- *Changing Contrast and Brightness*
- *Manage Clips with Clip Organizer*
- *Deleting a Clip from the Clip Organizer*
- *Renaming a Collection*
- *Adding Keywords or Captions to Clips*
- *Search for Clip Art on the Web*
- *Working with Objects*
- *Display Grid and Guides*
- *Use Format Painter*
- *Use Graphs*
- *Working with a Chart in Microsoft Graph*
- *Working with an Excel Graph/ Chart*
- *Enter Chart Data*
- *Select the Type of Chart*
- *Insert Leader Lines on a Pie Chart*
- *Format Charts*

Chapter 6 Working with Clip Art and Graphs

This chapter looks at how you can add some pizzazz to your presentation by using clip art, graphs, and charts to make your presentations more interesting and informative. These are some of the tools you can use to add information to your presentation, balancing the narrative parts with visual effects. In this way, you reach more viewers with complete information, as it is easier to absorb pictures than numbers or words.

You will see how to work with clip art and the Clip Organizer to manage your libraries of clip art. Then this chapter will present how to insert and format graphs in your presentation. You will insert charts from scratch or import them from Microsoft Excel. You will learn how to perfect them by entering your own data, selecting your own type of chart, formatting chart components, such as titles, data series, *x*- and *y*-axes, plot area, text, and axis numbers.

Work with Clip Art

PowerPoint is installed with many "clips." Clips can be media files, such as sound, graphics, videos, and animation.

In this section, we look at "*clip art*," which is comprised of photos, drawings, and bitmaps. You will see how to find clip art on your own computer and online, then how to insert it, position it, and modify it to get the results you want. You will see how to place it using a grid and ruler lines to help you position clip art precisely. You will see how to change the image color, resize it, crop pictures to refine the image, and delete clip art when necessary. You will learn how to improve an image by increasing or decreasing contrast and brightness, and about the Clip Organizer, which enables you to find clips easily.

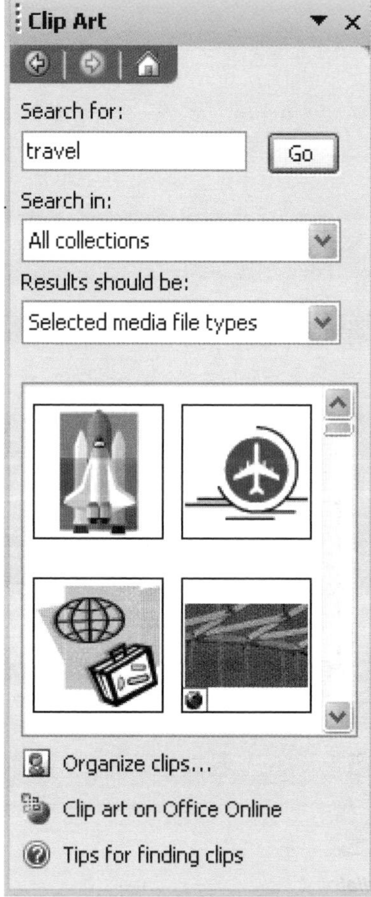

Figure 6-1a: The Clip Art task pane allows you to search for and organize clip art

Find and Insert Clip Art

With your presentation open, you find clip art using the Clip Art task pane.

1. Click the **Insert Clip Art** on the Drawing Toolbar. (You can also open **Insert**, select **Picture**, and click **Clip Art**.) The Clip Art task pane will open, as shown in Figure 6-1a. (Your beginning subject and thumbnails previewed probably will be different.)
2. Under Search For, fill in whatever subject you are looking for (for example, meetings, family, cars, or holidays.)
3. Open the **Search In** drop-down list box and click the appropriate check box to search Everywhere, My Collections, Office Collections, or Web Collections.

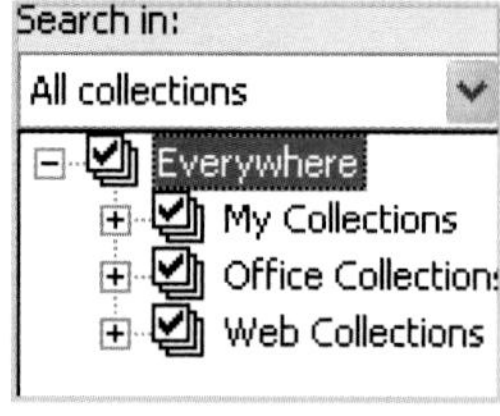

4. Under Results Should Be, open the drop-down list box and verify that the check marks are in the appropriate boxes. If a check mark is in a box, that media type will be searched for. (By default, all choices are selected.)

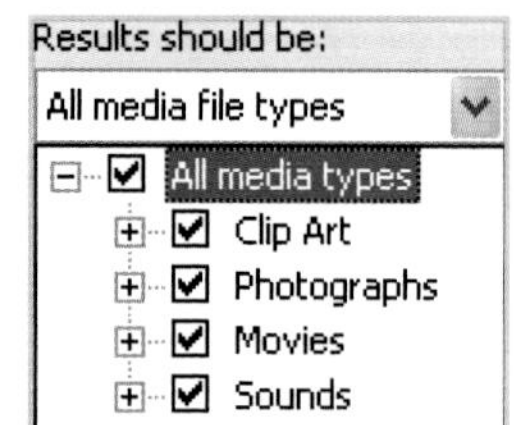

Figure 6-1b: Thumbnails of search results are displayed so that you can see them with a click

Thumbnails display the results of a search

5. The search result will be displayed as thumbnails in the preview pane, as shown in Fig. 6-1b. Scroll through the list. Click the thumbnail of the picture you want to insert. (Alternatively, you can right-click the thumbnail, and click **Insert**.)

Change the Color of Clip Art

To change the color of clip art:

1. Display the Picture toolbar (shown on next page) if it is not showing by opening **View**, selecting **Toolbars**, and clicking **Picture**.
2. To select it, click the clip art whose color you want to change.
3. Click the **Recolor Picture** button on the Picture toolbar. The Recolor Picture dialog box will be displayed, as shown in Figure 6-2.

You can change individual colors and/or the background fill. If you find that a color you want to change is only available in one or the other, you may have to experiment to see which option contains the colors you want to change.

1. Click either the **Colors** or the **Fills** option buttons to select it.

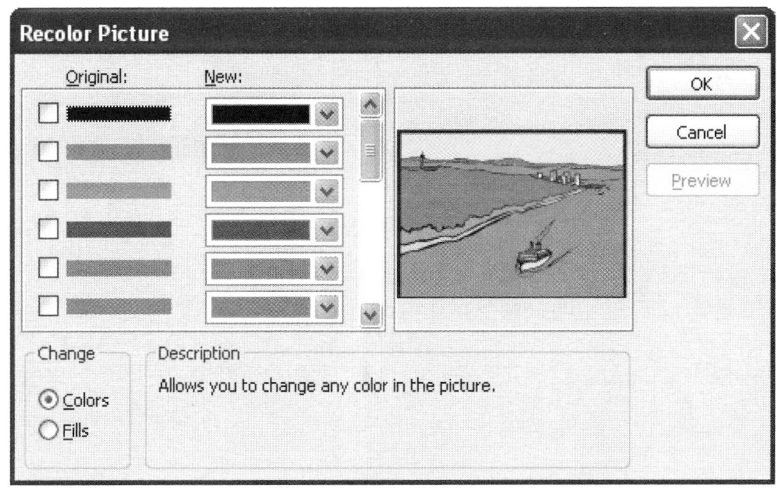

Figure 6-2: Use the Recolor Picture dialog box to change colors in clipart

NOTE

If you deselect an Original check box by removing the check mark, the color in the picture will be returned to its original color.

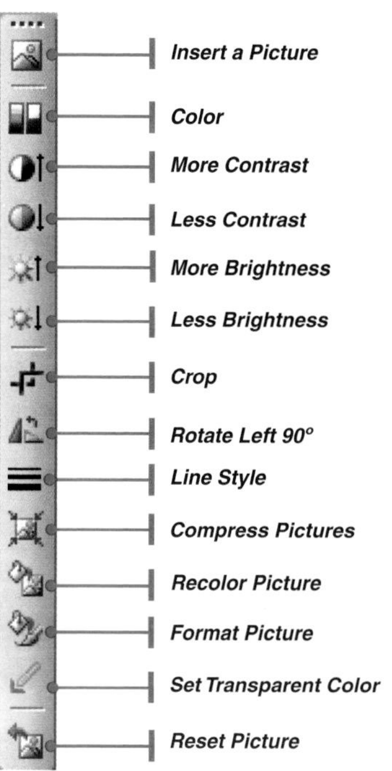

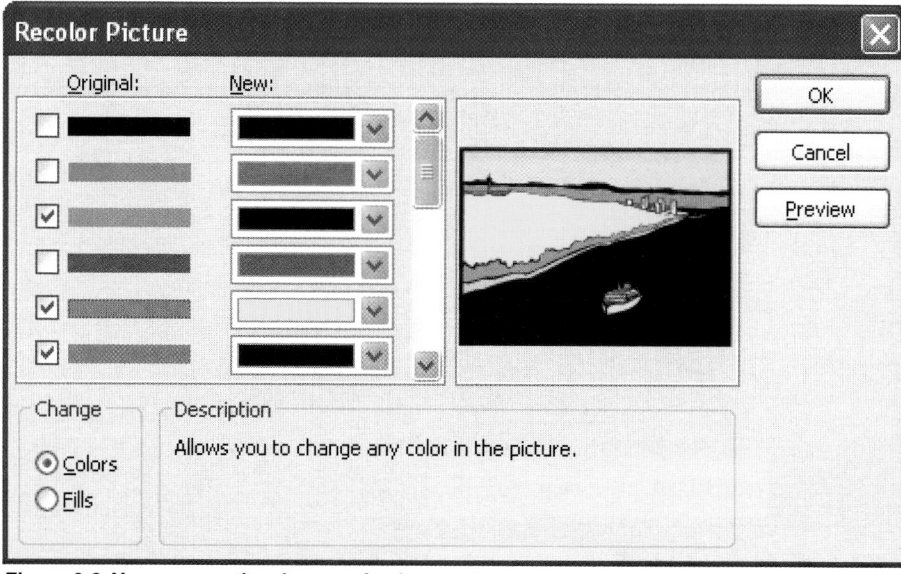

Figure 6-3: You can see the change of colors made selecting the choices in the Recolor Picture dialog box

2. Place a check mark in the **Original** color check boxes that you want to change.
3. Under New, click the down arrow to select the color you want to substitute for the corresponding original color. You will see the results in the preview pane, as shown in Figure 6-3.
4. Click **Preview** to change the clip art on the slide.
5. Click **OK** when you are ready to close the dialog box.

Crop a Picture

Cropping a picture allows you to zero in on the essential focus in a picture. You can cut the irrelevant part of the picture and retain the part you want to focus on. Here's how:

1. Click **Insert Picture** on the Picture toolbar. The Insert Picture dialog box will open.
2. Find the picture you want and click **Insert**.

NOTE

An image must be a vector image, not a bitmap image, before it can be colored with Recolor Picture. If you draw a picture, for instance, depending on the drawing product and the choices you make about the saved image, your image may be saved as a group of pixels which define the image as a set of points only (bitmap image), or as mathematical expressions which define the image by a series of lines and points (vector image). Files extensions of .tif, .jpg, .bmp, and .gif are common bitmap files. Common vector extensions are .eps, .cdr, .wmf, and .emf.

TIP

As the picture is reduced in size by cropping, you might alternate between resizing the picture and cropping it to gain a better idea of what else to crop. To do that, you need to click outside the picture to change from cropping to sizing, drag the sizing handles, click the **Crop** tool, drag the cropping handles, and so on.

3. Click the picture to select it so that you can see the sizing handles on all four edges of it. You may need to hide the task pane and Outline/Slides tabs to do this.
4. Click the **Crop** tool. Cropping marks will appear where the sizing handles are, and the pointer will morph between a four-headed arrow and a crop tool depending on where it is pointing. Use the cropping tool in this way:
   - Place the four-headed arrow on top of the cropping handles. It will turn into a cropping tool (an "elbow" or "T" shape, depending on the cropping handle it is on top of) when it is accurately placed.

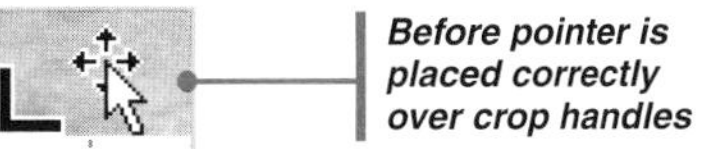

Before pointer is placed correctly over crop handles

After pointer is correctly placed

   - To cut an unwanted portion from one side of the picture, place the crop tool on a cropping handle and drag it inward (vertically or horizontally) until the picture is reduced to what you want to see.
   - If you want to cut unwanted portions equally from both sides of the picture (vertically or horizontally), press **CTRL** while dragging the crop tool. Figure 6-4 shows an example of a picture being cropped.

2. When you have finished cropping your picture, click **ESC** to clear the cropping tool mode, and save your presentation.

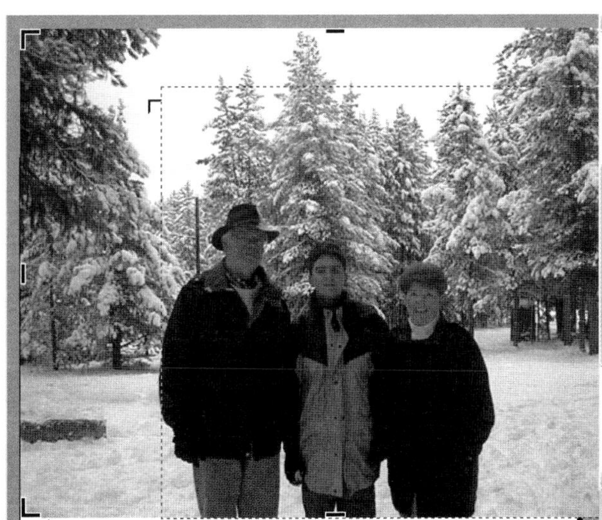

Figure 6-4: Cropping a picture lets you narrow the focus of a picture to what you want to see

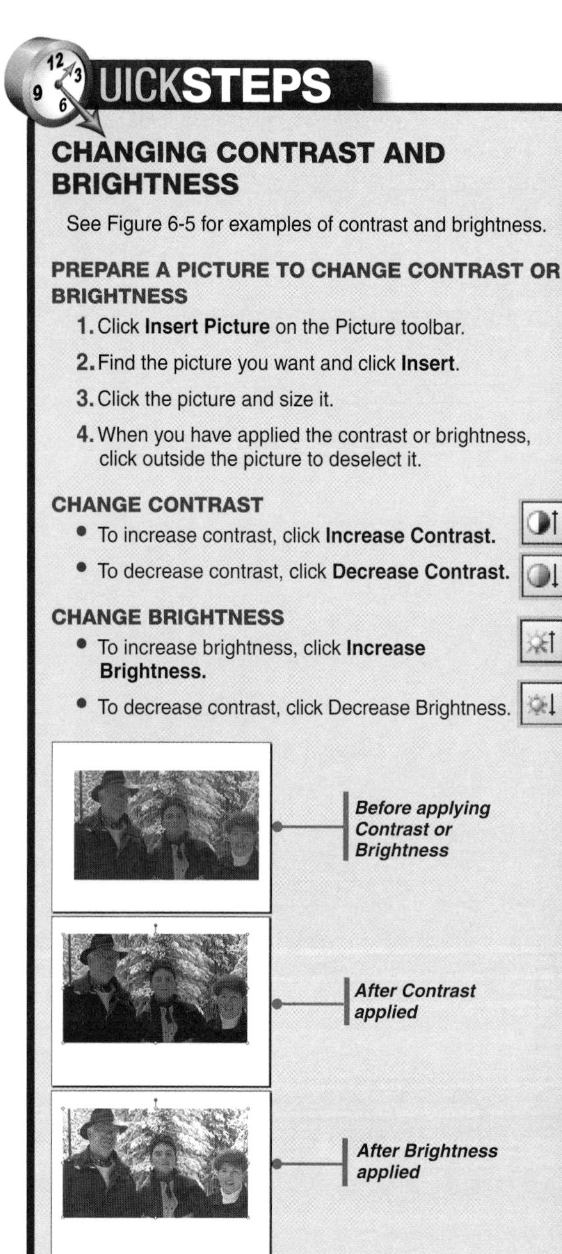

QUICKSTEPS

CHANGING CONTRAST AND BRIGHTNESS

See Figure 6-5 for examples of contrast and brightness.

PREPARE A PICTURE TO CHANGE CONTRAST OR BRIGHTNESS

1. Click **Insert Picture** on the Picture toolbar.
2. Find the picture you want and click **Insert**.
3. Click the picture and size it.
4. When you have applied the contrast or brightness, click outside the picture to deselect it.

CHANGE CONTRAST

- To increase contrast, click **Increase Contrast.**
- To decrease contrast, click **Decrease Contrast.**

CHANGE BRIGHTNESS

- To increase brightness, click **Increase Brightness.**
- To decrease contrast, click Decrease Brightness.

Before applying Contrast or Brightness

After Contrast applied

After Brightness applied

Figure 6-5: Examples of before and after increasing both contrast and brightness

Manage Clips with Clip Organizer

Clip Organizer is an application that works with other Microsoft Office applications and is used to organize your clips into a list of readily searchable collections. (Another way to see this: a list of folders currently containing your clips is organized into collections of shortcuts.) The collection names are taken from the folder name containing the clip art. The clips and folders are not physically moved to the collection list; a shortcut to the clips is created and organized within the list, which can be searched. The clips include any art, audio, movies, or animation files.

ORGANIZE CLIPS

1. Bring up Clip Organizer by opening **Insert** and selecting **Picture**. Then click **Clip Art**. The Clip Art task pane will be displayed.
2. On the bottom of the task pane, click **Organize Clips**. An Add Clips To Organizer dialog box will be displayed, such as in Figure 6-6.

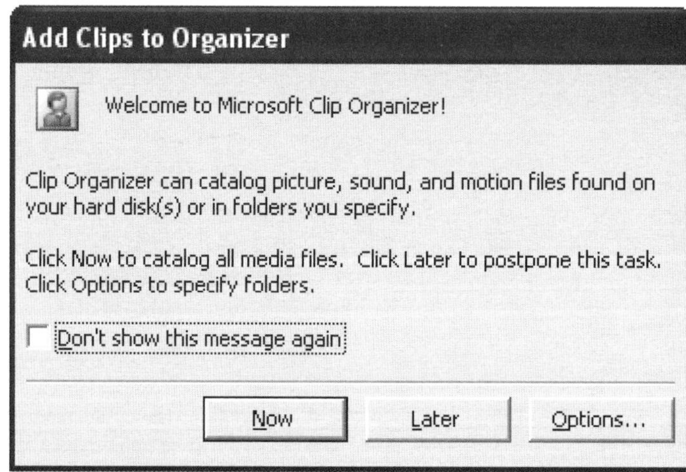

Figure 6-6: You may choose to have Clip Organizer automatically organize all your clips into a catalog or to organize only those folders you specify

3. To have Clip Organizer automatically search your entire computer for clips to catalog, click **Now**. Clip Organizer will take several seconds to do this. When it is done, it will display the completed catalog for you.

   –Or–

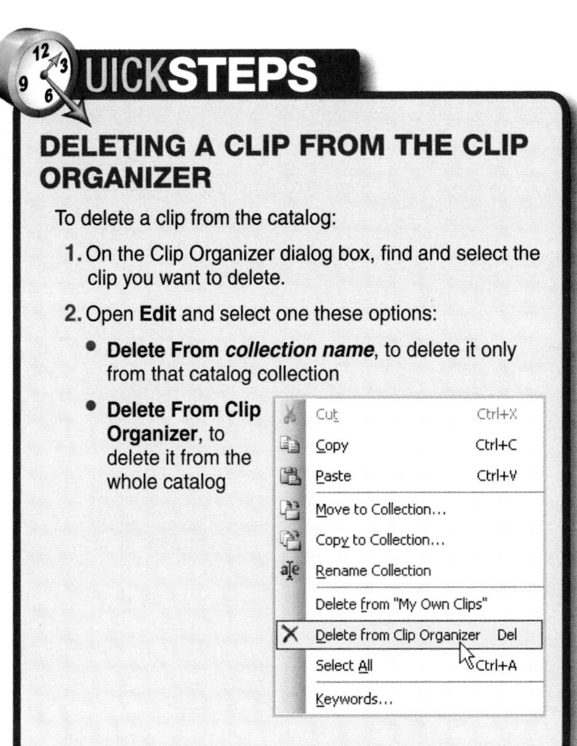

QUICKSTEPS

DELETING A CLIP FROM THE CLIP ORGANIZER

To delete a clip from the catalog:

1. On the Clip Organizer dialog box, find and select the clip you want to delete.
2. Open **Edit** and select one these options:
   - **Delete From *collection name***, to delete it only from that catalog collection
   - **Delete From Clip Organizer**, to delete it from the whole catalog

NOTE

The clip is not deleted from your computer. It is only removed from the collection reference, or its shortcut is removed from Clip Organizer. To delete the clip completely, you must delete it as you would any other file.

To specify which folders you want in the catalog, click **Options**. The Auto Import Settings dialog box, shown in Figure 6-7, will be displayed. Place check marks next to the folders which you would like to see in a catalog. Then click **Catalog**. The catalog will be created and displayed for you to see. (If you don't select any folders, all folders will be searched when you click **Catalog**.)

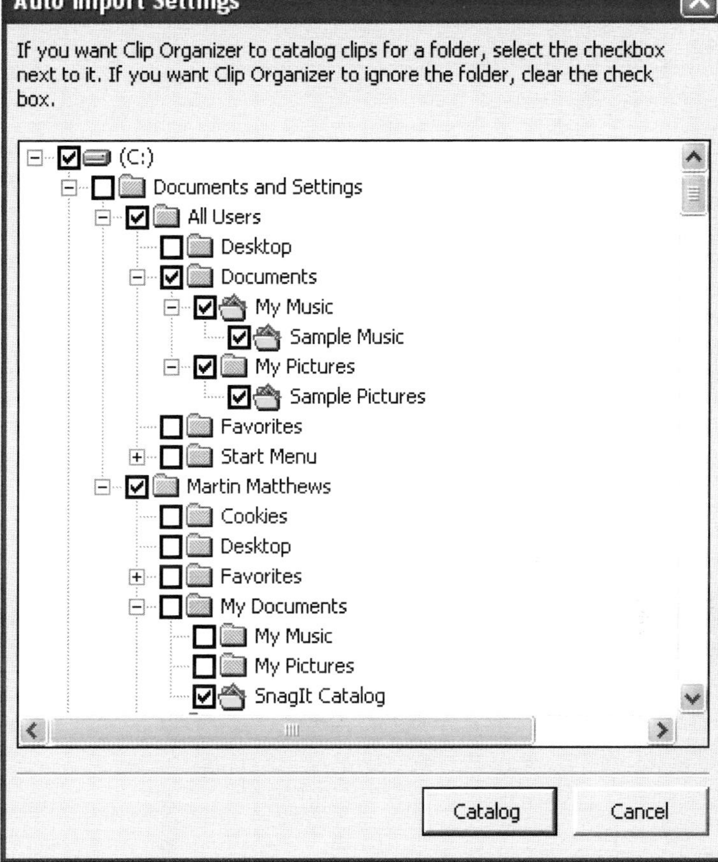

Figure 6-7: By placing check marks next to folders containing the clips you want to catalog, you can specify which folders are included

1 2 3 4 5 6 7 8 9 10

NOTE

You can bring up Clip Organizer without being in a Microsoft application. Open **Start** and point to **All Programs**, select **Microsoft Office**, select **Microsoft Office Tools**, and click **Microsoft Clip Organizer**. Although some of the functions may not work or may work differently, you can still use it to find your most used clips.

QUICKSTEPS

RENAMING A COLLECTION

To change the name of a collection of photos:

1. Under Collection List in the Clip Organizer dialog box, select the collection to be renamed.
2. Open **Edit** and click **Rename Collection**.
3. Type over the collection name in the Collection List. Press **ENTER**.

Rename Collection

TIP

On the Import to Collection dialog box, you can create the name of a new collection folder for a selected clip. Click **New** and the New Collection dialog box will open. In the **Name** text box, type the name of the new collection folder. Under **Select Where To Place The Collection**, find and click where you want the new folder to be placed. Click **OK**.

ADD MORE CLIPS TO THE CLIP ORGANIZER

To add a new clip to the catalog:

1. In the Clip Organizer dialog box, open **File**, select **Add Clips to Organizer**, and click **On My Own**. The Add Clips To Organizer dialog box will open, as seen in Figure 6-8.

Figure 6-8: Use this dialog box to find a clip and add it to a collection in the catalog

2. Open **Look In** to find the clip you want to add to the catalog. Click the clip to select it.
3. Click **Add To**. The Import To Collection dialog box will be displayed. Find the destination collection and select it. Click **OK**. (Note that you can click **New** to add a new collection to the catalog.)
4. Click **Add** to complete the cataloging of the clip.

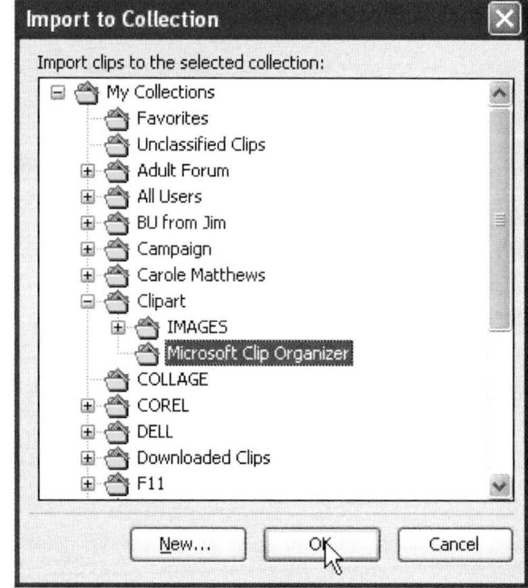

QUICKSTEPS

ADDING KEYWORDS OR CAPTIONS TO CLIPS

To add a keyword or a caption to the clips.

1. In the Clip Organizer find and select the clip you want to add keywords to.
2. Open **Edit** and click **Keywords.** In the Keywords dialog box the clip is displayed in the Preview pane; an example is seen in Figure 6-9. These options are:

ADD KEYWORDS

1. Under Keyword, type the keyword you want to associate with the clip. It will be added to the list of keywords that are already in the catalog.
2. Click **Add** to add the keyword to the list of keywords for the clip.
3. Click **Apply** when you are finished.
4. Click **OK** when you want to close the Keyword dialog box.

DELETE KEYWORDS

1. To delete a keyword, select it under Keyword, and click **Delete**.
2. Click **Apply** to make the change final. Click **OK** to close the dialog box.

MODIFY A KEYWORD

1. Select the keyword to be modified.
2. Under Keyword, type the keyword as you would like it to be.
3. Click **Modify**. Click **OK** to close the dialog box.

ADD A CAPTION TO A CLIP

1. Under Caption, type the caption you want to assign to the clip.
2. Click **Apply** to make the change. Click **OK** to close the dialog box.

REVIEW OTHER CLIPS FOR KEYWORDS OR CAPTIONS

1. Press **Previous** to view the previous clip.
2. Press **Next** to view the next one.

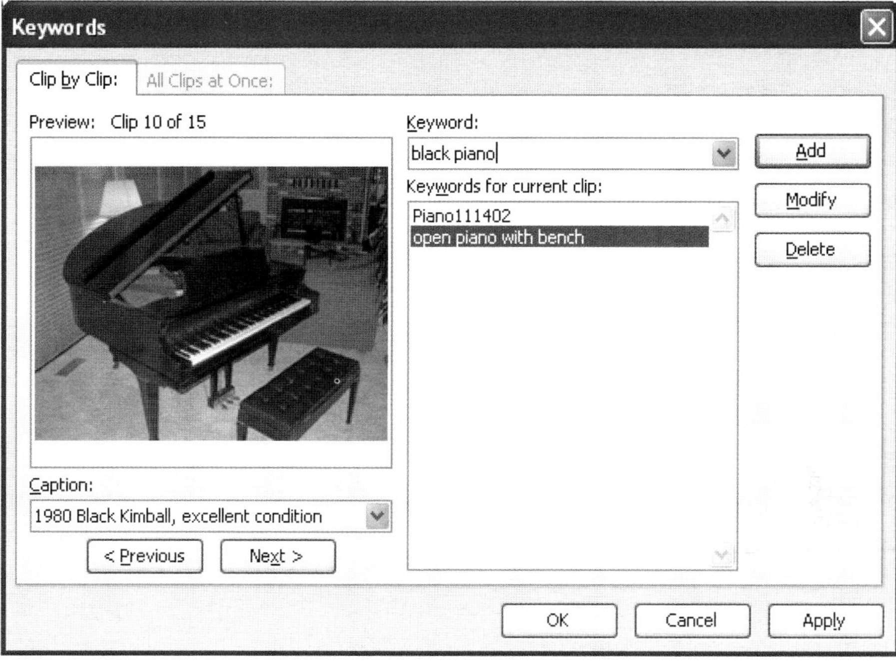

Figure 6-9: Entering keywords and captions for your clips enables you to track and find them more easily

Search for Clip Art on the Web

To search the Internet for clip art, display the Clip Art task pane, then:

1. Click **Clip Art On Office Online** to search for clip art online. Internet Explorer will open the Microsoft Online Clip Art And Media web site. Continue searching for the art you want.
2. Use Search to display categories of clip art.
3. When you find a clip that you want to keep, right-click it or open the menu on the side and click **Copy**, then right-click the slide where you want the clip and click **Paste**.

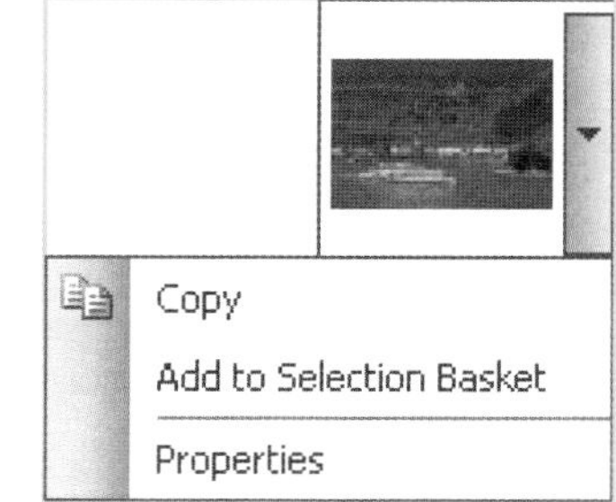

QUICKSTEPS

WORKING WITH OBJECTS

An object is something added to a slide that can be selected, such as clip art, photos, a graph or chart, a table, a drawing, or text.

SELECT OBJECTS

- Click an object with the pointer. You will know it is selected when the sizing handles and rotating handle are visible.

–Or–

- Press **TAB**. If several objects are on the screen, tab to the one you want.

MOVE OBJECTS

1. Select the object by clicking it.
2. Place the pointer on the selected object (but not on the sizing handles). The pointer will morph into a four-headed arrow.
3. Drag the object to its new location.

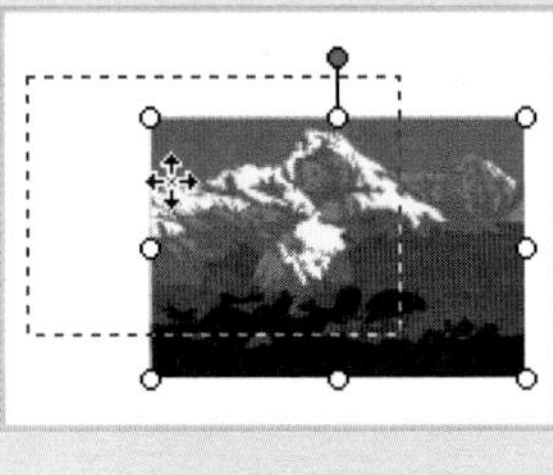

Continued...

Display Grid and Guides

Grids and guides can help you align objects very precisely. Figure 6-10 shows an example of a slide with grid and guides showing.

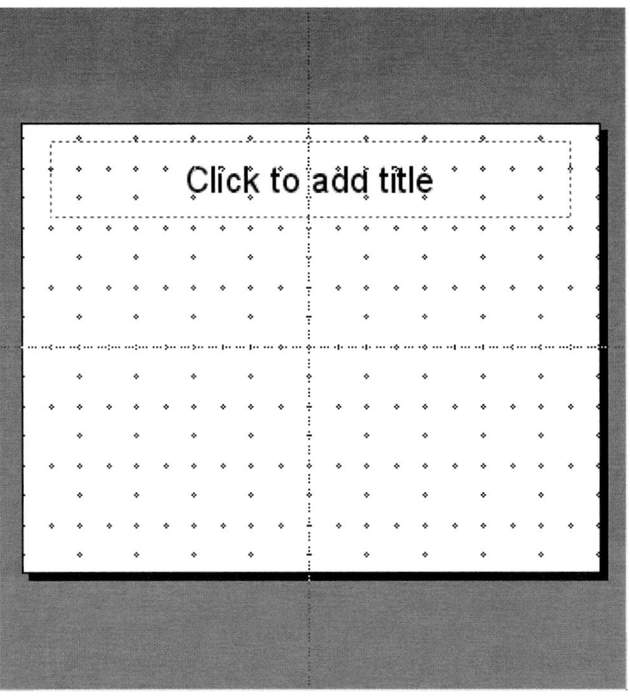

Figure 6-10: Grid and guides divide the slide so that you can position objects and text boxes precisely

1. Click the slide to select it.

WORKING WITH OBJECTS

(Continued)

RESIZE OBJECTS

1. Select the object by clicking it.
2. Place the pointer on any of the sizing handles so that the pointer arrow morphs into a two-headed arrow.

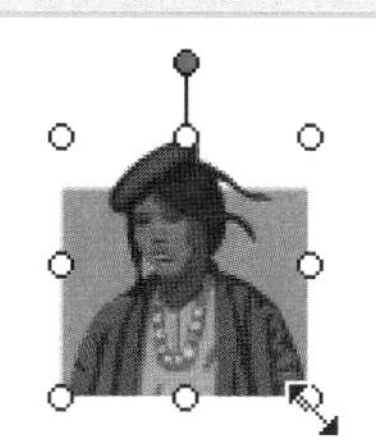

3. Click and hold the pointer so that it morphs into a cross.
4. Drag the border of the object inward or outward to the size you want.

DELETE OBJECTS

Select the object by clicking it and then press **DELETE**.

TIP

You can disable Snap To for one specific action by pressing **ALT** while you drag an object.

2. Open **View** and click **Grid And Guides**. The Grid and Guides dialog box will open, as shown here.

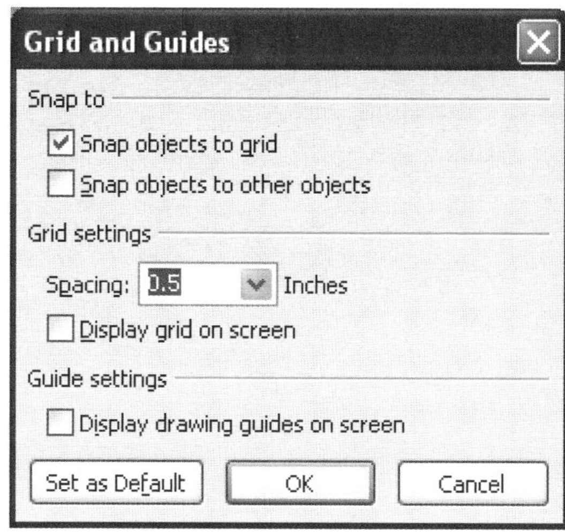

3. Select one or more of the following options by placing a check mark in the check box::
   - **Snap Objects To Grid**, to have objects pulled to a gridline
   - **Snap Objects To Other Objects**, to have objects pulled to other adjacent objects
   - **Spacing** drop-down list box, to select a setting specifying exact grid spacing
   - **Display Grid On Screen**, to display the grid on the screen
   - **Display Drawing Guides On Screen**, to display the Guide Settings on screen
   - **Set As Default**, to make your current Grid and Guides settings the default settings
4. Click **OK** to close the Grid And Guides dialog box.

NOTE

An object, as mentioned in the QuickSteps, is clip art, photos, a graph or chart, a table, a drawing, or text, and so on. Objects that we get from the Insert Object dialog box are specific types of objects, OLE (Objects Linked or Embedded) objects. This type of object, such as a spreadsheet, is either linked or embedded from another application, such as Excel, and works in a slightly different way, as you'll see later in this chapter.

TIP

If you have imported clip art, you may need to convert it to a Microsoft Office drawing object before it can be separated into the individual drawing shapes. To do this click the clip art, open **Draw** on the Drawing toolbar, and click **Ungroup**. Then you can click on the specific shape that you want to apply the color to.

Use Format Painter

Use the Format Painter to copy attributes from one object to another. All attributes will be copied, such as color, border formatting, and text formatting. If the object is not ungrouped (see Chapter 8 for a discussion on Grouping/ Ungrouping), the entire image will receive the copied attributes. In addition, if the object is a photo, the formatting doesn't take. Here's how it works:

1. Select the object, whether it is a picture, clip art, AutoShape, or Word Art (see Chapter 8), containing the attributes to be copied.
2. Click **Format Painter** on the Standard toolbar. 
3. Click the place on the receiving object where you want the formatting to be copied.

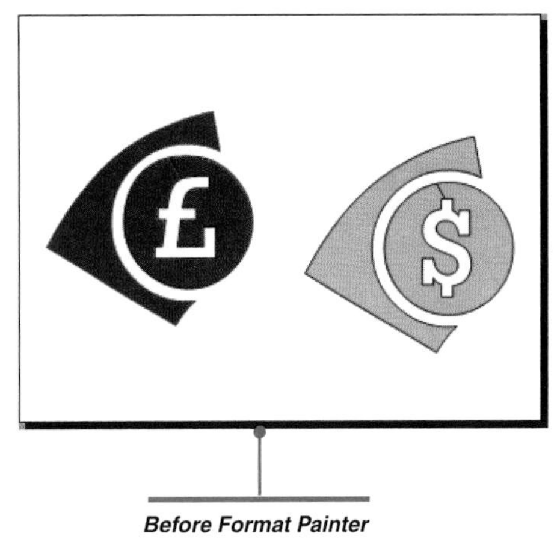

Before Format Painter

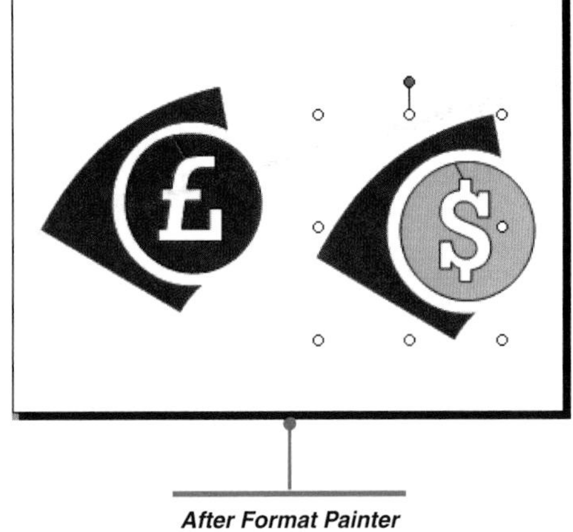

After Format Painter

NOTE

Here is some chart terminology: ***x*-axis** is the horizontal axis that normally contains the categories or types of data in a chart; ***y*-axis** is the vertical axis that normally contains the value or quantities of a chart; ***z*-axis** is the depth axis that is present in a -three-dimensional chart

Work with Graphs/Charts

You can create a chart or graph from scratch within PowerPoint or import one from Excel. PowerPoint uses Microsoft Graph to create charts. (Charts and graphs refer to the same component.) When you work with Microsoft Graph, a separate window opens with the toolbars and menus of that application. If the data or chart comes from Excel, that application is opened and its menus and toolbars are available, integrated with PowerPoint's, to modify its own component.

Use Graphs

When you first insert a chart, PowerPoint inserts a sample chart with a datasheet. You replace the data in the datasheet with your own data. You can also replace the graph with one of a different type, i.e., pie or radial for a bar chart. You'll have plenty of room. A chart can contain up to 255 *data series*. A data series is a group of related data points that are plotted on a chart. Each data series can have up to 4,000 data points.

INSERT A GRAPH FROM SCRATCH

To insert a graph from scratch:

1. Display the slide that is to contain the chart or graph. Find a layout (See Chapter 4) that contains the layout format and enough space for the chart you want.
2. If the layout contains a chart, click the **Insert Chart** icon. Otherwise, click **Insert Chart** on the Standard toolbar. (You can also open **Insert** and select **Insert Chart**.) The Slides pane will contain a chart with its associated datasheet, as shown in Figure 6-11.

Figure 6-11: When you insert a chart within PowerPoint, a sample chart and its datasheet are displayed for you to modify according to your own needs

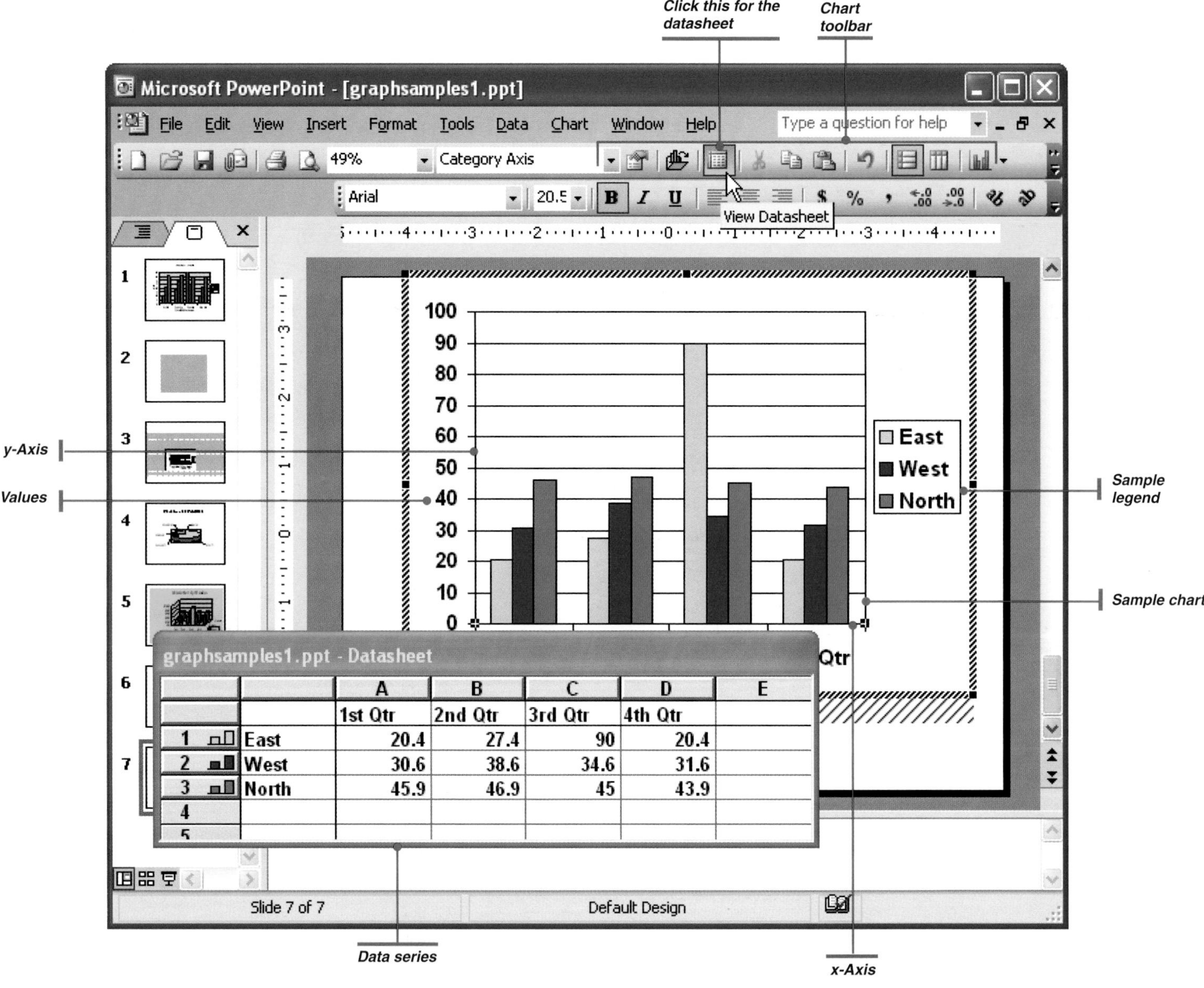

QUICKSTEPS

WORKING WITH A CHART IN MICROSOFT GRAPH

BRING UP THE MICROSOFT GRAPH WINDOW

From PowerPoint, double-click the Microsoft Graph chart to display its window with associated menus and toolbars. To return to PowerPoint, click outside the Microsoft Graph window.

DISPLAY THE EDITING TOOLBARS

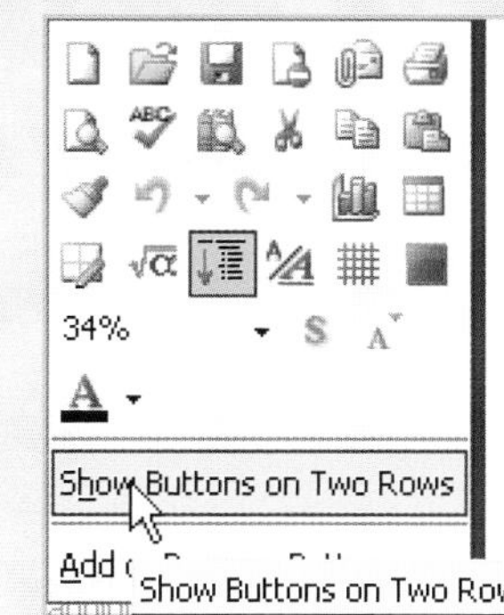

- From the Microsoft Graph window, open **View**, select **Toolbars**, and click **Standard** and **Formatting** if they are not currently showing.
- To show all options on a toolbar, click **Toolbar Options** on the end of a toolbar, and click **Show Buttons On Two Rows**.

SELECT CHART ELEMENT TO BE CHANGED

To select the chart element:

- Click the element itself.

  –Or–

- Click the button on the Standard toolbar to choose the element to be selected.

  –Or–

- Open the **Chart Objects** drop-down list on the Standard toolbar and select an object. (The name on the drop-down list will be the last object selected, such as Wall, shown here. Your list box may have another name, or may be blank.)

Category Axis

3. Modify the chart and datasheet as needed. (See the QuickSteps, "Working with a Chart in Microsoft Graph.")
4. Click outside the chart and datasheet objects to return to PowerPoint's window.

USE A GRAPH FROM EXCEL

To use a chart from Excel:

1. Display the slide with a *placeholder* (part of the layout selected for the slide) where you want the Excel chart and click it.
2. Open **Insert** and click **Object**. The Insert Object dialog box will open, as seen here. You can create a new chart within Excel at this point, or import an existing one:

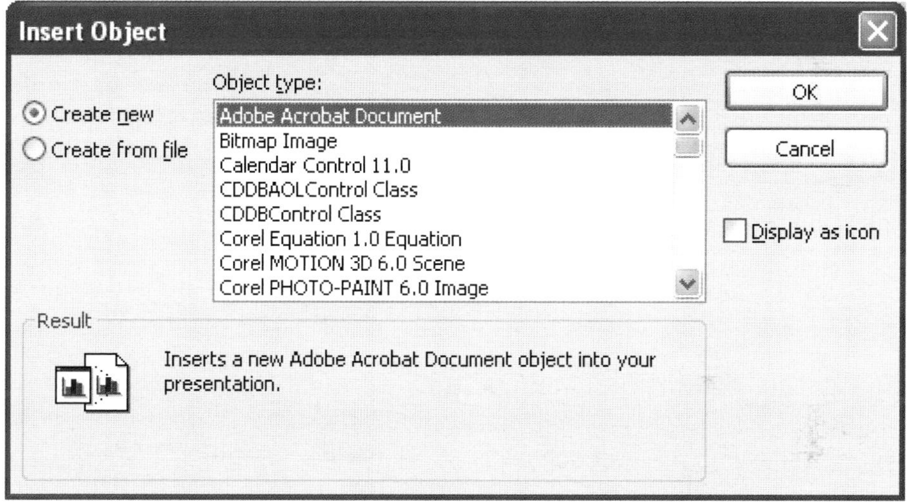

CREATE A NEW CHART WITHIN EXCEL

1. Select **Create New**, choose **Microsoft Excel Chart** in the Object Type list box, and click **OK**. A sample chart and datasheet, and a Chart toolbar will be displayed.
2. Click **Sheet1** to open the data worksheet. To increase the size of the datasheet, open **View** and click **Zoom**. Set the Zoom to the percentage you want to be able to see while modifying the data. Click **OK**. When you have entered the data, you may want to reset the zoom to **Fit**, which will allow you to see the original chart in one window.

CAUTION

When you insert a file linked to an Excel document, you must make all modifications to the source Excel document. If the PowerPoint chart is open at the same time, the linked chart will be updated at the same time. However, if you only make changes to the chart in PowerPoint, those changes will be only temporary and will be lost when you close the program.

3. Modify the chart and datasheet as needed. (If necessary, use Excel Help.)
4. To exit the Excel chart window, click outside the chart placeholder. To see the Excel chart window again, double-click the chart or datasheet.

IMPORT A CHART FROM EXCEL

Here you choose whether to import a linked file, which will remain linked to its source file and be capable of being updated when the source is updated, or to import an embedded file, which will become part of the PowerPoint presentation, now still connected to the creating program (Excel), but not to the source file.

1. Select **Create From File**. In the File box, type the file name of the chart you want, or use **Browse** to search for it.
2. If you want a linked file, click the **Link** check box. If the file contains linked information, and you have chosen not to select Link, you will see a Microsoft Excel message again asking if you want to update the linked information. Click **No** to disconnect the link.
3. Click **OK**. The chart will be displayed.
4. Double-click the graph to get Excel. An example is seen in Figure 6-12.
5. Modify the chart and datasheet as needed. (See Excel Help, if necessary.)
6. To exit the Excel chart window, click the background.

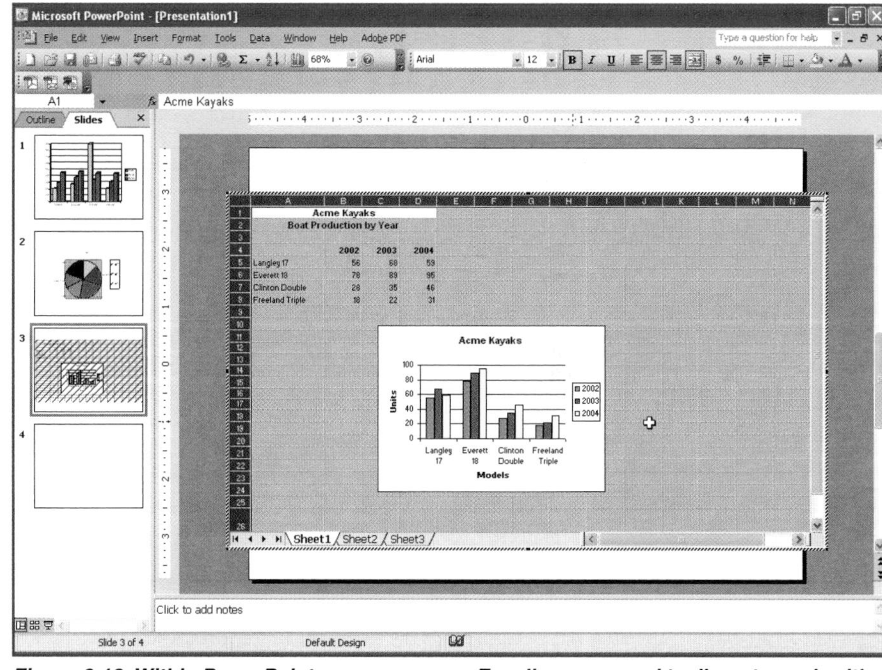

***Figure 6-12:** Within PowerPoint you can access Excel's menus and toolbars to work with an imported chart from Excel*

QUICKSTEPS

WORKING WITH AN EXCEL GRAPH/CHART

BRING UP THE EXCEL WINDOW

From PowerPoint, double-click the Excel created chart to display the Excel window with its associated menus and toolbars. To return to PowerPoint, click outside the Excel window.

DISPLAY THE CHART TOOLBAR

From the Excel window, open **View**, select **Toolbars**, and click **Chart**.

SELECT THE CHART ELEMENT TO BE CHANGED

To select the chart element either:

- Click the element itself.

  –Or–

- Click the Chart toolbar **Chart Objects** drop-down list box and choose the element to be selected.

Enter Chart Data

You will need to replace the sample data that comes with Microsoft Graph with your own data. Be sure to replace all the data and delete the contents of any leftover cells; otherwise, any remaining data will still be used to generate the chart.

1. If you are not in the Microsoft Graph window, double-click the chart to bring it up. Figure 6-12 shows the sample datasheet automatically inserted.

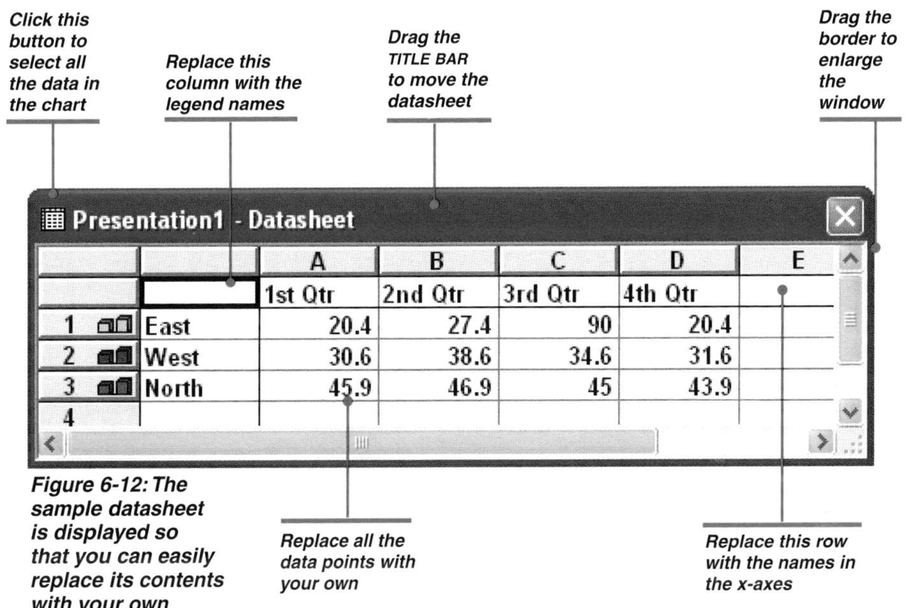

Figure 6-12: The sample datasheet is displayed so that you can easily replace its contents with your own

> **TIP**
>
> The intersection between a horizontal row and a vertical column is a cell. You can identify it by the column and row letter/number designation for all charts, such as A1, or by the column and row labels for a particular chart, for example, 1st Qtr East.

2. To clear the current contents, click the **Select All** button on the top left corner of the datasheet, then press **DELETE**.

		A	B	C	D	E
		1st Qtr	2nd Qtr	3rd Qtr	4th Qtr	
1	East	20.4	27.4	90	20.4	
2	West	30.6	38.6	34.6	31.6	
3	North	45.9	46.9	45	43.9	
4						

3. Enter the titles of your *x*-axes on the top row by clicking in a cell and typing. Enter your legend titles on the left-most column. As you make your changes, you will see the chart instantly change.
4. Enter the data series points; that is, the series of data pertaining to one row or column on the datasheet.

Select the Type of Chart

Microsoft Graph automatically creates a bar chart. You can change this to many other types of charts, depending on your data and how you want it displayed:

1. To display the menu of chart types, click the **Chart Type** down arrow 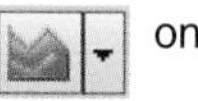 on the Standard toolbar. A menu of options will be displayed.

2. Click the chart type from the menu. You will see the chart immediately presented as shown in Figure 6-13.

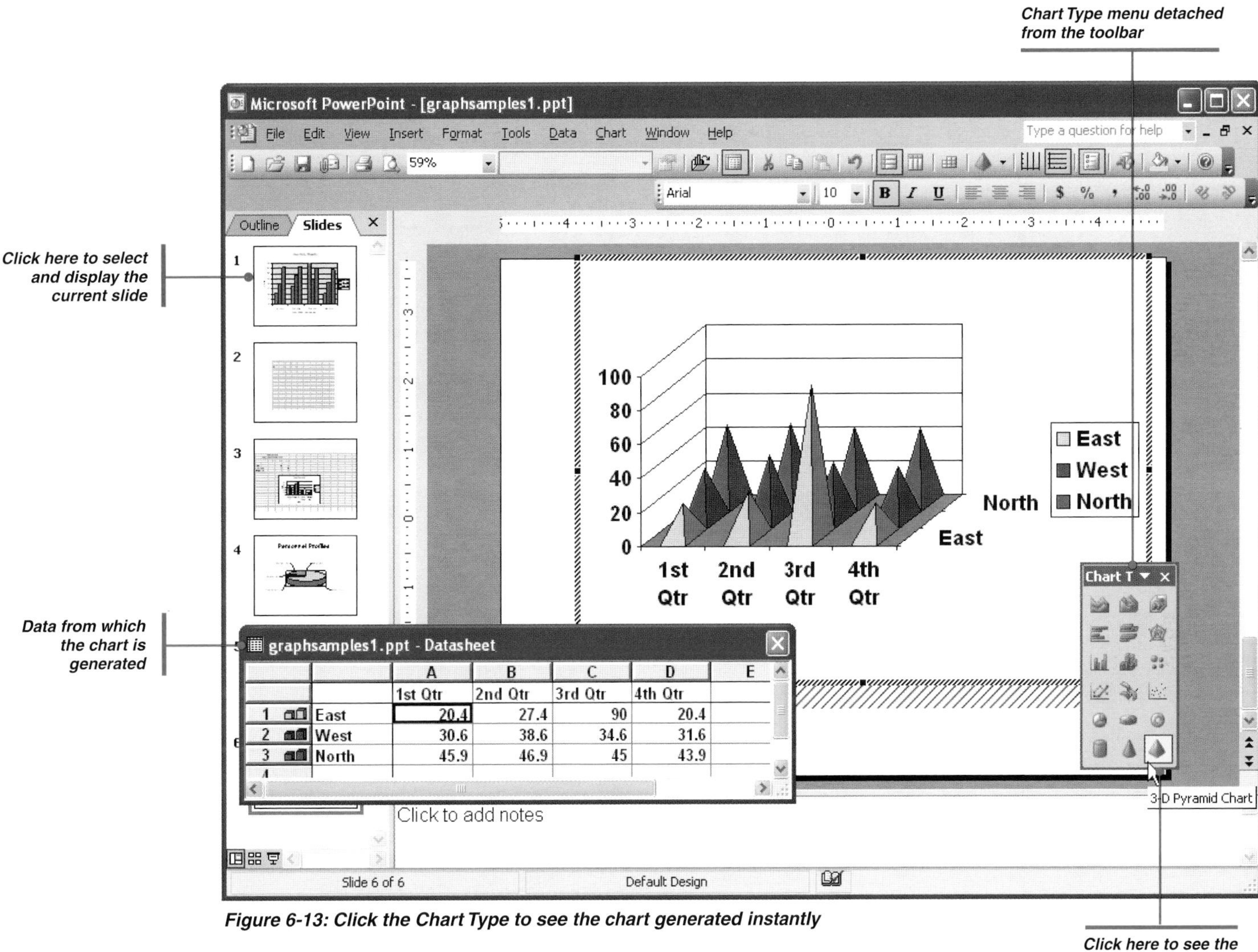

Figure 6-13: Click the Chart Type to see the chart generated instantly

> **NOTE**
>
> You can click the **Custom Types** tab to see a selection of built-in "designer" charts. These are specialty charts that may be used to add some excitement to your presentation. If you have designed your own chart type, you can view and select it here as well.

–Or–

Display the options for chart types by opening **Chart** and selecting **Chart Type**. The Chart Type dialog box will be display, as shown in Figure 6-14.

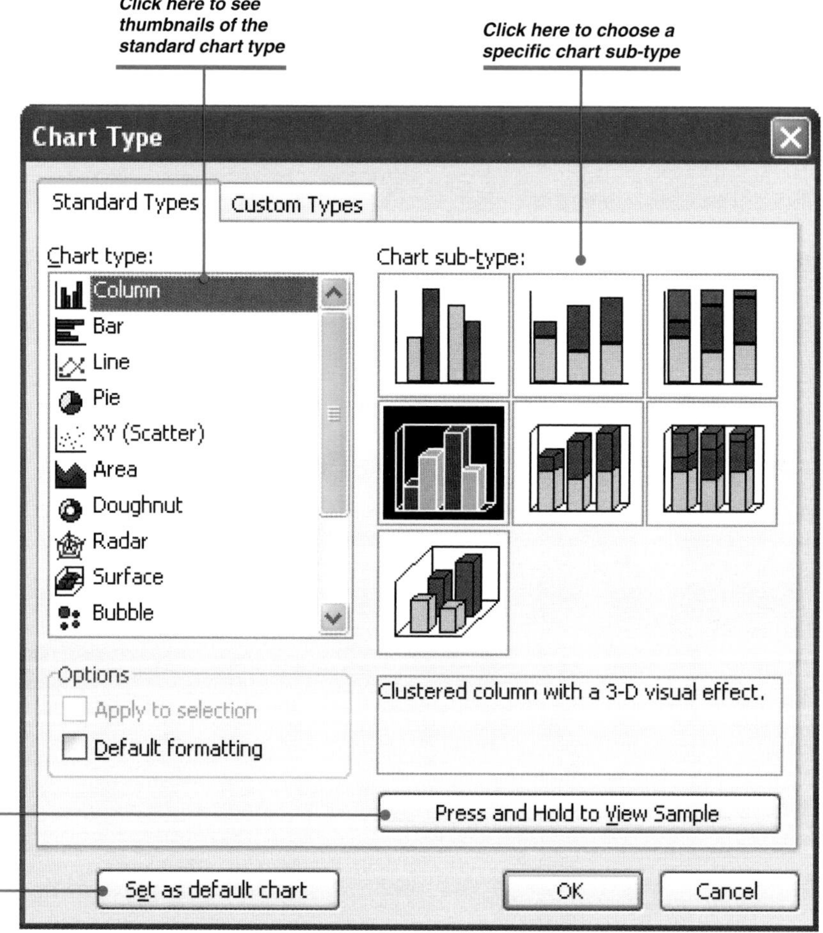

Click this to see the chart with the current datasheet

Click here to Set As Default Chart

Figure 6-14: See the types of charts available by clicking a Chart Type and viewing samples in the thumbnail preview

CAUTION

If the data labels are placed too close to the chart, the leader lines will not appear. Move your data labels away from the chart, allowing enough space for leader lines to make a difference.

NOTE

If leader lines do not appear, drag the data labels away from the chart. They may be too close for the leader lines to be formed.

3. Click **Standard Type** to see the sub-types available for each type. For example, by clicking **Column** you will see seven sub-types of column charts that may be created.
4. To see what the chart would look like with your data, click **Press And Hold To View Sample**.
5. When you have selected your chart type, click **OK**.

Insert Leader Lines on a Pie Chart

Leader lines connect the chart to data labels, which identify the data being viewed. (See the example illustration below.) Inserting leader lines is a two-step process. First, you move the data labels to where you want them on the chart; then you create the leader lines.

1. Select the pie chart and, if you already have them, drag the data labels to where you want them. If you don't have data labels on your chart, you'll create them in Step 3.
2. Open **Chart** and select **Chart Options**. Click **Data Labels**.
3. If you already have labels, skip this step. Otherwise, select the type of labels you want, and select a separator if you have more than one label per slice of pie.
4. Place a check mark in the **Show Leader Lines** check box. ☑ Show leader lines
5. Click **OK**. The chart will be displayed with leader lines, as shown here.

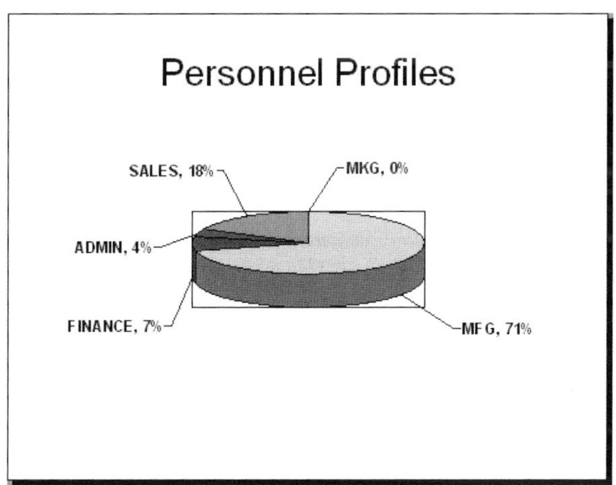

1 2 3 4 5 6 7 8 9 10

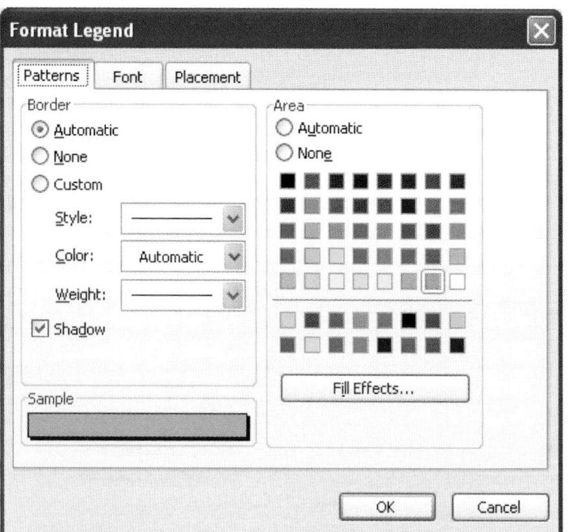

Figure 6-15: The Format Legend dialog box is used to format a chart legend's border, area color, text, and placement

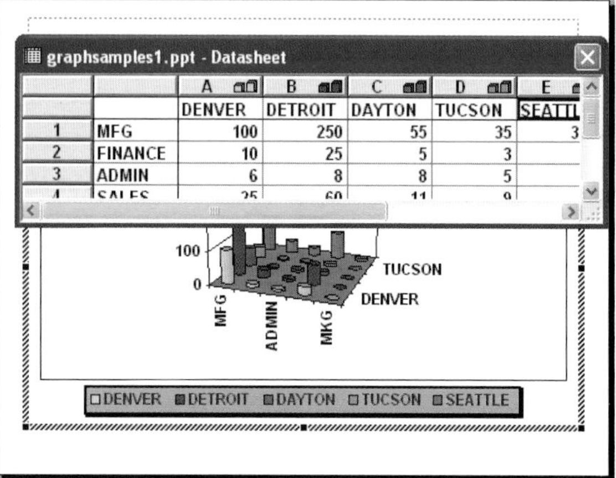

Figure 6-16: The legend at the bottom of the chart has been formatted to contain area color, its border has been thickened and shadowed, and its font, font size, and font color have been changed

Format Charts

Formatting a chart is used to change color, contents, text font and size, chart lines, and plot area. The chart must be open in Microsoft Graph in order to perform the following options.

FORMAT LEGENDS

1. To select the legend, double-click it. (Alternatively, you may click the legend to select it, open **Format,** and click **Selected Legend**.) The Format Legend dialog box will open, as shown in Figure 6-15.
2. Select one of the following options:
   - **To format the border of the legend,** do one or more of the following: Click **Patterns** and select the Border line thickness. Click **Automatic** for what the standard is; Click **None** for no border lines. Click **Custom** to select the Style, Color, and Weight from the drop-down list boxes. Click **Shadow** to have a shadow be applied to the border line.

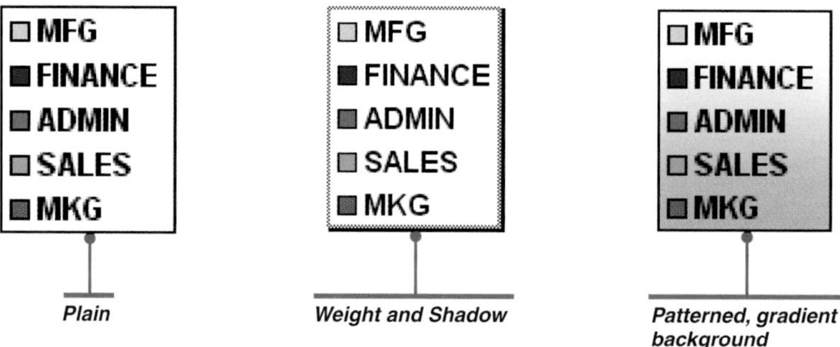

   - **To add color to the legend**, click **Patterns**. Under Area, select the color to be applied to the legend background. To add fill effects, refer to the Special Effects section in this chapter. Figure 6-16 shows legend changes.
   - **To format the text**, click **Font**. Change the Font, Font Style, Size, Color, or Effects as you wish. As you change the text formatting, the results will be displayed in the Preview box.
   - **To change the placement of the legend**, click **Placement**. Choose between Bottom, Corner, Top, Right, or Left. An example of Bottom is shown in Figure 6-16. (You can also drag the legend into position.)
3. Click **OK** to close the Format Legend dialog box.

ENTER A TITLE

To create or change the title of a chart:

1. Select the chart in Microsoft Graph.
2. Open **Chart** and click **Chart Options**. The Chart Options dialog box will open, as shown here.
3. Click the **Titles** tab. Then do one or more of the following:
   - For a chart title, type a name in the **Chart Title** text box.
   - To give the *x*-axis a name, type the name in the **Category (X) Axis** text box.
   - To give the *y*-axis a name, type the name in the **Value (Y) Axis** text box.

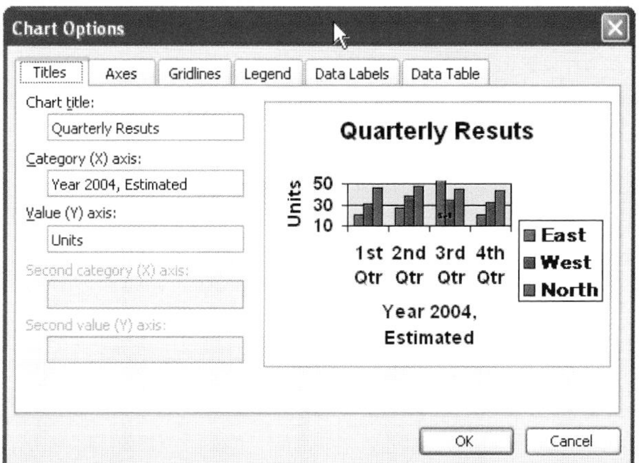

   - If you have a 3-D chart, you may name the *z*-axis by typing a name in the **Value (Z) Axis** text box.
4. Click **OK** to close the Chart Options dialog box.

CHANGE THE COLOR OF A DATA SERIES

To change the color of a data series:

1. Select the graph with Microsoft Graph.
2. To display the Format Data Series dialog box, shown in Figure 6-17, double-click a data series you want to color. All data series of the same color will display a selection "dot" on them, and the dialog box will open.

Figure 6-17: You can format the data series of a chart with the Format Data Series dialog box.

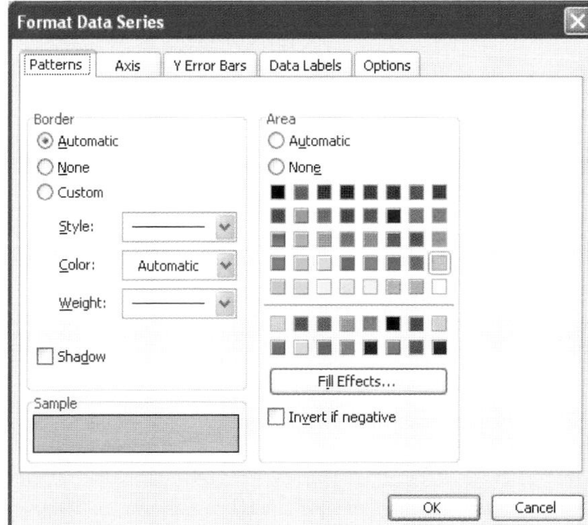

1 2 3 4 5 6 7 8 9 10

1st Qtr

Column before color applied

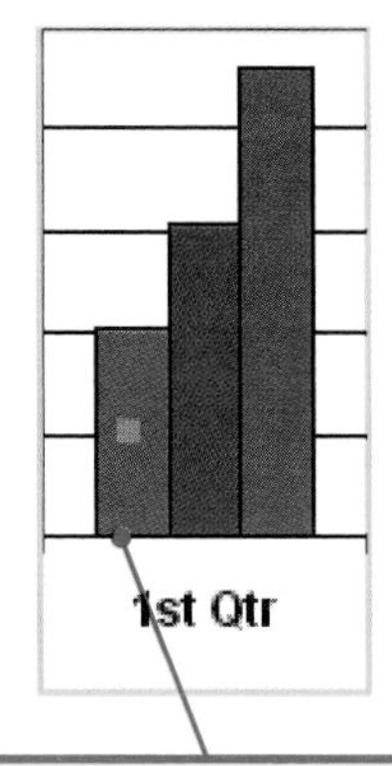

Column after color applied

> **TIP**
>
> When you select an element on the chart, the Selected option on the Format menu changes. For example, when you select a column, the option will be Format Selected Data Series; when you select an axis, the option will be Format Selected Axis; when you select gridlines, the option will be Format Selected Gridlines.

3. Open the **Patterns** tab.
4. Click the color you want the data series to be.
5. Click **OK**.

LABEL A DATA SERIES

To label a data series:

1. Select the chart within Microsoft Graph.
2. Open **Chart** and click **Chart Options**.
3. Click the **Data Labels** tab.
4. Place a check mark in the check box for the type of label you want. (Figure 6-18 shows a chart with the Value check box selected.)

Values assigned to columns

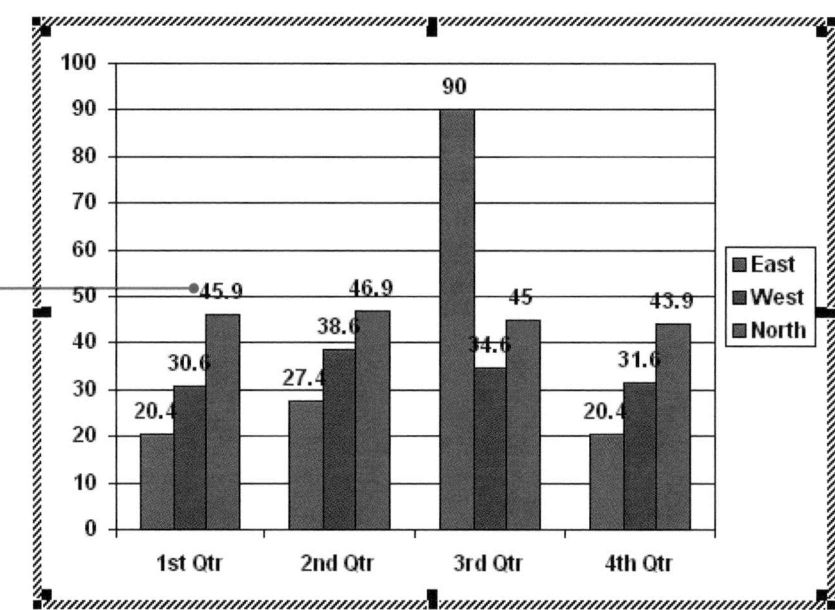

Figure 6-18: The columns in each data series can be labeled with a series name or category name, or with its value name, as this one is

5. If you want more than one label for a data series, open the **Separator** drop-down list box and choose the type of separator you want between labels.
6. Click **OK** to close the dialog box and see the results.

SCALE A *Y*-AXIS

To change the maximum, minimum, and incremental values of a *y*-axis:

1. Select the chart within Microsoft Graph.
2. Select the *y*-axis by clicking it. The axis line will have handles on each end when it is selected as shown to the left.
3. Open **Format** and click **Selected Axis**. The Format Axis dialog box will be displayed, as shown in Figure 6-19. Click the **Scale** tab.

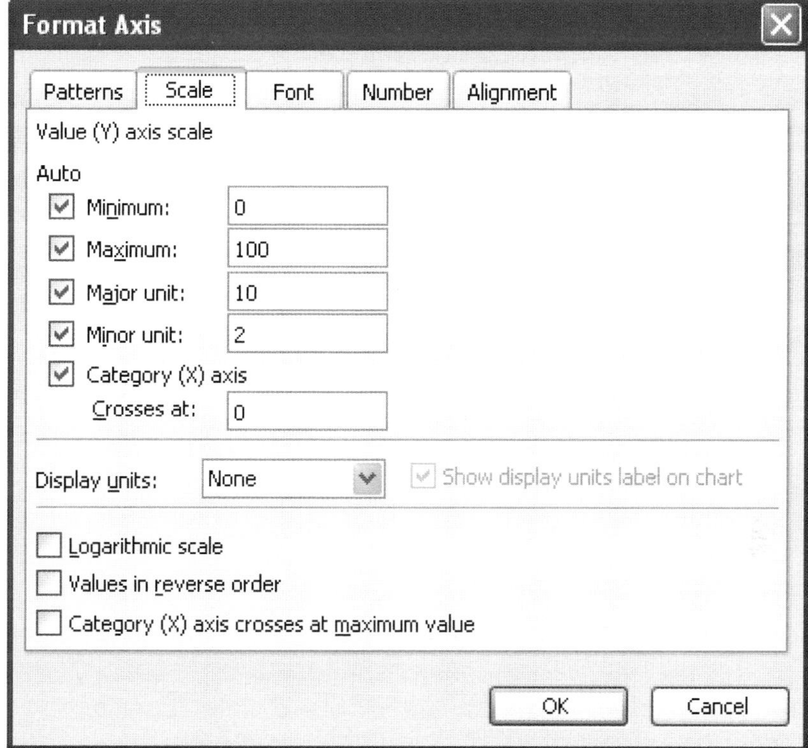

Figure 6-19: With the Format Axis dialog box, you can change many features of a y-axis, such as its scale, shown here

NOTE

To change the scale of the *x*-axis, select the *x*-axis, open **Format**, and click **Selected Axis**. Click the **Scales** tab. You can change the value where the *x*- and *y*-axes cross, the scale of the tick marks on the *x*-axis, and reverse the display of the categories, as shown in Figure 6-20.

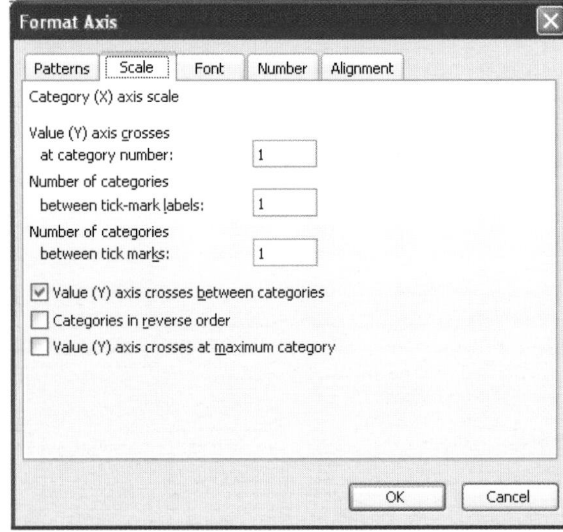

Figure 6-20: The x-axis scale is changed in the Format Axis dialog box with the x-axis selected

4. To change aspects of the *y*-axis scale, choose among these options:
   - **Minimum**, to change the lowest value
   - **Maximum**, to change the highest value
   - **Major Unit**, to show the largest increments displayed
   - **Minor Unit**, to show the smallest increments displayed
   - **Category X Axis Crosses At**, **to** establish the point on the *y*-axis where the *x*-axis will cross it
   - **Display Units**, to display a menu of units that may be displayed

   - **Logarithmic Scale**, to display the values in a logarithmic relationship, rather than an arithmetic one
   - **Values in Reverse Order**, to display the largest value at the bottom of the axis and the smallest at the top
   - **Category (X) Axis Crosses At Maximum Value**, to establish the point on the *x*-axis where the largest value will cross the *y*-axis
5. Click **OK** to close the dialog box and see the results.

FORMAT THE PLOT AREA

The plot area is the background of the chart, upon which the chart rests. It can be formatted with color and fill effects and its border can be formatted to take on a different style, thickness, or color.

1. Select the chart within Microsoft Graph.
2. Select the plot area by clicking the chart, outside of any lines or text.

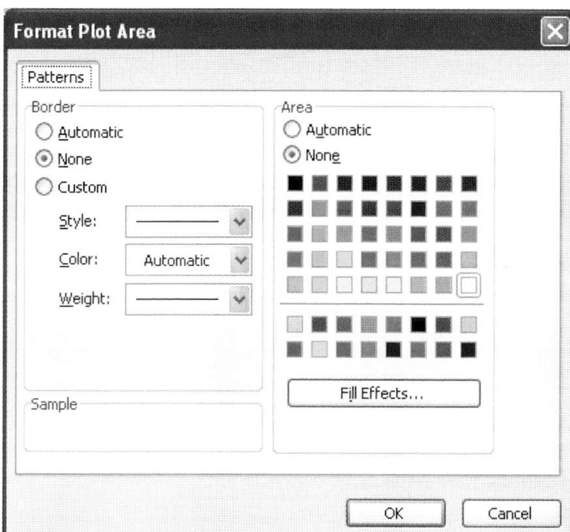

Figure 6-21: The plot area can be formatted with color, gradient colors, patterns, textures, or a picture, and the borders can be formatted as well

3. Open **Format** and click **Selected Plot Area**. The Format Plot Area dialog box will be displayed, as shown in Figure 6-21.
4. Choose the elements you want to change:
   - **To change the Border**, choose among the default settings of **Automatic**, **None** (for no border**)**, and **Custom**. If you choose Custom, select among changing the **Style**, **Color**, or **Weight** of the border.
   - **To change the area color**, choose **Automatic** (for default colors), **None** (for no color in the plot area), or select a color to apply to the plot area. Select **Fill Effects** to fill the plot area with gradient color, patterns, textures, or a picture (see Special Effects in Chapter 7).
5. Click **OK** to close the dialog box. Figure 6-22 shows a chart with a colored plot area.

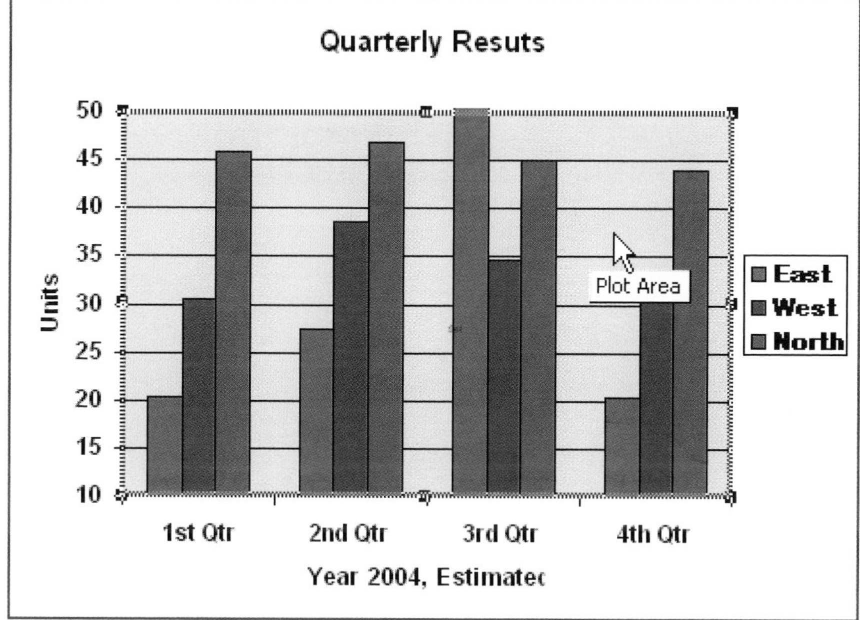

Figure 6-22: Plot areas can be colored

FORMAT TEXT

You can format text in a chart by changing its font, font style, font size, and color.

1. Select the chart within Microsoft Graph.
2. Select the chart element that contains text to be formatted. To select all text in the chart, open the **Chart Object** drop-down list box on the toolbar, and click **Chart Area**.
3. Open **Format** and click **Font**. The Font dialog box will open with the Font tab displayed, as shown in Figure 6-23.

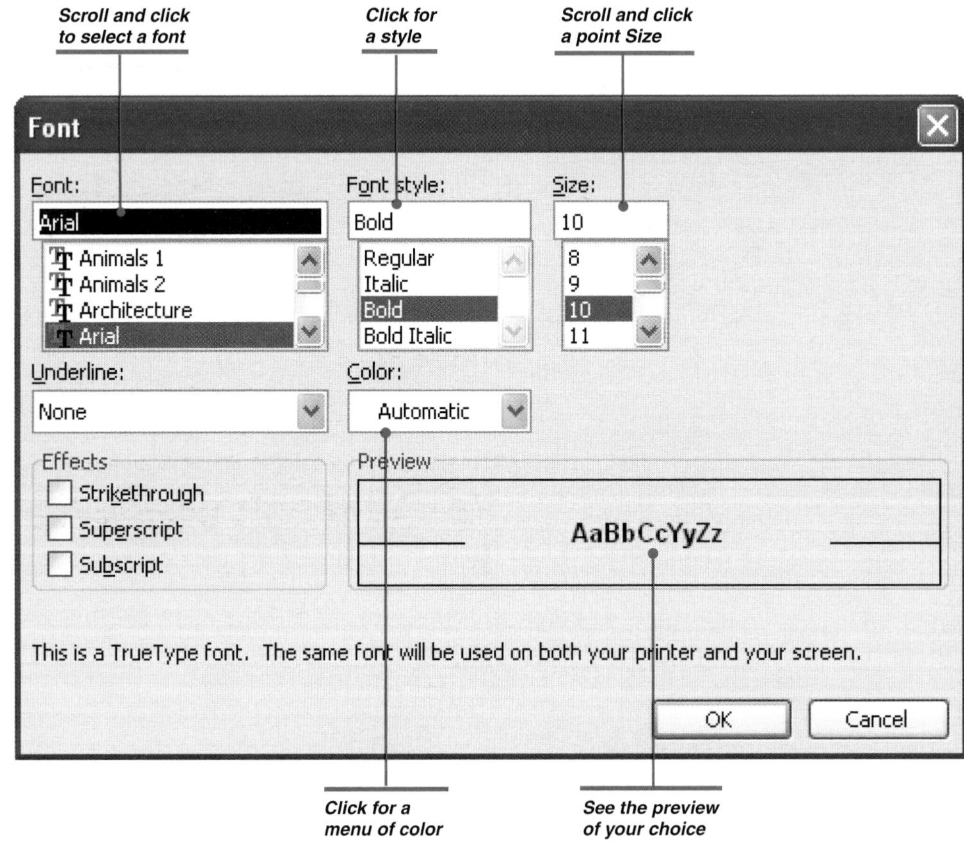

***Figure 6-23:** This dialog box is used to format all chart text and changes font, font style, size, color, and color background*

4. Choose your formatting option and click **OK**.

TIP

Common errors occur from selecting the wrong element in a crowded chart and from selecting one single element, such as one column, when you want to select all columns. To select specific chart elements, open the **Chart Object** drop-down list box, and click the element you want.

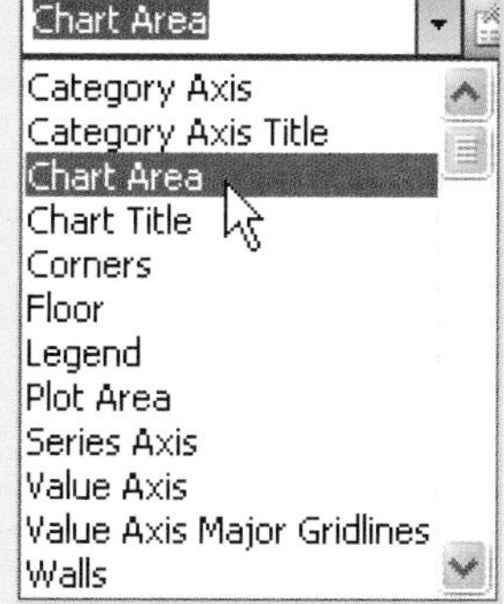

FORMAT AXIS NUMBERS

To format numbers, such as currency, dates, and percentages:

1. Select the chart within Microsoft Graph.
2. Select the numbers to be formatted, or simply double-click them. The Format Axis dialog box will open, as shown in Figure 6-24.

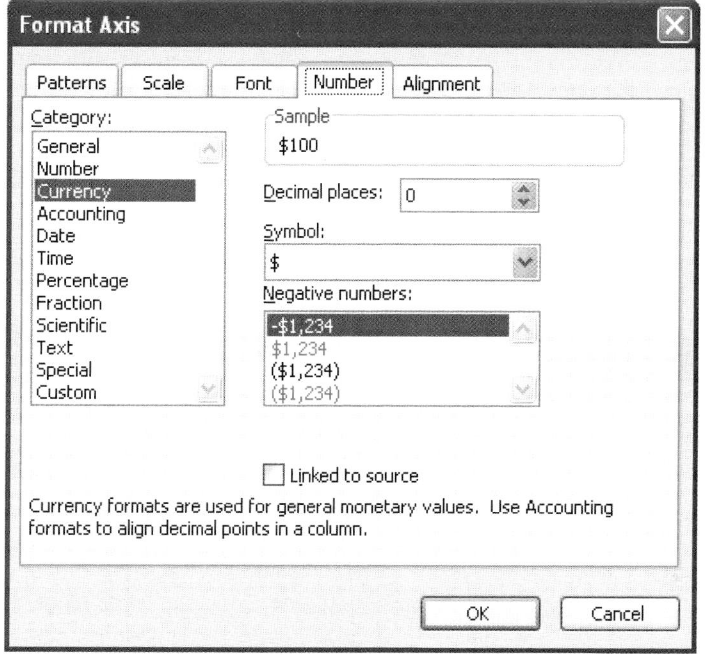

Figure 6-24: Numbers can be formatted to represent what they are, and the number of decimal points can be specified

3. Click the **Number** tab if it is not selected.
4. The formatting you apply depends on the numeric category you desire to format. If you choose Currency, for example, you might format as follows:
   - Under Category, click **Currency**.
   - Drag the **Decimal Places** slider to increase or decrease the number of decimals.
   - If you're not using U.S. currency, click the **Symbol** down arrow and choose the appropriate symbol.

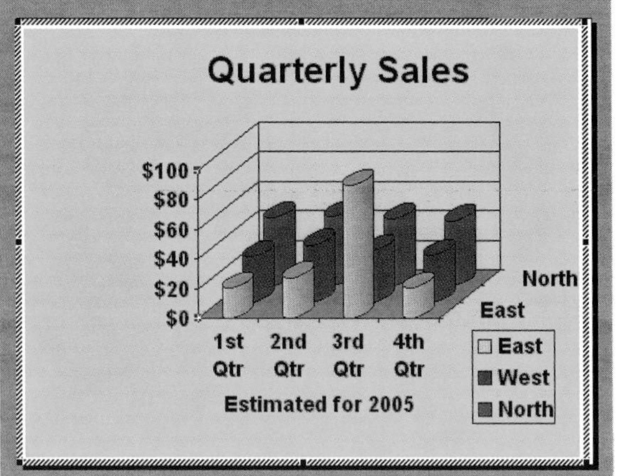

Figure 6-25: This charted image shows the y-axis formatted as currency

- Drag the slider for **Negative Numbers** to choose a format.
- If your numbers are linked to another source for updating, click **Linked To Source**.

5. Click **OK** to close the dialog box. (Figure 6-25 shows a chart formatted with currency.)

FORMAT GRID LINES

To make gridlines less obvious or more apparent (usually, in order to help viewers visually):

1. Select the chart within Microsoft Graph.
2. Open **Chart Objects** and select **Value Axis Major Gridlines**. You can also click a gridline to select it.
3. Open **Format** and click **Selected Gridlines**. The Format Gridlines dialog box will open, as shown in Figure 6-26.
4. Choose among these options:
   - **Automatic**, to restore default values
   - **None**, to remove gridlines
   - **Custom Style**, to choose the style of line, such as a solid line or a dotted line
   - **Custom Color**, to choose from a menu of colors
   - **Custom Weight**, to choose from a menu of line thicknesses
5. Click **OK** when you have made your choices.

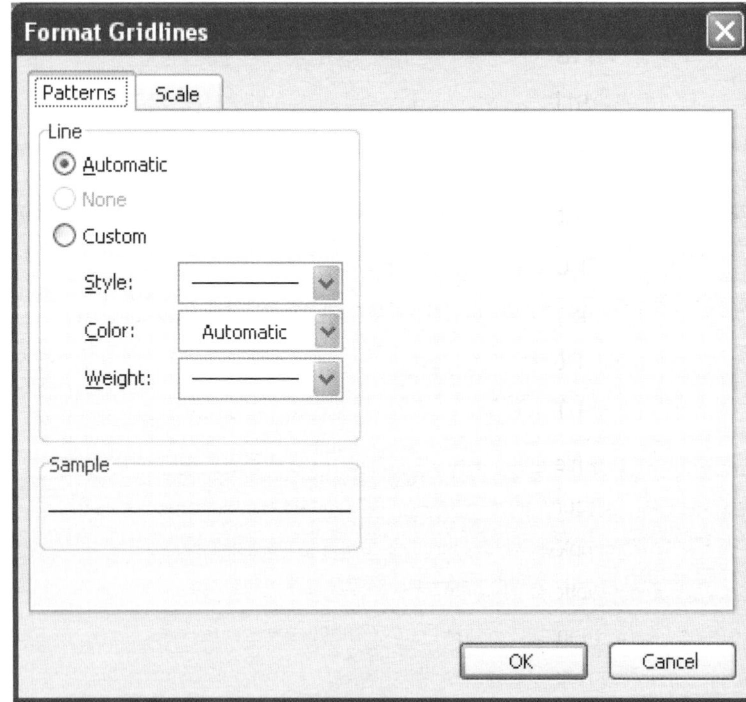

Figure 6-26: Gridlines can be made more or less apparent with this dialog box

How to...

- *Begin an Organization Chart*
- *Modify Text in Boxes*
- *Insert a Box*
- *Insert Complex Org Chart Templates*
- *Use an AutoFormat Style*
- *Insert Multiple Boxes*
- *Selecting Boxes*
- *Rearrange Boxes*
- *Change the Layout of an Org Chart*
- *Format Boxes and Box Outlines*
- *Format Connecting Lines*
- *Format Text*
- *Use Zoom*
- *Using the Diagram Toolbar*
- *Insert a Diagram*

Chapter 7

Working with Organization Charts and Diagrams

In addition to all the charts and graphs available, PowerPoint also offers a diagram feature that enables you to create organization (org) charts and other "relationship-type" diagrams. This chapter tells you how to use these diagrams.

The Diagram Gallery contains six types of diagrams, as seen in Figure 7-1. You can use these in your presentations to describe organizations, processes, and other subjects that have relationships to other subjects. This list gives you some ideas about how you might want to use these diagrams:

- **Organization Charts** show hierarchical relationships, as in a company or family tree.
- **Cycle Diagrams** show reoccurring processes or relationships.
- **Radial Diagrams** display spoke-like relationships with a central hub.
- **Pyramid Diagrams** show bottom-up, base to pinnacle, relationships.
- **Venn Diagrams** illustrate connections and shared relationships between parties.
- **Target Diagrams** display levels of processes or relationships leading to a central goal.

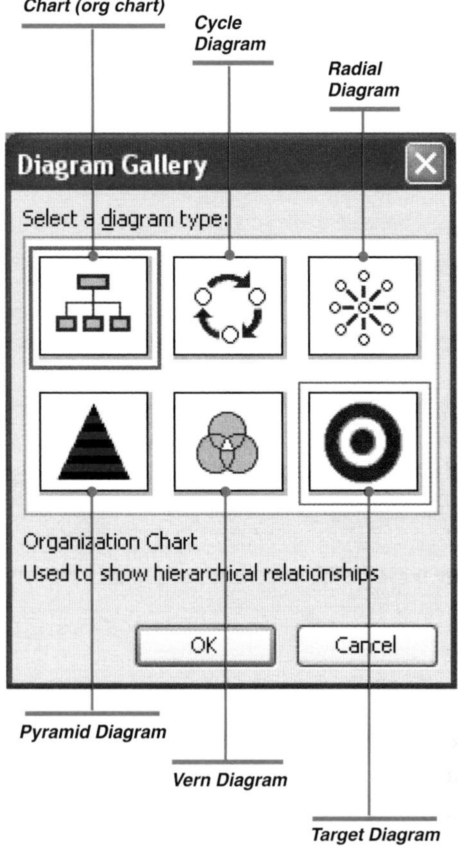

Figure 7-1: The Diagram Gallery offers a menu of diagrams and charts that you can insert into your presentation

Create an Organization Chart

Creating an org chart requires placing an org chart on your slide and then modifying it to meet your own needs. You can get the original org chart by using a template that comes with PowerPoint, downloading one from Microsoft, or making your own using the Drawing tools (see Chapter 8). You can then add org boxes and connecting lines, change colors or box borders or connecting lines, fill boxes with colors, and place your own labels in the org text boxes.

Begin an Organization Chart

You can use PowerPoint to create simple organization charts. By simple, I mean org charts that do not reflect deep or complex relationships. (Microsoft suggests Visio for complex org charts.) PowerPoint org charts do have the benefit of being able to incorporate the design elements and colors of your regular presentation. To insert an org chart on a slide:

1. Bring up the Diagram Gallery dialog box.
   - Open **Insert** and choose **Diagram**. 

   –Or–
   - Click **Insert Diagram** from the Drawing toolbar.

   –Or–
   - Bring up the Slide Layout task pane, and choose a layout with content. Click the Insert Diagram Or Organization Chart icon.

2. Double-click the Organization Chart icon. The org chart will be inserted on your slide, as shown in Figure 7-2.
3. Choose a layout that is appropriate for the slide you are creating, perhaps the Title And Content layout template.

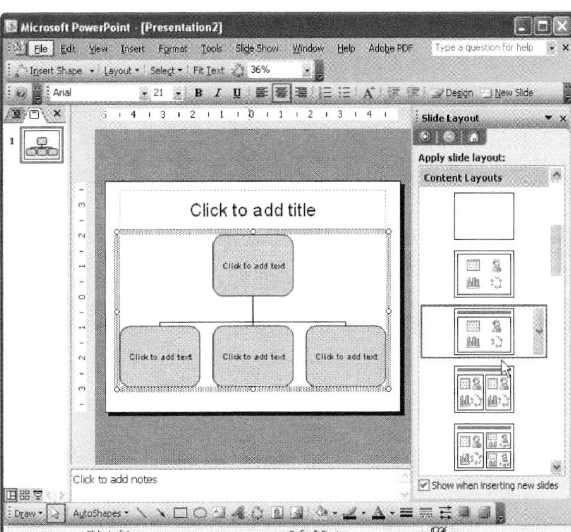

Figure 7-2: The original org chart is very simple but contains the basic patterns for you to modify and create your own, more complex org chart

NOTE

As you type in more text, you may see the font size decrease so that the text can fit in the box without the box changing shape.

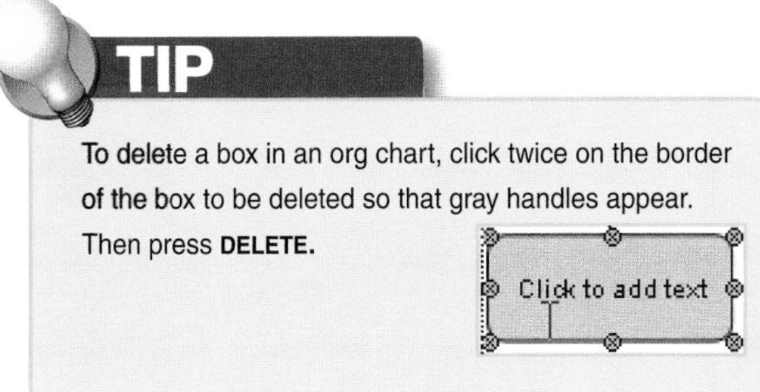

TIP

To delete a box in an org chart, click twice on the border of the box to be deleted so that gray handles appear. Then press **DELETE.**

Modify Text in Boxes

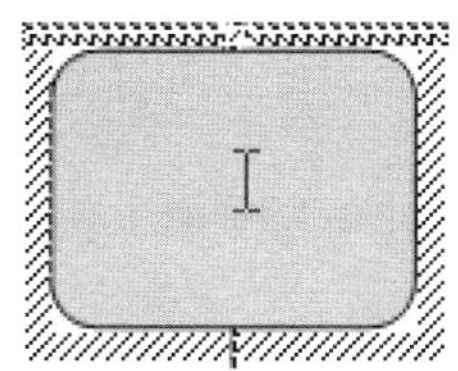

To enter or edit text in org chart boxes:

1. Click in the box to be edited. The text editing border automatically appears around it, indicating that you can now enter text.
2. Type in the text you want.
3. To skip to the next line, press **ENTER**.

Insert a Box

You can insert three types of boxes into an org chart: subordinate, assistant, or coworker boxes. Subordinate boxes will appear below the manager box you have currently selected. (A manager box may represent the head of a family in a family tree or a product or process in another kind of chart. The use of these charts varies, but I am using "manager" for clarity and because it will be the most common use of this type of chart.) Coworker boxes will be at the same level as the currently selected box. Assistant boxes will be inserted between the currently selected manager box and any already existing subordinate boxes. To insert boxes:

1. First, you want to select a box that will act as a reference point for the one being inserted. Select the box above the place where you want to insert the new box.

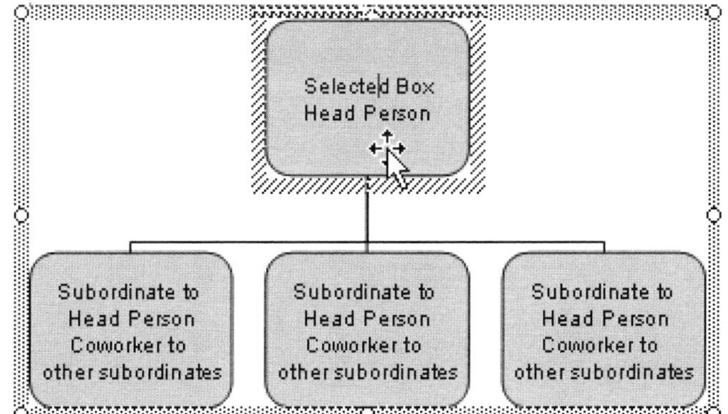

Figure 7-3: The Search Results task pane offers "designer" templates

2. Open **Insert Shape** on the Organization Chart toolbar, which appears when an org chart is selected.

- To place a box below the selected box, click **Subordinate**
- To place a box below the selected box but above any subordinates, click **Assistant**
- To place a box at the same level as a selected box, click **Coworker**.

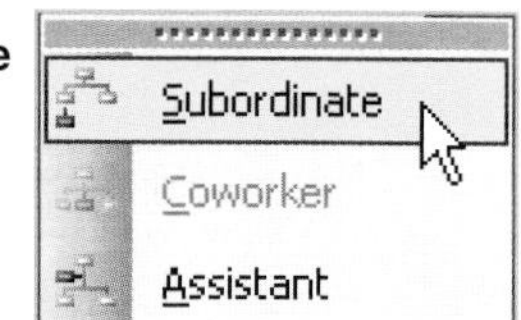

3. The box will be inserted. Continue to add boxes until you have the org chart you want.
4. Click each box to type the name or function of each person represented in the org chart.

Insert Complex Org Chart Templates

To insert more complex org charts, you can start with those that Microsoft offers on its web site. To access these charts:

1. Bring up the Search Results task pane by clicking the task pane title bar and clicking **Search Results**. The Search Results task pane will be displayed.
2. Type org charts under Search, and click the Go arrow. The task pane will be displayed with the search results.
3. Find and click **Complex Organization Chart**, as seen in Figure 7-3.
4. The Template Preview of org chart templates will be displayed, as shown in Figure 7-4. You can scroll back and forth through them by clicking the **Previous** and **Next** arrows.
5. When you find a chart you like, click **Download**. The template will be downloaded into a fresh slide, along with instructions on how to modify it.

Figure 7-4: An example of a template for an org chart that you can find online at Microsoft

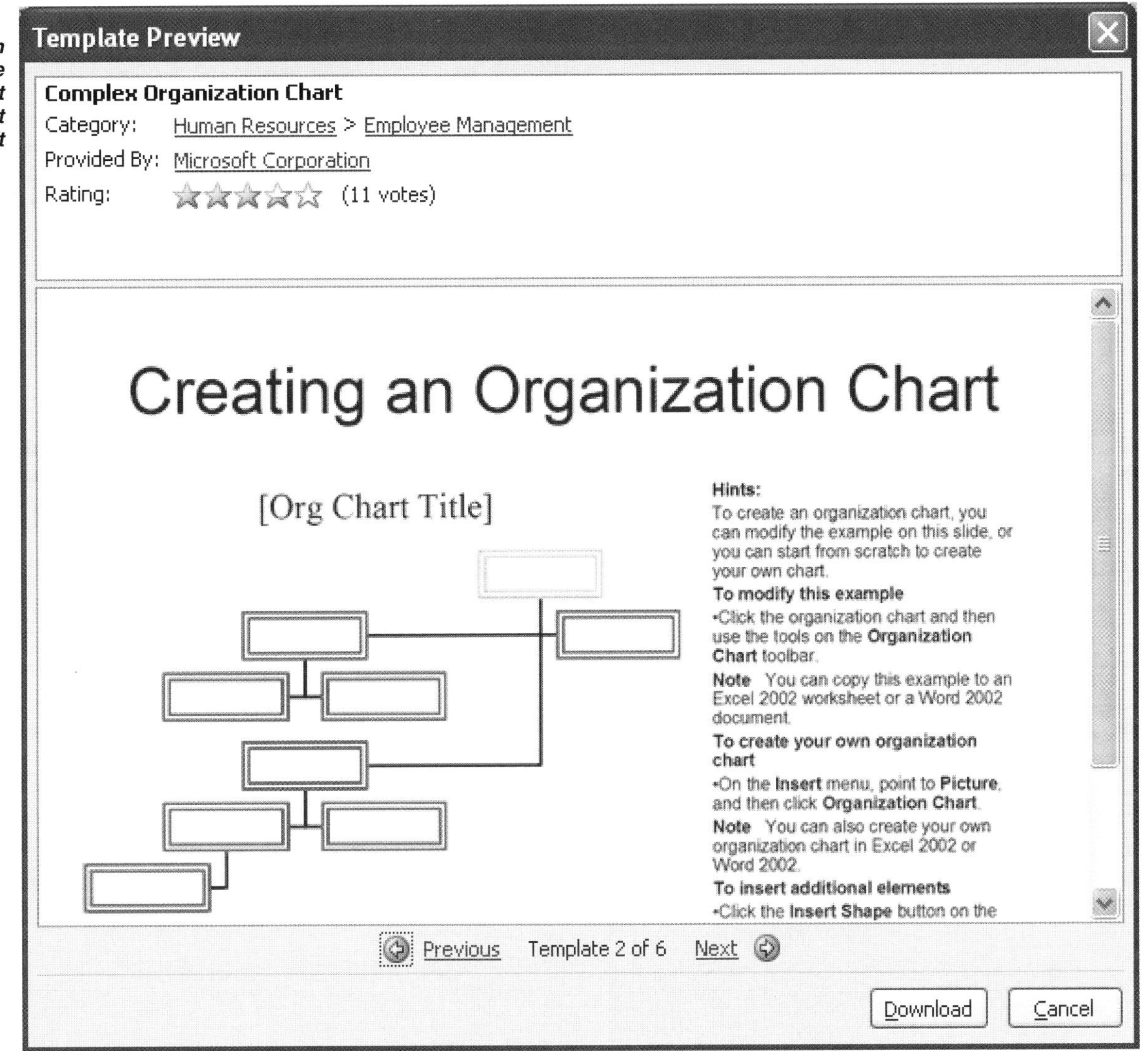

1 2 3 4 5 6 7 8 9 10

Use an AutoFormat Style

PowerPoint offers you a selection of already formatted org charts in a variety of styles and colors. To choose one:

1. Insert an org chart onto a slide, as explained in Begin an Organization Chart.
2. Click your org chart to select it and to display the Organization Chart toolbar.
3. Click **AutoFormat** on the toolbar. The Organization Chart Style Gallery dialog box will be displayed, as shown in the Fire example in Figure 7-5.

4. Click the styles to see them displayed in the preview pane. When you find one you like, click it and click **OK**. The style will be applied to the org chart on your slide.

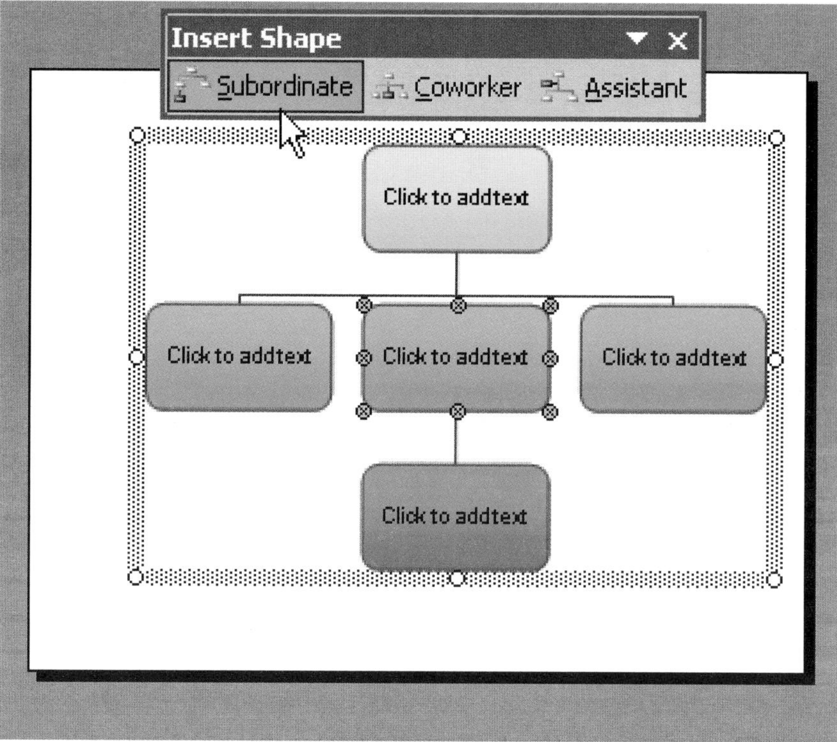

Figure 7-5: You can use prepackaged styles with the Style Gallery dialog box, such as this Fire style

> **TIP**
>
> The toolbar options will remain unavailable (indicated by being grayed out) until you select the org chart or a box within it.

Insert Multiple Boxes

You can insert more than one box at a time by detaching the Insert Shape menu.

1. To detach the Insert Shape menu, open the menu and place your pointer on the menu handle. It will turn into a four-headed arrow, like this:

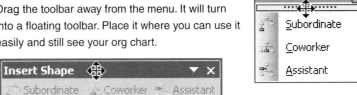

2. Drag the toolbar away from the menu. It will turn into a floating toolbar. Place it where you can use it easily and still see your org chart.

3. Select the box that will act as the reference point, and then click multiple times the desired tool on the toolbar. For instance, if you want to add two subordinates to a selected box, you click Subordinate two times. Figure 7-6 shows a chart after I have selected a box and have clicked Subordinate one time and when I am about to click it a second time.

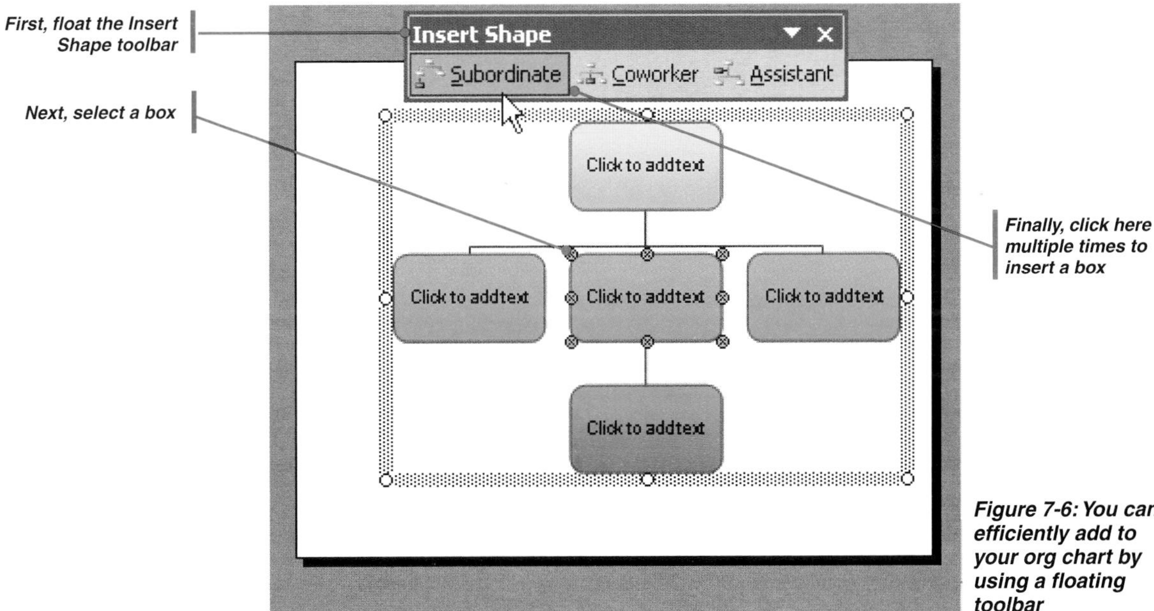

***Figure 7-6:** You can efficiently add to your org chart by using a floating toolbar*

QUICKSTEPS

SELECTING BOXES

You can select one box by simply clicking it. If you need to select multiple boxes on the same level, boxes that are in a branch, or the connecting lines, you use the Select tool.

SELECT A SINGLE BOX

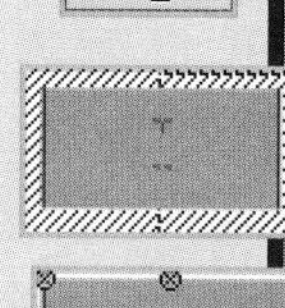

- To select a box for text entry or edit, click the box once. The text selection border will appear.
- To select a box to move or change its size or shape, click the box border twice. Gray handles appear.

SELECT MULTIPLE BOXES

To select multiple boxes not in a branch or on the same level, press and hold **CTRL** while you click each box to be selected.

SELECT ALL BOXES

To select all boxes in an org chart:

- Select the top box in the org chart, open **Select**, and click **Branch**.

  –Or–

- Click in the background of the org chart to deselect all boxes in the org chart. Open **Edit** and click **Select All**.

Continued...

TIP

You can move a branch of an org chart by opening **Select** on the toolbar, clicking **Branch** to select the branch, and dragging the head box. Subordinates follow a manager.

Rearrange Boxes

To rearrange the boxes on the org chart, simply drag them to a new location.

1. Clear any selections on the org chart by clicking off the chart or by pressing **ESC**.
2. Click the box you want to move, and drag it over the next level up on the branch. In other words, drag a subordinate over its new manager.

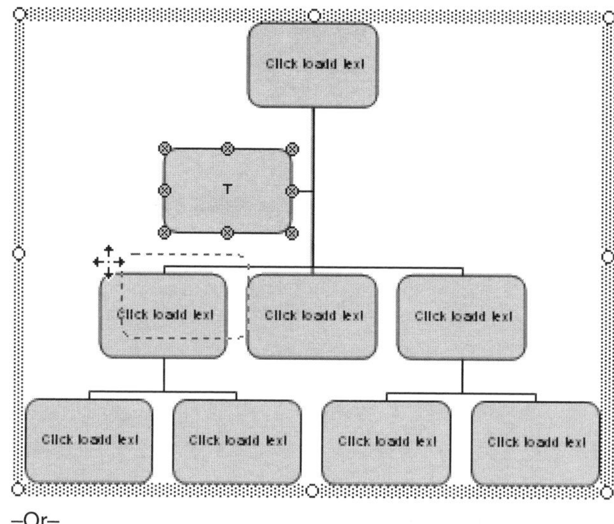

–Or–

3. Select a box (gray handles appear). Open **Edit** and click **Cut**.
4. Select the new manager of the box. Open **Edit** and click **Paste**.

SELECTING BOXES *(Continued)*

SELECT A BRANCH

1. Select the top box in the branch.
2. Open **Select** on the Organization Chart toolbar, and click **Branch**.

SELECT A LEVEL

1. Select a box at the level you want to select.
2. Open **Select** on the Organization Chart toolbar, and click **Level**.

SELECT CONNECTING LINES

1. Select any box in the org chart.
2. Open **Select** on the Organization Chart toolbar, and click **All Connecting Lines**.

Continued...

Change the Layout of an Org Chart

You can change the way a branch appears on an org chart by changing its layout. Figure 7-7 shows an example of left hanging, right hanging, and standard layouts.

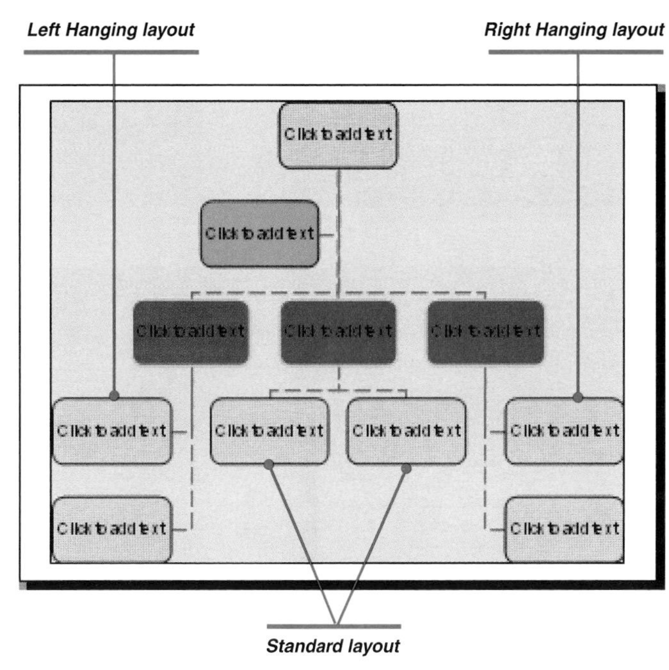

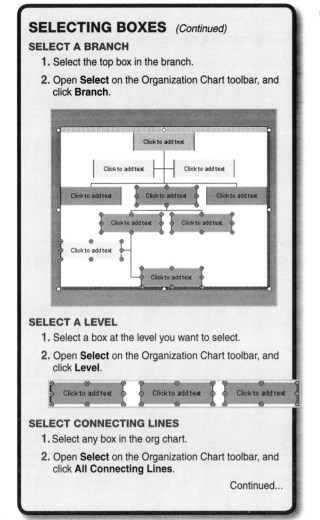

Figure 7-7: An example of how you can change the layout of an org chart

1. To change the layout, select the head of the branch.
2. Open **Layout** on the Organization Chart toolbar, and make sure that **AutoLayout** is selected.
3. Click the layout style you want.

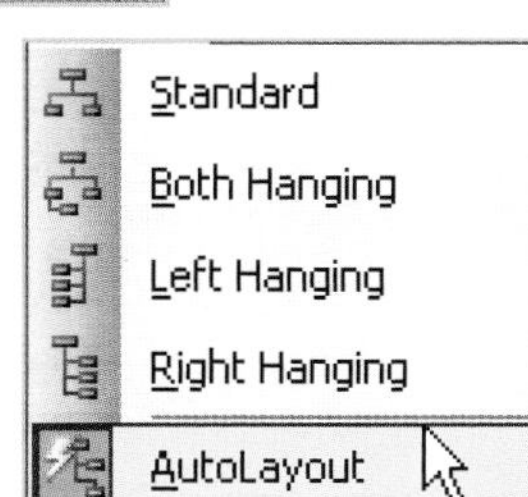

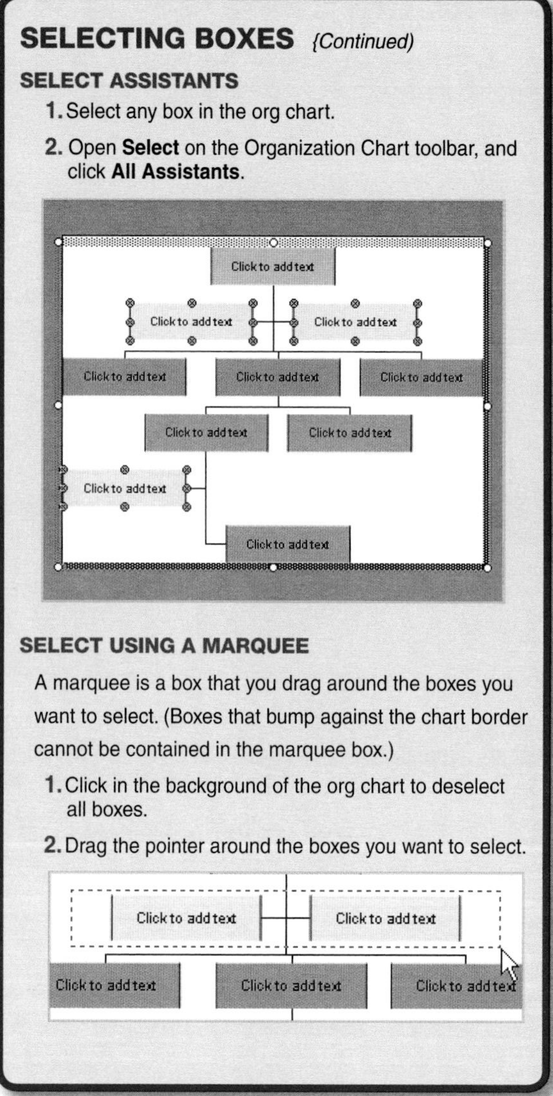

SELECTING BOXES *(Continued)*

SELECT ASSISTANTS

1. Select any box in the org chart.
2. Open **Select** on the Organization Chart toolbar, and click **All Assistants**.

SELECT USING A MARQUEE

A marquee is a box that you drag around the boxes you want to select. (Boxes that bump against the chart border cannot be contained in the marquee box.)

1. Click in the background of the org chart to deselect all boxes.
2. Drag the pointer around the boxes you want to select.

Format Boxes and Box Outlines

You can change the colors of boxes and of box outlines.

1. Select the box or the series of boxes to be modified. (You can use Select on the Organization Chart toolbar to select a branch or level.)
2. Double-click the border of one of the selected boxes. (Or you can open **Format**, and click **AutoShapes**). The Format AutoShape dialog box will open, as seen in Figure 7-8.

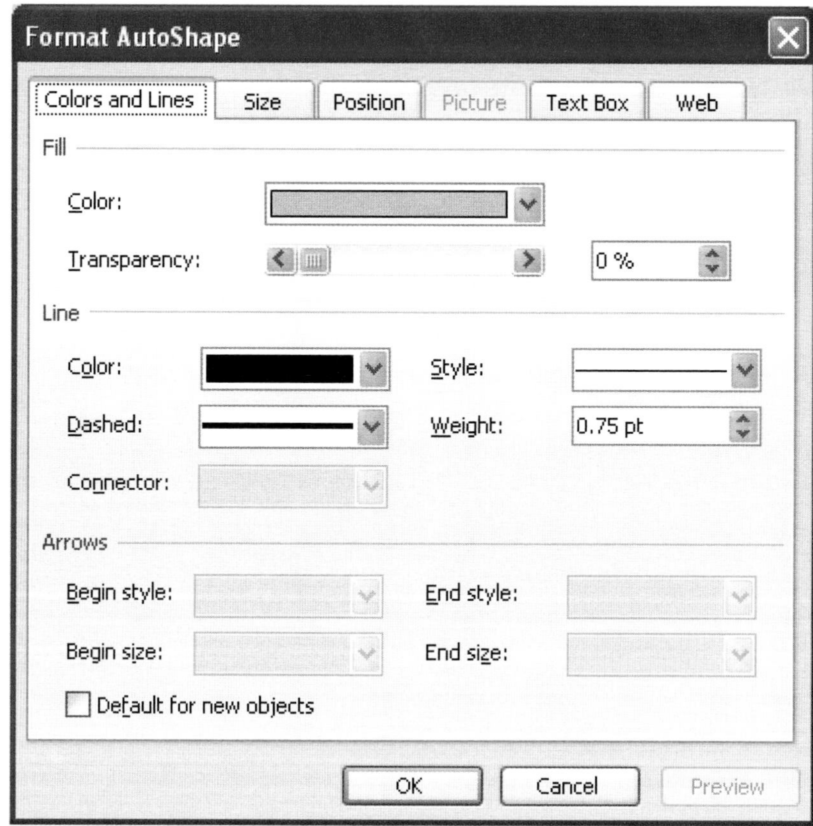

Figure 7-8: The Format AutoShape dialog box is used to format boxes with color and line definitions

TIP

You can click **More Colors** to view an alternative selection of colors or **Fill Effects** to fill your box with a gradient effect, patterns, texture, or a background picture. See Chapter 8 for additional information on how to use these special effects.

3. Click the **Colors and Lines** tab if it is not already open, and select one of these options:
   - Open **Fill Color** and click a color to fill the background of the box.
   - Drag the **Fill Transparency** slider to increase the "see-throughness" of the color or effect.

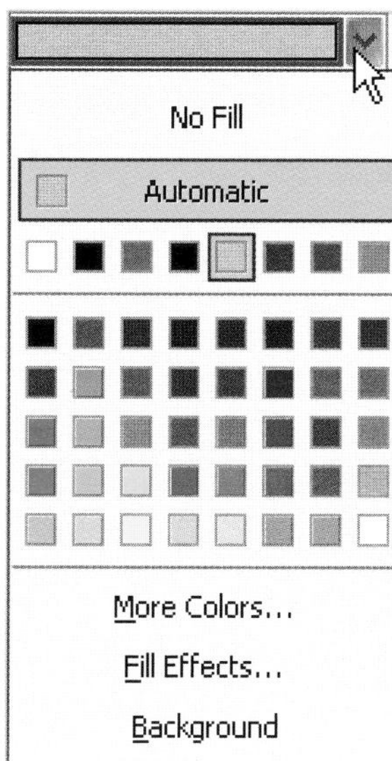

   - To change the outline of a box, open **Line Color** and click a color for the lines that define the boxes.
   - If you want a dashed-line style, open **Dashed** and click a line style.

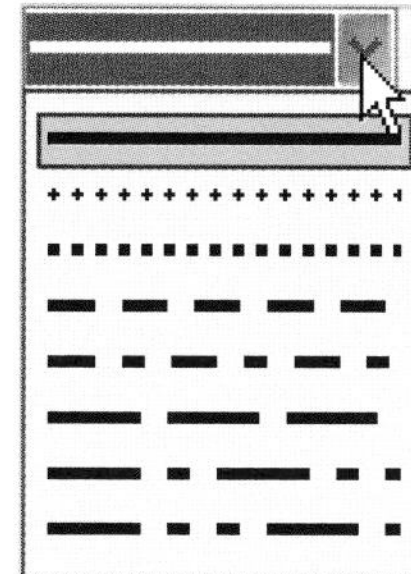

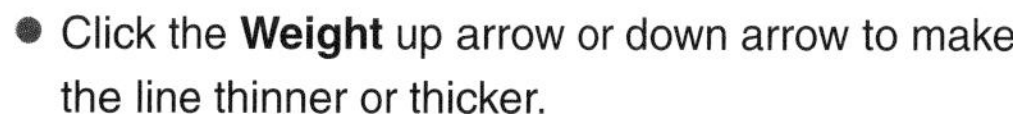

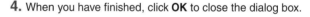

   - Click the **Weight** up arrow or down arrow to make the line thinner or thicker.

4. When you have finished, click **OK** to close the dialog box.

Format Connecting Lines

To format the connecting lines of an org chart:

1. Select anything, a box or a line, within the org chart.
2. Open **Select** on the Organization Chart toolbar, and click **All Connecting Lines**.
3. Double-click a connecting line (or open **Format** and click **AutoShape**). The Format AutoShape dialog box will open, as shown in Figure 7-9.

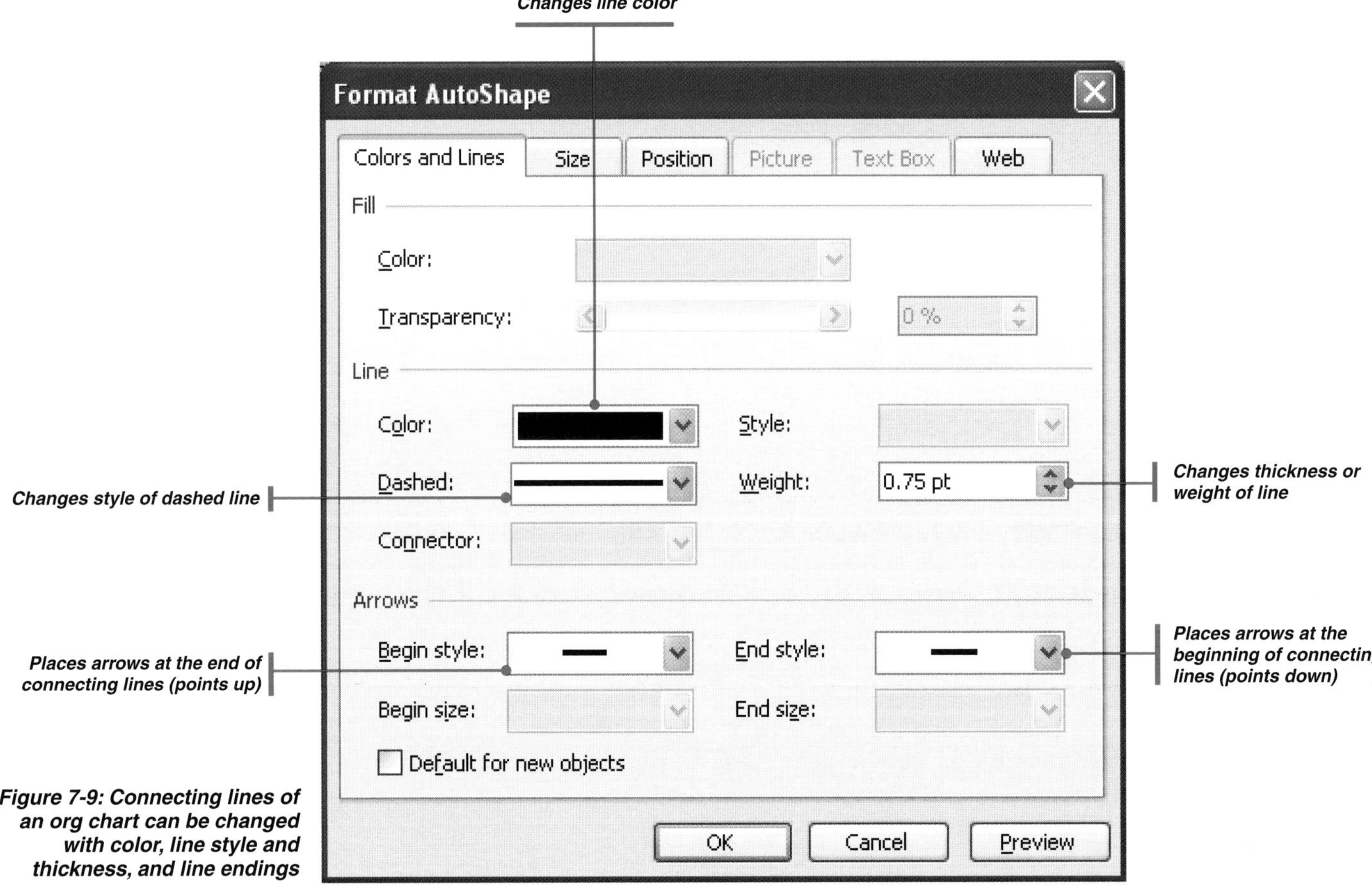

Figure 7-9: Connecting lines of an org chart can be changed with color, line style and thickness, and line endings

4. Choose one of the **Line** options:

- Open **Color**, and click the color of the line.
- Open **Dashed,** and choose a line style.
- Click the **Weight** up arrow or down arrow to set the line thickness
- To select a "to" line ending, open **Begin Style**, and click an option.

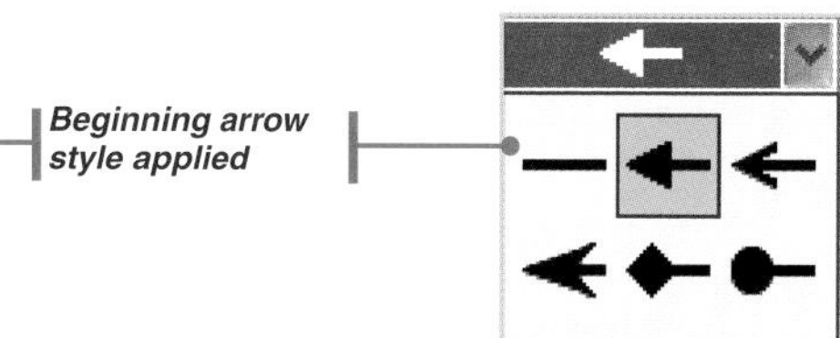

Beginning arrow style applied

- Open **End Style** to select a "from" line ending, and click an option.

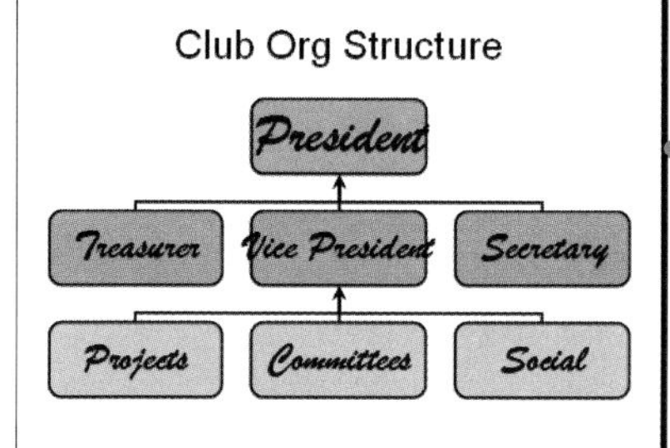

Ending arrow style applied

- Choose the **Begin Size** and **End Size** for the line endings.

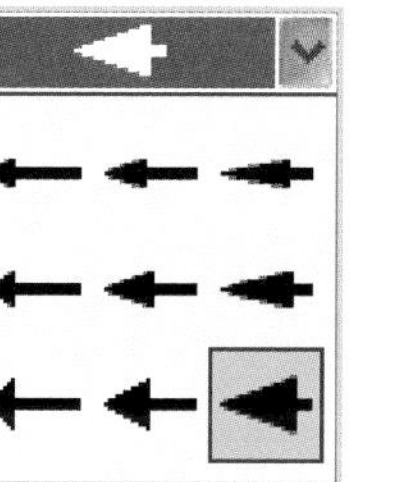

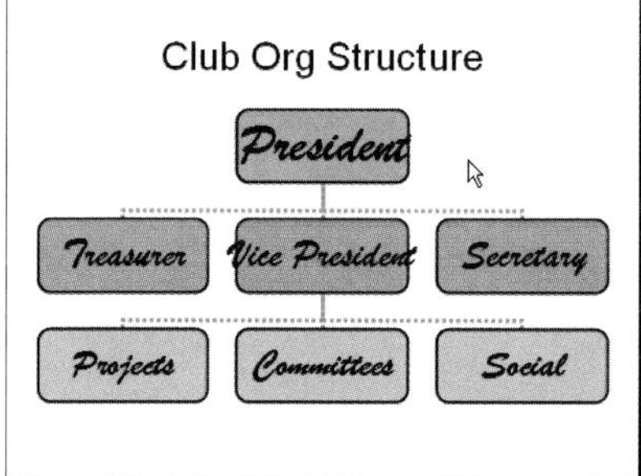

Color and dashed line style applied

5. Click **OK** to close the dialog box.

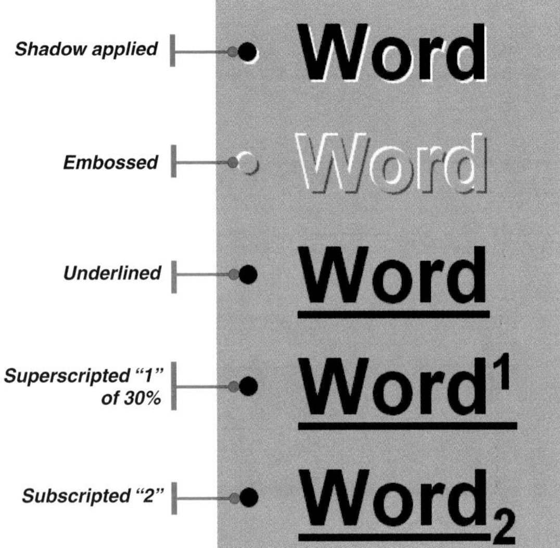

Format Text

The text in an org chart box can be changed in a number of ways. You can change the font, font style and size, color of text, and implement special effects, such as underline, shadow, or embossing.

1. Click on the text in a box to select the box.
2. Drag over the text you want to select, or press **CTRL+A** to select all the text in the box.
3. Open **Format** and click **Font**. The Font dialog box will open, as shown in Figure 7-10.

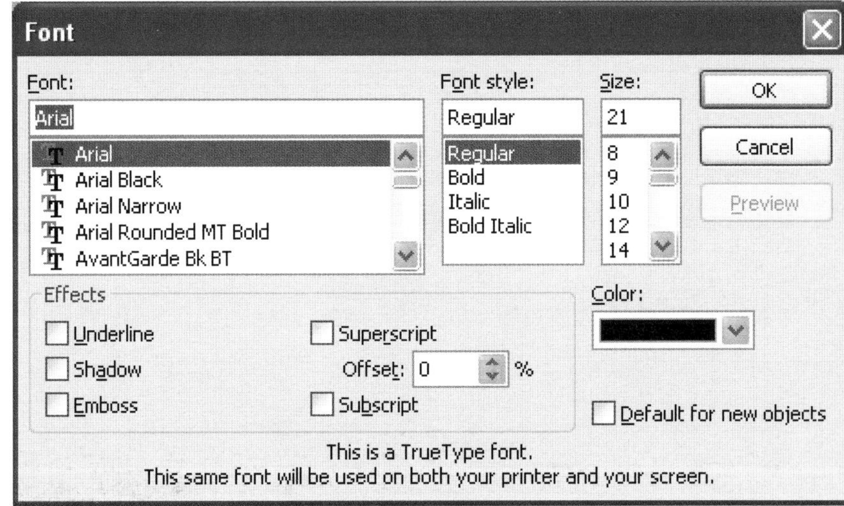

Figure 7-10: The Font dialog box offers you options in font, style, size and color, plus some effects

4. Select your options:
   - To select another font, scroll the Font scroll bar and click a choice.
   - To select a Font Style, click an entry.
   - Scroll the Size list box, and click the point size you want.

- For another color, open the **Color** drop-down list box and click the color. You can also click **More Colors** to have additional choices, or click **Automatic** for the original default color.

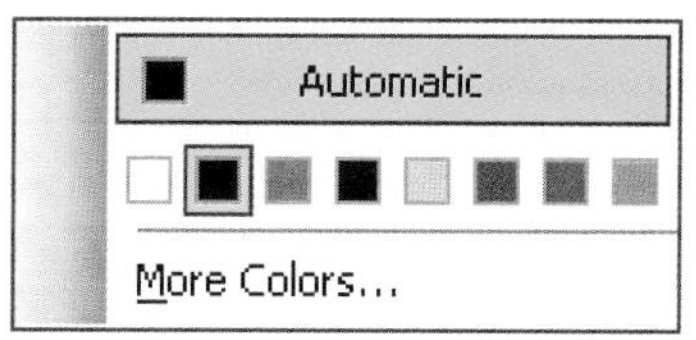

- To select a choice, place a check mark in one of the **Effects** check boxes.
- To make these selections the default for future entries, place a check mark in **Default For New Objects**.

5. Click **OK** to close the Font dialog box.

Use Zoom

Sometimes the text in the org chart boxes is too small to edit. Use Zoom to increase the size.

1. Click the box to select the org chart.

2. Open **Zoom** on the Organization Chart toolbar, and click the magnification you want.

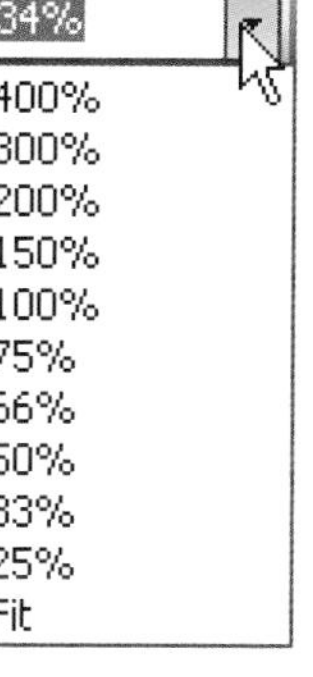

3. To return the zoom magnification to normal size, open **Zoom** and click **Fit**.

1 2 3 4 5 6 7 8 9 10

QUICKSTEPS

USING THE DIAGRAM TOOLBAR

INSERT SHAPES

Click **Insert Shape** to insert an additional arrow, circle, or layer to the diagram. Figure 7-11 shows additional shapes added to each of the diagrams.

MOVE SHAPE BACKWARD, MOVE SHAPE FORWARD

Click **Move Shape Backward** or **Move Shape Forward** to move the selected object.

- **Radial Diagram** moves the selection counter-clockwise and clockwise.

- **Pyramid** moves the selection up or down one layer.

- **Venn** moves the selection clockwise or counter-clockwise.

- **Target** moves the selection out or in one layer.

Continued...

NOTE

The other diagrams are very similar to the Cycle Diagram. Use the above steps to work with other diagrams, and refer to Using the Diagram Toolbar for additional help with the differences in the toolbar.

Use a Diagram

In addition to organization charts, PowerPoint provides five other diagram possibilities. Figure 7-11 shows examples of five diagrams, modified with color and added shapes. All of these diagrams use the same Diagram toolbar and contain the same types of sizing handles and drawing border.

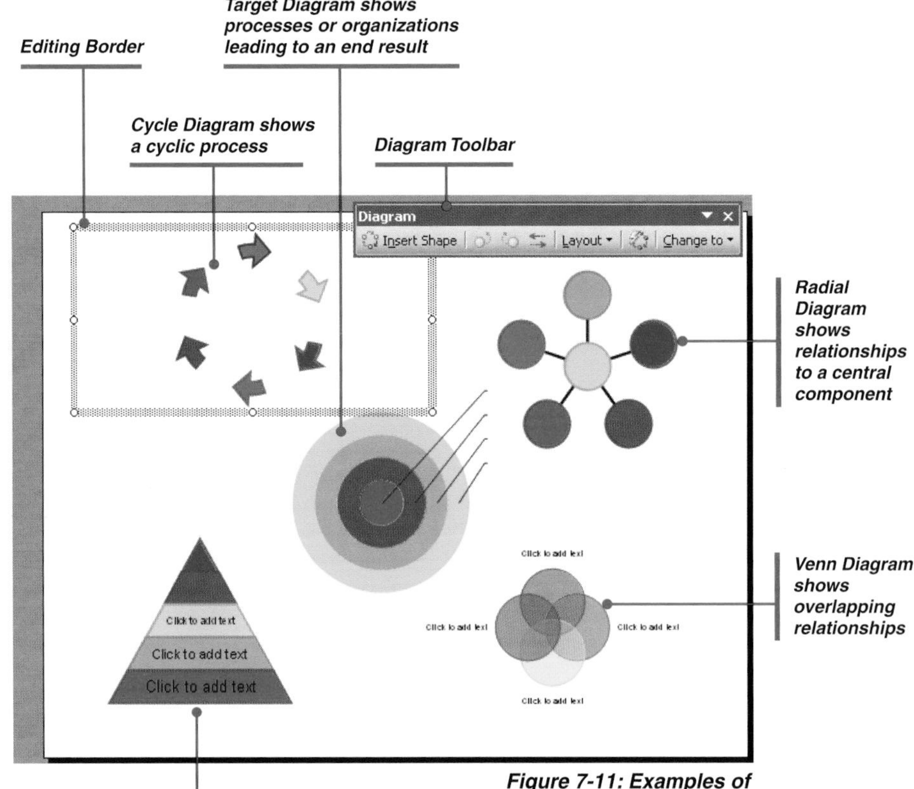

Figure 7-11: Examples of diagrams (modified with color and added shapes) that appear when you insert one on a slide

USING THE DIAGRAM TOOLBAR

(Continued)

REVERSE DIRECTION

Click **Reverse Direction** to move a circle, arrow, bubble, or layer in the reverse direction. The effects will differ depending on the type of diagram being reversed.

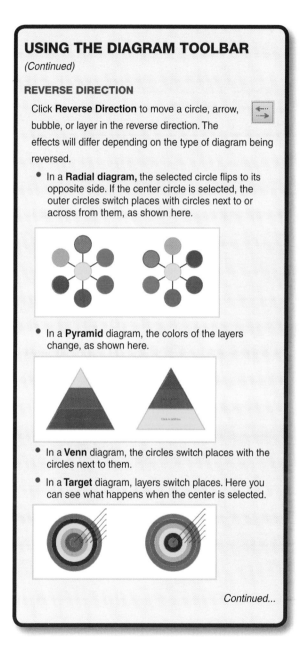

- In a **Radial diagram,** the selected circle flips to its opposite side. If the center circle is selected, the outer circles switch places with circles next to or across from them, as shown here.
- In a **Pyramid** diagram, the colors of the layers change, as shown here.
- In a **Venn** diagram, the circles switch places with the circles next to them.
- In a **Target** diagram, layers switch places. Here you can see what happens when the center is selected.

Continued...

Insert a Diagram

To insert a diagram:

1. Click New Slide, and select a layout with content.
2. Double click the **Insert Diagram** icon. (You can also open **Insert**, and click **Diagram**.) The Diagram Gallery dialog box will appear.

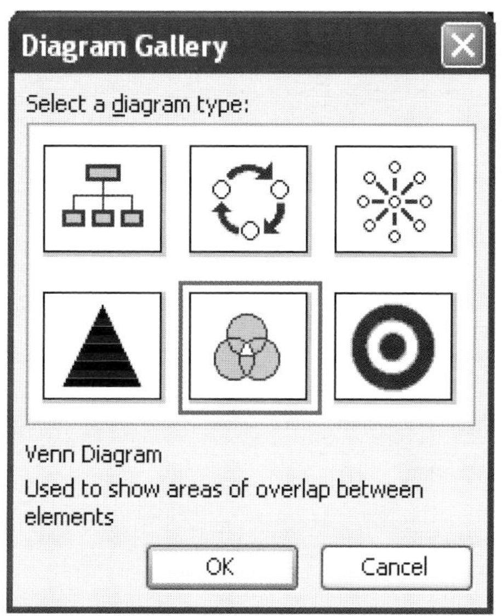

Used to show areas of overlap between elements

3. To show a cyclic process, shown in Figure 7-12, double-click **Cycle Diagram**.
4. Select among the options described in Using the Diagram Toolbar.

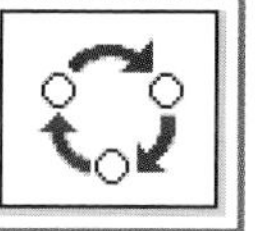

You can build a chart or diagram, such as a flowchart, from scratch by using the Drawing toolbar. See Chapter 8 to learn about the tools in the Drawing toolbar.

USING THE DIAGRAM TOOLBAR

(Continued)

LAYOUT

Click **Layout** to vary the size of the selection box. The Layout menu is displayed.

- Fit Diagram to Contents
- Expand Diagram
- Resize Diagram
- AutoLayout

- **Fit Diagram To Contents** makes the selected box fit the diagram contents.
- **Expand Diagram** expands the box that houses the diagram. It does not make the diagram larger.
- **Resize Diagram** displays sizing handles so that you can manually resize the diagram.
- **AutoLayout** turns the options on and off.

AUTOFORMAT

Click **AutoFormat** to select an alternate style for a diagram. Figure 7-13 shows an example of the Diagram Style Gallery using a pyramid diagram.

CHANGE TO

Click **Change To** to convert the selected diagram to another type.

Change to
- Cycle
- Radial
- Pyramid
- Venn
- Target

Figure 7-12: You can add processes to the cycle

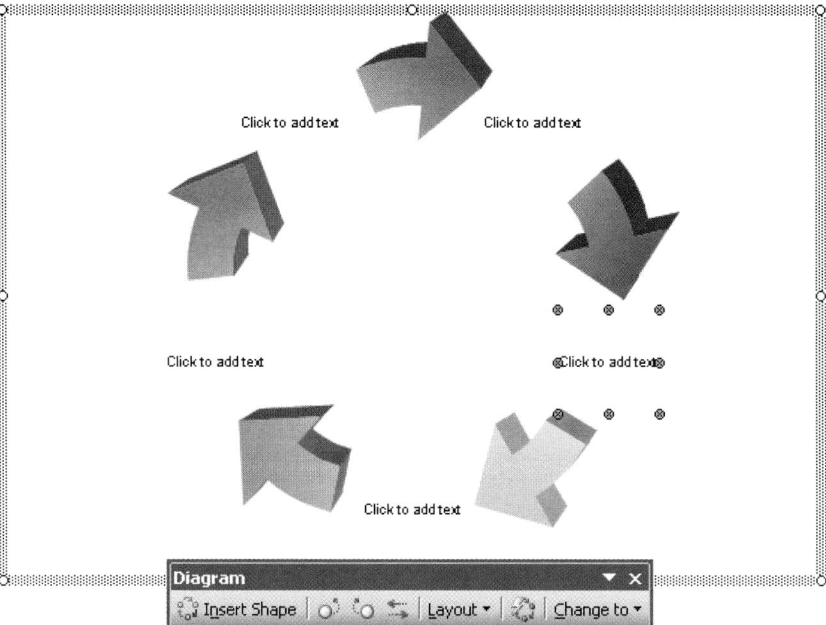

How to...

- *Transition between Slides*
- *Animate Objects and Slides*
- *Use Special Effects in the Slide Background*
- *Hide Master Background Graphics*
- *Use Special Effects with Text*
- *Using the WordArt Toolbar*
- *Draw a Shape*
- *Draw a Line or Arrow*
- *Use AutoShapes*
- *Combine Shapes by Grouping*
- *Working with Curves*
- *Create a Mirror Image*
- *Positioning Shapes*
- *Format Shapes*
- *Add Shadows to Shapes*
- *Add 3-D Effects*
- *Rotate and Flip Shapes*
- *Insert a Text Box*
- *Use Zoom*

Chapter 8 Special Effects and Drawing in PowerPoint

This chapter works with two interesting and creative parts of PowerPoint: its special effects capabilities and its drawing features. Special effects make your slides more interesting, allowing transitioning between slides, animation of objects or slides, and creation of engaging backgrounds. With the drawing features, you can create shapes or use predefined shapes to create your own diagrams, charts, clip art, and other objects to enhance your presentations.

Work with Special Effects

Special effects add that touch of "professionalism" that dresses up your presentation and makes it look professional. For example, transitions between slides are easy to implement and add interest when moving from one slide to the next. Animation also makes a presentation come alive. It adds movement and action to your slides. Finally, as you saw in Chapter 5, you can add gradient colors, textures, patterns, or pictures to your slide background.

Figure 8-1: The Slide Transition task pane allows you to assign transitions to selected slides or to the entire presentation

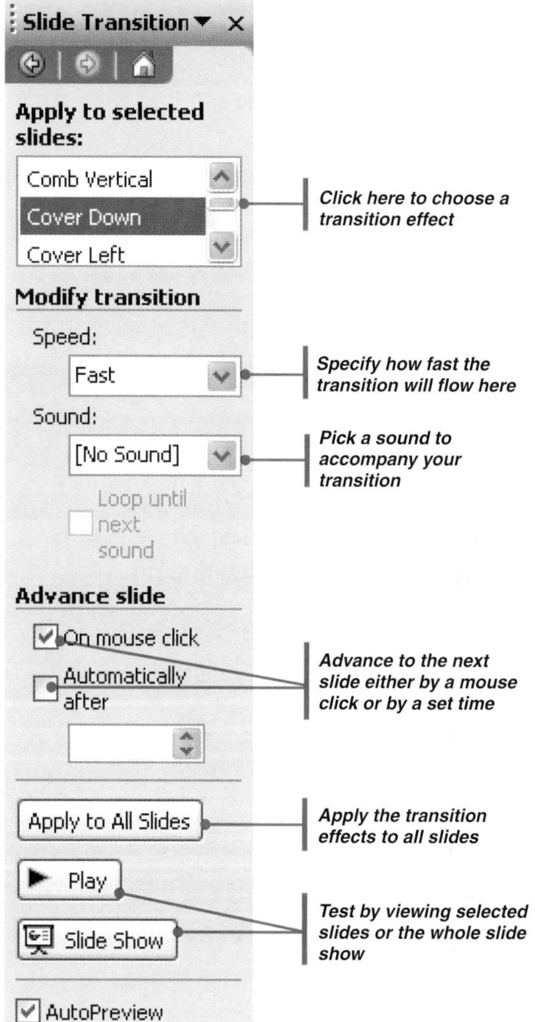

Transition between Slides

Transitions are used to lead from one slide to the next. For example, you can have one slide dissolve and another emerge and have slides slip in from the side or explode from the center. There are many more possibilities, all easy to implement.

1. First, display the slides in Slide Sorter View by clicking **Slide Sorter View**. This will make it easier to see the slides to which you will apply the transitions.
2. Click **Transition** on the Slide Sorter toolbar. The Slide Transition task pane will be displayed, as shown in Figure 8-1. (You can also open **Slide Show** and click **Slide Transition**.)
3. Select one or more slides. To select adjacent slides, press and hold **SHIFT** while you click the first and last slides in the range. To select noncontiguous slides, press and hold **CTRL** while you click the desired slides.
4. Select from these options:
   - Scroll through the list of transitions under **Apply To Selected Slides**, and click a transition for the slides selected in Step 3.
   - Click the **Speed** drop-down list box, and choose between Slow, Medium, and Fast speeds.
   - Click the **Sound** drop-down list box, and choose a sound to accompany the transition. (You might get a message informing you that you need to install the sound feature.)

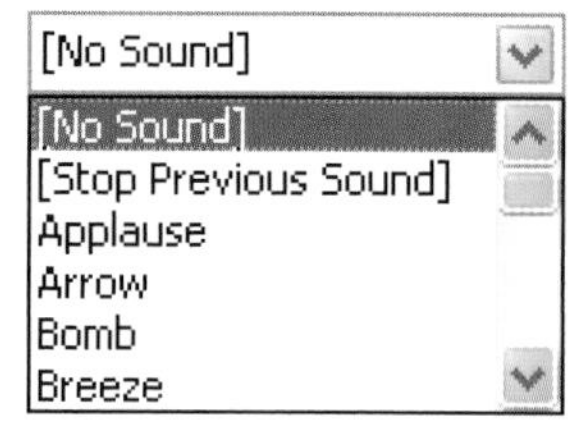

   - Click **Loop Until Next Sound** if you want the selected sound to remain on until the next sound is encountered.
   - Click **On Mouse Click** if you want to advance to the next slide by clicking the mouse.
   - Click **Automatically After** and fill in the time if you want the slides to automatically advance.

Figure 8-2: Use Animation Schemes for a lively look, increased interest, and to draw attention to priority items

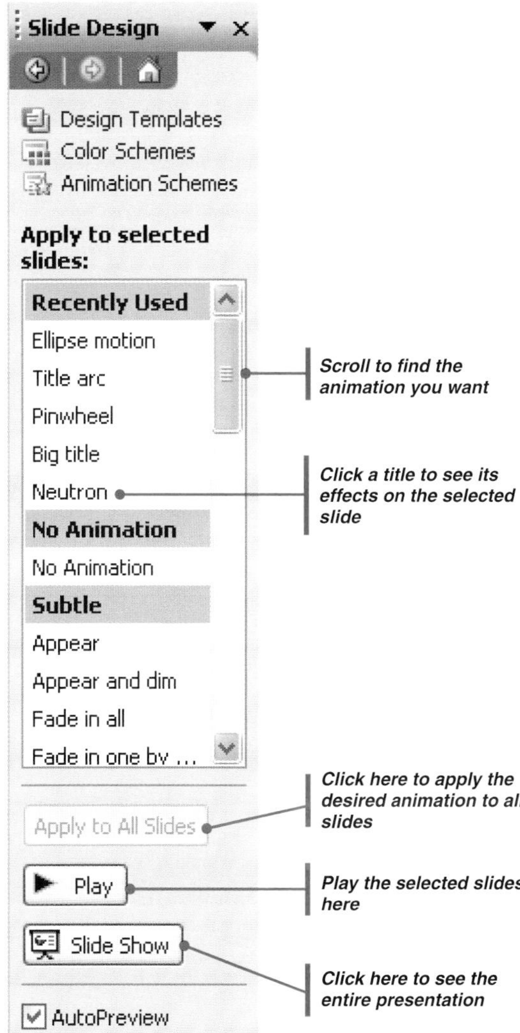

- Click **Apply To All Slides** to assign the transition effects and sound to the whole presentation.
- Place a check mark next to **AutoPreview** to see the transitions displayed as you scroll through the list.

5. Click **Play** to test your transition choice. 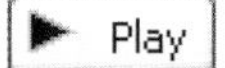

6. Click **Slide Show** to start the slide show with transition effects. 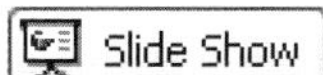

Animate Objects and Slides

Transitions apply when one slide is advanced to another. Animation, on the other hand, is applied to objects on a slide. You can animate text, graphics, charts, and other objects. You can apply animation to all the text, bullets, and graphics on a slide or to selected objects. (To apply animation selectively, see "Use Custom Animation.")

APPLY ANIMATION TO SLIDES

1. Display the slide in **Normal View** so that you can easily see what needs to be animated. Select the object or text on the slide that you want to animate.
2. Click the task pane title bar, and click **Slide Design – Animation Schemes** to bring up some animation schemes, as shown in Figure 8-2. (You can also open **Slide Show** and click **Animation Schemes**.)
3. Choose from among these options:
   - Click under **Apply To Selected Slides** to select an animation that will be applied to the select text or object. As you scroll through the options, you will see Subtle, Moderate, and Exciting offerings.
   - Click **Apply To All Slides** to use the animation on all slides in the presentation.
   - Click **Play** to see the animation played on the selected slides.
   - Click **Slide Show** to play the presentation.

1 2 3 4 5 6 7 8 9 10

Figure 8-3: The Custom Animation task pane allows you to identify specific objects or text to apply an animation scheme to

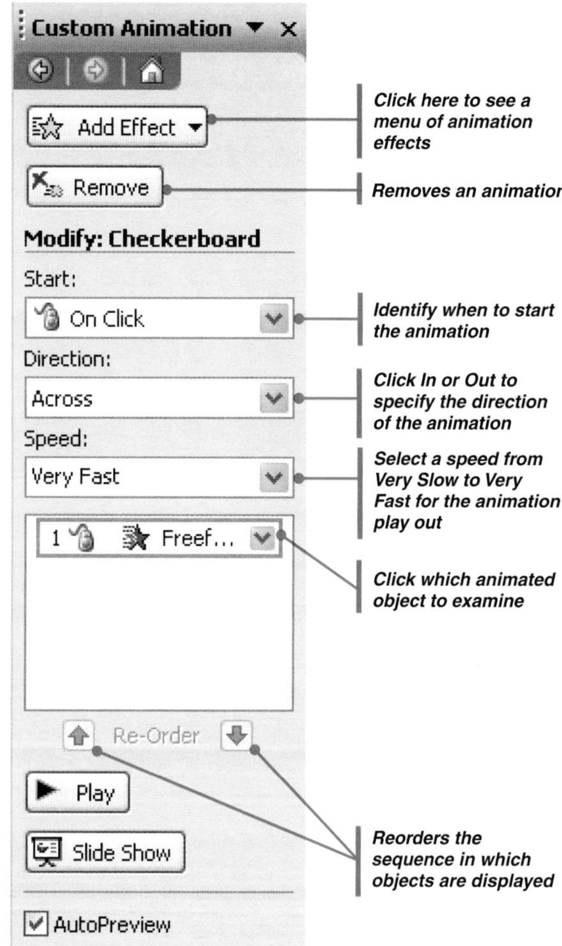

4. Remove the check mark from **AutoPreview** if you do not want to see the automatic preview when you click an animation option.

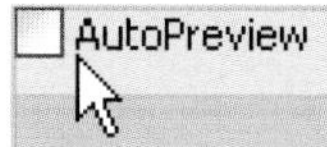

USE CUSTOM ANIMATION

Using Custom Animation, you can select specific objects to be animated:

1. Display the slide in **Normal View**.
2. Open the task pane title bar, and click **Custom Animation**. The task pane will open. Figure 8-3 shows the task pane after an animation effect has been selected.
3. Select the item on the slide to be animated. If you want all text in a text box to be animated the same way, just click in the text box. If you want to have different effects or timing, select each section of text individually by dragging over it.
4. To add an effect, open the **Add Effect** drop-down list box and click a choice. You can choose from animation that is used for an Entrance or Exit to the slide or for Emphasis and select the Motion Path that determines which direction the motion will take. Each of these displays another menu with several animation choices. You may see a fifth choice, Object Actions, if you select an object (such as a chart).
5. To change or delete an animation, first select the object to be changed from the task pane effects list, shown in Figure 8-4. (You can also click the tag number of the effect on the slide.) Then select from these options:

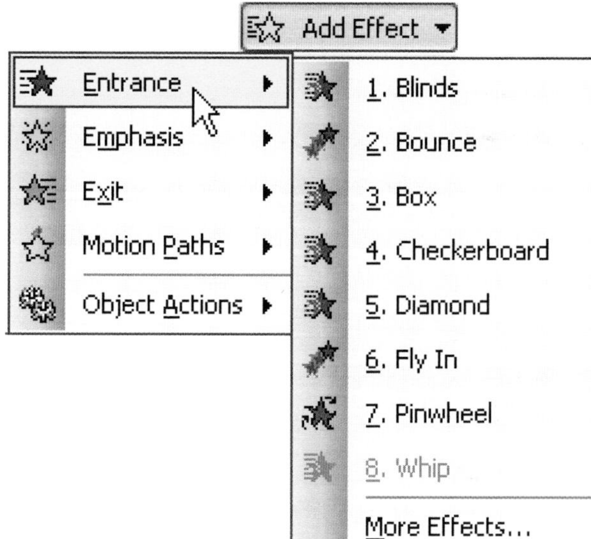

NOTE

As you add animation effects you will see each one listed below in a scrollable list. The icons describe the effects: a mouse is for "On Click" timing; a clock, for "After Previous"; a yellow star, for "Emphasis"; a green star, for "Entrance"; a red star, for "Exit"; a white star, for "Motion Path"; and cogs, for "Object Actions."

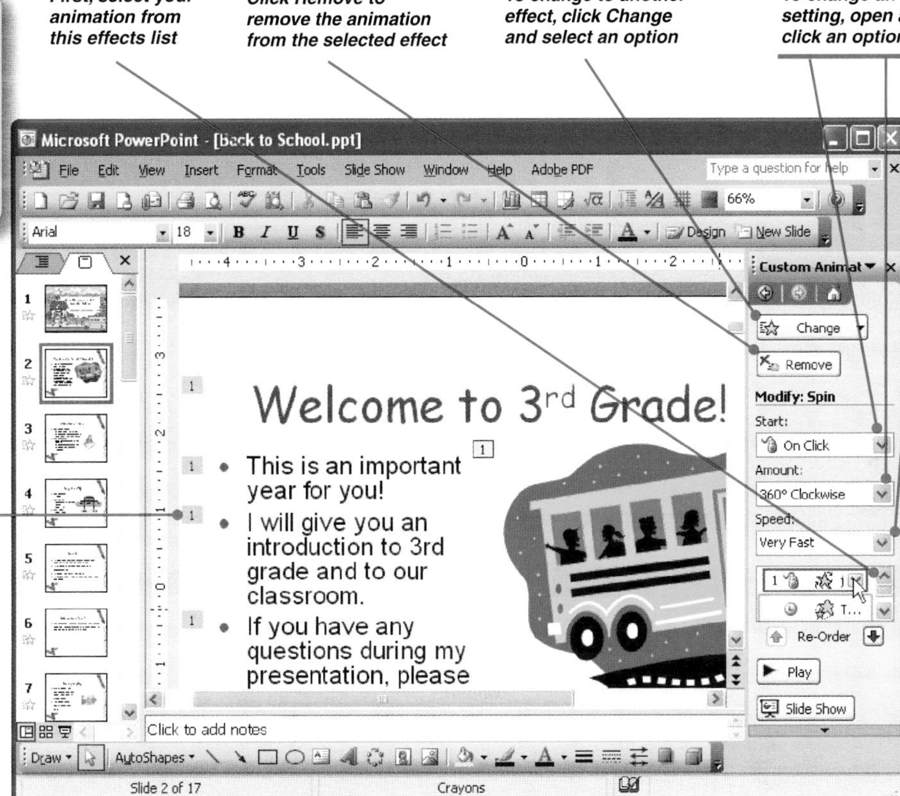

Figure 8-4: Changing an animation is done on the task pane

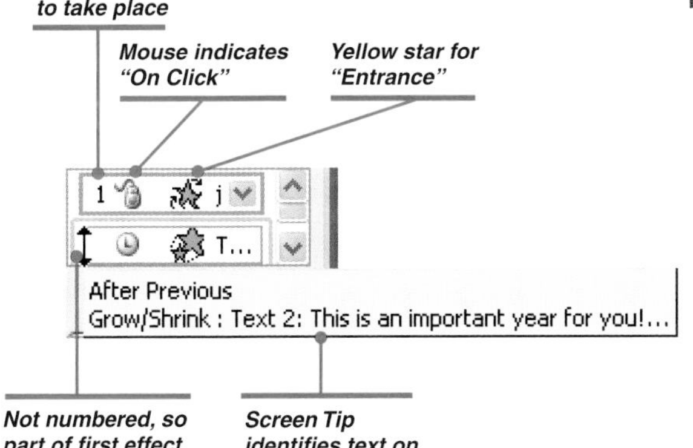

- Click **Change** to switch to another effect.
- Click **Remove** to delete an animation.
- Under Modify, open **Start**, and select when to start the animation.
- Depending on the effects chosen, the options under Modify might differ. You may find Font, Path, Direction, or Size. Select what makes sense.

On Click
On Click
With Previous
After Previous

TIP

If you place the pointer over an item, you will see a Screen Tip that describes the effect. The effects are listed and numbered in the sequence in which they will occur, and the slide items contain tags with the same numbers. So you can look at the tags on the slide and identify which effect is on each item.

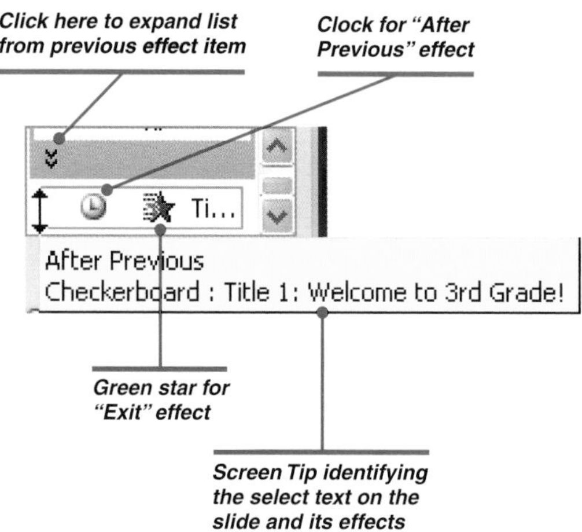

- The third option under Modify will probably be Speed or Duration. The options on the menu may differ as well. Again, click the option that makes sense for the effect you have chosen.

6. Click **Play** to see the effect played out for one slide. Click **Slide Show** to see the whole presentation.

ANIMATE BULLETED TEXT

You can animate a bulleted list so that you can display one bullet at a time, based on when you finish speaking about one item and want to move to the next bullet. Using the following steps, each bullet will be displayed on a click of the mouse button, in the sequence you choose. The bulleted text will be displayed in a different color when you have moved on to the next bullet:

1. Display the task pane by clicking the task pane title bar and clicking **Custom Animation**.
2. Display the slide in **Normal View**.
3. Select the text in the first bullet to be animated.
4. From the task pane, open **Add Effect**, and choose an **Entrance** style. Add any timing, sound, and direction needed for the effect.

5. Open **Start** and click **On Click**.
6. Click the down arrow by the effects list on the task pane, and choose **Effect Options**.

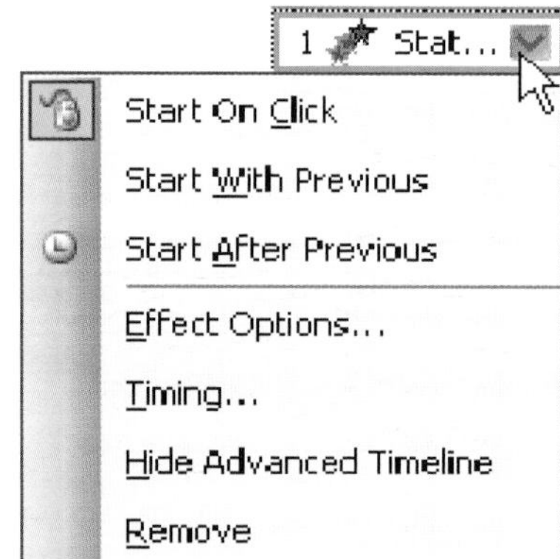

NOTE

You will not see any animations based on "On Click" until you view the presentation with Slide Show. Play does not show them.

7. Click the **Effect** tab, and open the **After Animation** drop-down list box.

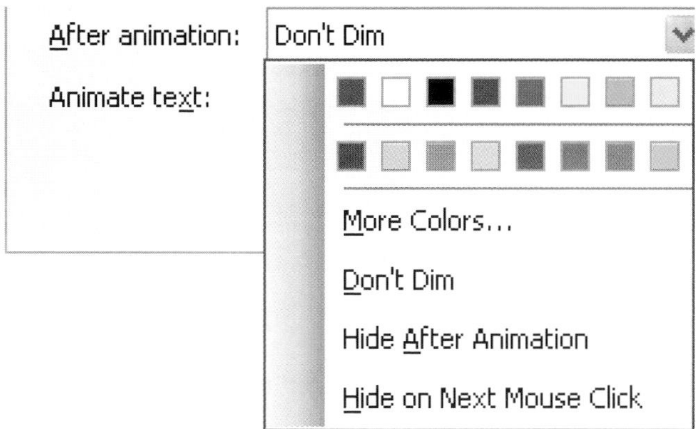

8. Click a color that is less dominant than the beginning text color. Click **OK**.
9. Repeat Steps 3 through 8 for each bulleted item. Be sure to choose **On Click** in Step 5.
10. When you are finished, click **Slide Show** to see how it works. Click the screen or slide image in Step 5. Click for each new bullet and for the next slide to be displayed. Figure 8-5 shows an example.

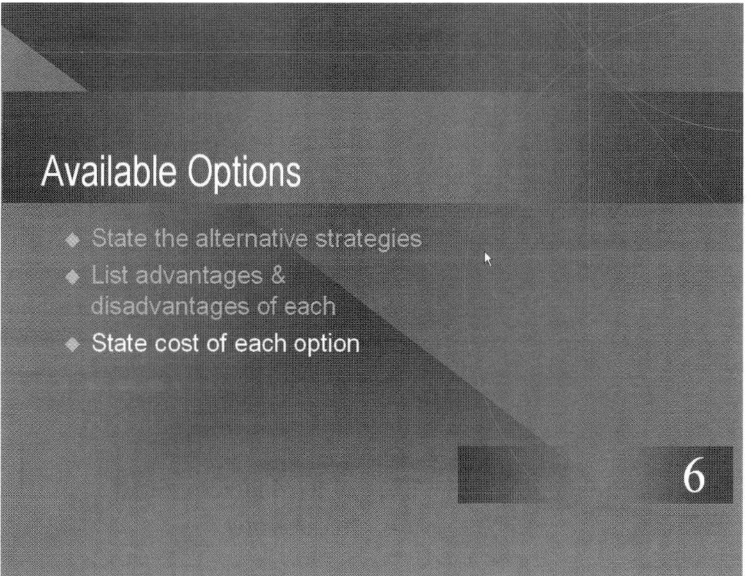

Figure 8-5: The third bullet is currently being discussed and will turn the same color as the other two bullets when the presenter clicks the mouse

Use Special Effects in the Slide Background

You can use special effects – such as gradient colors, texture, and patterns – in slide or placeholder backgrounds. (See Chapter 5 for how to create these special effects with tables.)

1. Select the slides or placeholder you want to receive the special effect.
2. Bring up the **Fill Effects** dialog box:
   - If you want to apply the special effects to a placeholder, click the **Fill Color** down arrow on the Drawing toolbar, and click **Fill Effects** (if the Drawing toolbar is not showing, open **View**, select **Toolbars**, and click **Drawing),**

   –Or–

   - If you want to apply the special effects to the slide background, open **Format** and click **Background**. The Background dialog box will open. Click the color drop-down box, and click **Fill Effects**, as shown in Figure 8-6.
3. The Fill Effects dialog box will be displayed. Click the tab you want: Gradient, Texture, Pattern, or Picture.

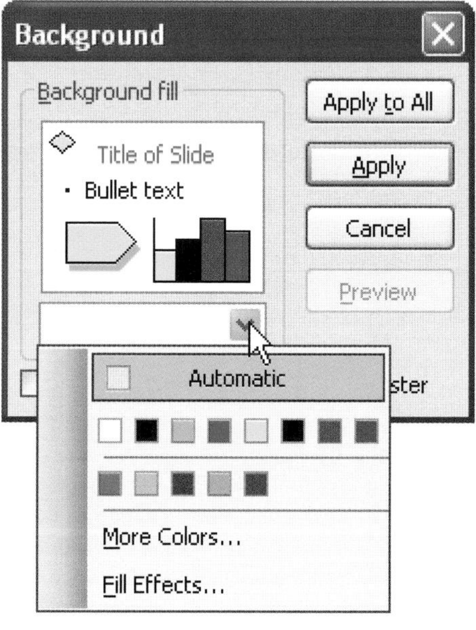

Figure 8-6: The Fill Effects dialog box is available from the Background dialog box, among other menu and toolbar options

CREATE A GRADIENT BACKGROUND FOR YOUR SLIDES

Figure 8-7 shows the Gradient tab, which you use to employ this special effect.

1. Select a **Colors** option:
   - **One Color** gives you a one-color gradient result. Click the color from the **Color 1** drop-down list. In this case, you can drag the slider between **Dark** and **Light** to get the lighting or shade you want. The Variants preview pane shows the results.
   - **Two Colors** gives you two colors blended into one gradient result. You can select from the Color 1 and Color 2 drop-down lists.
   - **Preset** allows you to select one of the gradient color schemes from the Preset Colors drop-down list box.
2. Select a Transparency percentage to set the degree of transparency, or "see throughness," of the color.
   - Click the horizontal arrows on **From** and **To** to change the relative extent to which each color will be transparent.
   - Click the spinners to set the degree of transparency more precisely.

Figure 8-7: The Gradient tab is used to blend, or graduate, the color of your slide background between one or two shades of color, which you select

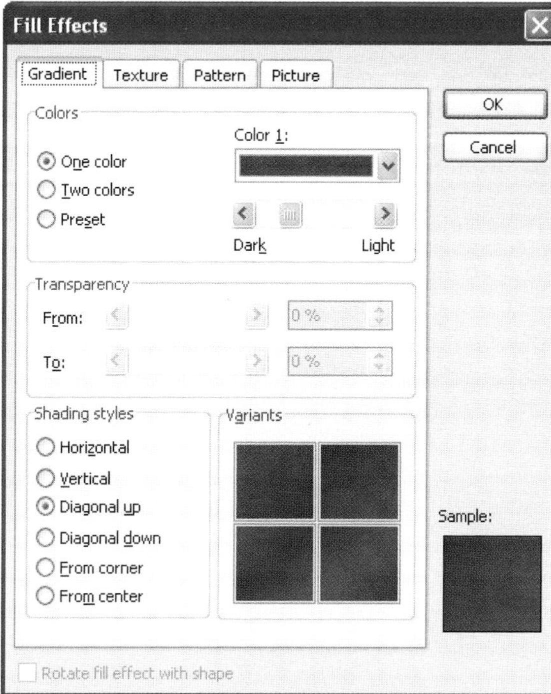

3. Select a Shading Style and Variants to determine in which direction the shading will fall across the slide. To see the differences, click each option.
4. When you are done, click **OK**. (If you entered the Fill Effect dialog box from the Background dialog box, you then need to click **Apply To All** or **Apply**.)

CREATE A TEXTURED BACKGROUND FOR YOUR SLIDES

To create a slide with a textured background, use the Texture tab, shown in Figure 8-8.

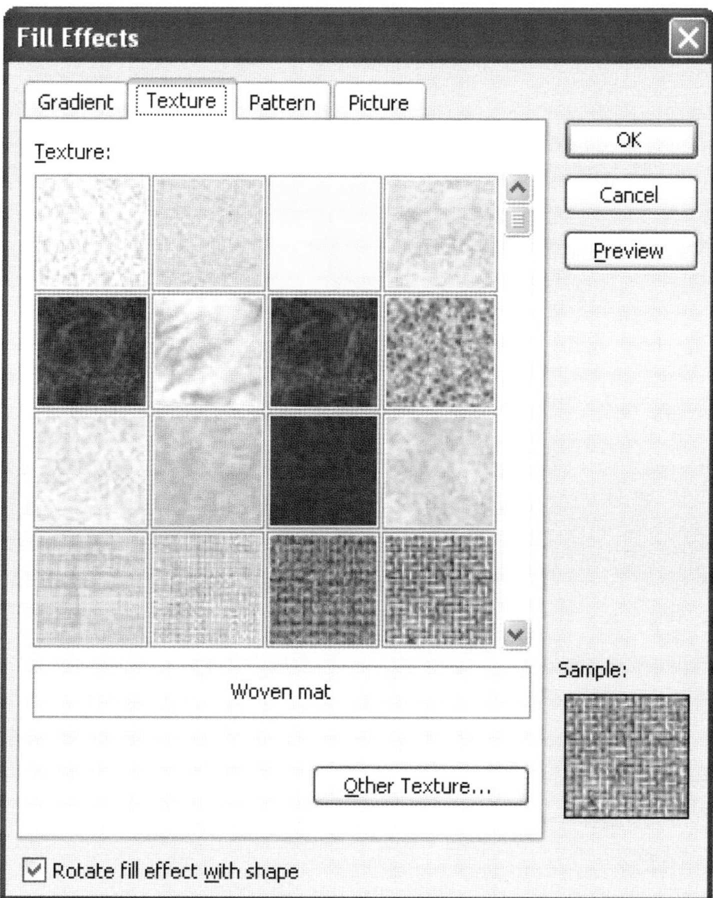

Figure 8-8: The Texture tab offers a selection of textures to provide interesting flavors to your slides

1
2
3
4
5
6
7
8
9
10

TIP

All of these effects can be previewed on the selected elements by clicking **Preview** in the respective tabs.

Figure 8-9: The Pattern tab provides blended colors in a patterned background

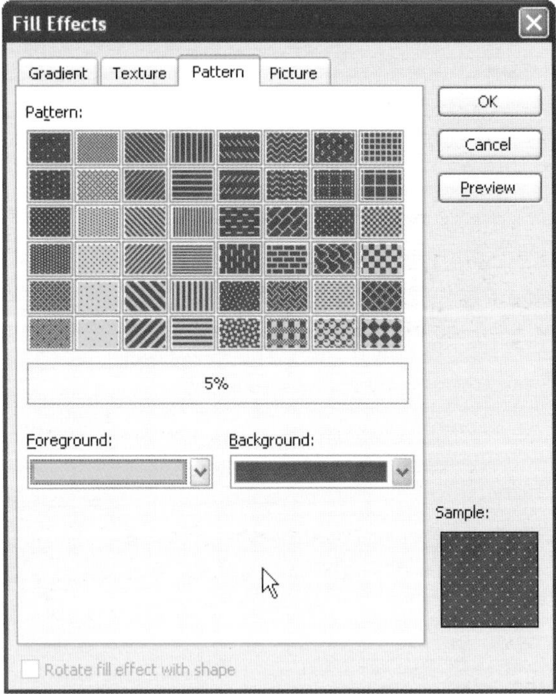

1. Click the texture that you want to fill your slide. An example is seen here:

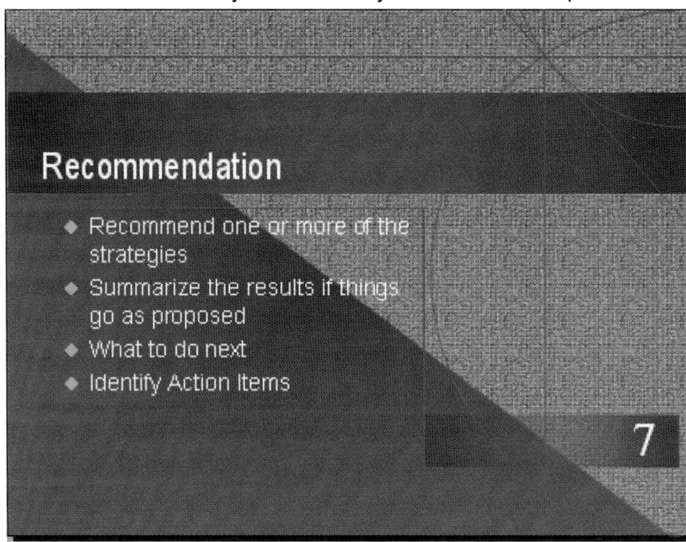

2. Click **Other Texture** to see additional samples of textures if you can't find THE one in the main pane.
3. Click **OK**. (If you entered the Fill Effect dialog box from the Background dialog box, you then need to click **Apply To All** or **Apply**.)

CREATE A PATTERNED BACKGROUND FOR YOUR SLIDE

To create a patterned background in your slides:

1. After clicking the **Pattern** tab, select your **Foreground** and **Background** colors. The resulting pattern will be reflected on the slide. An example is shown in Figure 8-9.
2. When you are finished, click **OK**. (If you entered the Fill Effect dialog box from the Background dialog box, you then need to click **Apply To All** or **Apply**.)

USE A PICTURE AS BACKGROUND ON A SLIDE OR PLACEHOLDER

You can add pictures to your slide as a background effect. The picture will be entered into a placeholder or onto the slide background, depending on how you select it.

TIP

To have the photo appear on all slides in a presentation, place it in a master slide. Open **View**, select **Masters**, click **Slide Master**. Click the master slide to select it. Then open **Format** and choose **Background**. Open the color drop-down box, and click **Fill Effects**. Click the **Picture** tab. As described in the picture section, insert a picture into the master slide. The photo will occupy the background of all slides in the presentation. If you want the picture to be only in a placeholder, select the placeholder and open the **Fill Colors** dialog box on the Drawing toolbar. Open **Fill Effects**, and click the **Picture** tab. Follow the directions in "Use a Picture as Background for a Slide or Placeholder." Then size the photo and drag it to where you want it positioned.

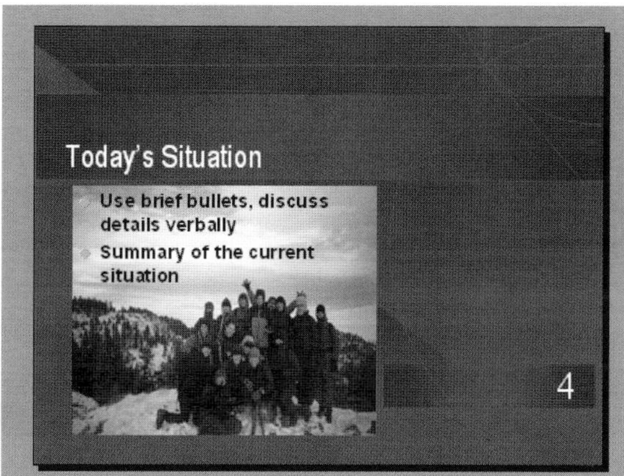

Figure 8-11: You can use a photo in a placeholder on your slide

1. Select the slide or the placeholder to contain the picture. (You get a placeholder from the layout assigned to the slide.)
2. If you want to place the picture in a placeholder, open the **Fill Color** menu on the Drawing toolbar. If the Drawing toolbar is not showing, open **View**, select **Toolbars**, and click **Drawing**.

   –Or–

   If you want to use a picture as background to the slide, open **Format** and choose **Background.**
3. Select **Fill Effects**, and click the **Picture** tab. 
4. Click **Select Picture**. The Select Picture dialog box will open.
5. Search for the picture you want. Select it, and choose **Insert**. The Fill Effects dialog box will appear with the picture, as can be seen in Figure 8-10.
6. Click **OK**, and the picture will be inserted into the placeholder of your slide or onto the slide background. You can see an example in Figure 8-11.
7. To resize the picture, if it is in a placeholder, drag the handles of the placeholder containing the picture.

Figure 8-10: An example of selecting a picture to insert in a slide

1
2
3
4
5
6
7
8
9
10

> **NOTE**
>
> To display hidden graphics, simply reverse the process. Select the slides, open **Format**, and click **Background**. On the dialog box, click **Omit Background Graphics From Master** to remove the check mark, and then click **Apply**.

Hide Master Background Graphics

You can hide all elements inserted into the Master Slide, such as graphics, the date/time, slide numbers, and so on, on all slides or selected slides. (To remove graphics or shapes from regular slides, simply select them and press DELETE.) To move graphics from the Master Slide:

1. In Normal View or Slide Sorter View, select the slides on which you want to hide the background graphics.
2. Select **Format** and click **Background**. The background dialog box will be displayed, as shown here:

- To hide all the graphics, click **Omit Background Graphics From Master**.
- Click **Apply** to make the changes to selected slides.
- Click **Apply To All** to make the changes to all slides.
- Click **Preview** to see the changes apply to the slide in the Slide Pane.

Use Special Effects with Text

Special effects can be easily added to text using WordArt to give a graphic artist's professional touch.

APPLY A WORDART EFFECT

1. If the Drawing toolbar is not showing, open **View**, select **Toolbars**, and click **Drawing**.
2. If you have text, perhaps a heading that you want styled, select it. You can also type it in later as part of these steps.
3. Click the **WordArt** button to display the WordArt gallery of text styles, shown in Figure 8-12.

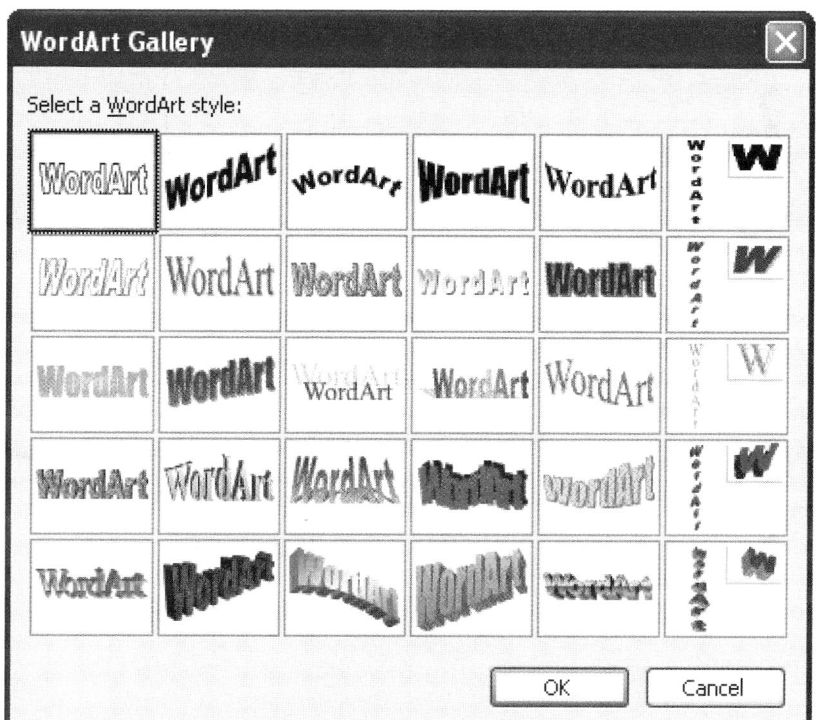

Figure 8-12: The WordArt Gallery offers many styles for your text

TIP

To determine whether a picture in your presentation is a bitmap or a vector image, select the picture and drag it. If it becomes blurry, or if you can see the pixels, it is a bitmap. If it becomes smoother, it is a vectored, or line-drawn, picture.

TIP

To change the text in a WordArt image, double-click the image so that the Edit WordArt dialog box appears. Type the changed text, and click **OK**.

USING THE WORDART TOOLBAR

- **Insert WordArt** to apply a WordArt effect to text (See "Apply a WordArt Effect.")
- **Edit Text** to enter or change the text and its font characteristics

- **WordArt Gallery** to get to the effects again
- **Format WordArt** to change formatting properties of colors and lines, size, position, and web alternative text (used while a web page is loading)
- **WordArt Shape** to re-contour the WordArt effect to that of 40 different shapes

- **WordArt Same Letter Heights** to adjust all WordArt characters to the same vertical size
- **WordArt Vertical Text** to shift the positioning of WordArt characters to a vertical orientation from the typical horizontal orientation
- **WordArt Alignment** to choose from several alignment formats
- **WordArt Character Spacing** to choose from several spacing options

4. Select a style that's close to what you want (you can "tweak" it later), and click **OK**.
5. If you have selected text previously, it will appear on the Edit WordArt dialog box. When you click OK, you will see the text inserted onto your slide as an object.

   –Or–

   If you have not selected the text previously, you can type it directly into the Edit WordArt Text dialog box. Click OK. The text will be displayed with the effect you selected.
6. Drag the object to where you want it. You can delete the original selected text.

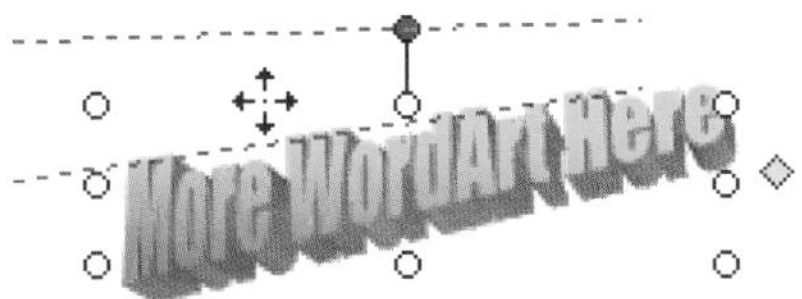

WORK WITH WORDART

A WordArt toolbar displays when you select text that has a WordArt effect applied to it. Use its buttons to edit, apply different styles, and change the contour of the effect. Click one or more of the following to achieve the indicated effects:

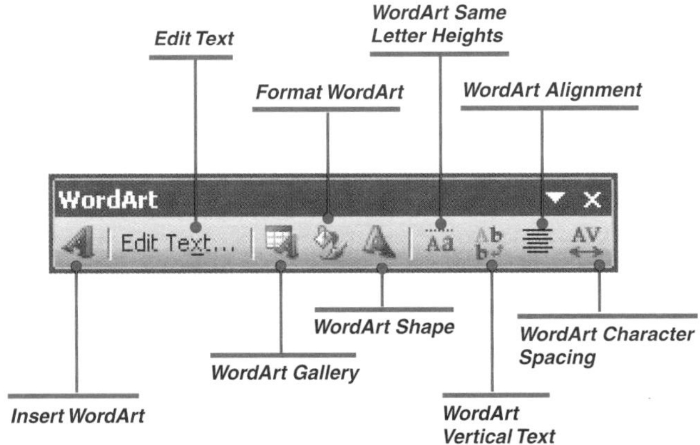

NOTE

A quick way to copy a shape is to press **CTRL** while you drag the shape. A copy will be moved, not the original shape.

Draw in PowerPoint

The drawing feature in PowerPoint enables you to create line drawings and art with simple-to-use tools. It presents tools to draw lines, circles, rectangles, and other shapes; and it contains predefined shapes for inserting a variety of arrows and other connecting symbols, flow-chart symbols, callouts, stars and banners, and other useful shapes. Table 8-1 lists the tools on the Drawing toolbar.

TABLE 8-1: THE DRAWING TOOLBAR

Draw ▾	Draw	Displays a menu of commands for working with objects
	Select Object	Turns the pointer into a selection tool
AutoShapes ▾	AutoShapes	Displays a menu of predefined shapes
	Line	Turns the pointer into a line-drawing tool
	Arrow	Turns the pointer into an arrow-drawing tool
	Rectangle	Enables the pointer to draw squares and rectangles
	Oval	Enables the pointer to draw circles and ovals
	Text Box	Enables the pointer to insert a text box
	Insert WordArt	Displays a menu of WordArt Styles
	Insert Diagram	Displays a gallery of diagrams (see Chapter 7)
	Insert Clip Art	Enables you to find and insert clip art (see Chapter 6)
	Insert Picture	Enables you to find and insert photos (see Chapter 6)
	Fill Color	Fills an object with a selected color

1

2

3

4

5

6

7

8

9

10

TABLE 8-1: THE DRAWING TOOLBAR CONTINUED

	Line Color	Allows you to choose a color for a selected line
	Font Color	Allows you to choose a color for selected text
	Line Style	Assigns a style to a selected line
	Dash Style	Assigns a style to a selected dashed line
	Arrow Style	Assigns a style to a selected arrow line
	Shadow Style	Places a shadow on a selected object
	3-D Style	Places a 3-D effect on a selected object

NOTE

To draw multiple occurrences of one shape with an AutoShape tool, double-click the button. That turns it on until you press **ESC** to turn it off.

TIP

To create a perfect square or circle, press **SHIFT** while you drag the Rectangle or Oval tool. To make the rectangle or oval larger or smaller, select it by clicking it, and then drag the sizing handles that appear on the shape.

Draw a Shape

You can draw a variety of shapes using the Drawing toolbar. These are contained within the AutoShapes (see AutoShapes Basic Shapes tool option), but they are so commonly used that they are also displayed on the Drawing toolbar. The Rectangle and Oval drawing tools can be used to create many other shapes. Use the following steps as a model for drawing whatever shape you want.

1. To draw a square or rectangle, click the **Rectangle** button. To draw a circle or an oval, click the **Oval** button.
2. Place the crosshair pointer where you want the edge of the shape to begin. Drag the pointer diagonally across the slide, shaping the rectangle or oval. Release the pointer when you are finished.

TIP

To change the length of a line or arrow, select it, and then drag the selection handle. Press SHIFT to change the length without changing the angle or direction of the line or arrow. You can select a line and drag it into another position. (See "Format AutoShapes" to see how to add color or vary the thickness or style of a line or arrow.

Draw a Line or Arrow

You can draw straight lines or connecting arrows with the Drawing toolbar. These are also part of the AutoShapes (see "Use AutoShapes") Lines tools, although they are also displayed on the Drawing menu.

1. To draw a straight line, click the **Line** button. To draw a connecting arrow, click the **Arrow** button.
2. Place the crosshair pointer where you want one end of the line or arrow to begin, and drag the pointer across the slide to where you want the line or arrow to end. Release the pointer when you are finished. To make the line perfectly straight, press **SHIFT** while you drag the pointer.

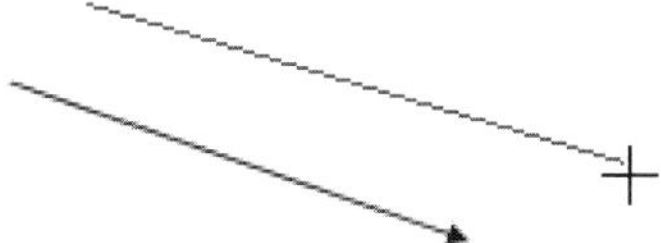

Use AutoShapes

AutoShapes are small prebuilt drawings you can select. You can also create your own drawings by modifying existing shapes or drawing freeform. The prebuilt AutoShapes and tools for creating your own drawings are located together on the Drawing toolbar. The following steps illustrate how to access the Basic Shapes of AutoShapes:

1. From the Drawing toolbar, click **AutoShape**. The AutoShapes menu will be displayed, as shown in Figure 8-13.
2. Select the tool type you want, and click the exact shape. The pointer will become a crosshair.
3. Drag your pointer in the approximate location and for the size you want. In the case of freeform tools, see the QuickSteps entitled "Working with Curves."

Figure 8-13: The AutoShapes menu offers many shapes you can insert into your own drawings

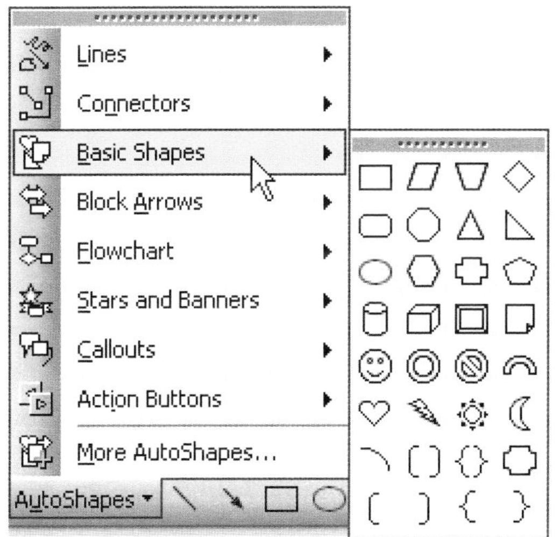

1 2 3 4 5 6 7 8 9 10

1 2 3 4 5 6 7 8 9 10

TIP

You can enter text directly into a selected shape. Just start typing. The text will be centered within the shape. However, it will not word wrap, so you must press **ENTER** to skip to the next line. The text becomes a part of the object.

NOTE

If you cannot easily ungroup an image,it may be a bitmap, which can't be ungrouped and converted to an object. In this case, use an imaging program to edit the image before placing it back into your table.

TIP

Click **More AutoShapes** to display the Clip Art search task pane so that you can search Microsoft Online for additional shapes. They will be automatically displayed. You can also type <u>autoshapes</u> in the Search For text box to search clip art collections. Choose to search in all collections, and click **Go**.

Combine Shapes by Grouping

You can combine shapes for any number of reasons, but typically you work with multiple shapes to build a more complex drawing. So you don't lose the positioning, sizing, and other characteristics of these components, you can group them. They are then treated as one object.

GROUP SHAPES

1. Select the shapes to be grouped by clicking the first shape and then pressing and holding **SHIFT** while selecting the other shapes.

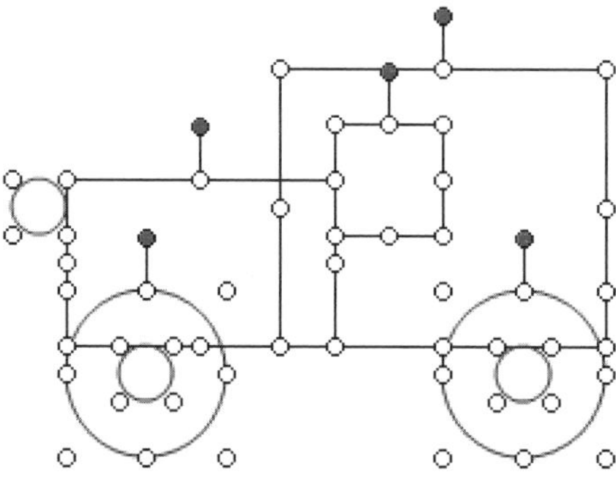

2. Open **Draw** on the Drawing toolbar, and click **Group**; or right-click one of the selected graphics, select **Grouping**, and click **Group**. A single set of selection handles surrounds the perimeter of the combined shapes. Coloring, positioning, sizing, and other actions now affect the shapes as a group, instead of individually.

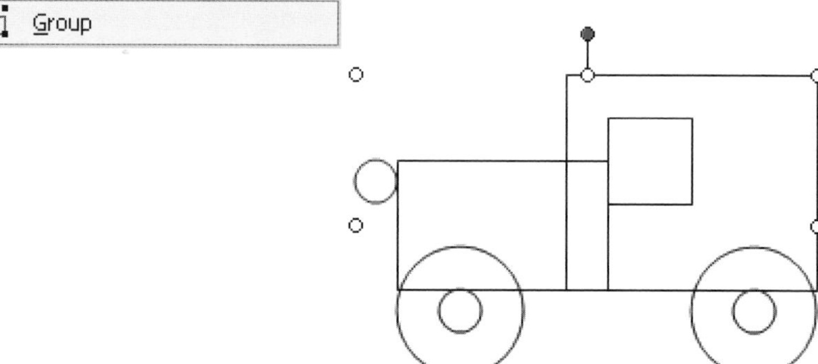

QUICKSTEPS

WORKING WITH CURVES

Freeform tools are available to draw curved AutoShapes.

CREATE A CURVE

On the Drawing toolbar, click **AutoShapes**, point at **Lines**, and click one of the following:

- **Curve** to create flowing shapes. Click the cross pointer to establish the curve's starting point. Move the pointer and click to continue creating other curvatures. Double-click to set the end point and complete the drawing.

  –Or–

- **Scribble** to create pencil-like lines. Drag the pencil icon to create the shape you want. Release the mouse button to complete the drawing.

  –Or–

- **Freeform** to use a combination of curve and scribble techniques. Click the cross pointer to establish curvature points and/or drag the pencil pointer to create other designs. Double-click to the set the end point and complete the drawing.

ADJUST A CURVE

1. Right-click a selection handle of the curve, and click **Edit Points**. Black rectangles (*vertices*) appear at the top of the curvature points.
2. Drag a vertex to reconfigure the curve's shape.

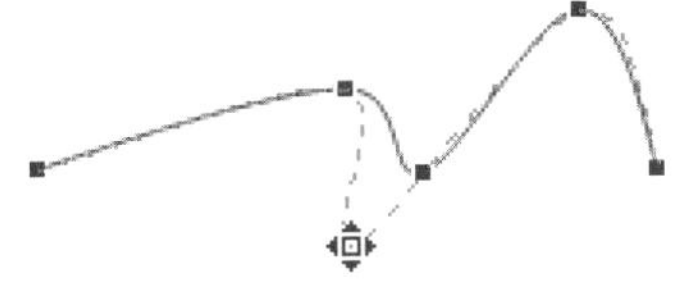

3. Change any other vertex, and click outside the curve when finished.

Continued...

UNGROUP SHAPES

To separate a group into individual shapes again, select the group, point at **Draw** on the Drawing toolbar, and click **Ungroup**; or right-click the group, point at **Grouping**, and click **Ungroup**.

RECOMBINE A GROUP AFTER UNGROUPING

After making a modification to a shape that was part of a group, you don't have to reselect each component shape to reestablish the group. Select any shape that was in the group, open **Draw** on the Drawing toolbar, and click **Regroup**; or right-click a member shape, point at **Grouping**, and click **Regroup**.

Create a Mirror Image

You can create a mirror image of a shape using some of the AutoShape tools.

1. Select the shape (not a placeholder) you want to be half of the mirror image, right-click, and from the context menu, click **Copy Here**. A second copy of the image is placed on top of the original and is selected.
2. Open **Draw**, select **Rotate Or Flip**, and click **Flip Horizontal** or **Flip Vertical** depending on how you want the image to look.
3. Press SHIFT and select the original graphic. (You may need to separate the two images in order to select both of them.) Both graphics should be selected.

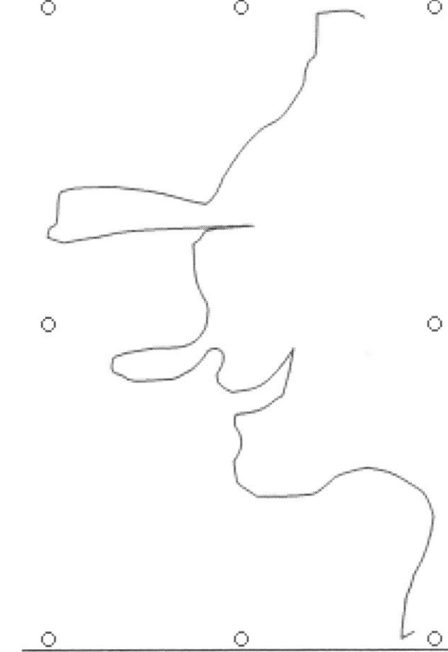

WORKING WITH CURVES *(Continued)*

ROTATE A CURVE

1. Click a curve to select it. A green rotate handle will appear on the curve.
2. Place the pointer over the handle, and drag it to rotate the curve in the way you want.

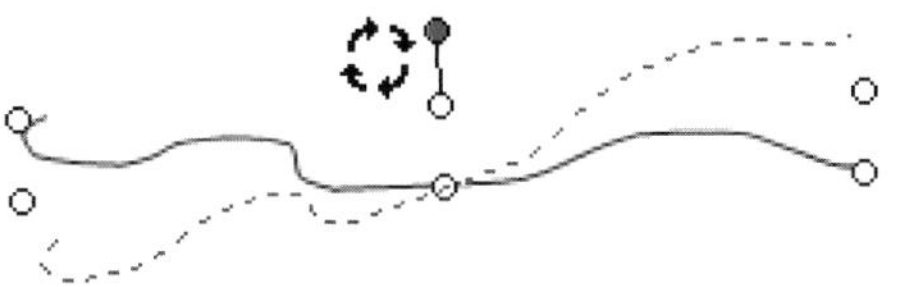

CLOSE A CURVE

Right-click a selection handle of the curve, and click **Close Path**.

OPEN A CURVE

Right-click a selection handle of a closed curve, and click **Open Path**.

TIP

If you cannot select the shape you want, send the shapes on top of the stack to the back, until the one you want is on top.

4. Open **Draw**, point at **Align Or Distribute**, and click an applicable alignment to make the graphics even. (In Figure 8-14, Distribute Horizontally was used.)
5. If you need to, select one shape, press and hold **CTRL**, and press the applicable arrow key to nudge the shape into a mirrored position.

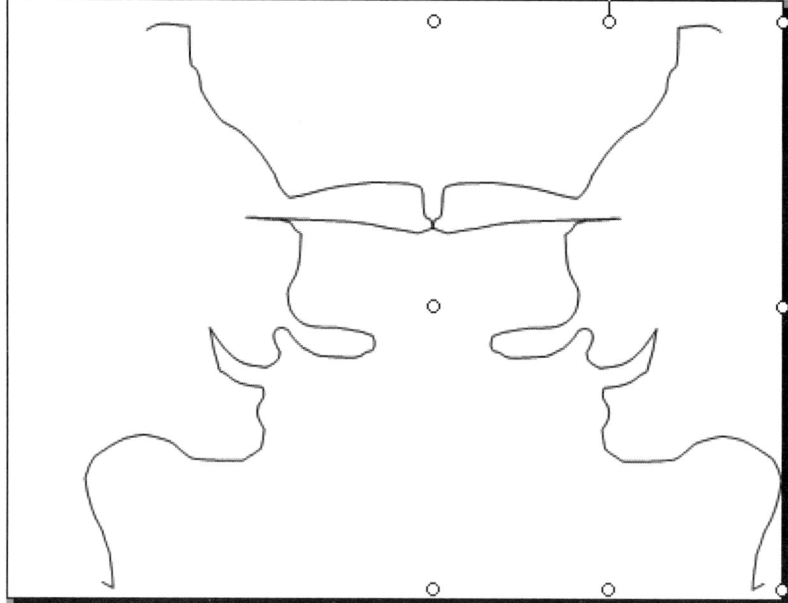

Figure 8-14: This mirror image was flipped horizontally and then aligned with Distribute Horizontally to get facing witches

See "Rotate and Flip Shapes" later in the chapter to learn more about those tools.

POSITIONING SHAPES

Shapes can be positioned by just dragging them, a technique with which you are probably familiar. However, PowerPoint also provides a number of other ways to help you adjust where a shape is in relation to other shapes and objects.

MOVE SHAPES INCREMENTALLY

- Select the shape or group, press and hold CTRL, and press the arrow key in the direction you want to move.

  –Or–

- Open **Draw** on the Drawing toolbar, point at **Nudge**, and click the direction you want the graphic moved.

REPOSITION THE ORDER OF STACKED SHAPES

You can stack graphics by simply dragging one on top of another. However, sometimes it is difficult to edit or format a shape within the stack. To reposition the order of the stack, right-click the shape you want to change, point at **Order**, and click one of these:

- **Bring To Front** to move the graphic to the top of the stack
- **Send To Back** to move the graphic to the bottom of the stack
- **Bring Forward** to move the graphic up one level (same as Bring To Front if there are only two graphics in the stack)
- **Send Backward** to move the graphic down one level (same as Send To Back if there are only two graphics in the stack)

Continued...

Format Shapes

You can use the buttons on the Drawing toolbar to format shapes or simply double-click the shape to get the Format AutoShape dialog box.

FORMAT AUTOSHAPES

1. Double-click the shape to be formatted. The Format AutoShape dialog box will be displayed, as shown in Figure 8-15.
2. For color and line attributes, click the Colors And Lines tab.
   - To fill the shape with color, open the **Color** drop-down box, and click the color you want.
   - To vary the line color, style, or shape, click open the appropriate drop-down box, and click the element you want.
   - To select an arrow style or size, click the beginning and ending style or size drop-down box, and click your choice.

Figure 8-15: The Colors And Lines tab in the Format AutoShape dialog box is used to add color and change the style or width of lines and arrows

3. To size, rotate, or scale the shape, click the **Size** tab.
   - Click the **Height** or **Width** up or down arrows to get a precise measurement.
   - To rotate the shape precisely, click the up and down arrows of the **Rotation** box.
   - To scale the shape, click the **Height** and **Width** up and down arrows to precisely change the scale. Click **Lock Aspect Ratio** to maintain the height-to-width ratio. Click **Relative To Original Picture Size** to have the change be in proportion to the original size. Click **Best Scale For Slide Show** to have PowerPoint determine the best scale for the presentation.

1 2 3 4 5 6 7 8 9 10

POSITIONING SHAPES *(Continued)*

ALIGN SHAPES

- To align a shape to an invisible grid, select the shape, open **Draw** on the Drawing toolbar, and click **Grid And Guides**. In the Grid And Guides dialog box, place a check mark next to **Snap Objects To Grid**.
- To align shapes to one another, select the shapes, open **Draw** on the Drawing toolbar, and click **Grid And Guides**. In the Grid And Guides dialog box, place a check mark next to **Snap Objects To Other Objects**. The shapes will be "attracted" to each other when they are moved close to each other. This is useful for stacking objects or for selecting and moving them as a unit.
- To display the grid or guides and establish grid and guide settings, open **Draw** and click **Grid And Guides**. In the dialog box, check or set the appropriate settings for **Grid Settings** and **Guide Settings**.

EVENLY SPACE SHAPES

Select the shapes, open **Draw** on the Drawing toolbar, point at **Align Or Distribute**, and click **Distribute Horizontally** or **Distribute Vertically**.

TIP

To restore the original color on a shape, line, or text, click **Automatic** of the color palette.

- Click the **Resolution** drop-down list box, and click the resolution you want for the shape.
- Click **Reset** to restore the original size of the Height and Width.

4. Click **OK** to close the dialog box.

FORMAT SHAPES AND LINES WITH COLOR

Working with the color palettes and dialog boxes is covered in detail in Chapter 3, "Create a Color Scheme."

- Click **Fill Color** to fill a selected shape with color. To see a menu of colors, click the arrow on the Fill Color button. A palette of colors will be displayed. Click the color you want, or click **More Fill Colors** for a complete color selection, as seen in Figures 8-16 and 8-17. Click **Fill Effects** to see how you can put gradient backgrounds, patterns, textures, and pictures in a shape. See "Use Special Effects in the Slide Background," earlier in this chapter, for more information on how to use the dialog boxes.

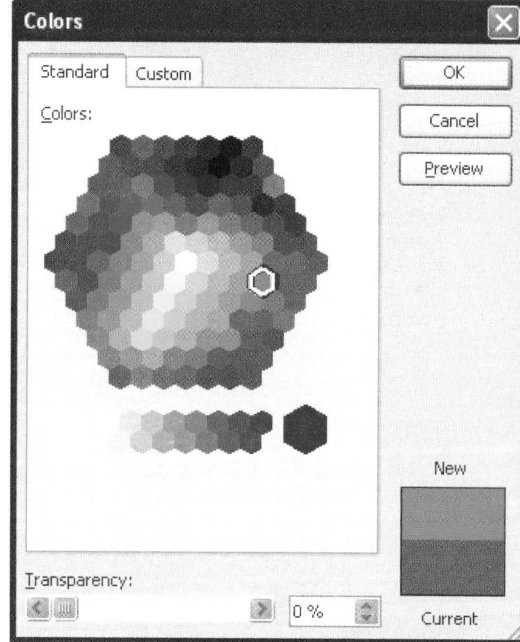

Figure 8-16: A complete selection of standard colors for fill, lines, and text is offered with this dialog box

Figure 8-17: You can create custom colors by clicking the hue and then dragging the slider to your precise color choice

- Click **Line Color** to assign a color to lines. To see a menu of colors, click the arrow on the Line Color button. From the palette, click the color you want, or click **More Line Colors** to see the complete color selection, as in Figures 8-16 and 8-17. Click **Patterned Lines** to see a menu of patterns that can be applied to the selected lines. (See "Create a Patterned Background for Your Slide" for information on how to use the Pattern tab.)

- Click **Font Color** to assign color to selected text. Click the arrow on the Font Color button to see a palette of colors. To see additional colors, click **More Colors**. The dialog box shown in Figures 8-16 and 8-17 will be displayed.

FORMAT LINES

- Click **Line Style** to see a menu of line styles, as shown in Figure 8-18. Click the style you like; or click **More Lines** to see the Format AutoShapes dialog box, shown in Figure 8-15, where you can be very precise in your line measurements.
- Click **Dash Style** to see a menu of dashed line styles. Click the style you want for your selected line.
- Click **Arrow Style** to see a list of varying arrow points and weights. Click the one you want for your selected line. To see additional styles, click **More Arrows**. The Format AutoShapes dialog box, shown earlier in Figure 8-15, will be displayed.

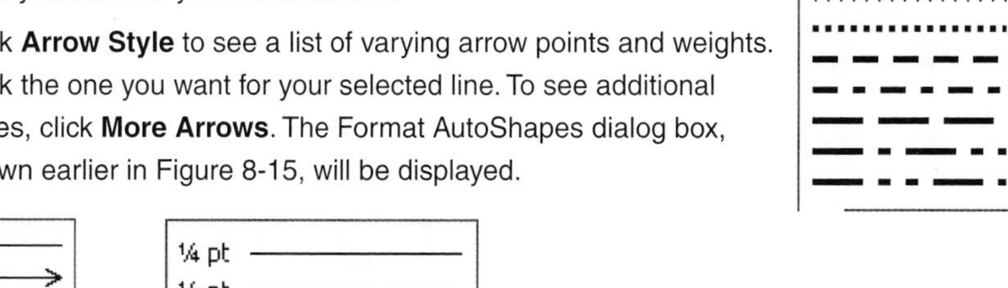

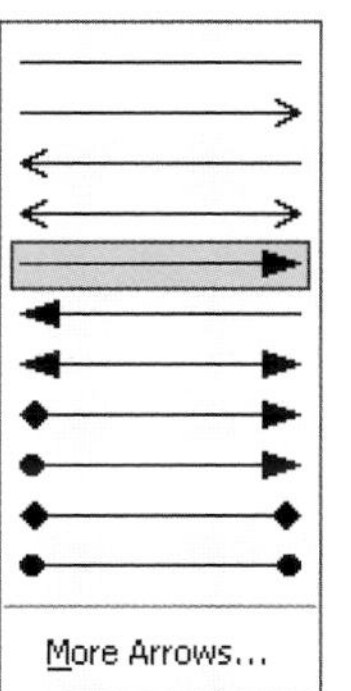

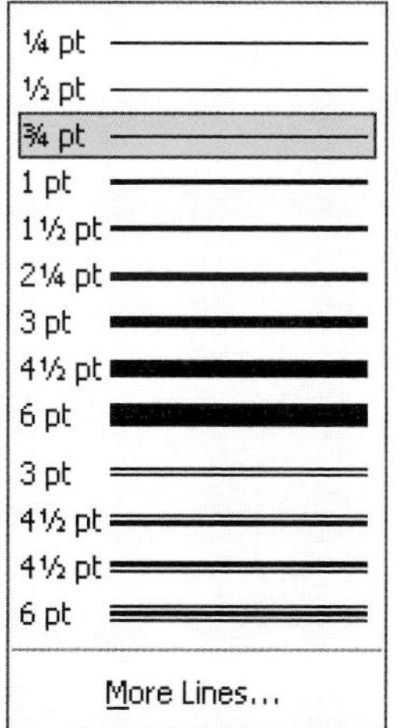

Figure 8-18: Line styles are varied by point size and by combinations of double or triple lines

CAUTION

Do not remove the line around a shape unless you have first added a fill. Without the line or a fill the graphic is invisible except for the handles that display when it's selected.

Shadow On/Off

Nudge Shadow Up

Nudge Shadow Left

Shadow Settings

Nudge Shadow Down

Shadow Color

Nudge Shadow Right

Figure 8-19: Shadows applied to shapes add dimension and suggest a light source

REMOVE EFFECTS

- To **remove a fill**, select the shape, choose the **Fill Color** down arrow on the Drawing toolbar, and click **No Fill**.
- To **remove the outline border** around a shape, select the shape, choose the **Line Color** down arrow on the Drawing toolbar, and click **No Line**.
- To **remove text coloring**, select the text, choose the **Font Color** down arrow, and click **Automatic** to display black.

Add Shadows to Shapes

To apply a shadow to a shape:

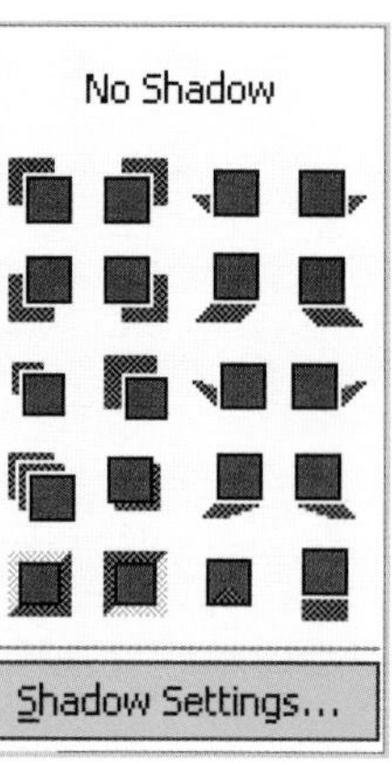

1. Select the shape by clicking it.
2. Click **Shadow Styles** on the Drawing toolbar. Click a style. The shadow will be applied. An example is shown in Figure 8-19.
3. Manipulate the shadow using one of the tools on the Shadow Settings toolbar. Click **Shadow Settings** on the Shadow Style menu to display the toolbar.
   - Click **Shadow On/Off** to hide or show the shadow on the selected shape.
   - Click **Nudge Shadow Up**, **Nudge Shadow Down**, **Nudge Shadow Left**, or **Nudge Shadow Right** to move the shadow by tiny increments up or down, left or right. As you click the button, the shadow on the selected shape will move.
   - Click **Shadow Color** to change the color of the shadow, such as has been done in Figure 8-19. When you click the down arrow, a color palette will appear, and on it you can select a color. You can also click **Semitransparent Shadow** to lighten the shade of the color selected or click **More Shadow Colors** to get the dialog box shown in Figure 8-16 and 8-17.

TIP

You can nudge a shape by pressing **CTRL** while you click a right, left, up or down arrow. The shape will move tiny increments, allowing you to align the shape exactly where you want it.

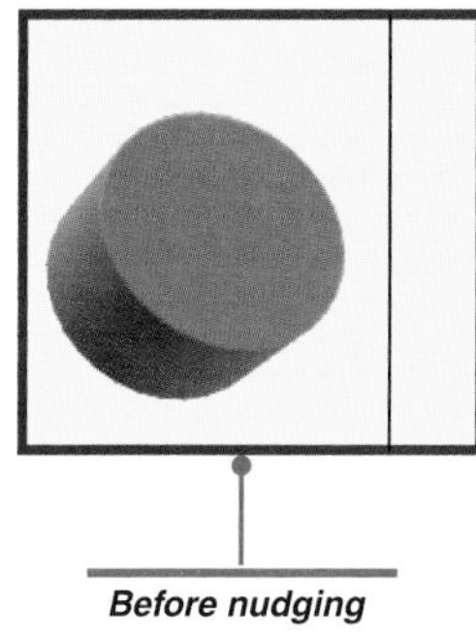

Before nudging

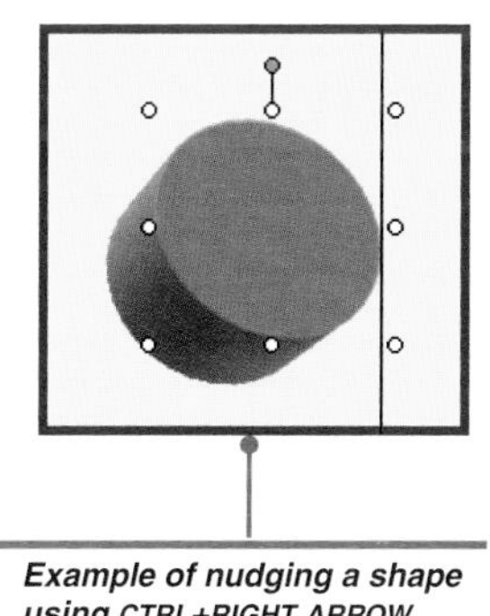

Example of nudging a shape using CTRL+RIGHT ARROW

Add 3-D Effects

You can add 3-D effects to your shapes to give them depth as well as height and width.

1. Select your shape by clicking it.

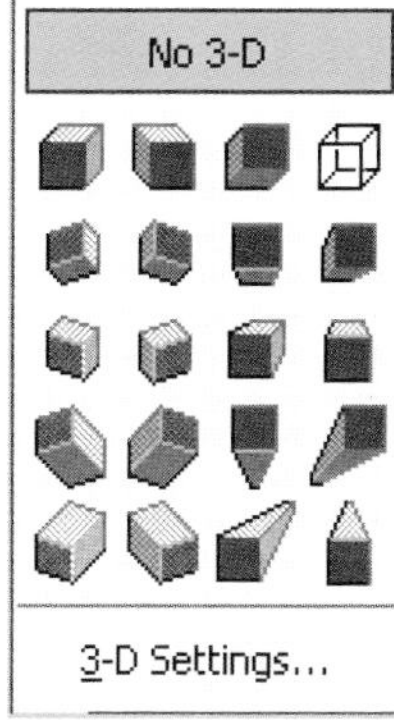

2. Click **3-D Styles** on the Drawing toolbar. A menu of 3-D effects will be displayed, as shown above:

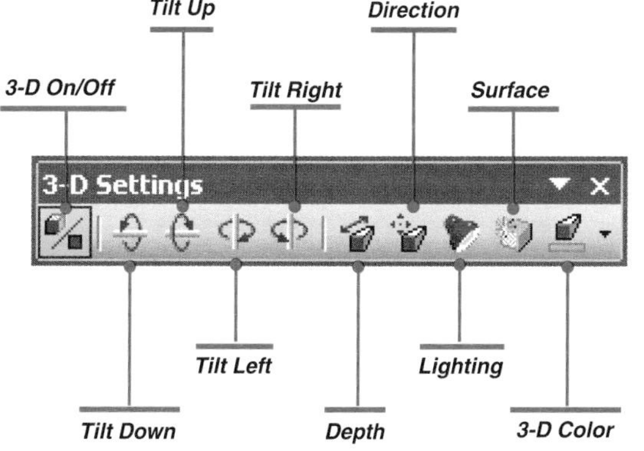

Figure 8-20: The 3-D Settings toolbar offers many ways to manipulate the effects

1 2 3 4 5 6 7 8 9 10

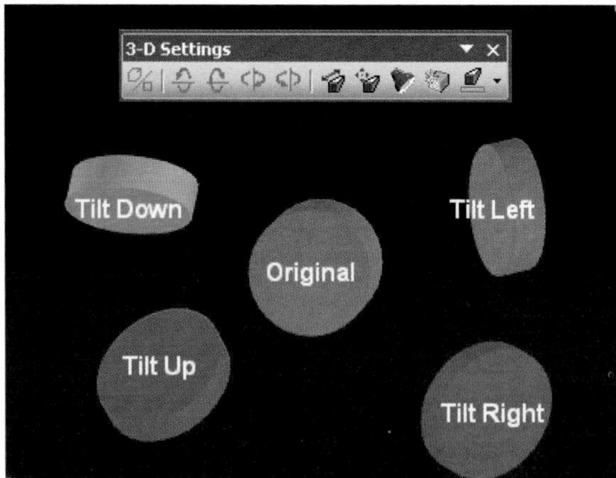

Figure 8-21: Tilting a shape allows you to orient it precisely to the "look" you want to display

- Click **D On/Off** to remove or display the effects.
- Click **Tilt Down**, **Tilt Up**, **Tilt Left**, or **Tilt Right** to turn or orient the shape in a different direction. Figure 8-21 shows the effects of using ten clicks of each button to tilt the shape.
- Click **Depth** to make the shape longer or deeper. You can specify how much depth to add, from 36 pt. (points) to Infinity or to a custom number.

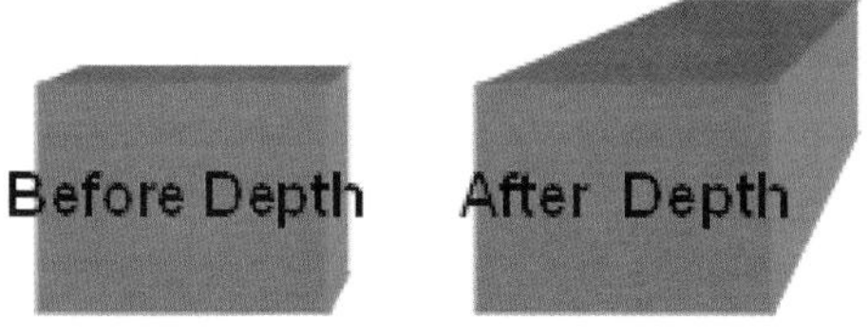

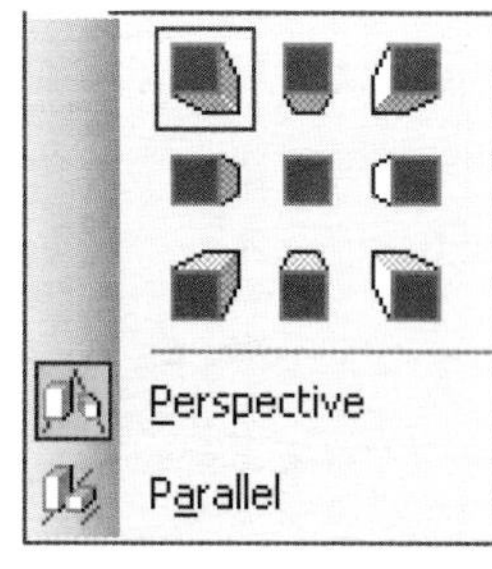

- Click **Direction** to turn the shape so it is facing straight-on, left to right, or up to down. By clicking **Perspective**, you can make one side of the shape smaller, giving the appearance that it is placed further away. Clicking **Parallel** gives the shape parallel lines, as if all parts were equally distant from the viewer.
- Click **Lighting** to display a menu with light-source options that places a light source in varying directions, as seen in Figure 8-22. As you pass the pointer over a lamp icon, you will see the effects on the box in the center and how it will change your selected shape. You can also control the degree of light by clicking **Bright**, **Normal**, or **Dim**.
- Click **Surface** to apply four "finishes" to a selected shape: Wire Frame, Matte, Plastic, or Metal.
- Click the **D Color** down arrow to display the standard palette of colors. If you want additional options, click **More D Colors** to see the dialog boxes shown in Figures 8-16 and 8-17.

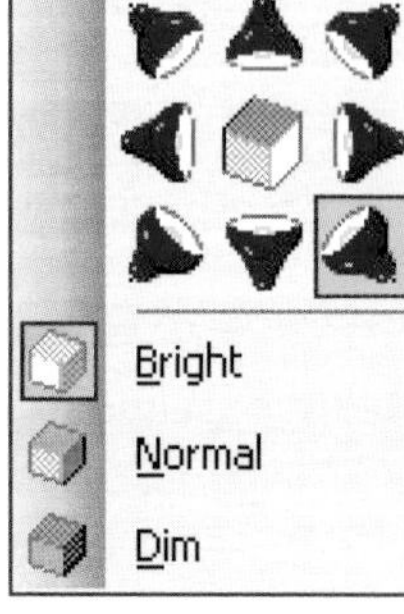

Figure 8-22: The Lighting option on the 3-D toolbar alters the light source on a shape

Rotate and Flip Shapes

Rotating is turning a shape clockwise or counterclockwise by a specific amount. Flipping is turning it upside down, vertically or horizontally. Figure 8-23 shows what happens with Rotate and Flip commands.

1. Select the shape to be rotated or flipped.
2. Open **Draw** on the Drawing toolbar, point at **Rotate And Flip**, and click your choice. Figure 8-23 shows all choices except Free Rotate, which allows you to rotate clockwise or counterclockwise as many degrees as you want.

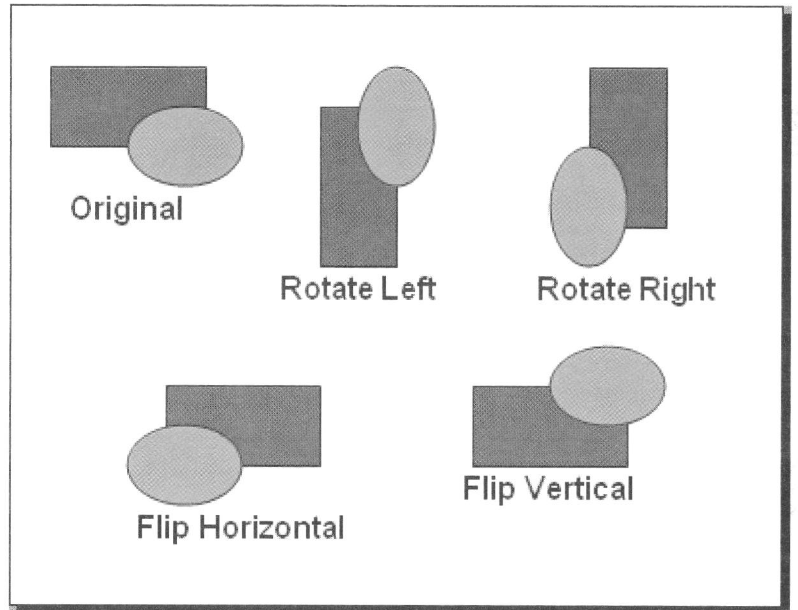

Figure 8-23: The ability to rotate and flip shapes adds power and speed to your drawing task

TIP

If you choose Rotate 90 degrees twice, you will turn the shape 180 degrees; three times, 270 degrees; four times, 360 degrees, or back to the original position. Similarly, if you Flip a shape twice, it will return to its original position.

Insert a Text Box

To insert a text box to contain a shape, perhaps for a label:

1. Open **Insert** and click **Text Box**. The pointer will be a straight line with a cross on the lower part of it.
2. Drag the pointer, which becomes a cross, across the slide to form a box.
3. Click in it and type.

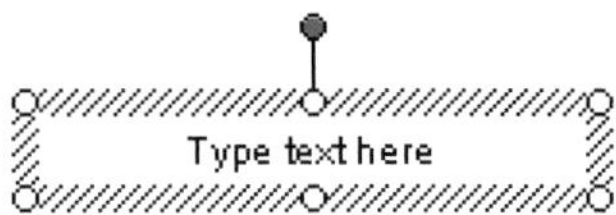

Use Zoom

Increasing and decreasing the size of an object may be essential to verifying that your work is accurate. In fact, you may find that you routinely flip in and out of Zoom view as you review your slides.

1. Click the selected shape to be magnified.
2. Open the Zoom drop-down list box on the Standard toolbar, and click the magnification you want.

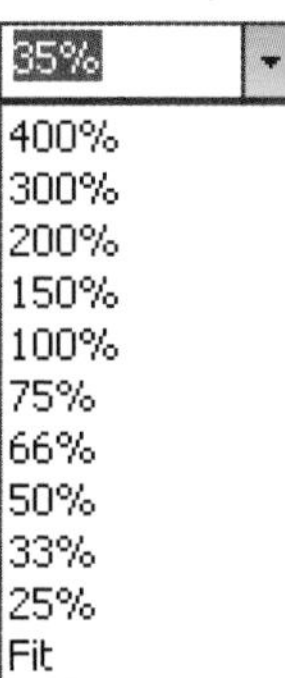

How to...

- *Insert Sounds from the Clip Organizer*
- *Insert Sound from a File*
- *Insert a CD Track*
- *Set Options for Sound Effects*
- *Change Size of Embedded Sound Files*
- *Record Sound Files*
- *Changing Video Options*
- *Use Video Files in Your Presentation*
- *Package Presentation Files*
- *Connect to Web Pages with Hyperlinks*
- *Use Action Buttons to Connect to a Web Page*
- *Transfer to an FTP Site*
- *Publish Your Presentation as a Web Page*
- *Changing Web Options*
- *Use the Web Toolbar*
- *View a Slide Show in a Default Browser*

Chapter 9
Working with Multimedia and the Internet

This chapter covers two very special and important areas: multimedia files and presentations on the Internet. You will see how to insert and play audio and video files and CD sound tracks in your presentation. You will see how to manage your sound files. You will then actually record sound files and package all linked files together with the presentation. Using the Internet, you will be able to make your presentation available to others who may not have PowerPoint. You will learn how to store the presentation as a web page on a local computer or an intranet or to a site on the Internet. You will see how to publish your files to an FTP (File Transfer Protocol) site. You will view your presentation with a browser.

1 2 3 4 5 6 7 8 9 10

NOTE

To hear multimedia files in PowerPoint, you must have a sound card and speakers, available from a wide variety of manufacturers. You can find out what sound equipment you have by opening **Start**, clicking **Control Panel**, and in Classic view, double-clicking **Sounds And Audio Devices**. Click the **Audio** and **Voice** tabs to find your hardware.

Figure 9-1: The Clip Art task pane is where you can find sound files on your computer or the Internet

Use Multimedia Files in Your Presentation

Music, sound, and video clips can be inserted on a slide or object on a slide. The clips can come from from files on your computer, Microsoft's Clip Organizer, the Internet, or from another network. You can record your own sounds and add them to the Clip Organizer or use tracks from a CD.

The sounds you insert can be made to start automatically when the slide is displayed or to start when you click the mouse.

Insert Sounds from the Clip Organizer

PowerPoint provides an inventory of sounds that you can use for your slides, or you can use files from Microsoft Online.

1. In Normal view, select the slide to have the sound.
2. Open **Insert**, choose **Movies And Sounds**, and click **Sound From Clip Organizer**.
3. Under **Search For** on the Clip Art task pane, shown in Figure 9-1, type the subject, such as "laugh," "airplane," or "fireworks," for which you want a sound.
4. In the **Search In** drop-down list box, click the sources you want to search. You may search for sounds in your own collections, from Microsoft Office, or from Microsoft Online.
5. In the **Results Should Be** drop-down list box, **Sounds** should be selected (if not, select it). If you want only certain types of files (AIFF, MIDI, or WAV), for instance, open the **Sounds** list by pressing the **+** (plus sign) and clearing the files you do not want by removing the check marks from the check boxes.

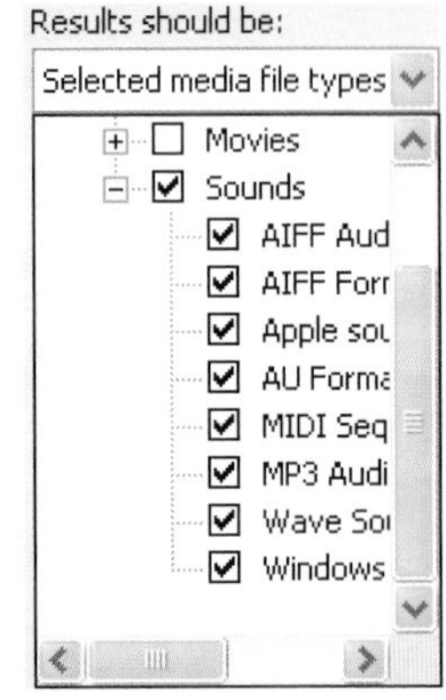

6. Click **Go.**
7. When the sound files are displayed in the preview of thumbnails, click the down arrow on the side of a thumbnail and click **Preview/Properties** to hear the sound.

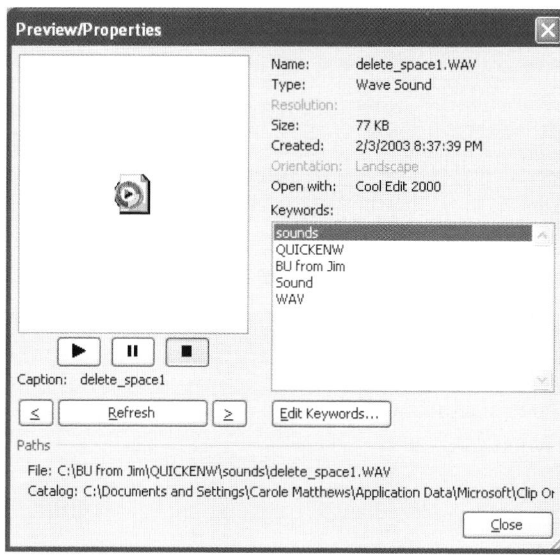

8. When the Preview/Properties dialog box opens, the sound is played. If you want to hear it again, press the **Play** button. Click **Close** when you are satisfied that you know that sound.

9. To insert the sound, double-click the thumbnail.

10. A message is displayed asking, "How Do You Want The Sound To Start In The Slide Show?" Click **Automatically** to have the sound played whenever the slide is displayed. Click **When Clicked** to have the sound played when you click. The sound will be assigned to the selected slide.

11. A sound icon will appear on the slide. Drag it to an "out-of-the-way" spot on the slide.

Insert Sound from a File

On your computer or network, you may have your own sound files that are not part of a Clip Organizer collection. You can also insert them in your slides:

1. In Normal view, select the slide to have the sound.
2. Open **Insert**, choose **Movies And Sounds**, and click **Sound From File**.
3. The Insert Sound dialog box will be displayed, as shown in Figure 9-2.
4. Find and select your sound file, and click **OK**. The sound icon will be displayed in the slide. Drag it to an inconspicuous spot on your slide.

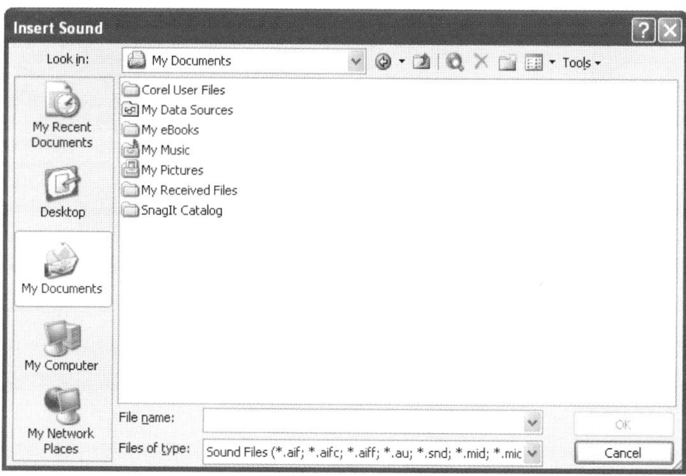

Figure 9-2: You can insert sound files from your own computer or a computer on a network

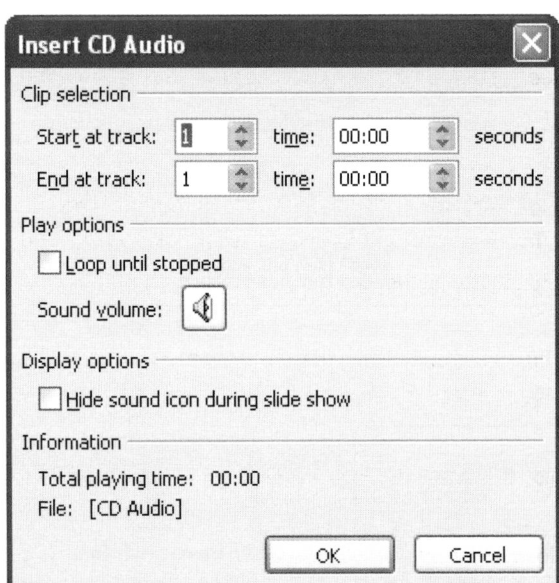

Figure 9-3: You can select specific tracks on a CD to assign to a slide

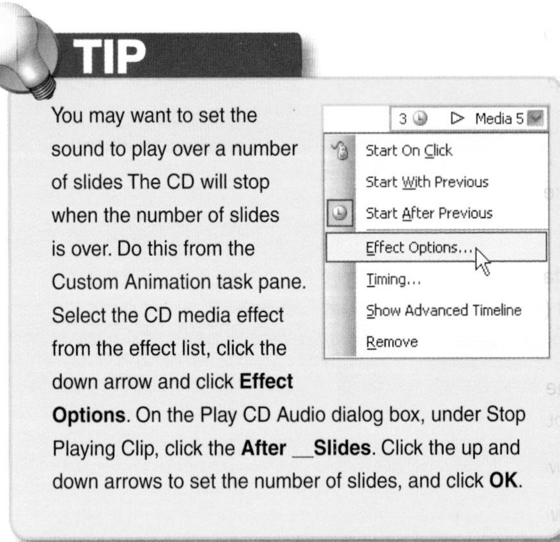

TIP

You may want to set the sound to play over a number of slides The CD will stop when the number of slides is over. Do this from the Custom Animation task pane. Select the CD media effect from the effect list, click the down arrow and click **Effect Options**. On the Play CD Audio dialog box, under Stop Playing Clip, click the **After __Slides**. Click the up and down arrows to set the number of slides, and click **OK**.

Insert a CD Track

To insert one or more sound tracks from a CD on your slide:

1. Insert your CD into the CD drive. Cancel the dialog box that may appear.
2. Select the slide that will contain the CD sounds.
3. Open **Insert**, choose **Movies And Sounds**, and click **Play CD Audio Track**. The Insert CD Audio dialog box will be displayed, as shown in Figure 9-3.
4. Select among these options:
   - In the **Start At** box, click the up and down arrows to set the beginning track number. For **Time**, set the number of seconds of delay before it should start to play.
   - In the **End At** box, click the up and down arrows to set the number of the last track to play. For **Time**, set the seconds that this track is to play.
   - Under Play Options, place a check mark next to **Loop Until Stopped** if you want the CD sound track to repeat itself until you click. Set the sound volume by clicking the sound icon and dragging the slider to the volume you want.
   - Under Display Options, click **Hide Sound Icon During Slide Show** if you want the CD icon to be hidden during the actual presentation.
   - For your information, the **Total Playing Time** is calculated so you will know how long the slide will take to play.
5. Click **OK**. A message asking how to play the sound will display. Click **Automatically** to play the CD track automatically when the slide displays. Click **When Clicked** to play the CD track when you click. The CD icon will be inserted onto the slide. Drag it to an inconspicuous spot.

6. To start the slide show, to see and hear it with the CD track, click the **Slide Show From Current slide** icon. To see the whole slide show, select a slide and press **F5**.

NOTE

Note: If you are using a CD track for your slides, you must insert a CD track for each slide unless you specify that the CD track is to loop or that it is to continue to play through a number of slides. The time for the CD to begin to play or to advance to the next track, compared to the display of the slides, is difficult to coordinate and cannot be done automatically.

Figure 9-4: The Custom Animation task pane allows you to select additional options for sound files

Set Options for Sound Effects

Once a sound has been inserted onto a slide, you can change or refine how and when it plays:

1. Select the sound icon for which you want to set options.
2. Click the task pane title bar, and select Custom Animation. (If the task pane is not showing, open **View** and click **Task Pane**.) The Custom Animation task pane will open.
3. Click the down arrow for the sound effect in the effect list, and a context menu will open, as shown in Figure 9-4.
4. Click **Effect Options** to open the Play Sound dialog box. The options may vary depending on the type of sound file you have selected.
5. On the **Effect** tab:
   - Under Start Playing Clip, click **From Beginning** to start playing the sound clip from the beginning.
   - Click **From Last Position** to continue playing the sound clip from the previous slide.
   - Click **From Time**, and click the up and down arrows to set the number of seconds to advance into the sound clip before beginning to play.
   - Under Stop Playing, click **On Click** to stop the sound when the slide is clicked.
   - Click **After Current Slide** to stop playing when the next slide is displayed.
   - Click **After**, and click the up and down arrows to set the number of slides during which the sound continues to play before stopping.
   - Under Enhancements, if the sound is connected to animation, open **After Animation** to indicate the action to take.
6. On the **Timing** tab:
   - Click the down arrow for **Start** to select whether the sound starts After Previous effect, With Previous effect (at the same time as another effect), or On Click (when you click the sound icon).
   - Set the **Delay** timer with the number of seconds that are to pass after the slide is displayed but before the sound plays.
   - Open the **Repeat** drop-down list to click the number of times the sound is to repeat.
   - Place a check mark in **Rewind When Done Playing** to return the sound clip to the beginning when the clip has completed playing.

1

2

3

4

5

6

7

8

9

10

TIP

You can apply sound to an animation. Select the animated object, and on the Custom Animation task pane, select the item from the effects list. Select **Effect Options**, and under **Enhancements** on the **Effect** tab, click the **Sound** drop-down list box and select a sound. See Chapter 8, "Special Effects and Drawing in PowerPoint," to read more about special effects and animation.

NOTE

When you are inserting multiple sound clips on a slide, the default is to play them in the order they are inserted onto the slide. You can change this order in the Effects and Timing tabs of the Effect Options dialog box.

- Open **Triggers** and click **Animate As Part Of Click Sequence** if the sound is to be a part of another effect or group of effects.
- Click **Start Effect On Click Of** to connect the sound with the click of another effect.

7. On the **Sound Settings** tab:
   - Click **Sound Volume** to set the slider to the volume you want.
   - Place a check mark next to **Hide Sound Icon During Slide Show** to hide the sound icon while the presentation is being played.
   - Use Information to learn how long the sound clip plays and whether it is an embedded file (contained in Presentation) or a linked file with the path to the source file listed.
8. Click OK to close the Play Sound dialog box.

Change Size of Embedded Sound Files

PowerPoint *embeds* .WAV sound files less than 100 KB in size. That is, it makes the files part of the presentation structure. All other file types and .WAV files larger than 100 KB are *linked*. That is, they are stored in their original location and loaded from there. To change the size of file that will be embedded within PowerPoint:

1. Open **Tools** and select **Options**. Click the **General** tab on the Options dialog box.
2. On **Link Sounds With File Size Greater Than**, drag the up and down arrows on the slider until you have, in KB, the file size you want.

Link sounds with file size greater than 100 Kb

Record Sound Files

There are at least three reasons you might want to record a narrative for your slide show. First, recording prior to the presentation enables the slide show to run without your presence. You can produce a web-based presentation or a kiosk trade show presentation this way. Secondly, recording during the

One potential problem with linked files is that if you move the presentation from its current location, you may lose linked sound files. So, it is important to keep the presentation and sound files together, in the same folder if possible.

presentation saves a record of your comments and the audience's response, if you choose. Finally, you might want to record short comments on just a few slides to note a change you'd like to make or to emphasize an important point. Before recording, however, you may need to set up and test your microphone equipment.

TEST YOUR MICROPHONE

To test your microphone's quality:

1. Open **Slide Show** and click **Record Narration**. The Record Narration dialog box will open, as seen in Figure 9-5.

Figure 9-5: The Record Narration dialog box enables you to set the quality and level of your microphone

2. To change the attributes of your sound, click Change Quality. The Sound Selection dialog box will appear.
   - Click the **Format** drop-down list box to change it. You may have only one possibility of PCM (Pulse Code Modulation).
   - Click the **Attributes** drop-down list box to change the quality of the sound being captured by your microphone. (Note that quality and file size are related; the higher the quality, the larger the file.)

1 2 3 4 5 6 7 8 9 10

- To save the sound selected, type a **Name** and click **Save As**. Enter the appropriate data, and click **OK**.

3. Click **Set Microphone Level** to test your microphone. The Microphone Check dialog box will be displayed.
   - Talk into the microphone, and see the sound meter reflect your voice. There is a message on the dialog box that you can read into the microphone.
   - Click **OK.**
4. Click **OK** to close the Record Narration dialog box..
5. You will see a message informing you that the timings, or the record of how long each slide took, will be saved with the narrations. Click **Save** to save the timings and the narrations. Click **Don't Save** to discard the timings.

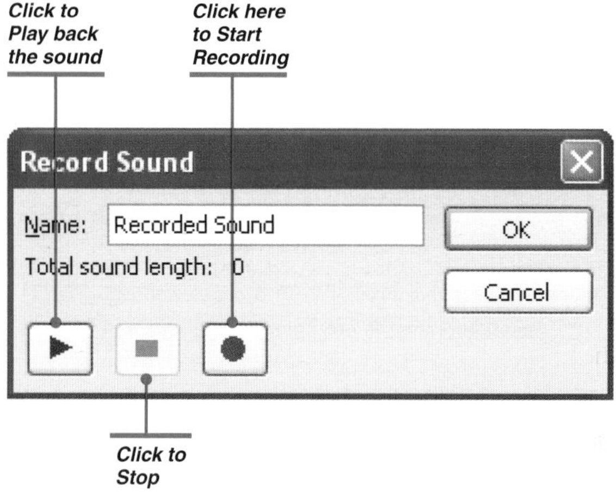

RECORD SHORT COMMENTS

To record a short comment on a single slide:

1. Select the slide that will have the comments.
2. Open **Insert**, choose **Movies And Sounds**, and click **Record Sound**. The Record Sound dialog box will open.
3. Type in a **Name** for the recording.
   - To begin the recording, click **Record**.
   - To stop, click **Stop**.
   - To play back the recording, click **Play**.
4. Click **OK** when you are done.

RECORD A NARRATIVE FOR YOUR PRESENTATION

You use the Slide Show menu to record a narrative for your presentation. You can record on selected slides or all slides.

1. Select the slide on which you will begin the narration.
2. Open the **Slide Show** menu, and select **Record Narration**. The Record Narration dialog box will be displayed.

NOTE

To record and hear sounds, you must have a sound card, speakers, and microphone.

CAUTION

A recorded narration is played instead of other sounds. So if you have inserted sounds and also recorded a narrative for a slide, the narration will be the only sound heard.

3. Click **Set Microphone Level** to test your microphone volume and quality. Click **OK**.
4. When you are ready to start recording, click **OK**. The Record Narration dialog box is displayed. (If you have already selected the first slide, this dialog box will not be displayed.)

   Record Narration...

   - Click **Current Slide** to start recording on the selected slide.

   –Or–

   - Click **First Slide** to start recording on the first slide in the presentation.

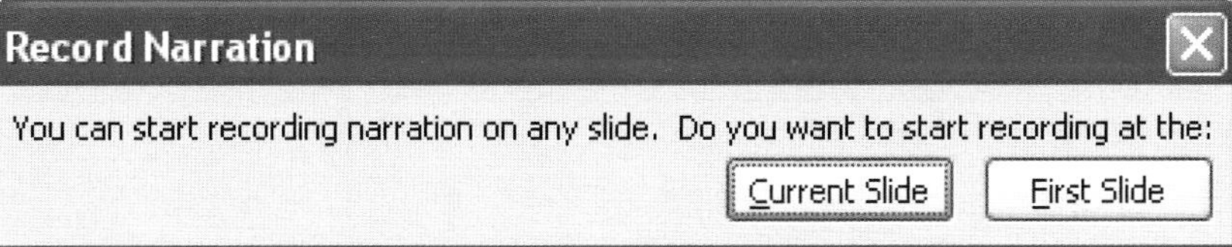

5. The slide will be displayed on the screen. Use these guidelines:
   - Be sure the microphone is on. Speak into it, stating your narrative. It will be recorded as you speak.
   - To move from one slide to the next, when you are finished recording on one, click the current slide.
   - To temporarily pause recording, right-click the slide and click **Pause Narration**.
   - To continue recording, right-click the slide and click **Resume Narration**.
6. To end recording, right-click the slide and click **End Show**. You will see the message below to save timings. Click **Save** to save the slide timings with the narrations. Click **Don't Save** to discard the timings.

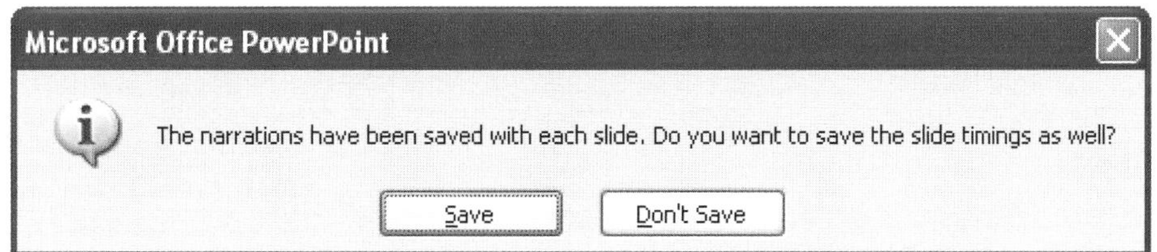

1 2 3 4 5 6 7 8 9 10

1

2

3

4

5

6

7

8

9

10

TIP

The narrative timings are used to time your slide display automatically without you needing to click to advance the slides. They can be turned off and on as you wish. (Open **Slide Show** and select **Set Up Show**. Under Show Options, click to set or clear the check mark for **Show Without Narration**.)

7. The Slide Sorter view will be displayed, if you chose to save timings, with the timings shown for each slide, as shown in Figure 9-6.
8. Refer to "Set Options for Sound Effects" to set up the directives for how your narrative will be played in the slide show. For example, if you want the slides to play automatically, all but the first can be set to Start After Previous. You may set the first to start On Click.

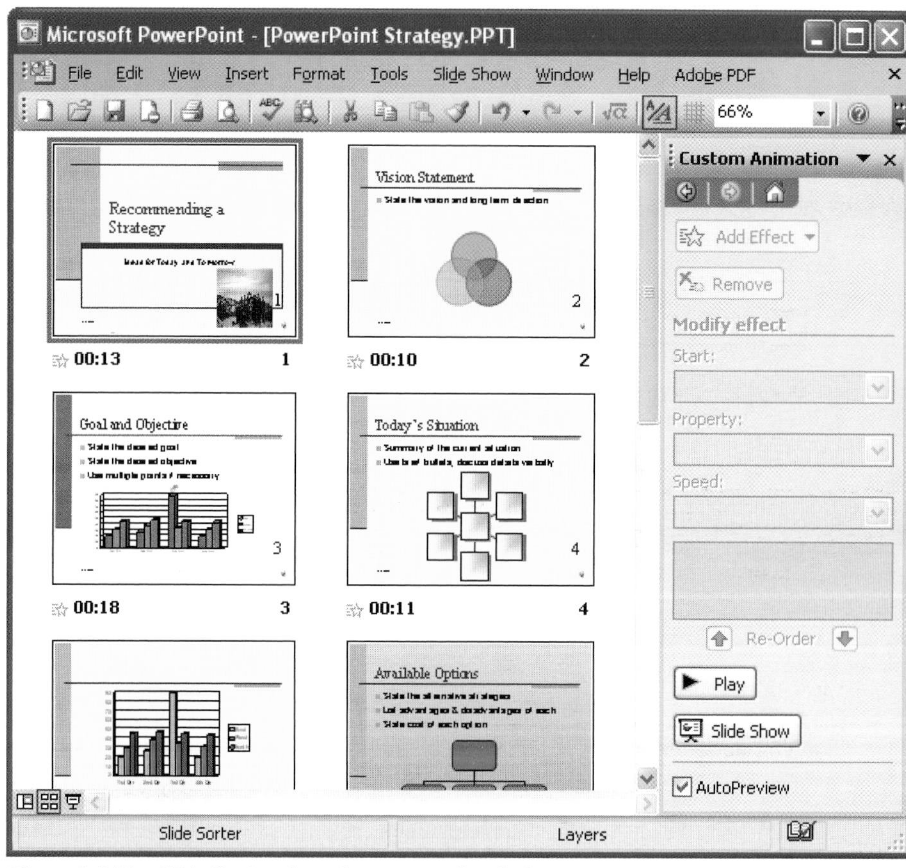

Figure 9-6: The Slide Sorter view shows narrative timings

CHANGING VIDEO OPTIONS

These options, set on the slide, determine how the video portion of your slide show will run.

LOOP OR REWIND A MOVIE

To cause a movie to play repeatedly or to rewind:

1. Right-click a movie and select **Edit Movie Object**.
   - Click **Loop Until Stopped** to cause the movie to repeat.
   - Click **Rewind Movie When Done Playing** to return to the beginning of the movie.
2. Click **OK**.

FILL THE SCREEN WITH THE MOVIE

To run the movie at full-screen size:

1. Right-click a movie and select **Edit Movie Object**.
2. Click **Zoom To Full Screen** under Display Options.
3. Click **OK**.

RESIZE THE MOVIE

Occasionally a video may look fuzzy at full-screen size. To fix this, you can resize the movie so that it plays in a smaller screen area during the slide show. To resize a movie, making it larger or smaller, select the movie and drag the sizing handles of the picture to the size you want.

SET VOLUME

To set the volume for the movie:

1. Right-click the selection handle of the movie, and click **Edit Movie Object**.
2. Click the **Sound Volume** icon.
3. Move the slider to the volume level you want.

Continued...

Use Video Files in Your Presentation

Similarly to sound files, you can insert video files and set options to vary the start, stop, timing, and other attributes of showing a video on your presentation. When you insert a video, you will see a picture of the beginning of the video rather than an icon.

INSERT A VIDEO

1. Select the slide to contain the video.
2. Open **Insert**, select **Movies And Sounds**, and click the source of your video file:
   - Click **Movie From Clip Organizer** to insert a video clip from Microsoft's Clip Organizer.
   - Click **Movie From File** to insert a video file from your own collections, not part of the Clip Organizer collection.
3. Using the Clip Art task pane for movies from the Clip Organizer or the Insert Movie dialog box for a video file in your collection, find your video file, and insert it into the selected slide.
4. You will see a message asking how to start the movie:
   - Click **Automatically** to start the movie when the slide displays.
   - Click **When Clicked** to start the movie when the video picture is clicked.

5. To preview the video on this slide, double-click the video picture or click the **Slide Show From Current Slide** icon. To see the whole slide show, select a slide and press **F5**.

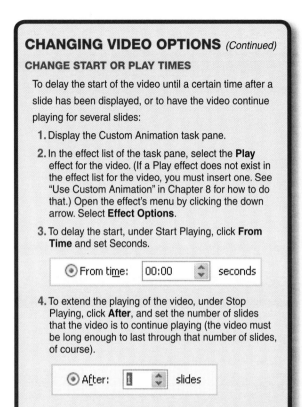

CHANGING VIDEO OPTIONS *(Continued)*

CHANGE START OR PLAY TIMES

To delay the start of the video until a certain time after a slide has been displayed, or to have the video continue playing for several slides:

1. Display the Custom Animation task pane.
2. In the effect list of the task pane, select the **Play** effect for the video. (If a Play effect does not exist in the effect list for the video, you must insert one. See "Use Custom Animation" in Chapter 8 for how to do that.) Open the effect's menu by clicking the down arrow. Select **Effect Options**.
3. To delay the start, under Start Playing, click **From Time** and set Seconds.

   From time: 00:00 seconds

4. To extend the playing of the video, under Stop Playing, click **After**, and set the number of slides that the video is to continue playing (the video must be long enough to last through that number of slides, of course).

   After: 1 slides

INSERT ACTION BUTTONS

Action buttons can be inserted on the beginning slide of a video to act as triggers for starting, pausing, and stopping the video. These replace the mouse clicks normally used to start, pause, and stop it. To insert an action button:

1. Click the slide containing the movie.
2. Open **Slide show**, point to **Action Buttons**, and click a button shape that fits your video scheme.

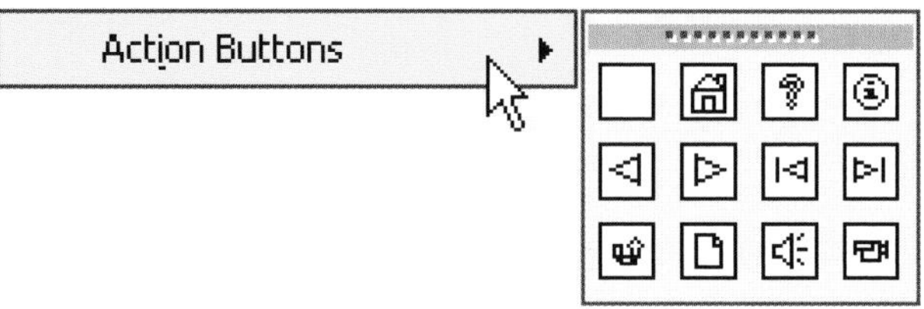

- Your pointer will become a cross. Drag it on the slide where you want the button shape. When you release the mouse, the Action Settings dialog box will appear.

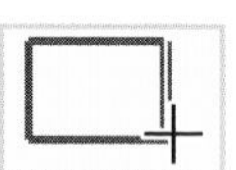

- On the Action Setting dialog box, under **Action On Click**, click **None**. Then click **OK**.

3. Open the Custom Animation task pane. Select the movie on your slide.
4. Add Play, Pause, and Stop effects to the movie. To do this, on the task pane, click **Add Effect**, select **Movie Actions**, and click the effect you want, for instance, **Play**. Repeat this for each action you want for the buttons.
5. Make the buttons the trigger for the actions. To do this:
   - In the effect list on the task pane, select each effect to be triggered by the button.
   - Click on its down arrow and select **Timing**.
   - Under **Triggers**, click **Start Effect On Click Of**, and click the action button you want, as shown in Figure 9-7.

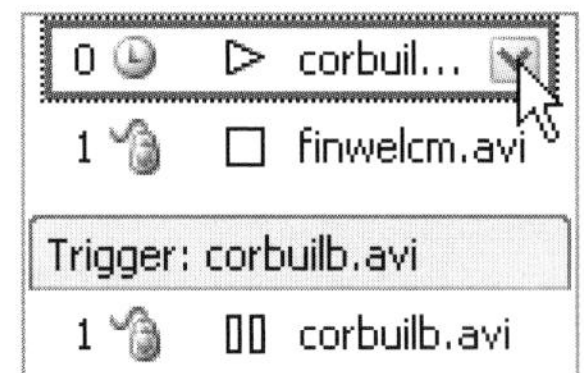

NOTE

If you want additional identical buttons (for example, buttons to start, stop and pause the video), make copies of the first button (right-click the button and click **Copy Here;** or use the traditional Copy and Paste menu options). Then, drag the copies in line with the first. Align them by selecting all the buttons (press and hold SHIFT while clicking each button), opening **Draw** on the Drawing toolbar, selecting **Align Or Distribute**, and clicking **Align Top/Bottom** or **Align Left/Right**. Then, select **Distribute Horizontally** or **Distribute Vertically,** depending on whether you want the buttons in a vertical or horizontal line.

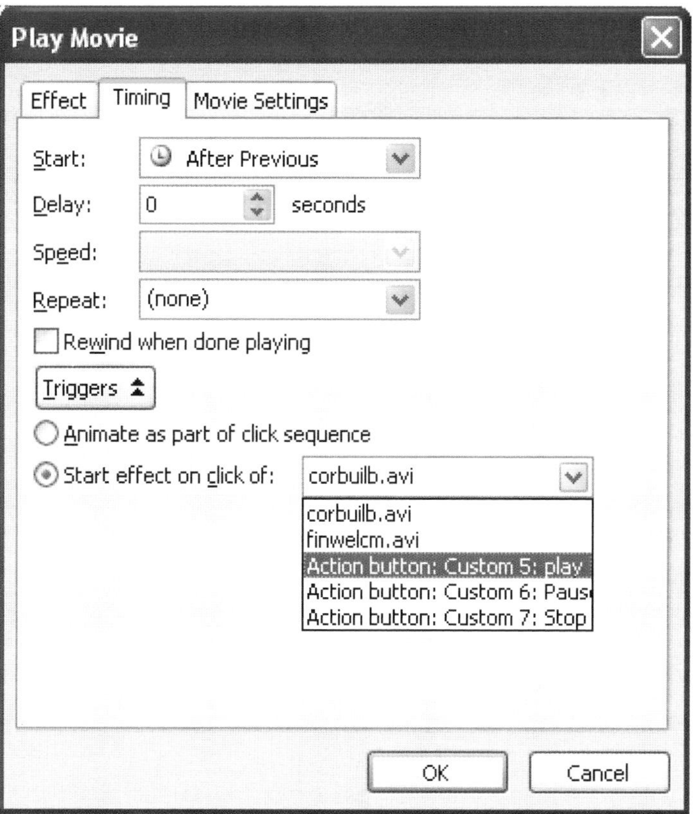

Figure 9-7: You can assign a button to be a trigger for an action on the video

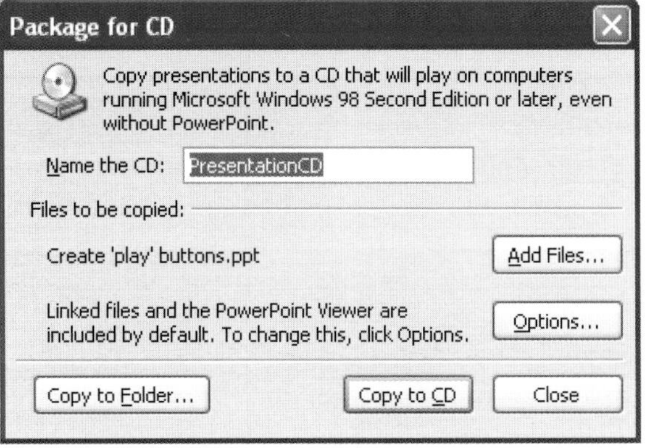

Package Presentation Files

You can copy all the presentation files to a folder or burn them on a CD in order to easily transport them to another computer to show a presentation. This is called packaging.

1. Open the presentation to be packaged.
2. Open **File** and select **Package For CD.** The Package For CD dialog box will open.
3. Type a name in the **Name the CD** text box.
4. Click **Add Files** if you need to add files other than those which are listed under Files To Be Copied. The Add Files dialog box will open. Find other files to include and click **Add**. They will be added to the list of files to be copied.
5. Click **Options** to specify whether PowerPoint Viewer will be used to view the slide show (the recipient may not have PowerPoint), which presentations to include and in which order, and whether to include linked or embedded TrueType fonts and to password protect the PowerPoint files.
6. Click **Copy To Folder** to copy the files to a unique folder.

   –Or–

   Click **Copy to CD** to burn the files onto a CD. You will be asked to insert a CD. A message will ask if you want to continue if comments and annotations are included in the slides. If you do, click **Yes**.
8. The files will be copied. If you want to copy the files to another folder or CD, click **Yes**.
9. Click **Close** to close the Package For CD dialog box.

Use the Internet with Your Presentations

You can use the Internet in several ways. You can insert a hyperlink to a web page that is embedded in your presentation. You can save your presentation to an FTP (File Transfer Protocol) location. You can save your presentation as a web page on a local computer, an intranet, or the Internet. Others can then view your presentation with a browser.

Connect to Web Pages with Hyperlinks

PowerPoint makes it easy to incorporate information stored on web sites as part of your slide show. A slide show can be published on the Internet or can allow the speaker access to web pages when making the presentation. You can connect to a web page by inserting a hyperlink directly into the presentation or by placing an action button, which connects to the web page when clicked, in your slide.

INSERT A HYPERLINK

To place a hyperlink directly on a slide:

1. Display the slide to contain the hyperlink in Normal view.
2. Type the text to become a hyperlink.
   - If the text is the URL of a web page, press **ENTER** or **SPACEBAR**, and the text will be recognized as a hyperlink, as shown below. Your task is done.
     ■ www.cofinances.org
   - If you want the hyperlink to be part of the text of the presentation, select it for the next step.
3. Open **Insert** and click **Hyperlink,** or click **Insert Hyperlink** from the Standard toolbar. The Insert Hyperlink dialog box will appear.

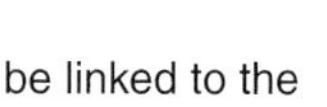

   - Enter the URL of the web site, either Internet or intranet, which will be linked to the selected text, as shown in Figure 9-8.
   - Click **E-mail Address** to enter a link to an e-mail address. Enter the address and subject.
   - Click **Place In This Document** to enter a hyperlink to another slide in the presentation.
   - Click **Create New Document** to enter a hyperlink to a new document yet to be created (you can edit it now or later).
   - Click **Existing File Or Web Page** to find a file on your computer, an intranet, or the Internet.
4. Click **OK**, and the text will be colored and underlined to show that it is a hyperlink such as: ■ Costs are being contained in most regions

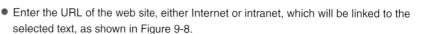

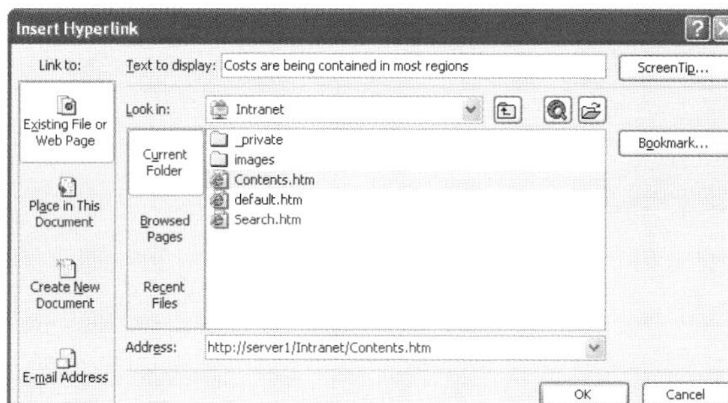

Figure 9-8: To insert a hyperlink in your presentation, you need to identify the text that will be the hyperlink and the URL to which it will be linked

NOTE

Hyperlinks only work during a slide show. You can create a link to the Internet, to intranet web pages, to pages on your own computer, or to other files, such as spreadsheets or Word documents, containing additional information for the presentation.

Use Action Buttons to Connect to a Web Page

You can insert a hyperlink in the form of an action button on a slide that, when clicked, connects to a web page:

1. In Normal view, display the slide that will contain the action button.
2. Open **Slide Show** and choose **Action Buttons**. (Or, you can click **AutoShapes** on the Drawing toolbar, and point at **Action Buttons** to get to the same place.) The Action Buttons menu will display, showing a variety of shapes.

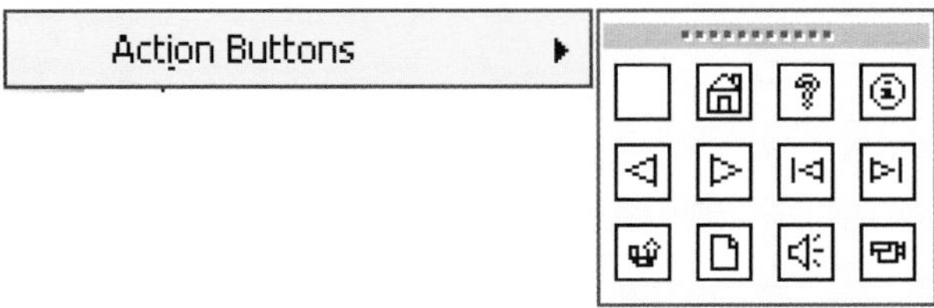

3. Click an action button shape. The pointer will become a cross which you drag diagonally across the slide to form a button shape. Click and release the pointer. The Action Settings dialog box will appear.
4. Click **Hyperlink To**.
5. Open the drop-down list box, and click the hyperlink connection. For a web site, click **URL**.

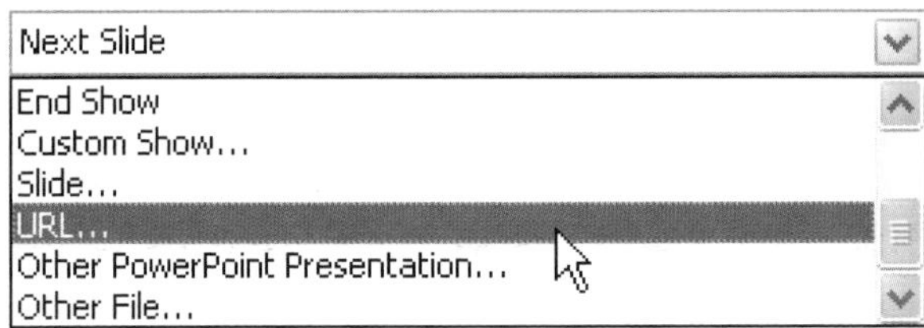

6. In the Hyperlink To URL dialog box, type the URL address (no need to put in the http://) and click **OK**. Click **OK** again to close the Action Settings dialog box. The hyperlink is now attached to the action button.

Figure 9-9: The action button can be used to connect to a web page on the Internet or intranet while you are giving a presentation

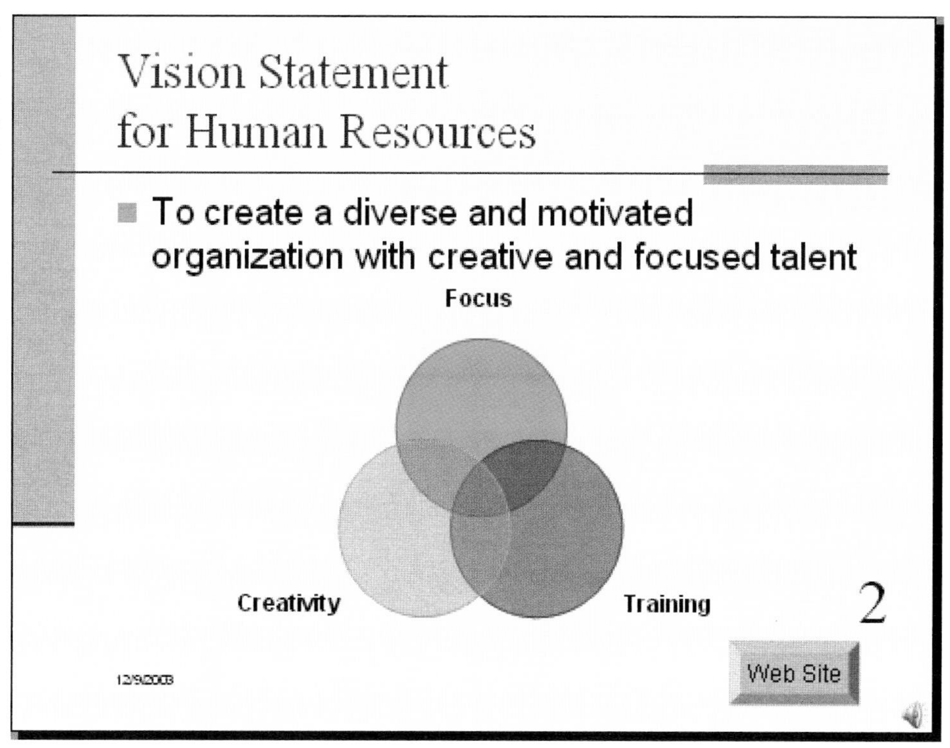

7. Format the button as needed. (Figure 9-9 shows an example of a slide with an action button connecting to a web page on an intranet.)
   - Click in the center of the button, and type the words you want to appear on the button.
   - Drag the diamond-shaped icon to create a 3-dimension button.
   - Using the sizing handles, size the button to the size you want.
   - Drag the button to where you want it placed on the slide.

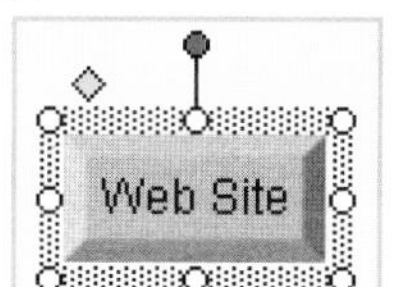

1 2 3 4 5 6 7 8 9 10

NOTE

FTP software also offers a way to publish a presentation to the Internet. To use it, you will need to have access to the software and know the address, user name, password, and other information.

TIP

To update a slide show that has been published to a web page format, simply make changes to the original presentation, not the published one, and go through the save steps to republish it as a web page.

Transfer to an FTP Site

You can save your presentation file to an FTP (File Transfer Protocol) location. This is a technique that lets you transfer large files to a protected site. People with access to the FTP site can then download the presentation and view it on their computers. This replaces sending it by e-mail, a bonus for large files that need to be distributed to a known group.

1. Connect to the Internet, and have ready the FTP address and password.
2. With the presentation displayed, open **File** and click **Save As**. The Save As dialog box will appear.
3. Open the **Look In** drop-down list.
   - If you do not have an FTP location set up, click **Add/Modify FTP Locations**. In the dialog box, enter the address of the FTP site in the **Name Of FTP Site**, click **User**, and type in a name and a password below. Click **Add** and then click **OK**. The FTP location will be displayed in the Save As dialog box.

   - If you have previously established an FTP location, click **FTP Locations,** and double-click the name of the FTP site.
4. When the FTP site is open, find the folder in which your presentation will be saved, and click **Save**. You will see a message telling you the file is being saved.

NOTE

When you "save" a file using Save As, you are creating a copy of the file that replaces the presentation currently on your screen with the copy. To update the copy, you make changes directly to it. The original and the copy go their separate ways. When you "publish" a file using Save As, you are creating an .htm file that can be viewed by a browser. Your original file remains on the screen. If you want to update the published file, you make changes to the original and publish it again.

Publish Your Presentation as a Web Page

You can publish your presentation as an HTML file, a web page. This enables viewers who do not have PowerPoint to view the presentation with a browser. Using this technique preserves the links, color schemes, and other design elements created with Power Point. You can save to a local computer, an intranet server, or to an Internet server.

1. Open the presentation that is to be saved to a web page, open **File**, and click **Save As**. (Don't click Save As Type Single File Web Page. That creates a single file of the presentation rather than a folder and file, as we're doing here.) The Save As dialog box will open.
2. Enter a **File Name**.
3. Open the **Save As Type** drop-down list box, and click **Web Page (*.htm; *.html).**
4. If you need a folder for the file, click **New Folder** on the toolbar and type a name.
5. To change the Title that will appear in the title bar of the browser, click **Change Title,** and in the Set Page Title dialog box, type a new **Page Title**. Click **OK**.
6. Click **Publish**, and the Publish As Web Page dialog box, as shown in Figure 9-10, will be displayed.
   - Under Publish What?, click **Complete Presentation** to save all slides; or click **Slide Number**, and use the up and down arrows to set the beginning and ending slide numbers.
   - To display the speaker notes with the presentation, place a check mark next to **Display Speaker Notes**. Clear the check mark to hide the notes.
   - See "Changing Web Options" for information on changing the most commonly used web options.
   - Under Browser Support, place a check mark next to the browsers that are supported in viewing the presentation.

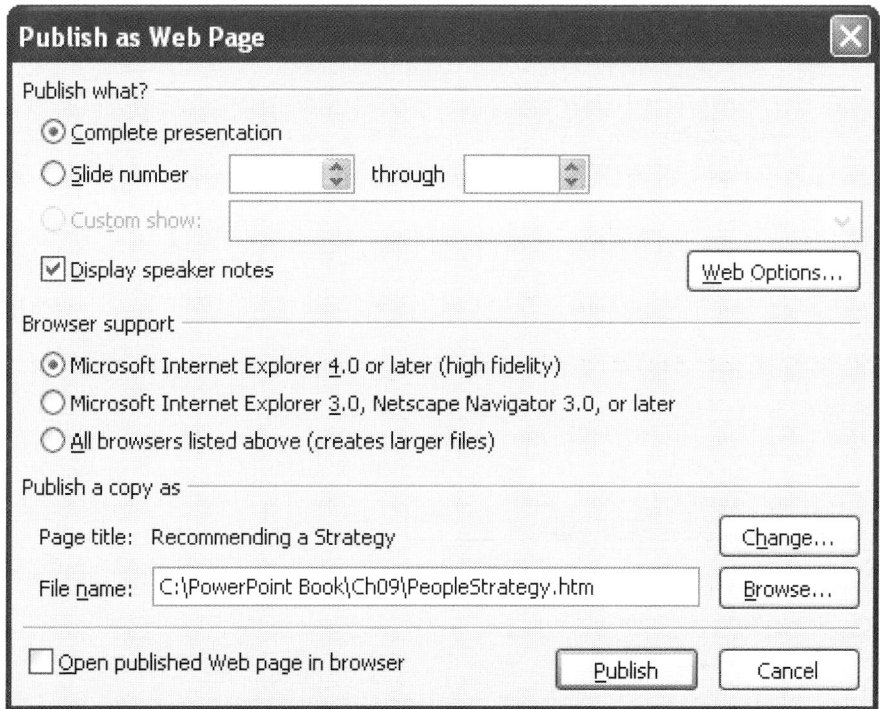

Figure 9-10: When you publish a presentation as a web page, this dialog box helps to establish exactly what is saved and how it will be supported

1 2 3 4 5 6 7 8 9 10

QUICKSTEPS

CHANGING WEB OPTIONS

ACCESS THE WEB OPTIONS DIALOG BOX

Most of the options in these QuickSteps will use the same dialog box. To display it, follow Steps 1 though 6 in "Save Your Presentation as a Web Page." Then, click **Web Options**.

SET WEB COLORS FOR NAVIGATIONAL CONTROLS

To set the way color is handled in the navigational controls displayed by the saved web page:

1. Click the **General** tab.
2. Place a check mark next to **Add Slide Navigation Controls**.

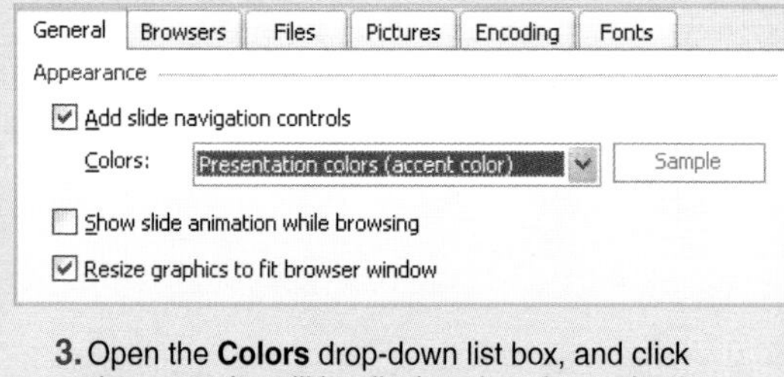

3. Open the **Colors** drop-down list box, and click the way color will be displayed on the navigation controls buttons. You will see a preview in the Sample box.
4. Click **OK**.

SHOW ANIMATION WITH BROWSER

To show animation while the presentation is being viewed on the browser:

1. Click the **General** tab.
2. Place a check mark next to **Show Slide Animation While Browsing**.
3. Click **OK**.

Continued...

- Under Publish A Copy As, click **Change** to change the Page Title. Use **Browse**, or type the path and name of the saved file if it is not already listed.
- Place a check mark in **Open Published Web Page In Browser** to open the saved web page automatically when the Save is complete.

7. Click **Publish** to save the presentation as a web page. A file and folder are created using the same file name. The folder contains all the slides and objects as .GIF and other file types. You need both the file and folder if moving or copying the presentation.

Use the Web Toolbar

The Web toolbar helps in finding and starting your web pages. To display the Web toolbar, open **View**, select **Toolbars**, and click **Web**. The Web toolbar will appear, as shown in Figure 9-11. You can choose the tools you need.

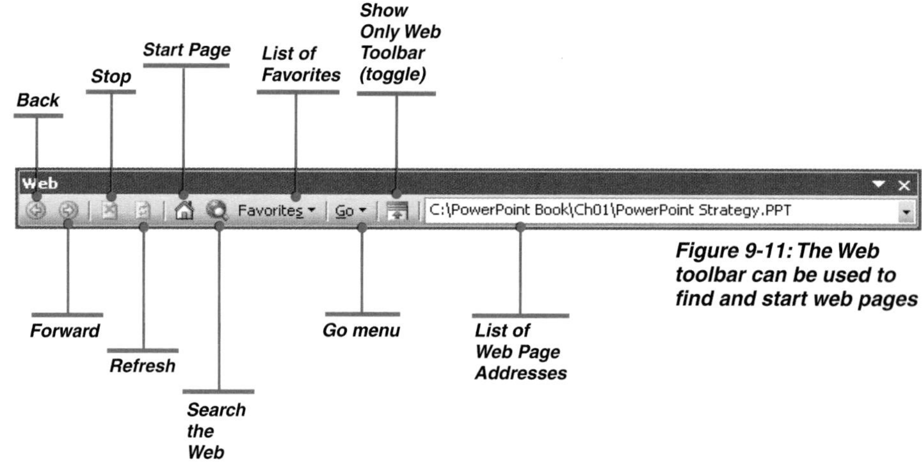

Figure 9-11: The Web toolbar can be used to find and start web pages

CHANGING WEB OPTIONS *(Continued)*

SELECT ADDITIONAL BROWSER CONTROLS

To specify additional browsers that may be used and to give additional specifications on saving the web page:

1. Click the **Browsers** tab. Under Target Browsers, open the **People Who View This Web Page Will Be Using** drop-down list box. Click the oldest browser that can be expected. Note the warning that the older choices display progressively smaller web pages.
2. Under Options:
   - Click **Allow PNG As A Graphics Format** to save the file in a more compressed file format, making file size smaller and the files faster to load. To use PNG (Portable Networks Graphics) file format, the browser must be a more recent one, at least Microsoft Internet Explorer 5.0 or later.
   - Click **Rely on VML** (Vector Markup Language) **For Displaying Graphics In Browsers** to generate vector-based images on the fly using some simple XML (Extensible Markup Language).
   - Click **Save An Additional Version Of The Presentation For Older Browsers** to save a copy for use with the older browsers. This is useful if you chose the PNG format.
   - Click **Save New Web Pages As Single File Web Pages** to save the files as .mhtm or .mhtml file formats.
3. Click **OK**.

Continued...

NOTE

If your presentation has been designed to run automatically, it will open and run itself when the hyperlink is clicked on a slide show.

View a Slide Show in a Default Browser

1. You can use the Web toolbar to look at a slide show saved as web pages. Display the Web toolbar as outlined in "Use the Web Toolbar."
2. If you know the address, type it in the address drop-down list box.

   –Or–

   If you do not know the address of your saved presentation, open **Go** on the Web Toolbar, and click **Open Hyperlink**. The Open Internet Address dialog box will be displayed.
3. Click **Browse**. In the Browse dialog box, find and select the presentation saved on your hard disk, and click **Open**.
4. Click **OK** to close the Open Internet Address dialog box. The presentation will start.
5. If the slide show does not automatically start up, the navigation pane on the left, shown in Figure 9-12, will help you scan your presentation by slides.

TIP

If you use a browser other than the default browser to view the saved web pages, the slide show may not automatically start up. In the nondefault browser, open **File** and click **Open**. In the Open dialog box, find the saved file and click the file name. Click **Open**. Use the Navigation pane to go through the slide show.

CHANGING WEB OPTIONS *(Continued)*

MANAGE SUPPORTING AND LINKED FILES DURING SAVE

To manage and pull together the most recent files:

1. Click the **Files** tab.
2. To pull together the supporting files of the presentation, place a check mark next to **Organize Supporting Files In A Folder**. This will make sure that all the sound and media files are together with the presentation.

File names and locations
- ☑ Organize supporting files in a folder
- ☑ Use long file names whenever possible
- ☑ Update links on save

3. To get the most recent updates of linked files, place a check mark next to **Update Links On Save**.
4. Click **OK**.

SET DEFAULT FONTS

To set the default fonts for the saved presentation:

1. Click the **Fonts** tab.
2. Under **Character Set**, click the language to use for the presentation.
3. Open the **Proportional Font** drop-down list box, and click the font to use on the saved file.
4. Set the **Size** and **Fixed-Width Font** if needed.
5. Click **OK**.

Figure 9-12: The presentation displays a slide pane, for viewing the slide show, and a navigation pane, to act like a table of contents, providing hyperlinks to the slides

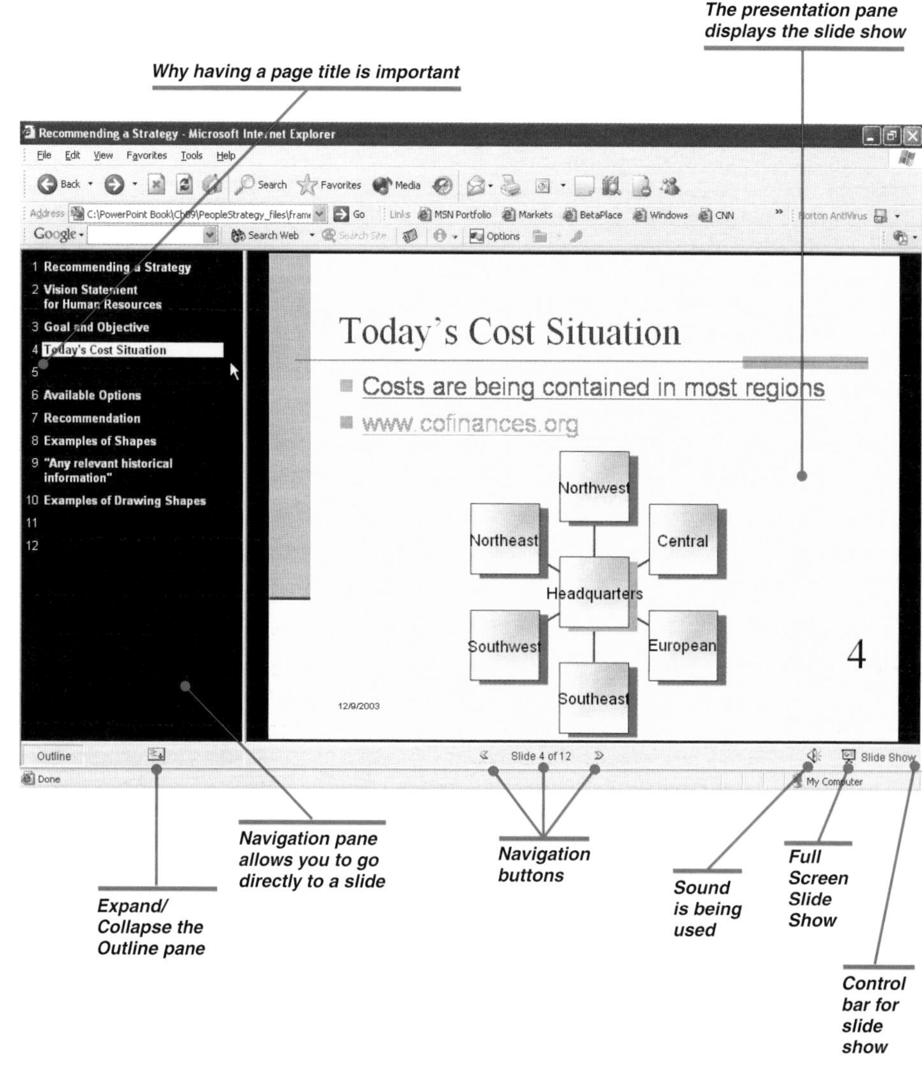

How to...

- *Automate a Slide Show*
- *Use a Laptop to Control the Presentation*
- *Setting Up a Slide Show*
- *Present a Dual-Monitor Slide Show*
- *Use a Pen Tool*
- *Navigating a Slide Show*
- *Rehearse Your Timing*
- *Display a Blank Screen*
- *Write Notes during the Presentation*
- *Setting Print Options*
- *Create a Custom Slide Show*
- *Place a Shortcut on Your Desktop*
- *Preview Slides before Printing*
- *Setting Print Preview Options*
- *Set Page Setup*
- *Print Grayscale or Black and White Slides*
- *Print Transparencies*
- *Print a PostScript File for 35mm Slides*
- *Stop Printing*
- *Change Printers*

Chapter 10 Printing and Running a Slide Show

This last chapter addresses how to display the output of a PowerPoint presentation. You may wish to present it as a slide show projected before an audience, on another monitor controlled by your laptop computer, or as a slide show running by itself on a standalone computer or kiosk. You may print it as transparencies, as a PostScript file for 35 mm slides, or simply as a printed handout. PowerPoint gives you much flexibility in how you offer your presentation.

Run a Slide Show

Designing a show to run by itself is often useful for trade shows or other places where you want a presentation to automatically run repeatedly with no presenter. The viewer watches, with limited or no ability to intervene with the presentation.

CAUTION

If you have set any animations to occur, they may also be included in the timing. For instance, if you have the automatic timing set for ten seconds and also have a heading that will be displayed, the slide will be displayed first, the heading will be displayed after ten seconds, and the next slide will appear ten seconds after that. If the animation does not advance the way you expect, it may be set for "on click," and you may have to click to start the animation.

NOTE

An example of the Loop Continuously option of an automated slide show is a marketing pitch at a trade show, where people pass by a booth and remain a few minutes to watch a repeating, automatic slide show. This is usually executed with a dual-monitor system controlled from "behind the scenes" by a laptop that is managed by someone who initiates the slide show and sees that it runs smoothly. See "Setting Up a Slide Show" for additional information.

Automate a Slide Show

In order to self-run a slide show, without any intervention from either the presenter or the viewer:

In order for a slide show to run itself, without any intervention from either the presenter or the viewer:

1. Open your presentation, and click a slide to select it.
2. Open the **Slide Transition** task pane. (If the task pane is not displayed, open **Slide Show** and click **Slide Transition**.)
3. Under Advance Slide, click **Automatically After** and set the number of seconds with the up and down arrows; or you can select the displayed time, and enter the time you want.
4. Click **Apply to All Slides**.
5. To allow the viewer to manipulate the slide show, open **Slide Show**, select **Set Up Show**, and click **Browsed At A Kiosk (Full Screen)**.

   –Or–

   To have the slide show automatically repeat and to prevent the viewer from manipulating it, place a check mark next to **Loop Continuously Until 'Esc'**.
6. Click **OK** to close the Set Up Show dialog box.

Use a Laptop to Control the Presentation

When you connect a laptop to a projector or monitor, you may need to fine-tune the resolution and audio before you can run the presentation from your laptop as you normally would.

SET RESOLUTION AND VOLUME

1. Connect the cables from the projector or monitor to the laptop and the audio cables from the speakers to the laptop, according to your laptop documentation.
2. To set the resolution on your laptop computer, right-click the **Desktop** and click **Properties**.

TIP

Loop Continuously and Browsed At A Kiosk are mutually exclusive. In Browsed At A Kiosk, the user is able to manipulate the show to see this, that, or whatever, moving as desired through the slide show. You can't do that AND have the show Loop Continuously. If you choose Browsed At A Kiosk, Loop Continuously is grayed (unavailable); if you choose Loop Continuously and then select Kiosk, you'll get Kiosk but Loop Continuously will become grayed. If you change your mind and want the presentation to loop, then deselect Browsed At A Kiosk, and Loop Continuously will again be available.

NOTE

To use a laptop computer as the control device for a projector or a monitor, you must have the presentation and all linked files on the laptop or have a CD/DVD in the disk drive. (If you intend to use PowerPoint Viewer, see "Package Presentation Files" in Chapter 9.) In addition, you must connect the laptop to the projector or other monitor. If you are going to be using sound, you must also connect an audio cable from your laptop to the projector or separate speakers. You may also need to connect a cable from the laptop to the projector to use a wireless mouse. Finally, you may need to activate the video-out port on the laptop. To connect the laptop to other devices, read the documentation for your laptop.

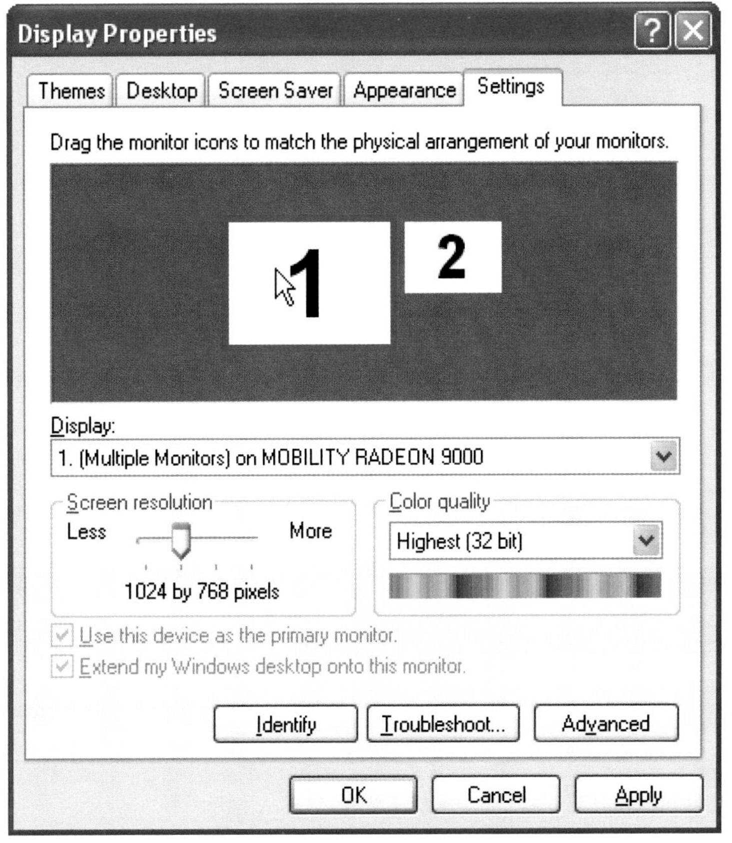

Figure 10-1: Adjust the resolution using the Display Settings dialog box

3. Click the **Settings** tab, as shown in Figure 10-1.
4. Under Screen Resolution, move the slider to the resolution that is common with the projector system (use 800x600 if you are unsure). You can flip back and forth between the monitor boxes shown in the dialog box to adjust the settings for both.
5. To set the volume, double-click the volume icon on the taskbar. Start the presentation.
6. Drag the volume slider where you want it.

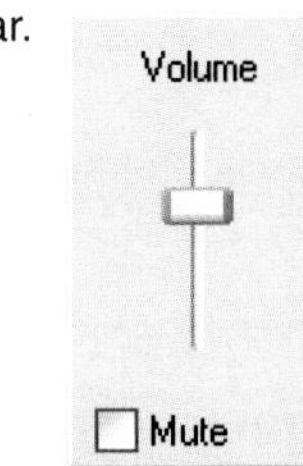

NOTE

Please note that if you use PowerPoint Viewer, you will not be able to edit the presentation.

NOTE

Microsoft PowerPoint supports only two monitors for a slide show. Even if your computer has the ability to use more than two monitors, PowerPoint will use only the primary and secondary monitors.

QUICKSTEPS

SETTING UP A SLIDE SHOW

All the topics in this QuickSteps require that the Set Up Show dialog box be displayed. To do so, open **Slide Show** and click **Set Up Show**. Figure 10-6 shows the Set Up Show dialog box.

SHOW SELECTED SLIDES

The default for a slide show is to show all slides in the presentation. To show a range of slides, under Show Slides, click the up and down arrows to set the **From** and **To** range.

DETERMINE THE TYPE OF PRESENTATION

To determine the type of presentation and how it will be run, select among these choices:

- Click **Presented By A Speaker (Full Screen)** to display a full-screen slide show that will have a speaker controlling the slide display.

Continued...

START THE PRESENTATION WITH POWERPOINT

Start the presentation exactly as you would on your own computer:

1. Bring up PowerPoint, and open your presentation.
2. Press **F5** to start the slide show from the beginning.

START THE PRESENTATION WITH POWERPOINT VIEWER

If your packaged presentation runs from a CD/DVD (see Chapter 9, "Package Presentation Files"), PowerPoint Viewer was installed as part of the packaging process. If you don't have PowerPoint and want to view slide shows, you can install the PowerPoint Viewer from the Microsoft Office Online web site. (You can find it on the PowerPoint Help task pane by clicking **Downloads** under Office Online.)

When you first bring up PowerPoint Viewer, you will need to go through the initial screens to accept the End User License Agreement for Microsoft Software. After that, the presentation may start automatically without your doing anything more. If it does not:

- To start PowerPoint Viewer with a packaged CD presentation, use Windows Explorer to find the packaged presentation, and double-click the PowerPoint Viewer file, **pptview.exe**. Find the presentation you want to run (use Browse if necessary), and select it. Then click **Open**.

  –Or–

- If you have installed PowerPoint Viewer from the Microsoft Online Web site, open **Start**, select **All Programs**, and click **Microsoft Office PowerPoint Viewer 2003**. Find the presentation you want to run (use Browse if necessary), and select it. Then click **Open**.

SETTING UP A SLIDE SHOW *(Continued)*

- Click **Browsed By An Individual (Window)** if the slide show will be run by the viewer. Click **Show Scrollbar** if the scroll bar will be displayed for the viewer to use.
- Click **Browsed At A Kiosk (Full Screen)** if the slide show is to run automatically with no intervention by the viewer.

USE TIMINGS TO ADVANCE SLIDES

To advance from one slide to the next by previously set timings (rather than advancing the slides manually), click **Using Timings, If Present**.

LOOP CONTINUOUSLY THROUGH PRESENTATION

Under Show Options, click **Loop Continuously Until "Esc"** to cause the presentation to repeat itself until ESC is pressed. This is used for a Kiosk show, for instance.

HIDE THE NARRATION DURING A SLIDE SHOW

To avoid sounding the narration during the slide show, click **Show Without Narration**.

HIDE THE ANIMATION DURING A SLIDE SHOW

To hide any animation in the presentation, click **Show Without Animation**. This can make the slide show faster and easier to control. You do not have to click the mouse repeatedly to initiate various animations as well as to advance the slide show or to wait for the animations to occur before continuing with the presentation.

SET THE SLIDE SHOW RESOLUTION

To set the resolution, click the **Slide Show Resolution** drop-down list box and click a setting.

Slide show resolution: [Use Current Resolution]
640x480 (Fastest, Lowest Fidelity)
800x600
1024x768 (Slowest, Highest Fidelity)
[Use Current Resolution]

Present a Dual-Monitor Slide Show

If you have a dual-monitor display card installed in your computer and are using a later version of Windows (2000 with Service Pack 3 or a later version, or XP), you can have different images of the slide show displayed on your primary monitor (perhaps a laptop) and on a projector or secondary monitor. For instance, your primary monitor can be showing speaker notes, the presentation outline, and scroll bars and buttons, while these are hidden on the projector or monitor, which sees only the full-screen display of the slide show.

There are two methods of viewing a slide show using two monitors. The first uses Presenter View. (See "Use Two Monitors with Presenter View.") This offers a structured way of controlling the slide show. What is seen on the secondary monitor is the full-screen slide show. On the primary monitor is a reduced slide show with tools, thumbnails of the slides, and speaker notes. The second method is more freeform. Both monitors see the full-screen slide show, but the presenter can use pen tools and other tools not available in Presenter View. (See "Use a Pen Tool.") In this second method, the presenter is actively working with the slides while showing them.

SET UP MULTIPLE MONITOR SUPPORT

First, you must enable one computer to echo its images to a secondary monitor device:

1. To open the Display Setting, right-click the Desktop and click **Properties**. On the Properties dialog box, click the **Settings** tab.
2. On the Display Settings dialog box, click the monitor that represents the primary monitor, usually 1.

TIP

When using a laptop and another monitor, you have a few different ways to control the secondary device. On a Dell, use the **FN** (blue) key under **F8**. After you have the laptop connected to a monitor or projector, press the keys appropriate to your machine (in the case of Dell, **FN** + **CRT/LCD**) a few times to cycle through the choices, e.g., just laptop, laptop and secondary synched, just secondary, back to laptop only.

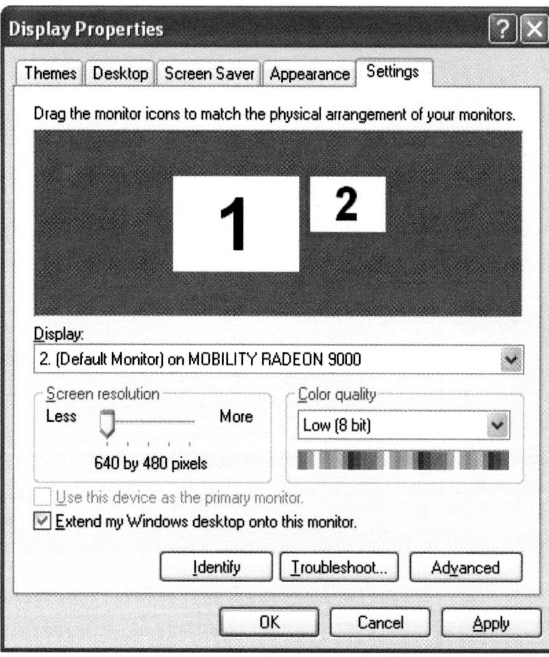

Figure 10-2: Set up your computer to handle dual-monitor displays

3. Place a check mark in the **Use This Device As The Primary Monitor**. If the option is unavailable (grayed out) but is selected, that option is set by default.

   Use this device as the primary monitor.
   Extend my Windows desktop onto this monitor.

4. Click the secondary monitor, usually 2.
5. If you are using Presenter View, place a check mark next to **Extend My Windows Desktop Onto This Monitor**, as shown in Figure 10-2. If you are using the full-screen slide show on both monitors, do not select this.
6. If needed, adjust the screen resolution and color quality to match the primary monitor.
7. Click **OK**.

USE TWO MONITORS WITH PRESENTER VIEW

After you have enabled the dual-monitor support, you can open your presentation. Presenter View offers some tools for navigating through the slides and for viewing speaker notes:

1. Open your presentation in PowerPoint.
2. Open **Slide Show** and click **Set Up Show**.
3. Under Multiple Monitors, open the **Display Slide Show On** drop-down list box, and click the monitor you want to be the one on which the presentation will be full screen, usually Monitor 2 Default Monitor.

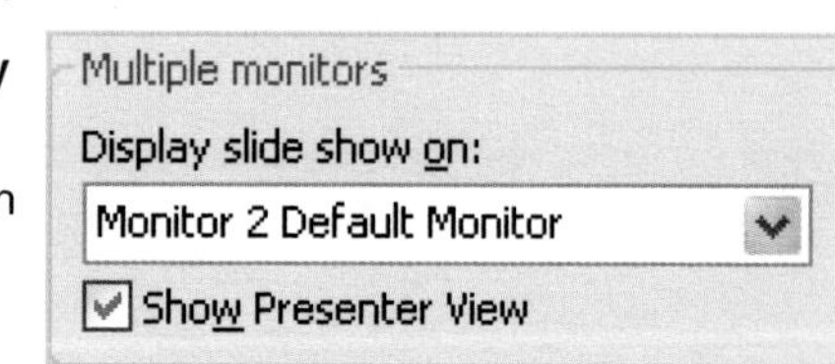

4. Place a check mark next to **Show Presenter View** to make the Presenter View tools available to you on the primary monitor.
5. Click **OK**.
6. Click **Slide Show From Current Slide** to test the display; or you can press **F5** to start the presentation from the beginning.

RUN A PRESENTER VIEW SHOW WITH DUAL MONITORS

When the support for the dual monitors has been established and you start the presentation, you have different screens available on the primary and secondary monitors. Figure 10-3 shows what the primary monitor looks like and the Presenter View tools for helping the presenter walk through the slide show.

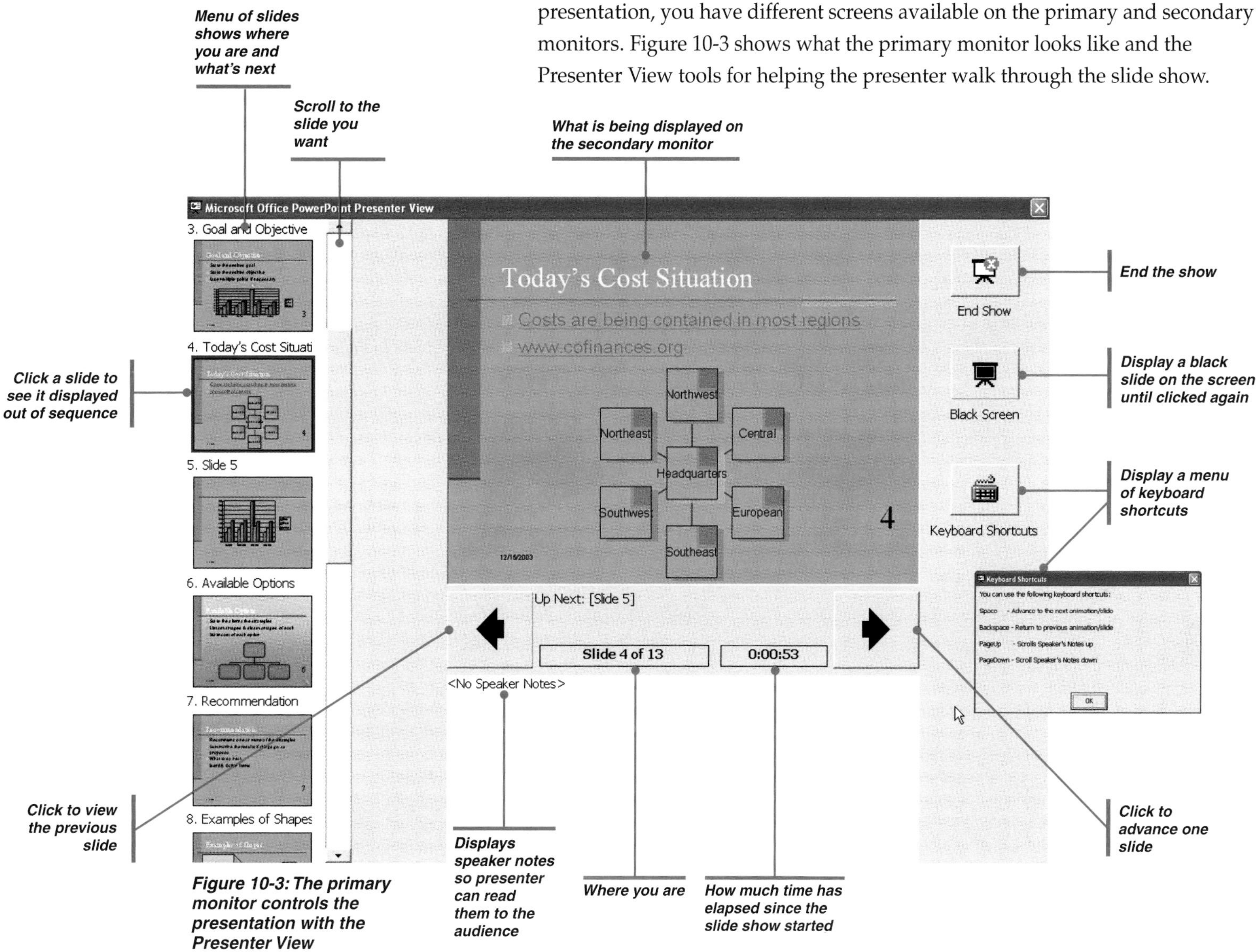

Menu of slides shows where you are and what's next
Scroll to the slide you want
What is being displayed on the secondary monitor
Microsoft Office PowerPoint Presenter View
3. Goal and Objective
4. Today's Cost Situati
5. Slide 5
6. Available Options
7. Recommendation
8. Examples of Shapes
Today's Cost Situation
Costs are being contained in most regions
www.cofinances.org
Northwest
Northeast
Central
Headquarters
Southwest
European
Southeast
4
12/16/2003
Up Next: [Slide 5]
Slide 4 of 13
0:00:53
<No Speaker Notes>
End Show
Black Screen
Keyboard Shortcuts
Keyboard Shortcuts
You can use the following keyboard shortcuts:
Space - Advance to the next animation/slide
Backspace - Return to previous animation/slide
PageUp - Scrolls Speaker's Notes up
PageDown - Scroll Speaker's Notes down
OK
End the show
Display a black slide on the screen until clicked again
Display a menu of keyboard shortcuts
Click a slide to see it displayed out of sequence
Click to view the previous slide
Click to advance one slide
Displays speaker notes so presenter can read them to the audience
Where you are
How much time has elapsed since the slide show started

Figure 10-3: The primary monitor controls the presentation with the Presenter View

RUN A FULL SCREEN SLIDE SHOW WITH DUAL MONITORS

If you prefer to see a full-screen slide show and use the pen or other tools that are available with the right-click menu rather than the tools on Presenter View (shown in Figure 10-3), do not place a check mark next to Show Presenter View. With that disabled, you will see the same display on both screens. You will also have the navigational buttons on the lower-left of the screen and the slide show menu available when you right-click the screen, as seen in Figure 10-4.

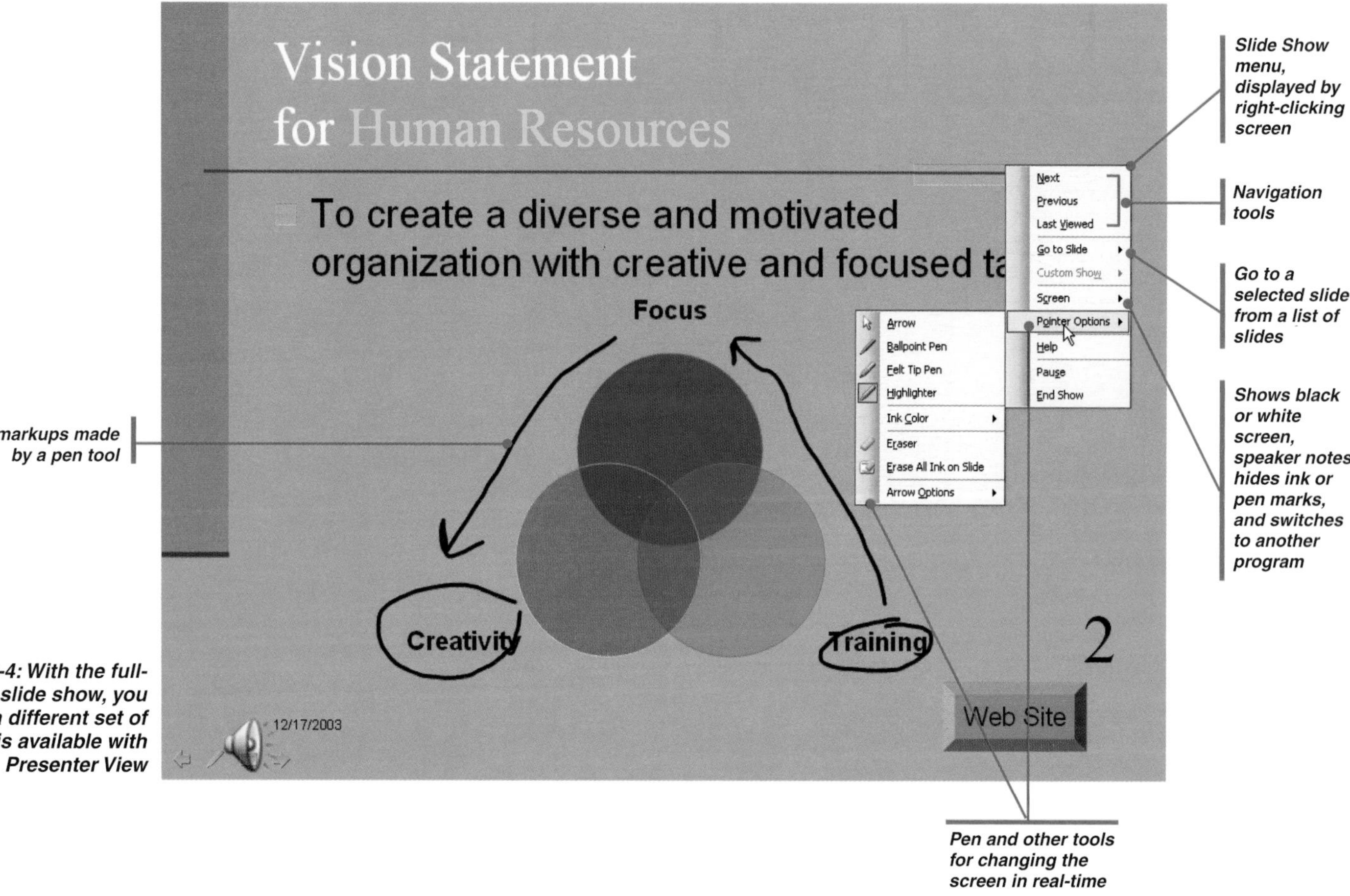

Figure 10-4: With the full-screen slide show, you can use a different set of tools than is available with Presenter View

Use a Pen Tool

When you are using dual monitors and not using Presenter View during a slide show, you can use a pen tool or highlighter to emphasize points, draw connecting lines, circle text you want to discuss, and more, as illustrated in Figure 10-5. Your marks will not be saved until you signal PowerPoint to do so. You must be in Slide Show view to do this.

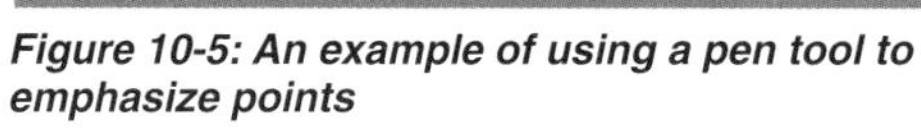

Figure 10-5: An example of using a pen tool to emphasize points

1. With your presentation in Slide Show view, right-click the slide, and click **Pointer Options**. (Or press CTRL+P to get an immediate pen.)
2. From the subsidiary menu, click the kind of pen you want.
   - **Ballpoint** for a thinner line
   - **Felt Tip Pen** for a thicker line
   - **Highlighter** for a broader highlighter effect
3. To select a different color, right-click the screen, select **Ink Color**, and click the color you want.

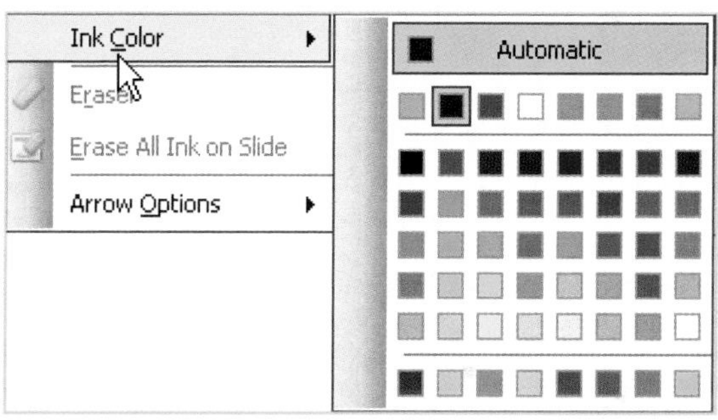

4. When the slide show is over, you will be asked if you want to keep your ink annotations. Click **Keep** to save the markings. Click **Discard** to do away with them.

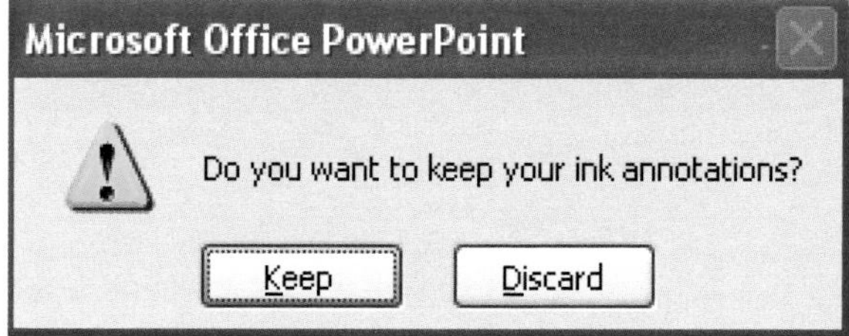

TIP

Press CTRL+U to return to an arrow pointer from a pen tool.

QUICKSTEPS

NAVIGATING A SLIDE SHOW

If your slide show is not run automatically, you can use these methods to navigate through your slide show.

START A SLIDE SHOW

- From within PowerPoint, click **Slide Show from Current Slide**.
- Open **Slide Show** and click **View Show**.

  –Or–
- Press **F5**.
- In My Computer or Windows Explorer, find the .ppt file and double-click it.

  –Or–
- Right-click the file name, and click **Show** on the context menu.
- In Internet Explorer, open **File**, click **Open**, find and select the file saved as a web page, click **Open,** and click **OK**.

  –Or–
- Open **File**, click **Open**, double-click the file name, and click **OK**.

ADVANCE TO NEXT/PREVIOUS SLIDE

To get to the next slide (or next animation if it is started by a mouse click), do one of the these:

- Click the slide.
- Press **ENTER.**
- Press **PAGE DOWN.**
- Press **DOWN ARROW.**
- Right-click and click **Next**.
- Click a Next navigation tool on the slide.

Continued...

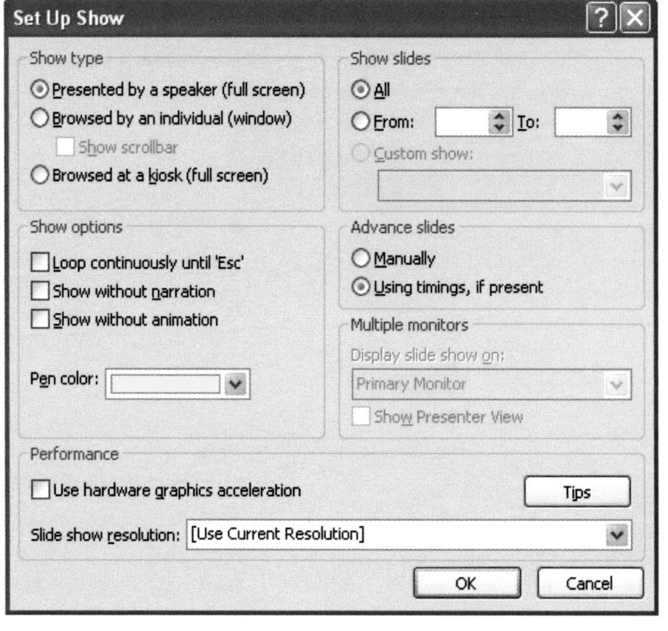

***Figure 10-6:** The Set Up Show dialog box controls many aspects of how a slide show is run*

Rehearse Your Timing

You can rehearse the length of time it takes you to present your slide show.

1. With your presentation in Normal or Slide Sorter view, open **Slide Show** and click **Rehearse Timings**.
2. The presentation will begin with a full-screen slide show and a timer in the top-left corner of the screen.

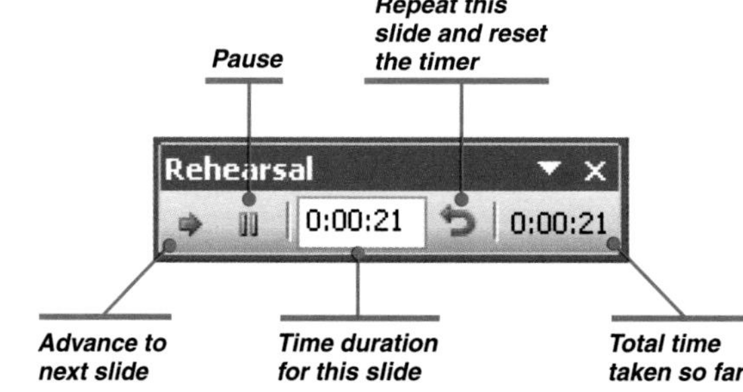

NAVIGATING A SLIDE SHOW *(Continued)*

To get to the previous slide (or previous animation if they are started by a mouse click), do one of these:

- Click **PAGE UP**.
- Press **UP ARROW**.
- Press **BACKSPACE**.
- Right-click and click **Previous**.
- Click a Previous navigation tool on the slide.

GO TO BEGINNING/END OF A SLIDE SHOW

- To go to the beginning of a slide show, press **HOME**.
- To go to the end of a slide show, press **END**.

GO TO A PARTICULAR SLIDE

- To go to the previously viewed slide, right-click the current slide, and click **Last Viewed**.
- To go to a specific slide number, right-click the current slide, click **Go To Slide**, and click the slide you want.

  –Or–
- Type the number of the slide, and press **ENTER**.

EXIT THE SLIDE SHOW

To exit a slide show, press **ESC**.

TIP

Try these tricks to speed up your presentation: reduce the screen resolution; use graphic hardware acceleration if it is available on your computer; reduce animation of individual objects and bullets or the size of animated pictures on a slide; simplify the animations you have; and avoid using background special effects, such as gradient, textured, or transparency enhanced backgrounds.

3. Go through your slide show as you expect to actually present it.
4. Use the scroll buttons on the timer to move to the next slide, or press **PAGE DOWN**. If you need to try a slide again, click **Repeat** and do it over. If you need to stop for a time, click **Pause**.
5. When you are done, PowerPoint will display a message stating the time you have taken and asking whether you want to record the slide timings for use in timing the display of the slides during the actual presentation.

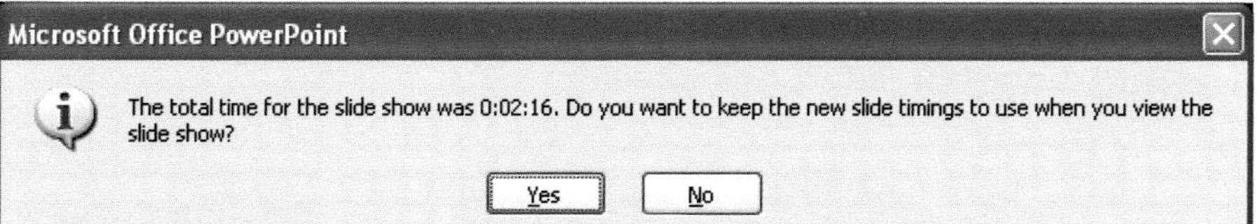

6. Click **Yes** to record the timings and create a timed presentation. The timings will appear on the bottom of the slides. Click **No** to discard the timings.

Display a Blank Screen

As you are making a presentation, you may want to pause for a moment and to hide the slide being displayed. You cannot be in Presenter View.

1. In Slide Show view, press **SHIFT F10** or right-click the slide. A menu will be displayed.
2. Click **Screen** and select from these choices:
   - Click **White Screen** to display a totally white screen.
   - Click **Black Screen** to display a totally black screen.
3. When you are ready to continue, click the blank screen.

Write Notes during the Presentation

While you are giving your presentation, you may want to type a few notes, perhaps to record what is being said by the audience about a particular slide or to remind yourself of a point to mention in future presentations. You can do this with Speaker Notes. You must not be in Presenter View.

TIP

To review slide show navigation options, right-click the show and click **Help**.

QUICKSTEPS

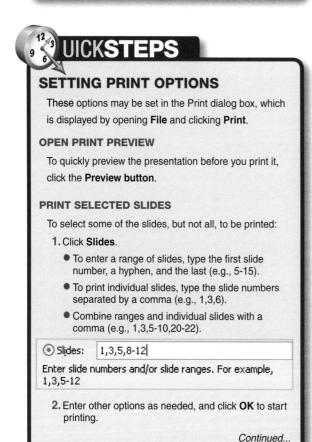

SETTING PRINT OPTIONS

These options may be set in the Print dialog box, which is displayed by opening **File** and clicking **Print**.

OPEN PRINT PREVIEW

To quickly preview the presentation before you print it, click the **Preview button**.

PRINT SELECTED SLIDES

To select some of the slides, but not all, to be printed:

1. Click **Slides**.
   - To enter a range of slides, type the first slide number, a hyphen, and the last (e.g., 5-15).
   - To print individual slides, type the slide numbers separated by a comma (e.g., 1,3,6).
   - Combine ranges and individual slides with a comma (e.g., 1,3,5-10,20-22).

Slides: 1,3,5,8-12
Enter slide numbers and/or slide ranges. For example, 1,3,5-12

2. Enter other options as needed, and click **OK** to start printing.

Continued...

1. During the slide show, right-click the slide being displayed.
2. Select **Screen** and click **Speaker Notes**. The Speaker Notes dialog box will open.

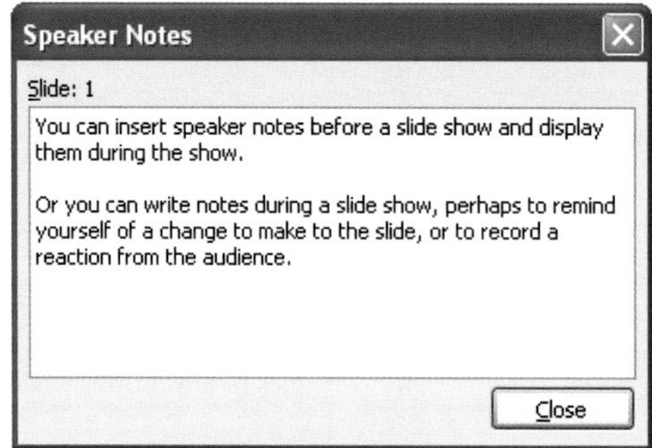

3. Type your notes and click **Close**.

Create a Custom Slide Show

You can create a custom show from your current presentation by adding, removing, or shuffling the slides. Your new custom presentation is a subset of the current one.

1. Open **Slide Show** and click **Custom Shows**. The Custom Show dialog box will open.
2. Click **New** to create a new presentation. The Define Custom Show dialog box will appear, as shown in Figure 10-7.

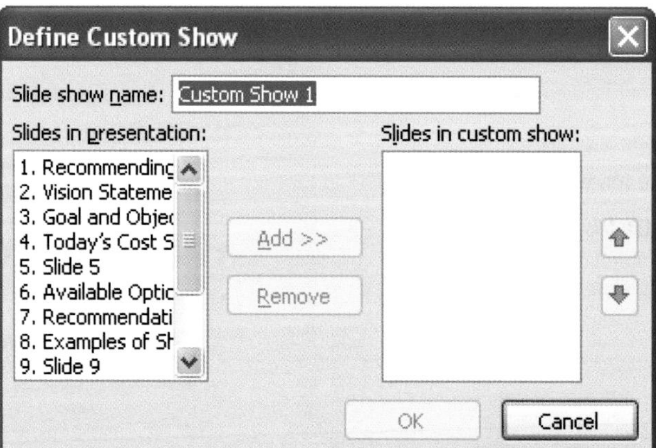

Figure 10-7: Create a new slide show by modifying the slides used and their order

SETTING PRINT OPTIONS *(Continued)*

PRINT DRAFT QUALITY

To select the quality of printing:

1. Click **Properties**. The Printer Document Properties dialog box will open.
2. Click the **Paper/Quality tab**.
3. Under Quality Settings, click **Draft** or the quality you want. Not all printers have the same properties. Yours may not have this same setting.

Quality Settings

Best Normal Draft Custom

4. Click **OK** to close the Printer Document Properties dialog box.
5. Enter other options as needed, and click **OK** to start printing.

PRINT A FRAME AROUND THE SLIDES

To print a frame around the slides, click Frame Slides. The frame will not appear on the Slide Show or Print Preview. It only appears on the printed copy.

Frame slides

PRINT MORE THAN ONE COPY

Under Copies, click the up and down arrows to select the number of copies you want. Place a check mark in Collate if you want the copies to be printed so that pages are automatically separated into complete, sequenced sets. (This is the default option.)

Copies

Number of copies: 12

Collate

3. Type a name in the **Slide Show Name** text box.
4. Select the titles of the slides you want from the Slides In Presentation list, and click **Add**.
5. To delete slides from the new slide show, select the slide from Slides In Custom Show, and click **Remove**.
6. When you are finished, click **OK**.
7. To review the new presentation, click **Show**; or to finish without viewing the slide show, click **Close**.

Place a Shortcut on Your Desktop

To place a shortcut to your presentation on the Desktop:

1. Find the file using My Computer or Windows Explorer.
2. Drag the file to the Desktop with the right mouse button.
3. Release the button, and click **Create Shortcut Here**.

Print Presentations in Various Ways

A presentation can be printed to paper (in color or grayscale), to transparencies or to a file for transfer to a 35mm slide-service bureau or for high-resolution printing. In this section, you will learn how to print to a printer or file to produce these types of output.

Preview Slides before Printing

As part of the print process, you can quickly preview your slides before printing them, as seen in Figure 10-8:

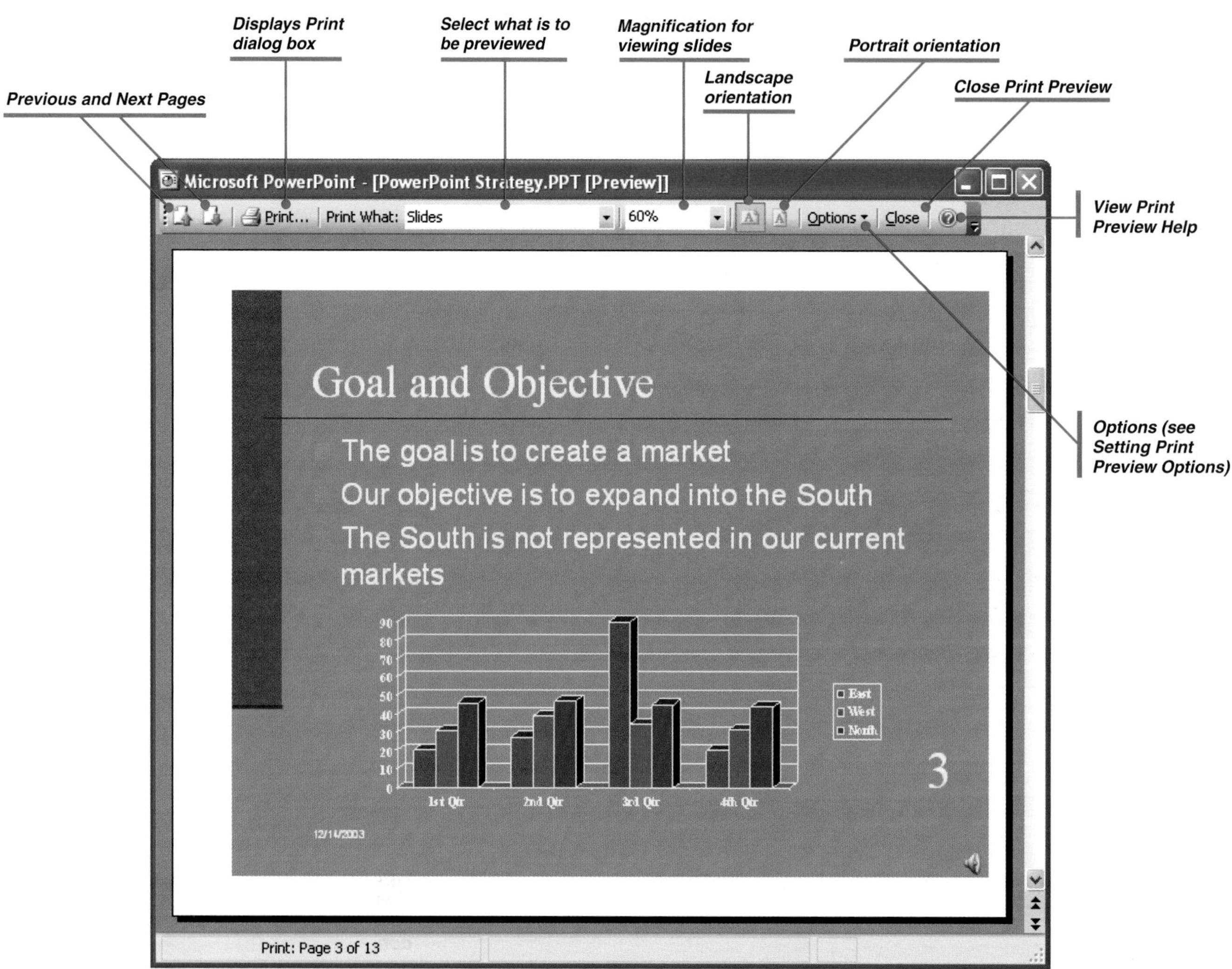

Figure 10-8: Print Preview gives you a chance to spot changes you want to make before printing

QUICKSTEPS

SETTING PRINT PREVIEW OPTIONS

You can set some of the printer options in the Print Preview screen. You might want to do this here instead of the Print dialog box in order to preview the effects of the options. Figure 10-9 shows the Options menu. Click **Print Preview** to display the Print Preview screen, and click **Options**.

ESTABLISH PRINT COLOR

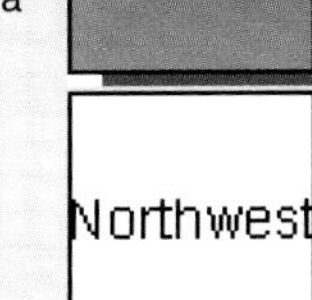

To designate the color in which the slides will be previewed and printed:

1. Open **Options**, and click **Color/ Grayscale** to open the subsidiary menu.
2. Click one of these option:
   - **Color** for color slides (requires a color printer)
   - **Grayscale** for grayscale slides
   - **Pure Black And White** for no gray tones

HIDE/PRINT COMMENTS, MARKINGS, AND HIDDEN SLIDES

Open the **Options** menu. You can toggle Print Hidden Slides and Print Comments And Ink Markup. A check mark beside the options means hidden slides, comments, and ink markups will appear in the preview and be printed. To deselect the options, remove the check marks. (If Print Hidden Slides is grayed, it means there are no hidden slides in the presentation.)

Continued...

1. Open **File** and click **Print Preview**, or click the **Print Preview** button on the Standard toolbar.
2. At the top of the window, open **Print What?** and click **Slides**. See Chapters 2 and 3 for further information on previewing Notes, Outline pages, and Handouts.
3. Open the **Zoom** drop-down list box and select a magnification if you want to see parts of the slides better. You can toggle back and forth between a selected magnification and the last one used by clicking the magnifying glass that the pointer morphs into.
4. Click the scroll bar to advance the slides one by one, or press **PAGE DOWN**.
5. If you decide to print the previewed slides, click **Print**.

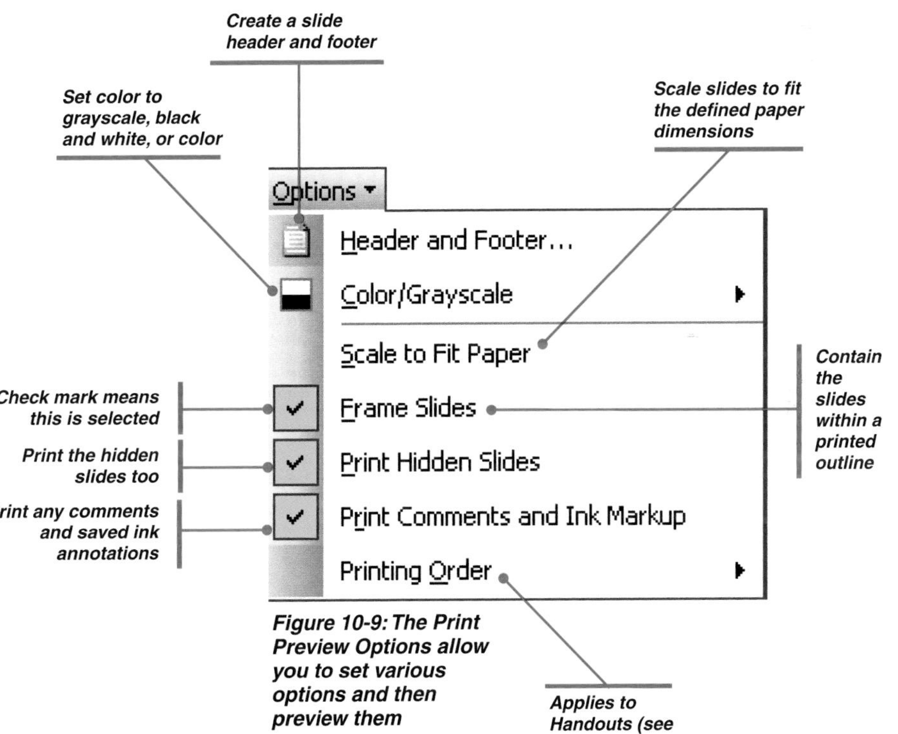

***Figure 10-9:** The Print Preview Options allow you to set various options and then preview them*

SETTING PRINT PREVIEW OPTIONS *(Continued)*

INSERT HEADERS AND FOOTERS

To insert a header or footer on a slide or on all slides, open **Options** and click **Header And Footer**. The Header And Footer dialog box will open.

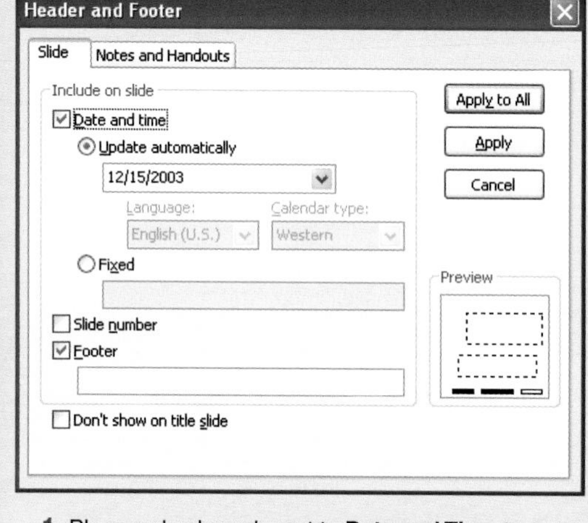

1. Place a check mark next to **Date and Time** to include the date and time on the slide.
   - Click **Update Automatically**, and click the drop-down list box to choose a style in which the current date and time should appear when automatically updated.
   - Click **Fixed**, and type in a date and time (or other text) that you want to appear on the slide without being updated.
2. Place a check mark next to **Slide Number** to have the slide number appear on the slide.
3. Place a check mark next to **Footer**, and fill in the text box with what you want the footer to be.

Continued...

Set Page Setup

Set up the slide width and height, page size, slide orientation, and the beginning slide number by using Page Setup.

1. Open **File** and click **Page Setup**. The Page Setup dialog box will open.

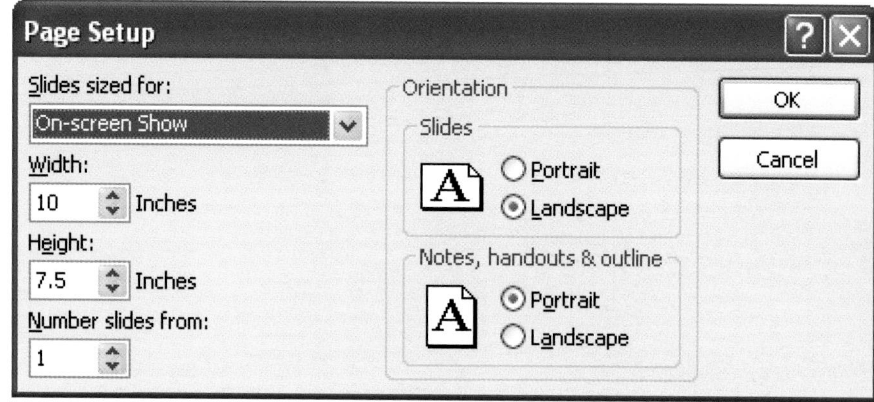

2. Select among these options:
   - To select a page size, open the **Slides Sized For** drop-down list box and click an option.
   - To precisely enter the slide size, use the up and down arrows to set **Width** and **Height**.
   - To set a starting slide number other than one, click the **Number Slides From** up and down arrows.
   - Under Slide Orientation, click **Portrait** to set the slide orientation to tall.
   - Click **Landscape** to set the slide orientation to wide.
3. Click **OK** to close Page Setup.

SETTING PRINT PREVIEW OPTIONS

(Continued)

4. Place a check mark next to **Don't Show On Title Slide** to prevent the selected information from being displayed on the first or title slide.
5. Click **Apply** to apply to only the selected slide or **Apply To All** to apply the options to all slides.

See Chapter 3 for information about headers and footers for notes and handouts.

SCALE SLIDES TO FIT PAPER

Since you can print the slides on a variety of paper sizes, you can scales the slides to fit the size, whatever it may be. To do so, open **Options** and place a check mark next to **Scale To Fit Paper**.

Print Grayscale or Black and White Slides

If you are using a black and white printer, PowerPoint will automatically set your slides to Grayscale; if you have selected a color printer, it will set them to Color. For a no-color printer, you can choose whether to use grayscale or black and white, which produces a more dramatic effect. To print:

1. Open **File** and choose **Print**, or press **CTRL+P**.
2. Under **Color/Grayscale**, open the drop-down list box and click your preference.
3. Set your other options, and click **OK** to print.

Print Transparencies

You may want to print your slides on transparencies to present the slide show with an overhead projector. Use the Print dialog box to set the type of output media. (Not all printers have a specified software option for printing transparencies. If yours doesn't, see your printer's manual for instruction on how to print transparencies.)

1. Open **File** and choose **Print**.
2. Click **Properties** to open the Printer Document Properties dialog box. Click the **Paper/ Quality** tab if it is not already selected.
3. Open the **Media** drop-down list, and click the type of transparency you want.
4. Click **OK** to close the dialog box.
5. Set your options as discussed in "Setting Print Options."
6. Click **OK** to begin printing.

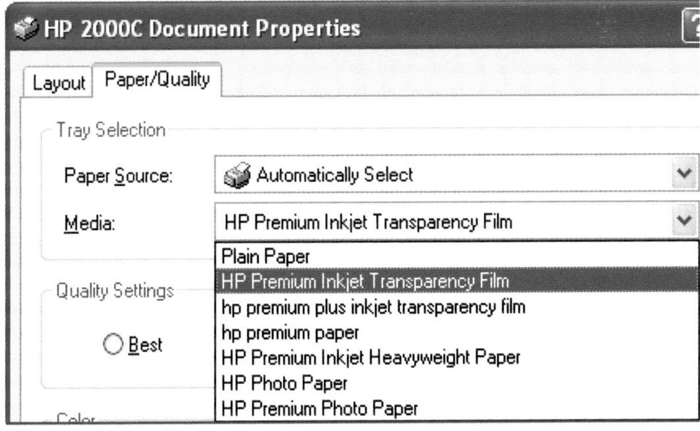

> **NOTE**
>
> If you do not have the required PostScript driver, get one from the service bureau you will be using, and install it from the Printer and Faxes (Windows XP) control panel using Add New Printer. To do this, open **Start**, click **Printers And Faxes** (your path to the Printers and Faxes control panel may vary depending on your operating system), and click **Add a Printer**.

> **TIP**
>
> Since Windows adds a .PRN file extension to the saved file, you may want to change it to .PS, for PostScript.

Print a PostScript File for 35mm Slides

You cannot print 35mm slides using PowerPoint with Windows. However, you can create a PostScript file to take to a business that creates 35mm slides from PostScript files. To create PostScript files, you must have a color PostScript driver installed on your computer. Many come with the Windows operating system, but your service bureau will have specific file types that you need to produce. After receiving those specifications, you may print a PostScript file this way:

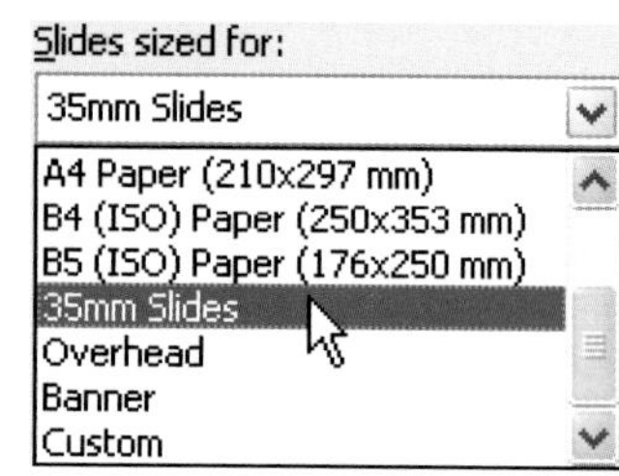

1. First, set the slide size. Open **File** and click **Page Setup**. The Page Setup dialog box will open.
2. Open the **Slides Sized For** drop-down list box, and click **35mm Slides**.
3. Click **OK** to close the dialog box.
4. Open **File** and click **Print**. The Print dialog box will appear.
5. Open the **Name** drop-down list, and click the name of your PostScript printer driver.
6. Click the options you want:
   - Select **Slides** in Print What?.
   - Select **Color** in the Color/Grayscale drop-down list box.
   - Remove the check mark in **Print Comments And Ink Markup**.
   - Remove the check mark for **Print Hidden Slides**, if available and if you want.
   - Look at the other options, and select the ones you want.
7. Place a check mark next to **Print To File**. Figure 10-10 shows an example of a Print dialog box you will see at this point.
8. Click **OK** to start the printing to a file. The Print To dialog box will be displayed.
9. In the Print To File dialog box, type your **File Name** and **Save In** location. Click **Save**.

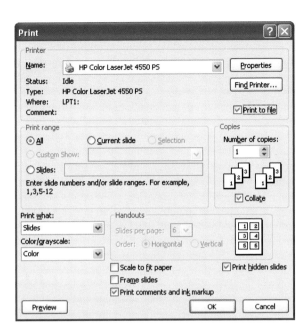

Figure 10-10: Printing to a file, formatted for a PostScript printer, can be used to produce 35mm slides by a service bureau

Stop Printing

To halt the printing of the slides while printing is in progress:

1. Double-click the printer icon in the taskbar. A dialog box for your printer will open.

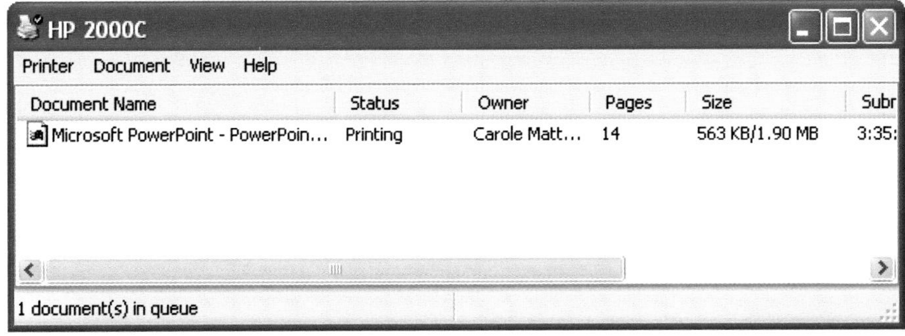

2. Click the presentation name to select it.
3. Open **Document** and click **Cancel**.
4. Click **Yes** to indicate that you really want to cancel the print job.
5. Click **Close** to close the dialog box.

Change Printers

To print to a printer that is not the default for your computer:

1. Open **File** and click **Print**. The Print dialog box will open.
2. Open the **Name** drop-down list, and click the printer you want to use.
   - If you are on an Active Directory domain and the printer is not there, click **Find Printers**, and follow the directions on the dialog box to search and find the printer.
   - If the printer is not on your computer or network, you must add it. Open **Start**, click **Printers And Faxes** (your path to the Printers and Faxes control box may vary depending on your operating system), and click **Add A Printer**. Follow the wizard or dialog box to install the printer on your computer or network.
3. When the correct printer name is in the Print dialog box and you have selected the options you want in the dialog box, click **OK** to begin printing.

TIP

Because the print queue fills so quickly, you may not be able to cancel printing of all the slides. Also, if your presentation is very short, the print icon will be present on the taskbar for a very short time. You may not be able to click it fast enough.

Index

A

B

C

R

S

T

V

W

International Contact Information

AUSTRALIA
McGraw-Hill Book Company Australia Pty. Ltd.
TEL +61-2-9900-1800
FAX +61-2-9878-8881
http://www.mcgraw-hill.com.au
books-it_sydney@mcgraw-hill.com

CANADA
McGraw-Hill Ryerson Ltd.
TEL +905-430-5000
FAX +905-430-5020
http://www.mcgraw-hill.ca

GREECE, MIDDLE EAST, & AFRICA
(Excluding South Africa)
McGraw-Hill Hellas
TEL +30-210-6560-990
TEL +30-210-6560-993
TEL +30-210-6560-994
FAX +30-210-6545-525

MEXICO (Also serving Latin America)
McGraw-Hill Interamericana Editores S.A. de C.V.
TEL +525-1500-5108
FAX +525-117-1589
http://www.mcgraw-hill.com.mx
carlos_ruiz@mcgraw-hill.com

SINGAPORE (Serving Asia)
McGraw-Hill Book Company
TEL +65-6863-1580
FAX +65-6862-3354
http://www.mcgraw-hill.com.sg
mghasia@mcgraw-hill.com

SOUTH AFRICA
McGraw-Hill South Africa
TEL +27-11-622-7512
FAX +27-11-622-9045
robyn_swanepoel@mcgraw-hill.com

SPAIN
McGraw-Hill/Interamericana de España, S.A.U.
TEL +34-91-180-3000
FAX +34-91-372-8513
http://www.mcgraw-hill.es
professional@mcgraw-hill.es

UNITED KINGDOM, NORTHERN,
EASTERN, & CENTRAL EUROPE
McGraw-Hill Education Europe
TEL +44-1-628-502500
FAX +44-1-628-770224
http://www.mcgraw-hill.co.uk
emea_queries@mcgraw-hill.com

ALL OTHER INQUIRIES Contact:
McGraw-Hill/Osborne
TEL +1-510-420-7700
FAX +1-510-420-7703
http://www.osborne.com
omg_international@mcgraw-hill.com